Post-Imperial Perspectives on Indigenous Education

This book explores the impact of the *United Nations Declaration on the Rights of Indigenous Peoples* in Japan and Australia, where it has heralded change in the rights of Indigenous Peoples to have their histories, cultures, and lifeways taught in culturally appropriate and respectful ways in mainstream education systems.

The book examines the impact of imposed education on Indigenous Peoples' pre-existing education values and systems, considers emergent approaches towards Indigenous education in the post-imperial context of migration, and critiques certain professional development, assessment, pedagogical approaches, and curriculum developments.

This book will be of great interest to researchers and lecturers of education specialising in Indigenous Education, as well as postgraduate students of education and teachers specialising in Indigenous Education.

Peter J. Anderson is Professor and Executive Director of the Carumba Institute at the Queensland University of Technology, Brisbane.

Koji Maeda is Professor at the Graduate School of Education, Waseda University, Tokyo.

Zane M. Diamond is Professor at the Faculty of Education, Monash University, Melbourne.

Chizu Sato is Professor at International Christian University, Tokyo.

Post-Imperial Perspectives on Indigenous Education

Lessons from Japan and Australia

Edited by
Peter J. Anderson, Koji Maeda,
Zane M. Diamond, and Chizu Sato

LONDON AND NEW YORK

First published 2021
by Routledge
2 Park Square, Milton Park, Abingdon, Oxon OX14 4RN

and by Routledge
605 Third Avenue, New York, NY 10017

First issued in paperback 2022

Routledge is an imprint of the Taylor & Francis Group, an informa business

© 2021 selection and editorial matter, Peter J. Anderson, Koji Maeda, Zane M. Diamond, and Chizu Sato; individual chapters, the contributors

The right of Peter J. Anderson, Koji Maeda, Zane M. Diamond, and Chizu Sato to be identified as the authors of the editorial material, and of the authors for their individual chapters, has been asserted in accordance with sections 77 and 78 of the Copyright, Designs and Patents Act 1988.

All rights reserved. No part of this book may be reprinted or reproduced or utilised in any form or by any electronic, mechanical, or other means, now known or hereafter invented, including photocopying and recording, or in any information storage or retrieval system, without permission in writing from the publishers.

Trademark notice: Product or corporate names may be trademarks or registered trademarks, and are used only for identification and explanation without intent to infringe.

Publisher's Note
The publisher has gone to great lengths to ensure the quality of this reprint but points out that some imperfections in the original copies may be apparent.

British Library Cataloguing-in-Publication Data
A catalogue record for this book is available from the British Library

Library of Congress Cataloging-in-Publication Data
Names: Anderson, Peter J. (Peter Joseph), editor. | Maeda, Koji, 1941– editor. | Diamond, Zane M., editor. | Sato, Chizu, editor.
Title: Post-imperial perspectives on indigenous education: lessons from Japan and Australia / [edited by] Peter J. Anderson, Koji Maeda, Zane M. Diamond, Chizu Sato.
Description: New York : Routledge, 2020. |
Includes bibliographical references and index.
Identifiers: LCCN 2020017661 (print) | LCCN 2020017662 (ebook) | ISBN 9780367001957 (hardback) | ISBN 9780429400834 (ebook)
Subjects: LCSH: Ainu–Education. | Aboriginal Australians–Education. | Torres Straight Islanders–Education. | Indigenous peoples–Education–Japan. | Indigenous peoples–Education–Australia. | United Nations.
General Assembly. Declaration on the Rights of Indigenous Peoples.
Classification: LCC LC3501.A56 P67 2020 (print) | LCC LC3501.A56 (ebook) | DDC 371.829/946–dc23
LC record available at https://lccn.loc.gov/2020017661
LC ebook record available at https://lccn.loc.gov/2020017662

ISBN: 978-0-367-00195-7 (hbk)
ISBN: 978-0-367-55307-4 (pbk)
ISBN: 978-0-429-40083-4 (ebk)

DOI: 10.4324/9780429400834

Typeset in Bembo
by Newgen Publishing UK

Dedication and cultural warning

We dedicate this book to all Indigenous peoples and, in particular, the Ainu and Aboriginal and Torres Strait Islander educators and all their ancestor educators. We pay respect to them and thank them for their struggle and for the footsteps they left for us to follow.

To Indigenous readers:

In Chapters 2 and 6, there are images of Indigenous people from Japan and Australia. Some of the images are of your ancestor educators and others who are no longer here with you. We have made our best efforts to acknowledge your ancestors in a positive and respectful manner. If you would like additional acknowledgements, please contact us, and in future editions we will ensure that these are included. We have used these images in the spirit of fair dealing for the purposes of review, including specific images of your ancestors to support our discussion of Indigenous teaching and learning contexts that would be difficult to portray in words alone.

To non-Indigenous readers:

We are providing this warning to highlight an important cultural protocol that has been adopted into the international publishing system to provide a cultural warning, as mentioned earlier, to Indigenous readers. We have included specific images to support our description of Indigenous teaching and learning contexts that are used to show specific examples in support of our discussion.

Contents

Foreword by Kayano Shiro and Gary Thomas   x
List of illustrations   xiii
Editor biographies   xv
Contributor biographies   xvii
Acknowledgements   xx
List of abbreviations   xxi
List of legislations   xxiii
Glossary   xxv

1. Introducing Indigenous education in Japan and Australia   1
   PETER J. ANDERSON, KOJI MAEDA, ZANE M. DIAMOND, AND CHIZU SATO

PART I
Historical perspectives on Indigenous education, Indigenous higher education, and teacher education in Japan and Australia   23

2. An Indigenous history of education in Japan and Australia   25
   CHIZU SATO AND ZANE M. DIAMOND

3. The place of Indigenous Peoples in multicultural education: Policies, debates, and practices in Australia and Japan   66
   KAORI OKANO

4. Higher education in Japan and the history of Ainu demands   80
   KOJI MAEDA

5. Indigenous higher education in historical context in Australia   91
   LEANNE HOLT

PART II
After UNDRIP: Japanese and Australian responses and possibilities — 111

6   Challenges and responses to UNDRIP in Australian and Japanese Indigenous education — 113
    ZANE M. DIAMOND AND CHIZU SATO

7   Embracing and resisting Indigenist perspectives in Australian pre-service teacher education — 126
    PETER J. ANDERSON, ZANE M. DIAMOND, AND JEANE F. DIAMOND

8   Teacher education issues in Okinawa — 151
    KENGO KAKAZU AND EISUKE SAITO

9   Questioning current issues in the higher education sector for Japan's Ainu People — 169
    JEFFREY J. GAYMAN AND MASAYUKI UENO

10 Stabilising and sustaining Indigenous leadership in Australian universities — 186
    PETER J. ANDERSON AND ZANE M. DIAMOND

PART III
Considering post-imperial Indigenous education in Japan and Australia — 209

11 The significance of building an Ainu-led higher education system and the empowerment of the Indigenous Ainu — 211
    KOJI MAEDA AND KAORI OKANO

12 The usefulness of the idea and concept of reconciliation for guiding Australian Indigenous higher education in the postcolonial, post-imperial world — 227
    VERONICA GOERKE AND PETER J. ANDERSON

Appendix — 255
Index — 258

Kaye Price, NAEC leader, talking to students in front of stone arrangement display on Aboriginal Day at Spence Primary School, Canberra, 9 May 1990.

Source: Photograph by Alana Harris. Courtesy of AIATSIS, HARRIS.A01.BW-N04967_14

Foreword

Kayano Shiro and Professor Gary Thomas

Nispautar katkematutar sineitak kuye kusnena.
Kurehe anakne Kayano Shiro ne ruwe ne.
Pipaushi kotan otta koapamaka kune wa, tane Kayanoshigeru Nibutani Siryoukan esapanekur ne ruwe ne.
Tan kampisos anakne Australian utar sisamutar 「先住民族研究者」 akar wa kuinu. Ne kampisos ani Australian otta hene sisammosr otta hene itak aeraman kusu kuyainu.
Nispautar katkematutar sineikinne neytapakno nisasnu kuni kamuypunki an nankon na.

ニシパウタラ　カッケマッウタラ　シネイタク　クイェ　クシネナ。

クレヘ　アナクネ　萱野志朗　ネ　ルウェ　ネ。

ピパウシコタノッタ　コアパマカ　クネ　ワ、タネ　萱野茂二風谷アイヌ資料館エサパネクル　ネ　ルウェ　ネ。

タン　カンピソシ　アナクネ　オーストラリアウタラ　シサムウタラ「先住民族研究者」アカラ　ワ　クイ。ネ　カンピソシ　アニ　オーストラリア　オッタ　ヘネ　シサムモシリ　オッタ　ヘネ　イタク　アエラマン　クス　クヤイヌ。

ニシパウタラ　カッケマッウタラ　シネイキンネ　ネイタパクノ　ニサシヌ　クニ　カムイプンキ　アン　ナンコン　ナ。

紳士・淑女の皆さん、一言ご挨拶申し上げます。私の名は萱野志朗です。ピパウシコタン（二風谷の古い地名）で生まれ、現在は萱野茂二風谷アイヌ資料館の館長を務めています。

この本はオーストラリアと日本両国の先住民族研究者が作ったと聞いています。この本によってオーストラリアや日本で言語の理解が深まると思います。

紳士・淑女の皆様、一様にいつまでも健康であることを神がお守りしてくださるでしょう。

Ladies and gentlemen, I would like to say a word of greeting.

I am Kayano Shiro, born in Nibutani, and currently serving as the Director of the Kayano Shigeru Nibutani Ainu Museum.

I have heard that this book has been written by scholars from Australia and Japan researching Indigenous matters. I am certain that this volume will contribute to understanding of language issues in both Australia and Japan.

May you, ladies and gentlemen, always and constantly be blessed with good health, overseen by the *kamuy* spiritual deities.

Kayano Shiro
Director, Kayano Shigeru Nibutani Ainu Museum
Japan
萱野茂二風谷アイヌ資料館　館長　萱野志朗

Post-Imperial Perspectives on Indigenous Education: Lessons from Japan and Australia is a refreshing examination of Australia and Japan as nations. This work tells the story of education history, policy, and practice using the ratification of the *United Nations Declaration on the Rights of Indigenous PPeoples* as the critical mid-point in the trajectories of relations between Australia and Aboriginal and Torres Strait Islander Peoples and between Japan and the Ainu people.

Educators and anyone with an interest in the process of education will be moved by the discussions. The authors take the reader on two similar yet distinct journeys of human beings seeking the expression of their human rights through education. By positioning the participation of Indigenous Peoples in education within a rights framework, the authors are challenging those associated with education planning, delivery, and assurance to act with responsibility through responsiveness.

The authors are both eclectic and adept in their presentation of a rich narrative that weaves historical, sociological, political, educational, and organisational theories and practice. Central to the discussion is privileging Indigenous Peoples' voices. This text is a lesson in listening first. Far from a re-telling of deficit tropes, the authors' provocations are hopeful and invite readers to act through increased understanding.

This work is a collaboration of academics who have committed themselves to demonstrating true and good partnerships. Their commitment to Indigenous Peoples, to each other, and to better education for all Peoples is evident. The pairing of Australia and Japan in the context of Indigenous education is exciting and provides opportunities for new questions, ideas, and revisiting accepted realities from a new comparative lens.

Post-Imperial Perspectives on Indigenous Education: Lessons from Japan and Australia will be one of those texts that readers will return to time and again for truth-telling, affirmation, and encouragement and to seed new imaginaries and creative endeavours in education.

Professor Gary Thomas (PhD WINU., Postgrad DipEd Qld., BA Qld.)
Dean, Indigenous Education and Engagement
University of the Sunshine Coast
Queensland, Australia

Illustrations

Figures

7.1	The 'Aboriginal' and 'respect' key concept maps	142
7.2	The 'student' and 'important' key concept maps	143
7.3	Difference of associated concepts with key word as 'Aboriginal' and 'student'	144
10.1	Indigenous and non-Indigenous academic employment trend data 2009–2018	201

Tables

3.1	Estimated population of minority groups in Japan	70
3.2	Retention of Ainu children to upper secondary school compared with that for the surveyed communities as a whole, 1972–2017	72
3.3	Retention of Ainu children to university compared with that for the surveyed communities as a whole, 1979–2017	73
4.1	The actual nature and extent of discrimination: Survey of 715 Ainu (aged 15 years or older)	85
4.2	Situation in which discrimination takes place: Survey of 201 Ainu (aged 15 years or older)	86
7.1	Focus Area 1.4: Strategies for teaching Aboriginal and Torres Strait Islander students	127
7.2	Focus Area 2.4: Understand and respect Aboriginal and Torres Strait Islander people to promote reconciliation between Indigenous and non-Indigenous Australians	128
7.3	An example of SETU feedback: University-wide items (summary)	145
8.1	Comparisons of three modes on teacher education in Okinawa	161

Images

2.1	Ainu telling *yukara* to a Wajin	29
2.2	Ainu in front of a house in 1877	30
2.3	Drawings of an Aboriginal feast and Aboriginal mothers	32
2.4	Example of mastery	33
2.5	Example of mastery learning and approximation	34
2.6	Deer hunting	35
2.7	Grass weaving	36
2.8	A New South Wales Family	37
2.9	Learning fire mastery	38
2.10	Ropemaking mastery	38
2.11	Learning formal education	41
2.12	Opening ceremony of a new *Tsuishikari kyōiku-sho* school building	43
2.13	William Cooper	44
2.14	Sarah Cooper	44
2.15	Cummeragunja school, c.1800s	45
2.16	Cummeragunja Aboriginal School, c. 1938	45
2.17	The 'Day of Mourning' Aboriginal meeting, 26 January 1938	48
2.18	Petition by the Victorian Aboriginal people presented by Doug Nicholls to the Minister of Aboriginal Affairs Ray Meagher	49
2.19	Hyllus Maris	50
2.20	Ballot paper 1967 Referendum	52
2.21	Shigeru Kayano's first attendance at the Diet	54
2.22	Takeshiro Matsuura in 1877	57
2.23	A junior high school teacher demonstrates methods for teaching students about Ainu culture at a teacher workshop	58
2.24	School teachers making a strap decorated with traditional Ainu patterns at a teacher workshop	59
6.1	Presentation Day 2019 at Worawa Aboriginal College	118
6.2	Dr Lois Peeler AM, executive director, Worawa Aboriginal College	119
6.3	University students visiting a museum to learn about the Ainu	120
6.4	University students learning about the history of the Ainu at a museum	121

Editor biographies

Peter J. Anderson, PhD, is from the Walpiri and Murinpatha First Nations in the Northern Territory. He is Professor and Executive Director of the Carumba Institute at Queensland University of Technology. His research theorises the understandings of the organisational value of academic freedom in Australian universities, more broadly in the polar south. His research spans the areas of organisational leadership, Indigenous Peoples' education, and teacher and academic professional development. His teaching philosophy is grounded in his understanding of the *sui generis* rights of Aboriginal and Torres Strait Islander Peoples as recognised in the *United Nations Declaration on the Rights of Indigenous Peoples* (UNDRIPs), in particular in education. A dynamic teacher, he employs modern Information and Communication Technologies (ICT) and blended learning opportunities that challenge, teach, disrupt, and inspire his students.

Koji Maeda, EdD, is Professor of Education at the Graduate School of Education, Waseda University, Tokyo. He has also been involved in education policy making and implementation, as the Vice Chancellor of Fujisawa City University of Lifelong Learning, Japan. He was also executive director of the Japan Society for the Study of Adult and Community Education and the ex-President of Japanese Association for the Study of Learning Society. As the ex-President of Japan International Education Society, he is also active in the field of international education. He has researched and published extensively in multicultural education and Indigenous education, including *Ōsutoraria senjūminzoku no shutai keisei to daigaku kaihō* [Autonomy development and higher education of the Australian indigenous community] (Akashi-shoten, 2019).

Zane M. Diamond, PhD, is Professor at the Faculty of Education, Monash University. Diamond's research investigates how wisdom might be developed in modern education systems, addressing the alienation from mainstream education that people from non-dominant cultures report, arguing that full participation as citizens is possible only when education enables inclusion of diverse student needs through understanding the impact of ancestry, ethnicity, and lifeways on the provision of mainstream education services. She employs theoretical perspectives drawn from Indigenist, social exchange, organisational change, and intelligent complex adaptive systems theories to develop an understanding of how to incorporate a diversity of ethnoreligious cultural perspectives within mainstream education and in the leadership and management of education services. She researches in the field of sociology of education (sub-fields of leadership and pedagogical reform of teacher education). International and comparativist in approach, her research encompasses: upholding Indigenous and traditional wisdom in modern universities and schools; negotiating traditional environmental knowledge into contemporary land, water, and food studies; embedding wise, culturally inclusive pedagogies; and an overarching study of the pedagogies of wisdom development in university and school students.

Chizu Sato, PhD, is Professor at International Christian University, Tokyo. Her research interests include teacher education, comparative and international education, and Indigenous education. She completed her doctoral studies at the University of Oxford, where she researched the nature of cultural awareness education in overseas Japanese schools in consideration of teachers' views on the nature of culture. One of her recent research focuses on systems and policies for the quality assurance of teacher education programmes. She is the President of the Japan International Education Society, the Vice President of the Japan Association for the Study of Learning Society, and an executive member of Board of Directors of the Japanese Society for the Study of Teacher Education.

Contributor biographies

Jeane F. Diamond is qualified in both Montessori and Primary Education and taught for many years in the United Kingdom. Subsequent to earning a Master's degree in California, she taught Leadership and Management in BBA and MBA programmes in Paris, France. She now brings this combination of teaching, leading, and managing expertise to early years education, focusing on ethical decision-making, risk management, and communication as core skills for Early Years Education (EYE). Jeane has been introduced to a number of Indigenous communities in Australia and internationally and has participated in several education research projects. She works with Professors Anderson and Diamond to deliver the Indigenous curriculum to pre-service teachers who are developing the skills to meet the new Australian Professional Teaching Standards in Australia. Her current PhD work examines the cognitive and affective components of resilience.

Jeffrey J. Gayman, PhD, is Professor at the Hokkaido University Research Faculty of Media and Communication and Hokkaido University Graduate School of Education. American by birth, he has been living, studying, and working in Japan for approximately 30 years. His research interests include Indigenous education, intercultural education, and education for human rights. Since coming to Hokkaido University, his efforts have shifted from research to more applied projects such as conceptualisation of how to systematise the empowerment of Ainu voice within higher education research and education in Japan, and consciousness-raising with regard to Indigenous issues within Japan. He is also involved in the support of Ainu rights recovery activism movements.

Veronica Goerke, PhD, is a descendant of people from the Valtellina in northern Italy and was born and lives with her family on Wadjuck Noongar Country, Western Australia. She is a senior lecturer working on academic development at Curtin University. She has previously been a secondary school teacher, a communication skills unit coordinator and lecturer working mainly with first year university students. Her current role includes facilitating staff to enhance and create quality, inclusive curriculum so they can deliver high-quality learning experiences for their students. Goerke especially enjoys working in collaboration with local First Nations colleagues to promote learning and research to include Australian Indigenous knowledges. She has recently completed her doctoral thesis on the place and impact of Reconciliation and Reconciliation Action Plans (RAPs) in universities.

Leanne Holt, PhD, is a Worimi woman with further connections to Biripai country on the eastern coast of New South Wales, Australia, and over twenty years of higher education experience. Holt is the current Pro-Vice Chancellor (Indigenous Strategy) and Director of Walanga Muru at Macquarie University. She is President, National Aboriginal and Torres Strait Islander Higher Education Consortium (NATSIHEC); co-Deputy Chairperson, World Indigenous Nations Higher Education Consortium (WINHEC); a member of Universities Australia Vice-Chancellor Plenary Committee; a member of the Department of Education's Equity, Research and Innovation Panel; and on the Panel of Experts for TEQSA.

Dr Holt's research interests relate to Aboriginal and Torres Strait Islander higher education policy and governance, with her PhD tracing the development of Aboriginal education policy in Australia. Recently she has led the development of a report on implementing a 'Whole of University approach' for Aboriginal and Torres Strait Islander higher education as part of a broader Accelerating Indigenous Higher Education report for the Department of Education. She was previously at the University of Newcastle as co-Director of the Wollotuka Institute where she led Wollotuka to be the first university in Australia to achieve international accreditation through the WINHEC. Dr Holt is an active member of a number of local, national, and international professional and community organisations.

Kengo Kakazu grew up in Naha city in Okinawa Prefecture, Japan. Kengo obtained his BA from the University of the Ryukyus and MA as well as PhD from Hiroshima University. Soon after completing the doctorate programme, he joined the Faculty of Humanities at Okinawa University in April 2011 as a full-time lecturer and promoted to be an associate professor in 2014. Research interests of Kengo include teacher education, quality assurance in teacher education, pedagogy of physical education. While working for Okinawa University, Kengo also served as a member of the Teacher Professional Development Committee for Okinawa Prefecture.

Kaori Okano is Professor of Asian Studies at La Trobe University, Melbourne, Australia. She researches on sociology/anthropology of education, inequality, multiculturalism, and more recently, the politics of eating at schools in Japan. Originally from Hiroshima, she worked as a secondary teacher in Australia and New Zealand prior to her academic career. From 2015 to 2017 she was the President of the Japanese Studies Association of Australia.

Her publications include *Education in contemporary Japan: Inequality and diversity* (1999, with M. Tsuchiya); *Minorities and education in Japan* (2011, with Tsuneyoshi & Boocock); *Asia Education Handbook* (2011, with Zhao et al.), and *Nonformal education and civil society in Japan* (2016). A recent work with Yoshio Sugimoto, *Rethinking Japanese Studies: Eurocentrism and the Asia-Pacific region* (2018), captures her recent thoughts about area studies.

She currently works on the Kobe Women Panel Study (working-class women's life courses, 1989–2019), which has produced two monographs to date: *Young women in Japan: Transitions to adulthood* (2009), which is the sequel to *School to work transition in Japan* (1993). This study has expanded to include an interdisciplinary project with sociolinguists, leading to its first book, *Discourse, gender and shifting identities in Japan* (2018, with Maree). Kaori also studies the politics of education about eating at Japanese schools.

Eisuke Saito currently works as a lecturer at the Faculty of Education, Monash University (Australia). Before joining Monash University, Eisuke served at the National Institute of Education, Singapore, and was a consultant for international educational development in developing Asian countries. Eisuke researches in School Reform, Teacher Professional Development, Education Policy, Educational Management and Leadership, and Pedagogical Reform.

Masayuki Ueno, PhD, is Assistant Professor of Toyo University, Department of Education, Faculty of Letters. He was born and raised in Tokyo. Participation in the movement to recover Ainu human rights, which he joined in the 1990s, allowed him to acquire an in-depth knowledge of the Ainu language and culture and prompted him to develop an interest in Ainu history and human rights which fed into his current focus as a researcher. One of the few Ainu researchers in the field of education in Japan, his research to date has focused on the restoration of Ainu culture and the Ainu language, and he received his doctorate for his research on Ainu education. At university, he teaches about Ainu culture as well as lectures in teacher education courses. His goals are to promote a multicultural Japanese society which accepts diverse values and ethnicities, and to establish the right for Indigenous people to preserve their own ethnic education.

Acknowledgements

The editors of this collection acknowledge that we live and work on the lands of Indigenous people. In the spirit of UNDRIP, and with respect to our work in partnership with Indigenous people, we affirm that we are committed to building respectful and equal partnerships with Ainu, Aboriginal, and Torres Strait Islander people, working together to create a culturally safe environment where educators and researchers, Ainu, Aboriginal, Torres Strait Islander, and non-Indigenous will make significant contribution to the field of Indigenous education. By developing culturally appropriate partnerships, positive role models, and through the preservation and maintenance of Indigenous lifeways in the mainstream formal education systems of Japan and Australia, we share an aspiration to support the economic and social sustainability of Indigenous communities and the development of the Indigenous faculty as a national and international leader in the field of Indigenous education teaching and research. We acknowledge the contributions by Indigenous experts in education who have led the field through their research, engagement with national governments, and scholarship over a significant time period. We have drawn on their wisdom throughout this book.

We are committed to a collaborative partnership approach in all of our research that works within international and national guidelines on the protocols for the conduct of research and evaluation with Indigenous people and to undertake research that is approved by our university Ethics Committees. We are also committed to developing meaningful partnerships to ensure that our conduct is at all times culturally sensitive, guided by Indigenous people, that there are accessible consultation opportunities, and that Indigenous views on all aspects of this work are represented accurately in our reporting.

Finally, we want to acknowledge and sincerely thank Miriam Verbeek and Jeane Diamond who have supported us through their thorough attention to the editing, revising, and proofing of the manuscript across its development.

Peter J. Anderson, Koji Maeda,
Zane M. Diamond, and Chizu Sato,
Australia and Japan, March 2020

Abbreviations

ACARA	Australian Curriculum, Assessment and Reporting Authority
ACER	Australian Council for Education Research
ACFAP	Advisory Council for Future Ainu Policy
ACPA	Ainu Cultural Promotion Act
AECC	Aboriginal Education Consultative Committee
AECG	Aboriginal Education Consultative Group
AHRC	Australian Human Rights Commission
AIAS	Australian Institute of Aboriginal Studies
AIATSIS	Australian Institute of Aboriginal and Torres Strait Islander Studies
AITSL	Australian Institute of Teaching and School Leadership
APB	Aboriginal Protection Board
APPA	Ainu Policy Promotion Act
APSC	Australian Public Service Commission
APST	Australian Professional Standards for Teachers
BLL	Buraku Liberation League
CALD	Culturally and linguistically diverse
CAR	Council for Aboriginal Reconciliation
CCP	Cross-curriculum priorities
CIA	Comparative institutional analysis
CSR	Corporate Social Responsibility
DET	Department of Education
EEATSIT	Education and Employment of Aboriginal and Torres Strait Islander Teachers
FCAATSI	Federal Council for the Advancement of Aborigines and Torres Strait Islanders
HEW	Higher Education Worker
HREOC	Human Rights and Equal Opportunity Commission
HUCAIS	Hokkaido University Centre for Ainu and Indigenous Studies
HUE	Hokkaido University of Education
IAHEA	Indigenous Australian Higher Education Association

IEA	International Association for the Evaluation of Educational Achievement
IHEAC	Indigenous Higher Education Advisory Council
ILO	International Labour Organization
ISP	Indigenous Support Programme
ITE	Initial Teacher Education
KPI	Key Performance Indicator
MATSITI	More Aboriginal and Torres Strait Islander Teachers Initiative
MCEETYA	Ministerial Council on Employment Education Training and Youth Affairs
MEXT	Ministry of Education, Culture, Sports, Science and Technology
NACC	National Aboriginal Consultative Council
NAEC	National Aboriginal Education Committee
NATSIHEC	National Aboriginal and Torres Strait Islander Higher Education Consortium
NCBE	Naha City Board of Education
NIAA	National Indigenous Australian Agency
NIHEN	National Indigenous Higher Education Network
NIHEWS	National Indigenous Higher Education Workforce Strategy
NITE	National Inquiry into Teacher Education
NSW	North South Wales
NTEU	National Tertiary Education Union
OJC	Okinawa Junior College
OKTSC	Okinawa University Teaching Support Centre
PIRLS	Progress in International Reading Literacy Study
RAPs	Reconciliation Action Plans
RCAGA	Royal Commission on Australian Government Administration
RSC	Reconciliation Spiralling Continuum
SETU	Student Evaluation of Teaching Units
TIMSS	Trends in International Mathematics and Science Study
TRC	Truth and Reconciliation Commission
UN	United Nations
UNPFII	United Nations Permanent Forum for Indigenous Issues
WGIP	Working Group on Indigenous Populations
WIPCE	World Indigenous Peoples Conference on Education

Legislations

Cases
Mabo v Queensland (No. 2) [1992] HCA 23; 175 CLR 1

International materials
Indigenous and Tribal Peoples Convention, 1969. Entered into force 5 September 1991. ILO, C169. (*ILO 169*)
International Convention on the Elimination of All Forms of Racial Discrimination, 21 December 1965, 660 UNTS 195 (entered into force 4 January 1969).
UN Declaration on the Rights of Indigenous Peoples (2007) A/RES/61/295. Retrieved 31 May 2020 from www.un.org/development/desa/indigenousPeoples/declaration-on-the-rights-of-indigenous-Peoples.html (*UNDRIP*)
The Coolangatta Statement: On Indigenous Peoples' Rights in Education. (6 August 1999). World Indigenous Peoples' Conference on Education, Hilo, Hawai'i. Retrieved 31 May 2020 from press-files.anu.edu.au/downloads/press/p15621/pdf/ch191.pdf (*Coolangatta Statement*)
Universal Declaration of Human Rights, GA Res 217A (III), UN GAOR, UN Doc A/810 (10 December 1948)

Legislation (draft and passed into law)
Japan
Family Register Act (1871)（戸籍法）
Hokkaido Former Aboriginal Protection Act (1899) (Meiji 32)（北海道旧土人保護法）
Regulations for the Education of Former Aboriginal Children (1901)（旧土人児童教育規程）
Nihon-koku Kenpō (Constitution of Japan [1947])（日本国憲法）
Private School Act (1949)（私立学校法）

Draft Law Concerning the Ainu People (1984) (General Assembly of the Ainu Association of Hokkaido) (Draft Law) (アイヌ民族に関する法律（案）)

Act on the Promotion of Ainu Culture and Dissemination and Enlightenment of Knowledge About Ainu Tradition, etc. (Act No. 52 of 1997) (*Ainu Cultural Promotion Act*) (アイヌ文化の振興並びにアイヌの伝統等に関する知識の普及及び啓発に関する法律)

Basic Act on Education (Act No. 120 of 2006) (教育基本法)

Act on Promoting Measures to Realize a Society in Which the Pride of the Ainu People Is Respected (Act No. 16 of 2019) (*Ainu Policy Promotion Act*) (アイヌの人々の誇りが尊重される社会を実現するための施策の推進に関する法律 [アイヌ政策推進法])

Australia

Commonwealth of Australia Constitution Act 1900 (UK) (Australian Constitution)
Aborigines Act No. 1905/014 (5 Edw.VII No.14)
Higher Education Support Act 2003 (Cth) (HESA)
Aboriginal Institute of Aboriginal Studies Act 1964 (Cth) (AIAS Act)
Australian Institute of Aboriginal and Torres Strait Islander Studies Act 1989 (Cth) (AIATSIS Act)

Glossary

All definitions are from *Oxford English Dictionary* [Online] (Oxford University Press, 2000) with additional commentary.

Please note:
  In this edited collection, 'Indigenous' with an upper case 'I' refers to Indigenous Peoples of Australia and Japan.
  Depending on the context of the discussions found in each chapter, Indigenous, Indigenous Peoples, First Nations people, First Peoples, Ainu people, Aboriginal people, and Torres Strait Islander people are used interchangeably and refer to the original inhabitants of Japan and Australia including the Torres Strait Islands lands and seas.

Indigenous Peoples

There is no general agreement on the definition of 'Indigenous' with respect to Indigenous peoples and their rights. The most common is the 'working definition' formulated by special rapporteur for the UN Sub-Commission, José Martinez Cobo, in his study of the problem of discrimination against Indigenous populations (Martínez Cobo, 1981, 1982, 1983). In 1996, Erica-Irene Daes, Chairperson of the Working Group on Indigenous Populations (WGIP), and Special Rapporteur of the UN Sub-Commission on Human Rights, adopted the working definition suggested by Martínez Cobo (1982):

> Indigenous communities, peoples and nations are those which, having a historical continuity with pre-invasion and pre-colonial societies that developed on their territories, consider themselves distinct from other sectors of the societies now prevailing in those territories, or parts of them. They form at present non-dominant sectors of society and are determined to preserve, develop and transmit to future generations their ancestral territories, and their ethnic identity, as the basis of their continued existence as peoples, in accordance with their own cultural patterns, social institutions and legal systems.[1]

The United Nations' WGIP used the following to guide its work (Martínez Cobo, 1982):

> In summary, the factors which modern international organizations and legal experts (including indigenous legal experts and members of the academic family) have considered relevant to understanding the concept of 'indigenous' include:
> - experience of subjugation, exclusion or discrimination, whether or not these conditions persist.
> - priority in time with respect the occupation and use of a specific territory;
> - self-identification, as well as recognition by other groups, or by State authorities, as a distinct collectivity; and
> - the voluntary perpetuation of cultural distinctiveness, which may include aspects of language, social organization, religion and spiritual values, modes of production, laws and institutions;

Interestingly, although both nations eventually endorsed UNDRIP, neither Australia nor Japan has adopted Convention 169 of the International Labour Organization (ILO). According to ILO, Indigenous Peoples constitute about 5 per cent of the world's population, or nearly 370 million people spread across over 70 countries, accounting for about 15 per cent of the world's poor. Indigenous Peoples care for an estimated 22 per cent of the Earth's surface and protect nearly 80 per cent of remaining biodiversity on the planet.[2] ILO explicitly highlights the importance of education for the world's Indigenous Peoples to support them to enter the mainstream labour market in a manner that does not exploit either their labour or their resources.

Thirty years ago, in 1989, the ILO's Convention No. 169 (1989) specified the following peoples to be recognised as being Indigenous and tribal Peoples:

> Article 1
> 1. This Convention applies to:
>   (a) tribal peoples in independent countries whose social, cultural and economic conditions distinguish them from other sections of the national community, and whose status is regulated wholly or partially by their own customs or traditions or by special laws or regulations;
>   (b) peoples in independent countries who are regarded as indigenous on account of their descent from the populations which inhabited the country, or a geographical region to which the country belongs, at the time of conquest or colonisation or the establishment of present state boundaries and who, irrespective of their legal status, retain some or all of their own social, economic, cultural and political institutions.

2. Self-identification as indigenous or tribal shall be regarded as a fundamental criterion for determining the groups to which the provisions of this Convention apply.

It can be seen that both the UN mechanism of UNDRIP and the ILO Convention 169 share common essential elements that are required for recognition as being an Indigenous person for the purposes of having their *sui generis* rights addressed.

Aboriginal

'First or earliest as recorded by history; present from the beginning; primitive. Of peoples, plants, and animals: inhabiting or existing in a land from earliest times; strictly native, indigenous' (Oxford University Press, 2000).

Commentary

'Aboriginal' was the word adopted by the English to collectively describe the Indigenous peoples of the lands they subsequently colonised in Australia, New Zealand, Malay Peninsula, the Americas, and Canada. Some of these nations no longer use this term but it is still commonly used in Australia.

Aboriginal Australians are one of two Indigenous Peoples recognised by the Australian government (see 'Torres Strait Islander'). This generic descriptor refers to the various Indigenous Peoples of the Australian mainland and Tasmania. The generic term 'Aboriginal' refers to those people who identify as Aboriginal according to the definition. In 1981, the Australian government's Department of Aboriginal Affairs developed a definition of an Aboriginal Australian person (see further explanation in Gardiner-Garden, 2003). Government agencies and community organisations usually accept three 'working criteria' as confirmation of Aboriginal heritage:

- being of Aboriginal descent
- identifying as an Aboriginal person
- being accepted as such by the community in which one lives, or formerly lived

All of these things must apply.

Ainu

A member of (the people descended from) an Aboriginal People of northern Japan, formerly also living in neighbouring islands and parts of the adjacent Kuril Islands.

Commentary

The term Ainu People is widely recognised globally, and now legally defined by the *Ainu Policy Promotion Act*, which came into force in 2019, is used in the research literature; therefore, we will use this term interchangeably with the phrase *Indigenous Peoples* that has been defined and recognised legally through UNDRIP.

Torres Strait Islander

These are the Indigenous people of the Torres Strait Islands. They are distinct from the Aboriginal people of the rest of Australia (see 'Aboriginal'), and are generally referred to separately (see further explanation in Gardiner-Garden, 2003).

Government agencies and community organisations usually accept three 'working criteria' as confirmation of Torres Strait Islander heritage:

- being of Torres Strait Islander descent
- identifying as a Torres Strait Islander person
- being accepted as such by the community in which one lives, or formerly lived.

All of these things must apply.

First Nations and First Peoples

Predominantly used in Canada, and a term recognised in the Canadian Constitution, 'First Nation' as a term became officially used beginning in 1980s to replace the term 'Indian band' in referring to groups of Indians with common government and language (Gibson, 2009). 'First Peoples' recognises the historical fact that Indigenous Peoples were the first people to occupy the lands and waterways of their estates. It reminds all others that they came later and therefore their claims must be considered as being less than the claims of 'First Peoples'.

Other key terms and phrases

Affirmative action

'Active measures taken by an employer, college, and so on, to provide opportunities for members of minority groups, women, or other people regarded as having suffered from discrimination. Often used to address the consequences of deficit education'.

Cultural diversity

'The condition or quality of being diverse, different, or varied; difference, unlikeness applied in particular to the distinctive ideas, customs, social behaviour, products, or way of life of a particular nation, society, people, or period'.

Commentary

We use this term to highlight an intra-group recognition of difference within the nation-state formation.

Deficit thinking in education

Originally deficit was widely understood as a financial term. The meaning of this word is 'the amount by which a sum of money, or the like, falls short of what is due or required'. The word has been borrowed into the field of Education Studies to describe education theories and practices that approach the learner as 'falling short, having a deficiency' rather than considering that it is the education system that might be failing the learner.

Commentary

Educationalists in Indigenous Education have pointed to deficit thinking by teachers and more broadly by education systems as being an approach that blames the child's cultural background for academic failure rather than asking questions of mainstream teaching and learning practices that might discriminate against Indigenous learners.

An important professional development programme for Australian educators (teachers and teacher educators in particular), *Respect, Relationships and Reconciliation*, says of deficit thinking in education:

> When students' academic outcomes are below expectations, teachers, or indeed the whole school, may view this as a problem characteristic within the child's cultural background or within their family or community.
> In challenging this kind of deficit thinking, it is important to look at the classroom and school environment.[3]

Lifeways

'A way through life, a course of life; a way or manner of life (in later use), especially one that is customary or traditional'.
Commentary
We use this term to express the totality of a person's way of living that is shaped by what is variously described in literature as: culture, history, language,

and so on. Lifeways are a composite of habits, customs, attitudes, behaviours both individually and socially constructed and expressed in ways that can be translated from lived experiences as tacit knowledge into formal knowledge through processes of knowledge production, legitimation, dissemination, and reproductions that can be used in teaching contexts.

Mainstream education

'Of or relating to the mainstream; belonging to or characteristic of an established tradition, field of activity, and so on; conventional'.

Commentary

This descriptor is used in education to denote the type of education system that is offered by the nation-state as its formal education system. Sometimes used conterminously with 'formal', these descriptors together describe an education system that is established by the state. This approach to education has been challenged by Indigenous Peoples as being hostile to their distinctiveness and as being one of the mechanisms by which attempts by the nation-state have been made to extinguish their cultural distinctiveness within the nation.

As a counterpoint to this observation, many Indigenous people in both Japan and Australia have achieved high academic success in formal mainstream education. The contemporary argument in education is that formal, mainstream education must be more inclusive of the diversity of the needs of its learners, especially those Indigenous students whose distinctive rights have been recognised in UNDRIP by both governments.

Marginal

'Of an individual or social group: isolated from or not conforming to the dominant society or culture; (perceived as being) on the edge of a society or social unit; belonging to a minority group (frequently with implications of consequent disadvantage). Also, partly belonging to two differing social groups or cultures but not fully integrated into either'.

Modernisation (Japan)

Begun during the early Meiji Restoration period, the Japanese government enacted sweeping reforms to social, political, and economic aspects of traditional Japanese and Ainu lifeways, explicitly aiming to modernise the country by adopting the Western style. This process of reform also attempted to extinguish the distinctiveness of the Ainu people. In 1899, the Japanese government passed an act labelling the Ainu as 'former aborigines', with the idea they would assimilate and they were granted automatic Japanese citizenship, effectively denying them their distinctiveness as an Indigenous group (Loos & Osanai, 1993).

Multicultural

'Of or relating to a society consisting of a number of cultural groups, especially in which the distinctive cultural identity of each group is maintained'.

Nation

'A large aggregate of communities and individuals united by factors such as common descent, language, culture, history, or occupation of the same territory, so as to form a distinct people' (Oxford University Press, 2000).

Nation-state

'An independent political state formed from a people who share a common national identity (historically, culturally, or ethnically); (more generally) any independent political state' (Oxford University Press, 2000).

Personhood

'The quality or condition of being a person; especially personal identity, selfhood'.

Commentary

In this book, we have ensured that the personhood of Indigenous peoples is reflected in the language that has been used. It is common in colonial and imperial education to use the descriptor (adjective) 'Aborigine' or 'Ainu' as a noun. In text, we use phrases such as 'Aboriginal person', 'Ainu people', and 'Indigenous Peoples'. We always capitalise the words Aboriginal, Ainu, Torres Strait Islander, and Indigenous in acknowledgement that we are speaking about distinct collectivities with *sui generis* rights who are becoming recognised in the Australian and Japanese education systems.

The capitalisation of the word 'Indigenous' also distinguishes Australia's Indigenous Peoples, the Aboriginal Peoples and the Torres Strait Islander Peoples, from anyone who was born in Australia, who are generally referred to with small 'i' 'indigenous'. Many computing packages now have a spell check function that recognises only the small 'I' indigenous, so it is something that writers and teachers need to pay attention to, over-riding the automated system to use the capital 'I'. Students will commonly say, 'but I was born here so that makes me indigenous!' That is true in the small 'I' sense but it does not make that person Indigenous in the sense recognised by UNDRIP in its definition (see 'Indigenous Peoples').

Reconciliation/reconciliation (Australia)

'The action or an act of bringing a thing or things to agreement, concord, or harmony; the fact of being made consistent or compatible. Reconciliation is recognised as being "the restoration of friendly relations" and "the action of making one view or belief compatible with another"'.

Commentary

In this book, we consider both the idea of 'reconciliation' and the concept of 'Reconciliation' as it has been employed in Australian universities as part of their social justice initiatives. The idea and the concept will be discussed more fully in Chapter 12 (this edition).

Sovereignty

'Supremacy in respect of power, domination, or rank; supreme dominion, authority, or rule'.

State

'A community of people living in a defined territory and organized under its own government; a commonwealth, a nation. Also, occasionally: the territory occupied by such a community' (Oxford University Press, 2000).

Sui generis

The term *sui generis* is used in the sense that Indigenous peoples have cultural and intellectual property rights that exist in their own right (which also means that they were not extinguished by later legal frameworks (Janke, Australian Institute of Aboriginal and Torres Strait Islander Studies, & Aboriginal and Torres Strait Islander Commission, 1998).

Traditional and traditionally oriented

'Of, or relating to, tradition, or a particular tradition; based on, derived from, or sanctioned by tradition; long-established, customary, conventional'.

References

Gardiner-Garden, J. (2003). *Defining Aboriginality in Australia*. Canberra, Australia: Australian Government. Retrieved 31 May 2020 from www.aph.gov.au/About_Parliament/Parliamentary_Departments/Parliamentary_Library/Publications_Archive/CIB/cib0203/03Cib10.

Gibson, G. (2009). *A new look at Canadian Indian policy: Respect the collective – Promote the individual.* Vancouver, Canada: Fraser Institute.

International Labour Organization (ILO). (1989). *C169 – Indigenous and tribal peoples convention, 1989 (No. 169).* Retrieved 31 May 2020 from https://www.ilo.org/dyn/normlex/en/f?p=NORMLEXPUB:12100:0::NO:12100:P12100_INSTRUMENT_ID:312314:NO.

Janke, T., Australian institute of Aboriginal and Torres Strait Islander studies, & Aboriginal and Torres Strait Islander commission. (1998). *Our culture our future: Report on Australian Indigenous cultural and intellectual property rights.* Sydney, Australia: Michael Frankel.

Loos, N., & Osanai, T. (Eds.). (1993). *Indigenous minorities and education: Australian and Japanese perspectives on their Indigenous Peoples, the Ainu, Aborigines and Torres Strait Islanders.* Tokyo, Japan: Sanyusha Publishing.

Martínez Cobo, J. R. (1981). *Study of the problem of discrimination against Indigenous populations: Final report submitted by the special rapporteur.* Geneva, Switzerland: United Nations. Retrieved 31 May 2020 from www.un.org/esa/socdev/unpfii/documents/MCS_intro_1981_en.pdf.

Martínez Cobo, J. R. (1982). *Study of the problem of discrimination against Indigenous populations: Final report submitted by the special rapporteur (Report No. E/CN.4/Sub.2/476).* (E/CN.4/Sub.2/1982/2). United Nations, Department of Economic and Social Affairs, Indigenous Peoples. Retrieved 31 May 2020 from www.un.org/esa/socdev/unpfii/documents/MCS_intro_1981_en.pdf.

Martínez Cobo, J. R. (1983). *Study of the problem of discrimination against Indigenous populations: Final report submitted by the special rapporteur.* (E/CN.4/Sub.2/476). Retrieved 31 May 2020 from www.un.org/esa/socdev/unpfii/documents/MCS_intro_1983_en.pdf

Oxford University Press. (2000). *Oxford English Dictionary.* Oxford, England: Oxford University Press; and Online.

Notes

1 E/CN.4/Sub.2/1986/7 Add.1–4, paragraph 379.
2 www.ilo.org/global/topics/indigenous-tribal/lang--en/index.htm.
3 https://rrr.edu.au/unit/module-2/topic-1/deficit-thinking/.

Chapter 1

Introducing Indigenous education in Japan and Australia

Peter J. Anderson, Koji Maeda, Zane M. Diamond, and Chizu Sato

Introduction

This chapter explains the background to the collection of chapters in this book, which stemmed from our shared interest in how ancestral and modern education approaches have shaped the education of Indigenous Peoples. We are a group of academics across the disciplines of Indigenous Education, Teacher Education, Indigenous Studies, Educational Anthropology, the Sociology of Education, and Educational Leadership who share a sub-field of interest in international and comparative perspectives within our chosen fields of expertise.

Historically, the nations of Japan and Australia have had little to compare directly in educational terms, except where they participate in global assessment comparisons such as those conducted by the International Association for the Evaluation of Educational Achievement (IEA), Progress in International Reading Literacy Study (PIRLS), and Trends in International Mathematics and Science Study (TIMSS). Modern education systems tend to focus on achieving goals set at the national level and are strongly influenced by local sociocultural, political, historical, and economic circumstances. Throughout the development of the modern system of studying and researching the provision of education services, the fields of the sociology and anthropology of education have provided some opportunities for comparative studies, but these have proved fraught because of the complexities of local and regional conditions. In the case of comparison between Japan and Australia, Loos (1993, p. 4) noted:

> Despite the distance that separates Australia and Japan and their very different societies and cultures, their histories intertwined [sic] – marginally prior to World War II and increasingly since then. Indeed, today, despite the fact that Japan is an economic giant while Australia is only a lower, middle order power, the relationship between the two nations has become symbiotic.

In 1993, during the UN's Year for the World's Indigenous People, Loos and Osanai (1993) published a collaborative report that investigated Australian and

Japanese perspectives on the education of Ainu, Aborigines, and Torres Strait Islanders. In doing so, they highlighted that such an international event as declared by the UN's Year enabled scholars to gather and compare the state of Indigenous matters in these two nations. Now, 27 years later, the Loos and Osanai publication provides a valuable collection of thinking to underpin this book. While our collection of chapters focuses on education, the weight is still firmly tilted towards the field of Indigenous Studies, with scholars trying to grapple with how to change mainstream formal education systems to include Indigenous perspectives (Ma Rhea & Russell, 2012).

Another initiative also led by the UN in the form of the *United Nations Declaration on the Rights of Indigenous Peoples* (UNDRIP) – a non-binding document adopted by the UN on 13 September 2007 – provides a further pivotal opportunity for Japanese and Australian scholars to collaborate in this field of research. In doing so, the authors of this book have extended and deepened the focus on education that draws on the field of Indigenous Studies. We observe that because of the impact of UNDRIP, there is now a stronger focus on the structural changes that have and have not yet occurred in the provision of educational services to the Indigenous Peoples of Australia and Japan. Arguably, this is the most significant shift between the approach taken by the authors in the Loos and Osanai collection of 1993 and this book's 2020 collection – a shift in education from an emphasis on Indigenous Studies in education towards an emphasis on systemic, organisational developments that embrace the aspirations of UNDRIP.

In 2008, the Government of Japan recognised the Ainu as an Indigenous People (Advisory Council for Future Ainu Policy [ACFAP], 2009) and began developing an Ainu policy that has now been formally ratified (the *Ainu Policy Promotion Act* (Act No. 16 of 2019). In 2009, the Australian government endorsed the UNDRIP (AHRC, 2009). In effect, Japan and Australia have officially recognised that Indigenous Peoples live within their respective nation-state boundaries. The endorsement of UNDRIP (United Nations, 2007) by both nations has provided the authors in this collection with a pivotal historical moment for examining the way this international rights mechanism has changed how Japan and Australia, in particular, have changed their approaches to the education of Indigenous citizens and how they educate non-Indigenous citizens about the lifeways of Indigenous Peoples.

As will be examined throughout the book, the historical circumstances by which Indigenous Peoples were brought into the modern nations of Japan and Australia continue to shape Indigenous education. The global Indigenous Peoples' Movement, which has become more publicly recognised following the adoption of UNDRIP, is working with national governments to increase recognition of the distinctive lifeways of Indigenous Peoples and, in particular, their rights in education. Globally, Indigenous Peoples are demanding that educationalists ask questions about the current arrangements in education systems that were developed to extinguish the distinctiveness of Indigenous Peoples for the sake of nation building and colonisation.

Since colonisation of the Australian landmass by the English in 1788, Australia continues to have an underpinning imperial structure governed by the British Queen, overlaid with a system of parliamentary democracy. Since the Meiji Restoration in 1868, Japan has evolved a strong, resident, imperial system together with a parliamentary democratic system of governance. In 1993, Loos observed:

> In Japan and Australia, it is clear that the comfortable, self-fulfilling assumption of the colonists, that their Indigenous peoples did not exist or would soon disappear, has been destroyed. The Ainu, Australian Aborigines and Torres Strait Islanders have tenaciously maintained their identity and continue to assert their human rights not only as individuals but also as three separate peoples emerging from the domination of colonialist expansion.
>
> (p. 4)

Indigenous Peoples lived on the lands and waterways prior to the colonial (Australia) and imperial (Japan) periods – lands and waterways now claimed as 'belonging' to the nation-state. We are not promoting an anti-imperial stance in this book but, rather, we are examining the nature of the education of Indigenous peoples before and after UNDRIP and whether the *sui generis* rights (rights *of themselves*, already existing before the formation of the nation-states of Japan and Australia) of Indigenous Peoples are now becoming recognised. Echoing the Loos and Osanai (1993) collection of essays, we examine the potential of the ancestral education systems of the Indigenous People of both nations to be brought into mainstream, formal education system. We focus on leadership issues and organisational development in higher education and teacher education, and we assess how UNDRIP has influenced approaches in both nations to the education of Indigenous students and how each is educating non-Indigenous students about Indigenous matters.

We note that Japanese and Australian histories are quite different in the manner in which they were territorially occupied, but efforts in both countries to educate Indigenous Peoples have followed similar assimilationist approaches. This collection of writings, drawn from research and teaching experience, seeks to revisit the impact of UNDRIP in changing the course of assimilation towards recognition of the lifeways of Indigenous Australian and Japanese Peoples and their integration into mainstream education systems.

The rest of this chapter begins with quoting the relevant sections of the UNDRIP before providing an overview of Indigenous education history in both countries. The chapter closes with a detailed summary of the structure and content of the rest of the book.

UNDRIP: Articles of direct relevance to education

The UNDRIP, in addition to its general all-encompassing recognition of Indigenous Peoples' rights, pays particular attention to rights in education. Articles 14, 15, 21, and 31 require modern education systems to work in partnership with knowledgeable Indigenous experts to further Indigenous People's rights in education (United Nations 2007).

> Article 14
> 1. Indigenous peoples have the right to establish and control their educational systems and institutions providing education in their own languages, in a manner appropriate to their cultural methods of teaching and learning.
> 2. Indigenous individuals, particularly children, have the right to all levels and forms of education of the State without discrimination.
> 3. States shall, in conjunction with Indigenous peoples, take effective measures, in order for Indigenous individuals, particularly children, including those living outside their communities, to have access, when possible, to an education in their own culture and provided in their own language.
>
> Article 15
> 1. Indigenous peoples have the right to the dignity and diversity of their cultures, traditions, histories and aspirations which shall be appropriately reflected in education and public information.
> 2. States shall take effective measures, in consultation and cooperation with the Indigenous peoples concerned, to combat prejudice and eliminate discrimination and to promote tolerance, understanding and good relations among Indigenous peoples and all other segments of society.
>
> Article 21
> 1. Indigenous peoples have the right, without discrimination, to the improvement of their economic and social conditions, including, inter alia, in the areas of education, employment, vocational training and retraining, housing, sanitation, health and social security.
> 2. States shall take effective measures and, where appropriate, special measures to ensure continuing improvement of their economic and social conditions. Particular attention shall be paid to the rights and special needs of Indigenous elders, women, youth, children and persons with disabilities.
>
> Article 31
> 1. Indigenous peoples have the right to maintain, control, protect and develop their cultural heritage, traditional knowledge and traditional

cultural expressions, as well as the manifestations of their sciences, technologies and cultures, including human and genetic resources, seeds, medicines, knowledge of the properties of fauna and flora, oral traditions, literatures, designs, sports and traditional games and visual and performing arts. They also have the 23 right to maintain, control, protect and develop their intellectual property over such cultural heritage, traditional knowledge, and traditional cultural expressions.

2. In conjunction with Indigenous peoples, States shall take effective measures to recognize and protect the exercise of these rights.

Both Japan and Australia have endorsed these Articles. Even so, such endorsement has been built on the preceding years of slowly building recognition derived from the concerted actions of Indigenous Peoples in both nations to make representations to key elected decision makers, law makers, and government bureaucrats to promote the recognition of their rights (ACFAP, 2009; AHRC, 2009).

Recognition of the special place of Indigenous peoples

The sub-section that follows presents a selected timeline that allows an understanding of how the modern nations of Japan and Australia have come to the recognition of the special place of Indigenous Peoples, beginning prior to the endorsement of UNDRIP and spanning numerous policies and actions designed to recognise the rights of Japanese Ainu, Australian Aboriginal People, and Torres Strait Islander People up to 2020 with the passing of the *Ainu Policy Promotion Act* in Japan.

We pay particular attention to those events that reflect how formal education systems, both schooling and universities, have responded to this recognition of distinctiveness. Formal education systems, in our analysis, have sometimes pre-empted and sometimes followed broader societal legal and government policy changes, albeit slowly and often dependent on the political will of those in charge of the provision of education services.

Timeline: Indigenous Education in Japan

After the Meiji Restoration in 1868, the Japanese government renamed the island of *Ezochi*, the traditional estates of Ainu people, calling it Hokkaido and transforming it into a state-owned land in 1869. Since then, the Japanese government has been principally responsible for the Ainu policy. In 2008, the Japanese government officially recognised the Ainu as Indigenous people. The Hokkaido prefectural government also has responsibility for the improvement of Ainu life, with the financial support being provided by the national government since 1974.

Other distinctive communities such as Okinawa people live on their traditional estates known as the Ryūkyū Kingdom. In 1879, the Satsuma Domain forced the Ryūkyū Kingdom to become part of Japan. Distinctive communities such as the Okinawans have not been recognised as Indigenous people by the Japanese government and, because of complex geopolitical forces, the matter of recognition as Indigenous Peoples continues to be debated among ethically distinctive communities in Japan who pre-exited the more recent formation of the Japanese nation. Hence, for the purposes of this chapter, we discuss Indigenous Education provisions which are officially concerned with Ainu people living mainly in Hokkaido and nearby areas.

1899

The government enacted the *Hokkaido Former Aboriginal Protection Act* with the expectation that Ainu people would become small farmers and assimilate as Japanese imperial subjects. The post-war Japanese state created a single category of Japanese citizens, which included Indigenous Ainu and Okinawan Peoples. In 1984, the Hokkaido Utari Association issued the law proposal:

> Universities will establish courses in Ainu culture and history. Teachers of these courses should be recruited from ethnic Ainu people who excel in these fields and are appointed as professors, associate professors and lecturers. Such appointments require a degree of flexibility in normal academic requirements. Universities should provide special consideration for Ainu children so that they can enter universities and focus on their respective studies.
> (Hokkaido Utari Association, 1984)

In effect, well before the endorsement of UNDRIP, Ainu people were promoting self-determination and expanding the possibilities of empowerment for Indigenous Peoples into Japanese higher education. The statement quoted conveys the Association's desire for tertiary-educated Ainu experts to actively participate in decision making concerning Ainu matters, and, ultimately, to pursue self-determination. In order to achieve such an outcome, the Association requires universities and/or governments to provide a quota for Ainu at universities.

1997

The government enacted the *Law for the Promotion of the Ainu Culture and for the Dissemination and Advocacy for the Traditions of the Ainu and the Ainu Culture (1997)* (*Ainu Cultural Promotion Act [ACPA]*) promoting measures which enabled both Ainu and the majority *Wajin* Japanese students to become enlightened about Ainu culture and tradition. At the time, this was an initiative of individual academics or universities rather than a systematic effort to promote Ainu culture or provide assistance to Ainu students to participate more inclusively in Japanese schooling or in higher education.

2007

UNDRIP provided a normative framework for policies on Indigenous Peoples and for multicultural and multi-ethnic societies in Japan.

2008

On 6 June 2008, in the 169th session of the DIET, both the House of Representatives and House of Councillors unanimously adopted the *Resolution to Recognize the Ainu as an Indigenous People*, stating:

> [T]he Ainu as an Indigenous people who have resided in the northern part of the Japanese archipelago, in particular, Hokkaido, and who maintain their own unique languages, religions and culture.

The government established the ACFAP, an expert study group on Ainu policies, and began research and discussion towards the formulation of Ainu policies which would include education (ACFAP, 2009).

2009

According to the report of ACFAP (2009), the Council for Ainu Policy Promotion (CAPP) was established with the cabinet secretary as its Chairperson, and it worked on the recommendations made by the former Advisory Council, which identified policy priorities. The Council consisted of 14 members in total, including five Ainu representatives, so that it might better reflect Ainu People's views on the policy agenda. It was then divided into two working groups with specific roles: one group to discuss multi-ethnic co-living to examine '[a] space that symbolizes ethnic coexistence' and the other group to research the lives of Ainu people living outside Hokkaido through the conduct of 'a survey of the living conditions of Ainu outside Hokkaido'. After these groups finished submitting their reports, a working group for 'Ainu Policy Promotion' was newly established, which led to a new *Ainu Policy Promotion Act* (CAPP, 2012).

2019

Because the *Ainu Culture Promotion Act* focused mainly on cultural aspects, a new law which recognised Ainu Indigenous rights after the UNDRIP was promulgated. The *Act on Promoting Measures to Realize a Society in Which the Pride of the Ainu People Is Respected* (Act No. 16 of 2019) (*Ainu Policy Promotion Act* [APPA]) became effective on 18 April 2019. It is worth noting that for the first time the Ainu are recognised as Indigenous People by law; however, there were objections from Ainu right groups that the law does not recognise Ainu Indigenous rights as an Indigenous right as recognised by the UNDRIP.

2020

The *National Ainu Museum and Park* opened in mid-2020.

Timeline: Indigenous Education in Australia

To compile this timeline of progress towards a greater understanding and incorporation of Indigenous Education in Australia, the authors have drawn on the work of Fletcher (1989a, 1989b), Cadzow (2010), and Burridge and Chodkiewicz (2012), as well as other authors specifically cited in the discussion. A number of examples here are drawn from New South Wales because it was here that many initiatives were developed that were later reproduced with local variations across the nation.

New South Wales was the first colony to be established in Australia and the methods it developed, particularly regarding the education of Indigenous children, guided many later approaches taken (Parbury, 1991). It is important to note here that, while the Australian government is the overarching national government, with a key role in the collection of taxes and the disbursement of funds according to its policies, it is the State governments of New South Wales, Victoria, Tasmania, South Australia, Western Australia, and Queensland and the Territory governments of Northern Territory and the Australian Capital Territory that are responsible for the provision of education services.

In the case of Indigenous Education, the Australian government is responsible for the provision of services to Indigenous Australians. Therefore – as will be discussed in later chapters – historically, there have been many instances of Indigenous Education becoming a political matter between various levels of government where policies and the funding for those policies have been cause for contention but having little to do with improving education services for Indigenous children.

1814

Governor of New South Wales Lachlan Macquarie developed a 15-point plan for the provision of education services to Indigenous children (Macquarie, 1814).

1815–1822

Governor Lachlan Macquarie and the Missionary William Shelley established the Native Institution as an 'experiment' to teach Aboriginal children how to be labourers and servants for colonists. Children were instructed in basic literacy skills, agriculture, and craft, and encouraged to convert to Christianity. Some students were brought to the school by force, and students were separated from their Aboriginal families and cultural influences (Brook & Kohen, 1991; Fletcher, 1989a, pp. 19–21; Read, 2006).

1837

The Select Committee of House of Commons (UK) inquired into the conditions of Indigenous People in British colonies. The Select Committee recommended a system of Protectors for Aboriginal people in Victoria, eventually extending such a committee to all the colonies. The Committee was influenced by the emerging anti-slavery movement in the UK. Education is regarded as an important mechanism to undertake the work of both protecting and educating Indigenous people into the new colonies.

1870s

Some Aboriginal parents began to enrol their children in schools. Population growth, the expansion of public schools, and increasing Aboriginal employment on rural properties contributed to higher Aboriginal student enrolments. Several parents wanted their children to learn skills to improve their children's economic and social prospects.

1905–1909

In 1905, the Australian government passed the *Aborigines Act* No. 1905/014 (5 Edw.VII No.14) into law. In 1909, for example, a law to protect Aboriginal people was passed in New South Wales as the *Aboriginal Protection Act* (NSW 1909). This Act like those then enacted in other states and territories increased the influence of the Aboriginal Protection Board (APB) over many areas of Aboriginal people's lives. The *Aboriginal Protection Act* (NSW 1909) stated that if Aboriginal children were found to be 'neglected', the Board could take custody of the children. This enabled the APB to remove children between the age of 14–21 from their families and 'apprentice' them. One of the specific locations used by the Protectors was schools. Many Indigenous children, not only in NSW but across Australia, were taken into the custody of the Protector directly from the school they attended.

1957

Federal Council for the Advancement of Aborigines & Torres Strait Islanders (FCAATSI) formed. This organisation, which initially had non-Aboriginal and Aboriginal membership, acted as a national organiser of local and state campaigns for rights for Aboriginal people. A strong focus of FCAATSI was to take the control of the education of Indigenous Australian children from the Australian State and Territory governments, particularly Ministers of Education, back into the hands of Aboriginal and Torres Strait Islander parents and communities.

1963

Aboriginal Education Consultative Committee (AECC) formed. This group consulted with Aboriginal people regarding their education desires and needs and conveyed this information to the NSW Education Department. They recognised that Aboriginal families needed to be involved in education.

1965

The *Aboriginal Institute of Aboriginal Studies Act 1964* (Cth) (AIAS Act) and the subsequent 1989 Act that included Torres Strait Islander people established a research institute to collect, publish, and research the cultures and societies of Aboriginal and Torres Strait Islander Peoples (Australian Institute of Aboriginal and Torres Strait Islander Studies (AIATSIS) (2018). AIATSIS continues to provide the most extensive collection of culturally appropriate material about Indigenous Australian lifeways. As later chapters will demonstrate, the material held by AIATSIS is an essential collection that can be reliably used (with permissions) by teachers and teacher educators to develop locally appropriate curriculum resources.

1979

The Australian Education Council endorsed the principle that Aboriginal and Torres Strait Islander Studies should be a core unit in all pre-service and teacher education programmes (Craven, 1979, p. 3).

1980

The National Aboriginal Education Committee (NAEC) produced the first Indigenous education policy, the *National Aboriginal Education Committee Policy* (1980), used as one of the key documents in subsequent government investigations (reproduced in full in Ruddock, Hand, & Blanchard, 1985, pp. 115–118, Appendix V). It emphasised the importance of building on cultural heritage, the importance of Indigenous Studies for all Australian people, promotion of cross-cultural understanding, skills acquisition, and Aboriginal people's involvement in managing their own education.

1980–1985

Following representation by the National Aboriginal Education Committee (NAEC), the Australian government's House of Representative Standing Committee on Aboriginal Affairs over the 32nd, 33rd, and 34th Parliaments undertook an extensive examination of Aboriginal education (Ruddock et al., 1985). Their report concluded that:

Education in Australia has as its central tenet the attainment of greater equality of educational opportunities and outcomes. Such equality does not yet exist for Aboriginal people and the Committee has concluded that there is a continuing need for special educational programs for Aboriginal people to enable improved educational attainments to be achieved.
(Ruddock et al., 1985, p. 1)

Further, they noted that:

These objectives were that Aboriginal people be able to obtain an education which allows them to function without disadvantage in the wider community while at the same time being able to retain their Aboriginal identity and lifestyle. The Committee endorses these as fundamental aims in Aboriginal education.
(Ruddock et al., 1985, p. 2)

1989–2008: Policy development

Over the course of almost 20 years, the Australian government – through the *Hobart Declaration* (Australian Government, 1989), *Adelaide Declaration* (Australian Government, 1999), and *Melbourne Declaration* (Australian Government, 2008) – established goals with expectations that teachers do more to improve their knowledge and skills in the education of their Aboriginal and Torres Strait Islander students and guide students, both Indigenous and non-Indigenous, towards a better understanding of Aboriginal and Torres Strait Islander societies.

1991

As an outcome of the *Royal Commission into Aboriginal Deaths in Custody* (*Royal Commission into Aboriginal Deaths in Custody* & Johnston, 1991), Recommendation 295 gave unambiguous direction to the government on the need for teachers to be better educated about Indigenous matters and that Aboriginal and Torres Strait Islander people etc.:

a. All teacher training courses include courses which will enable student teachers to understand that Australia has an Aboriginal history and Aboriginal viewpoints on social, cultural and historical matters, and to teach the curriculum which reflects those matters;
b. In-service training courses for teachers be provided so that teachers may improve their skill, knowledge and understanding to teach curricula which incorporate Aboriginal viewpoints on social, cultural and historical
c. Aboriginal people should he involved in the training courses both at student teacher and in-service level (Dodson, Johnston, O'Dea, Wootten, & Wyvill, 1991).

1991

Federal Council for Aboriginal Reconciliation formed in recognition that through education, there would come to be a deeper understanding of Aboriginal and Torres Strait Islander history and contemporary cultures, assisting the process of Reconciliation.

1995

The Ministerial Council on Employment Education Training and Youth Affairs (MCEETYA), a national partnership of Commonwealth, State, and Territory governments, developed a taskforce on Indigenous education and agreed upon national goals for schooling. The outcome was the *National Education Policy* (Cadzow, 2010) shaped substantially by the initial nine objectives identified in the 1980 NAEC policy document (Dodson et al., 1991).

1995–2002

Indigenous education leader and member of NAEC, Paul Hughes, undertook the drafting of what became the guiding policy document for Indigenous Education in Australia (Hughes, 1995). Known as the *National Strategy for the Education of Aboriginal and Torres Strait Islander Peoples* (NATSIEP) 1996–2002, this nationally agreed policy was launched with a key agreed aim to have all Aboriginal and Torres Strait Islander peoples' children completing school able to read, write, spell, and add in English.

2003–2004

Following the development of the national NATSIEP policy, in New South Wales, an extensive review of the effectiveness of Aboriginal education and training was conducted by the NSW Department of Education (DET) and the NSW Aboriginal Education Consultative Group (NSW AECG). The report 'raised concerns about the consistency with which the Aboriginal Education Policy had been implemented in New South Wales and recommended that the Aboriginal Education Policy be updated in partnership with the NSW AECG Inc.'. Such work as the NATSIEP and the policy development and implementation that occurred in all the State and Territory jurisdictions laid the groundwork for Australia's endorsement of UNDRIP.

2009

The Australian Government endorses UNDRIP on 3 April 2009.

Overview of book chapters

Overall, this book comprises three sections: Part I: *Historical perspectives on Indigenous education, Indigenous higher education, and teacher education in Japan and Australia* comprises four chapters; Part II: *After UNDRIP – Japanese and Australian responses and possibilities* comprises five chapters that considers the impact of UNDRIP, particularly regarding developments in the provision of education services to Indigenous Peoples in Japan and Australia; Part III – *Considering post-imperial Indigenous education in Japan and Australia* comprises two chapters and considers future challenges and opportunities for mainstream education systems in both nations as they improve their system-level response to these matters.

Chapter 2 (Part I), by Sato and Diamond, provides a history of Indigenous education in Japan and Australia prior to the endorsement in each country of UNDRIP. They argue that Indigenous Peoples the world over have always educated their young people to learn those things considered important. Socialisation of children is a complex matter and the relationship between socialisation and formal schooling requires us to think about the ways that Indigenous Japanese and Australian families and communities might have educated their young prior to the formation of the nations of Japan and Australia. In this chapter, the authors focus on the history of attempts to formally educate Indigenous children in both separate and mainstream schools up to the time when Japan and Australia endorsed UNDRIP. The authors note differences and similarities in the Japanese and Australian systems. Japan developed its imperial system through a prolonged period of consolidation of many feudal fiefdoms. This process swept up Japanese Indigenous tribal groups such as the Ainu whose claims to land pre-existed many arrangements made subsequently under fiefdoms and annulled any a priori claims and arrangements that had been recognised before the imperial process of consolidation.

After the establishment of the Meiji Restoration in 1868, the early school system was developed during the period known as the *Dai Nippon Teikoku* (Empire of Japan). From the time of the enactment of the 1947 constitution of modern Japan, formal schooling has continued to educate to a monocultural aspiration of one-Japan-ness. Unlike the situation in Japan, the Australian landmass was territorially colonised by the British Crown and the English education system was transplanted to the new colony and imposed upon Indigenous people.

In Chapter 3, Okano examines the place of Indigenous Peoples in multicultural education, analysing multicultural policy debates and practices in both Australia and Japan for how Indigenous People's education needs have been met or obscured within such debates. She observes that how Indigenous Peoples are understood and treated in multicultural education policies and practices varies significantly across societies. The dominant idea of liberal multiculturalism, which focuses on diversity and equality of opportunity, emerged, at least initially, in response to the impact of transnational migration on the population composition of first world countries. Indigenous Peoples in Australia and Japan are both marginalised minority groups as a result of their colonial experience. This chapter examines how differences and similarities have emerged in the two societies, why and with what consequences in order to advance our understanding of the place of Indigenous Peoples in multiculturalism debates.

Chapters 4 and 5 move the book's discussion to the education of Indigenous people in higher education institutions in Japan and Australia. In Chapter 4, Maeda examines whether higher education in Japan before the proclamation of the UNDRIP included the Ainu. He considers the direction of university reform in Japan after the 1991 University Council report on improving university education in what is also termed the 'third wave' of educational reform. Maeda undertakes a critical examination of the state of higher education reform in Japan from the perspective of equity and fairness – in particular, what sort of institutional arrangements were made to support higher education for those including the Ainu who were disadvantaged in the opportunity to access higher education. He uses the *Draft Law Concerning the Ainu People* adopted in 1984 by the General Assembly of the Utari Association of Hokkaido as a framework for consideration. The Draft Law has provided some suggestions for the government's higher education policy, which is discussed more fully in Chapter 11.

In Chapter 5, Holt examines pre-UNDRIP developments for Indigenous Australians in Australian higher education. She notes that while education has been integral to the progress and sustainability of Australian Aboriginal and Torres Strait Islander societies since time immemorial, the impacts of post-invasion, of disempowering policies, and the removal of access to both traditional and contemporary education had devastating long-term effects. Holt presents a summary of the historical context of Australian Indigenous higher education from invasion to Australia's endorsement of UNDRIP. In particular, she examines the impact of the assimilative policies of post-English invasion and pre-1970s and moves through to an era where Aboriginal and Torres Strait Islander Peoples demanded a voice in their educational endeavours. Holt argues that the 1970s marked a significant turning point with the appointment of Aboriginal people to form NAEC. The Aboriginal education experts who led policy development and direction provided a foundational framework that would guide Aboriginal and Torres Strait Islander education into the future. A major influence of the emergence of Aboriginal and Torres Strait Islander peoples into higher education was NAEC's policy directive to graduate '1,000 Aboriginal Teachers by 1990', which resulted in the forging of pathways into and through higher education. The chapter concludes with the most significant international milestone, the implementation of the UNDRIP. Holt's presentation of this history recognises the contribution of Aboriginal and Torres Strait

Islander Peoples in their past and continuing fight for ensuring that their voices are heard within the endeavours to make higher education accessible and conducive to successful outcomes for future generations – at times under extremely challenging circumstances.

The first chapter of Part II, Chapter 6, by Diamond and Sato examines challenges and responses to UNDRIP in Australian and Japanese Indigenous education. In Chapter 2, they observed that Indigenous Peoples the world over have always educated their young people to learn those things considered important, and they discussed the ancestral legacy of the Indigenous education systems that continues to be preserved and maintained into the modern era. In Chapter 6, they examine the developments since the endorsement of UNDRIP by Australia and Japan. Diamond and Sato argue that UNDRIP represented a circuit break in the imperial and colonial narratives of both nations, recognising the rights of Indigenous Peoples to educate their children according to their own needs and aspirations rather than having an education system imposed from imperial and colonising powers into the future. The authors find that the consequence of UNDRIP is that education systems in pluricultural, postcolonial democracies worldwide are grappling with the incommensurability of the aspirations of UNDRIP with older imperial and colonial legacies embedded within education systems. Chapter 6 examines the impact of UNDRIP on these imperial and colonial approaches to the education of Indigenous children in Australia and Japan in terms of policy, pedagogical, and curriculum changes.

In Chapter 7, Anderson, Diamond, and Diamond examine research of attempts to embed Indigenist perspectives into Australian pre-service teacher education. Australian teachers currently must demonstrate competence in seven professional standards, known as the Australian Professional Standards for Teachers. Each provides several Focus Areas. After lengthy nation-wide consultation with Aboriginal elders and educators, the Australian Institute of Teaching and School Leadership (AITSL) formulated two Focus Areas (1.4 and 2.4) for teachers concerning Indigenous education in Australia to address the chronic lack of skills, knowledge, or understanding demonstrated by primary and secondary teachers in Aboriginal and Torres Strait Islander matters: Focus Area 1.4 addresses the teaching of Australian Indigenous students; Focus Area 2.4 addresses the teaching about the histories, cultures, or lifeways of Indigenous Australians. Chapter 7 provides the background to these standards and a case study of the best practice arising from research on an approach designed to help pre-service teachers build confidence in their professional and personal skills, knowledge, and understanding in Indigenous education.

Kakazu and Saito discuss the Okinawan people of Japan in Chapter 8 and how the Okinawans have maintained their social, cultural, and political characteristics. Because of their strong ethnic identity, which is independent of the majority Japanese, the Okinawans are often treated as cultural others by the majority Japanese. Nevertheless, the Government of Japan does not recognise Okinawans as Indigenous people (Ministry of Foreign Affairs, 2014). Chapter 8 examines how teacher education has shifted from a period of self-adaptation with the majority Japanese to that of establishment of self-identity in Okinawa after the Second World War. To discuss this question, the authors use the comparative institutional analysis (CIA) framework for their analysis. They find that the development of the teacher education programmes in Okinawa can be divided into three modes: 'rehabilitation mode' under the US rules, 'standardisation mode' after re-integration to Japan, and 'localisation mode' since 2010s for greater awareness of Okinawan identities. Developments in teacher education programmes in Okinawa University shows the potential to create a deeper understanding about local needs and contexts among student teachers. The authors' findings suggest that, should the Okinawans seek more autonomy in the sense of their Indigenous rights, UNDRIP could be utilised.

In Chapter 9, Gayman and Ueno question current issues in the higher education sector for Japan's Ainu people through the lens of the two rights to education enshrined in Article 14 of the UNDRIP: the right of Indigenous Peoples to establishment and control of education through their own language and culture; the right to access to education provided by the state. In order to understand the implications of higher education for Indigenous Peoples, the authors first overview the standards and frameworks for Indigenous education before reviewing the standards and frameworks for Indigenous higher education. Next, the authors evaluate background information, statistics on Ainu higher education matriculation, primary economic sector of employment, and so on to provide the reasons for the need for improved educational measures in the higher education sector. The authors also overview higher education initiatives in Ainu Studies and compare the general situation of Ainu Studies and Indigenous Education generally in higher education in Japan with that of other countries. Gayman and Ueno conclude that higher education for Japan's Ainu people varies greatly, with some programmes containing inchoate elements of higher education programmes for Indigenous Peoples found in countries considered to have advanced Indigenous education standards, and there is much room for improvement in terms of international standards.

In Chapter 10, Anderson and Diamond discuss the challenges facing Australian universities post-UNDRIP in attempts by universities to stabilise and sustain Indigenous leadership. This chapter builds on Holt's (Chapter 5) discussion of the history of Australian Aboriginal and Torres Strait Islander peoples' participation in higher education and examines the impact of UNDRIP on supporting the acceleration of Indigenous participation in Australia's universities. Bringing together the academic fields of Educational Leadership, Educational Administration, and Strategic Change Management, Anderson and Diamond argue that the enormity and complexity of the task of indigenising an entire education system demands simultaneously addressing community governance and leadership capacity building, offering culturally appropriate professional development and developing explicit approaches to the leadership and management of policy development. The authors problematise the concept of the leadership pipeline for accelerating employment of Indigenous people in Australia's universities, exploring senior leadership, professional, and academic roles in Australian universities from the perspective of Aboriginal and Torres Strait Islander employees. They argue that conventional organisational approaches practised by universities that assume a proper, functioning 'pipeline' are unable to achieve the espoused Australian government targets for Indigenous employment growth to parity. More importantly, such approaches fall short of ever being able to address the aspirations of Indigenous people given the historical and ongoing difficulties for Australian universities in attracting sufficient Indigenous people with the necessary skills to take up senior leadership.

Part III considers challenges facing the education systems of Japan and Australia, especially in their post-imperial, postcolonial responses to *UNDRIP* and other international Indigenous rights mechanisms endorsed by both nations.

In Chapter 11, Maeda and Okano revisit research they undertook in 2013 to examine the significance of building Ainu-led higher educational systems and the empowerment of the Indigenous Ainu. The authors examine how collaboration among university, Indigenous community, and private sector companies can promote Ainu participation in higher education, drawing on a case study of the Urespa Project in Sapporo University, Japan. In this project, the university offers scholarships to Ainu students, requiring them to take a special course in Ainu culture and history and develop collaborations with partner private sector companies. The authors suggest that the mutual learning approach that the Urespa Project advocates signifies a challenge to the conventional approach to Ainu education, which has long centred on the majority *Wajin* providing unidirectional assistance to the Ainu in order to help them achieve the national educational benchmarks. The 'mutual learning' approach (*sodateai* in Japanese, *urespa* in the Ainu language) stresses a nurturing environment in which both Ainu and non-Ainu students feel included. That such initiatives came from private universities, rather than the national government, is indicative of how Ainu education is perceived as a local, rather than a national issue in Japan.

In the final chapter of this collection, Chapter 12, Goerke and Anderson examine the strengths and limitations of the idea of reconciliation and the concept of Reconciliation for guiding Australian Indigenous higher education into the 21st century. Drawing on research and discussions over the past 20 years and, in particular, the findings of a recent study by Goerke, the authors report on the views of prominent Indigenous and non-Indigenous Australian political and educational leaders about universities in Australia and their engagement with the aspirations of the Indigenous Peoples of Australia. Complimenting Chapters 5 and 10, Goerke and Anderson explore a particular concept known internationally as 'Reconciliation' and its policy lever that has been operationalised in some Australia universities to guide this work – the 'Reconciliation Action Plan'.

The authors conclude that the concept of Reconciliation in universities needs to be founded on establishing the 'right' relationship between the majority non-Indigenous peoples and First Nations Peoples. However, Reconciliation exists along a complex and dynamic continuum which spans well-intentioned though sometimes assimilationist practices through to reciprocal partnerships and Indigenous rights-based reconciliation.

Conclusion

Historical events, in both Japan and Australia, still cast a shadow over recent government policies on Indigenous matters. In Australia, Indigenous people have asserted their special place in debates on multicultural symbiosis and, therefore, Indigenous issues, having a distinctive claim based on their First Peoples' status, are differentiated from those of other minority groups. In Japan, however, Indigenous people, the Ainu, were left behind in the discussion when the government discussed multicultural symbiosis; Japanese government policies focused predominantly on living well with people who came from outside Japan.

Among the provisions in the UNDRIP, Article 14(2), which specifies 'right to all levels and forms of education of the State without discrimination', can be interpreted as the 'right to independently and actively seek education' and thus includes the right to demand changes in Indigenous education as it stands. For that reason, while avoiding direct mention, these provisions imply that scholarship systems must be improved to guarantee opportunities for access to higher education institutions by Indigenous youth who would otherwise be prevented due to financial or other reasons. One possible interpretation is that the state needs to take proactive measures to provide scholarships under affirmative action. Such provisions have proven to be an indispensable approach for building higher education systems to help empower Indigenous People's participation and engagement in universities. They point to the need for Japanese and Australian university leaders to establish conditions that promote creation of mutual collaborative networks with Indigenous people to eliminate discrimination and shift to an education system that reflects Indigenous lifeways and aspirations.

With the importance of the rights of Indigenous Peoples to self-determination becoming recognised, the expression '*Indigenous rights*' has been coined. How to actually guarantee such rights is an important global issue. In particular, Indigenous Peoples are increasingly making claims and taking action regarding the right to participate in social decision making, which is one of the rights derived from the right to self-determination, that is, participating in decisions on matters that affect them. In light of the foregoing discussion, government recognitions, such as the *Ainu Policy Promotion Act* (2019), in Japan and the longer-term Reconciliation movement in Australia have a shortcoming: the lack of a perspective to ensure higher education rights that promote the Indigenous People's self-determination as envisaged by the UNDRIP.

As a consequence of endorsement of UNDRIP by nations, the nations of Japan and Australia are entering a new phase of Indigenous education and we have approached this new post-UNDRIP phase with a new perspective and a new theoretical framework. This book draws on organisational development and education theories to make the link between the motherhood statements found in the UNDRIP mechanism and the manner in which the Japan and Australian governments have developed policies to require their respective higher education systems to be proactive in the provision of programmes for capacity building and professional development. The authors use Indigenous Peoples' right to education, as recognised by the global community in the UNDRIP, as a benchmark for comparative analysis and a normative framework to examine the significance of developing Indigenous-led higher educational arrangements.

We hope this collection of chapters will provide impetus for a sustained scholarly engagement with international and comparative perspectives on the development of higher education globally that meets the aspirations and needs of Indigenous Peoples.

References

Advisory Council for Future Ainu Policy (ACFAP). (2009). *Final report*. Tokyo, Japan: Government of Japan (Provisional translation into English on 14 November 2011). Retrieved 31 May 2020 from www.kantei.go.jp/jp/singi/ainu/dai10/siryou1_en.pdf.

Australian Government. (1989). *Hobart Declaration*. Retrieved 31 May 2020 from www.educationcouncil.edu.au/EC-Publications/EC-Publications-archive/EC-The-Hobart-Declaration-on-Schooling-1989.aspx.

Australian Government. (1999). *The Adelaide Declaration*. Retrieved 31 May 2020 from www.educationcouncil.edu.au/EC-Publications/EC-Publications-archive/EC-The-Adelaide-Declaration.aspx.

Australian Government. (2008). *Melbourne Declaration*. Retrieved 31 May 2020 from www.curriculum.edu.au/verve/_resources/National_Declaration_on_the_Educational_Goals_for_Young_Australians.pdf.

Australian Human Rights Commission (AHRC). (2009). *United we stand – Support for United Nations Indigenous Rights Declaration a watershed moment for Australia*. Canberra, ACT: Australian Human Rights Commission. Retrieved 31 May 2020 from www.humanrights.gov.au/about/news/media-releases/2009-media-release-united-we-stand-support-united-nations-indigenous.

Australian Institute for Aboriginal and Torres Strait Islander Studies (AIATSIS). (2018). *Our history*. Retrieved 31 May 2020 from https://aiatsis.gov.au/about-us/our-history.

Brook, J., & Kohen, J. L. (1991). *The Parramatta native institution and the black town: A history*. Sydney, Australia: UNSW Press.

Burridge, N., & Chodkiewicz, A. (2012). An historical overview of Aboriginal education policies in the Australian context. In N. Burridge, F. Whalan, & K. Vaughan (Eds.).

Indigenous education: Transgressions (Vol. 86). Rotterdam, The Netherlands: Sense Publishers.

Cadzow, A. (2010). *A NSW Aboriginal education timeline 1788–2007*. Retrieved 31 May 2020 from https://ab-ed.nesa.nsw.edu.au/go/aboriginal-studies/timeline.

Council for Ainu Policy Promotion. (2012). *Council for Ainu policy promotion: Meetings and topics*. Retrieved 31 May 2020 from www.kantei.go.jp/jp/singi/ainusuishin/index_e.html#about.

Craven, R. (1979). *Teaching the teachers Indigenous Australian studies: A national priority!* Paper presented at the AARE Annual Conference, Brisbane.

Dodson, P., Johnston, E., O'Dea, D. J., Wootten, H., & Wyvill, L. F. (1991). *Royal commission into Aboriginal deaths in custody: Recommendations* (Volume 5). Canberra, Australia: AGPS. Retrieved 31 May 2020 from www.austlii.edu.au/au/other/IndigLRes/rciadic/national/vol5/.

Fletcher, J. J. (1989a). *Clean, clad and courteous: A history of Aboriginal education in New South Wales*. Sydney, Australia: J. J. Fletcher.

Fletcher, J. J. (1989b). *Documents in the history of Aboriginal education in NSW*. Sydney, Australia: J. J. Fletcher.

Hokkaido Utari Association. (1984). Ainu minzoku ni kansuru hōritsu-an [Law proposal concerning the Ainu community]. In Ainu Association of Hokkaido (Ed.). *Ainu minzoku no gaisetsu – Hokkaido Ainu Kyōkai no katsudō o fukume* [Overview of the Ainu: History of the Ainu Association of Hokkaido] (2017 ed.). Retrieved 31 May 2020 from www.ainu-assn.or.jp/public/files/1d05c1dd9ceb9cf70478cd757622d3075a2c94b7.pdf.

Hughes, P. (1995). *A national strategy for the education of Aboriginal and Torres Strait Islander Peoples 1996–2002*. Ministerial Council on Education, Employment, Training and Youth Affairs. Retrieved 31 May 2020 from www.educationcouncil.edu.au/site/DefaultSite/filesystem/documents/Reports%20and%20publications/Publications/Cultural%20inclusion%20and%20ATSI/National%20Strategy%20for%20the%20Education%20of%20Aboriginal%20and%20Torres%20Strait%20Islander%20Peoples%201996–2002.pdf.

Loos, N. (1993). Australia, Japan and their Indigenous peoples: An introduction. In N. Loos & T. Osanai (Eds.). *Indigenous minorities and education: Australian and Japanese perspectives on their Indigenous peoples, the Ainu, Aborigines and Torres Strait Islanders* (pp. 2–10). Tokyo, Japan: Sanyusha.

Loos, N., & Osanai, T. (Eds.). (1993). Indigenous minorities and education: Australian and Japanese perspectives on their Indigenous peoples, the Ainu, Aborigines and Torres Strait Islanders. Tokyo, Japan: Sanyusha.

Macquarie, L. (1814). 'Establishment of the native institution 1814'. NRS 1046 [SZ759, pages 11–14; Reel 6038]. Online. Retrieved 31 May 2020 from www.records.nsw.gov.au/state-archives/digital-gallery/lachlan-macquarie-visionary-and-builder/public-notices/full-transcript-establishment-of-the-native-institution-1814.

Ma Rhea, Z., & Russell, L. (2012). The invisible hand of pedagogy in Australian Indigenous studies and Indigenous education. *Australian Journal of Indigenous Education*, 41(1), 18–25. doi:10.1017/jie.2012.4

United Nations. (2012). International covenant on civil and political rights. Consideration of reports submitted by States parties under article 40 of the Covenant: Sixth periodic report of States Parties: Japan. CCPR/C/JPN/6, Geneva: United Nations. Retrieved from www.mofa.go.jp/policy/human/cove_civil/index.html.

Parbury, N. (1991). *Survival: A history of Aboriginal life in New South Wales.* Surry Hills, Australia: New South Wales Department of Aboriginal Affairs.

Read, P. (2006). Shelly's mistake: The Parramatta native institution. In M. Crotty & D. A. Roberts (Eds.). *The great mistakes of Australian history* (pp. 32–47). Sydney, Australia: UNSW Press.

Royal Commission into Aboriginal Deaths in Custody, & Johnston, E. C. (1991). *National report: Overview and recommendations.* (0644144076). Canberra, ACT: Australian Govt. Pub. Service

Ruddock, P. M., Hand, G. L., & Blanchard, C. A. (1985). *Aboriginal education.* Canberra, ACT: AGPS. Retrieved 31 May 2020 from www.aph.gov.au/Parliamentary_Business/Committees/House_of_Representatives_Committees?url=reports/1985/1985_pp357report.htm.

United Nations. (2007). *United Nations Declaration on the Rights of Indigenous Peoples.* Retrieved 31 May 2020 from www.un.org/development/desa/indigenouspeoples/wp-content/uploads/sites/19/2018/11/UNDRIP_E_web.pdf.

Legislation

Japan

Family Register Act (1871)（戸籍法）
Hokkaido Former Aboriginal Protection Act (1899) (Meiji 32)（北海道旧土人保護法）
Regulations for the Education of Former Aboriginal Children (1901)（旧土人児童教育規程）
Nihon-koku Kenpō (Constitution of Japan [1947])（日本国憲法）
Private School Act (1949)（私立学校法）
Draft Law Concerning the Ainu People (1984) (General Assembly of the Ainu Association of Hokkaido) (Draft Law)（アイヌ民族に関する法律（案））
Act on the Promotion of Ainu Culture and Dissemination and Enlightenment of Knowledge About Ainu Tradition, etc. (Act No. 52 of 1997) (*Ainu Cultural Promotion Act*)（アイヌ文化の振興並びにアイヌの伝統等に関する知識の普及及び啓発に関する法律[アイヌ文化振興法]）
Basic Act on Education (Act No. 120 of 2006)（教育基本法）
Act on Promoting Measures to Realize a Society in Which the Pride of the Ainu People Is Respected (Act No. 16 of 2019) (*Ainu Policy Promotion Act*)（アイヌの人々の誇りが尊重される社会を実現するための施策の推進に関する法律 [アイヌ政策推進法]）

Australia

Commonwealth of Australia Constitution Act 1900 (UK) (Australian Constitution)
Aborigines Act No. 1905/014 (5 Edw. VII No.14)
Higher Education Support Act 2003 (Cth) (HESA)
Aboriginal Institute of Aboriginal Studies Act 1964 (Cth) (AIAS Act)
Australian Institute of Aboriginal and Torres Strait Islander Studies Act 1989 (Cth) (AIATSIS Act)

Part I

Historical perspectives on Indigenous education, Indigenous higher education, and teacher education in Japan and Australia

Chapter 2

An Indigenous history of education in Japan and Australia

Chizu Sato and Zane M. Diamond

Introduction

In this chapter, we examine the period prior to and including the imperial colonising periods of Japan and Australia and its impact on Indigenous Peoples, especially in the socialisation and education of non-Indigenous young Ainu, Aboriginal, and Torres Strait Islander children and non-Indigenous young adults. We also examine the transition of Australia and Japan from being countries run by imperial power to formal enactment of a national constitution that moved both countries into being recognised as independent democratic nations led by elected governments and through legal mechanisms.

In this chapter, we focus on the history of the education of Indigenous Peoples and on the attempts to encourage Indigenous children to be involved in education up to the time when Japan and Australia endorsed the *United Nations Declaration on the Rights of Indigenous Peoples* (UNDRIP). We have employed the narrative style in this chapter to highlight that we want to engage with you, the reader, whether you identify as Indigenous or non-Indigenous, with the ideas in the chapter in a way that speaks directly to how young people learn to absorb, build their knowledge of their world, and how they can engage in the joy of learning. We have found, over many years, that it can be the impersonal academic style that allows readers to slide over the amazing human activity that is teaching and learning, and to miss out on understanding the deep implications for Indigenous Peoples of how their ancestral educational approaches were severely disrupted by imperial and colonial education policies and practices. Such policies have been central to the attempts at assimilating Indigenous People into the dominant culture. We demonstrate here and in Chapter 6 that it is our classrooms, our choice of curriculum content and resources, and our pedagogical practices as educationalists that maintain or challenge the imperial, colonial mindset at the heart of mainstream approaches to Indigenous Education.

A warning and an explanation

An acknowledgement and a warning for Indigenous readers:

> There are images of Indigenous Peoples of both Japan and Australia in this chapter, some who have passed away. We pay respect to them and thank them for their struggle and for the footsteps that they left for us to follow. We dedicate this chapter to all Indigenous Peoples and, in particular, to the Ainu and Aboriginal and Torres Strait Islander educators and all those ancestor educators.

A warning for non-Indigenous readers:

> The stories here are about Indigenous People, containing images of ancestors and their descendants. As a non-Indigenous person, while you may not relate to these images as being memories of family, you might imagine how it would be for you to come across photos of your ancestors and descendants in an academic book such as this. If you are a teacher or teacher educator, please make sure to seek permission from Indigenous People before using their images in teaching materials.

Indigenous Peoples have requested that when authors use images of people who might be deceased, they insert a warning note before showing the image. Teacher educators in Indigenous Education know that if they use images of Indigenous People in their classes, they must model best practice and remind their students of this fact. Indigenous people often tell of images being indiscriminately flashed up as part of a PowerPoint presentation without the lecturer understanding that it is easy for them to forget that these photos and other images might be relatives of students in the class or their grandparents or parents because, often, they do not know Indigenous People personally.

We note that because the media draws on images of Indigenous People as stock photos and, as consumers, they may not know any Indigenous People in their social or familial network, it can become so disconnected for non-Indigenous People that they fail to recognise the image as being of a person – a human with the same humanity as themselves.

We highlight that the images we have chosen are images of Indigenous People who might be someone's relatives or ancestors from the past. Hereby we would like to note that just as how a non-Indigenous person might feel a jolt of sadness, pain, fond memory, or some negative memory if they suddenly saw an image of one of their ancestors used in a classroom, if a non-Indigenous person is fortunate enough to have Indigenous students in their class, images of the students' ancestors might cause those same emotions. So, be careful when using such images. We are showing images in this chapter because of the historical discussions that we want to have with our readers and in recognition of the place of the people shown in an Indigenous history of education. In 1976, Colin Bourke reminded us:

> Unfortunately, the beliefs and expectations of the mostly middle-class: white teachers, school-administrators, fellow students and other significant white Australians are, that Aboriginals are poor social outcasts, no matter how well the views are hidden nor how hard people try not to be chauvinistic.
>
> (Bourke, 1976, p. 15)

Dr M. Yunupiŋu (1956–2013), arguing against the closure of the Northern Territory government's bilingual program in remote Aboriginal communities, remarked just days before he died:

> I want to talk about strength, either in English or the Yolngu Matha speaking domain. We learnt from our elders that language is sacred. Yolngu kids think in their own language which can then inform them about English, about its meanings and its values. I consider Yolngu children in Yolngu schools to be as clever as anyone else in the wide world, and I don't want that cleverness left outside the classroom door. Not for my kids or my grandkids. They should have equal rights, the same rights as any kids in the world, whether they are Chinese, or Balanda, the equal right to learn in their own language.
>
> (Recorded by Reconciliation Australia, 2013)

In 2019, attitudes are slowly changing but still many non-Indigenous People do not know about Indigenous approaches to education or the historical impact of imperial and colonial schooling that continues into the present. While beyond the limits of this chapter, the following argument draws on a range of theorists across the academic fields of educational leadership, educational administration, strategic change management, and Indigenous education internationally to examine the key problematic of systemically embedded and, arguably, racially determined failure. Reflecting on the evidence, this chapter aims to educate non-Indigenous readers with reliable knowledge and, in particular, if they are a teacher or teacher educator, when they are teaching Indigenous students or when they are teaching about Indigenous histories.

Socialisation and education of Indigenous children prior to the imperial colonial period

Indigenous Peoples have always educated their children, socialising them into the lifeways of their ancestors. Socialisation of children began from the earliest time in a child's life: the child was taught to know their place of belonging in their family, community, world, and universe constellations. Regarded as a spirit inhabiting a body, each child was granted autonomy to grow and reveal that spirit. Note that the word 'child' is immediately problematic because it is not a life stage that is fixed but one that is determined culturally. In many pre-colonial societies, the young person was regarded in the same way as an older person – just another spirit becoming human albeit needing to be educated into the ways of the family, wider community, and region.

Elder knowledge-keepers, language, and story

Similar to many Indigenous languages, the language of Ainu was not a written one, so there are few written accounts of their child-rearing. What is known is that Ainu have many forms of oral traditions. Their narrative genres can be grouped into two categories depending on the contents of speaking: (1) narratives about events and (2) narratives about the wisdom of their Elders, which provide information and lessons for life (Strong, 2011).

The first type of stories can be told in an almost normal speaking voice, including old stories called *uepeker*, or *tu-itak* in some regions. Such stories were different from *yukara* or *kamui yukara*, which are told with a melody and told as though they were about human beings who had actually lived rather than simply being fantasy stories (Ainu Museum, 1997). As for *uepeker*, Kayano (1988) reported that when Ainu heard an old *uepeker* story, they were easily able to imagine that there was a small village, *kotan*, and people living in the village were depicted somewhere in the story. Because Ainu stories were so familiar, they could believe that they were not fictitious but real stories. Batchelor (1901) gave an example of a legend when Ainu taught about respect for elderly persons:

> At the head of Japan there was a metal (i.e. very hard) pine tree. Now, the ancients, both noble and ignoble, came together and broke and bent their swords (upon that tree). Then there came a very old man and a very old woman upon the scene. The old man had a useless old axe in his girdle, and the old woman a useless old reaping-hook. So, they caused the ancients to laugh at them. (…) 'We have only come that we may see'. As the old man said this he drew his useless old axe, and, striking the metal pine tree, cut a little way into it. And the old woman drawing her useless old reaping-hook, struck the tree and cut it through. (…) Therefore, the Ainu say: Let not the younger laugh at the elder, for even very old people can teach juniors a great deal, even in so simple a matter as felling trees.
>
> (pp. 258–259)

Okuda (1996) argues that, given Ainu passed such stories down from generation to generation, and that the stories are inseparable from life itself, a way of examining Ainu lives before colonisation is through their stories. That is, it might be possible to discover some Ainu child-rearing wisdom by analysing their *uepeker*, such as the story that explains how a boy learned about hunting.

Indigenous education history 29

Image 2.1 Ainu telling *yukara* to a Wajin.
Source: Nishikawa, n.d.

Even today, when asked about the life of Ainu in former times, some Ainu might add stories to supplement their explanations.

Observation and repetition

Observation and repetition among Ainu are an outgrowth of the fact that the older people were highly respected teachers of Law, Philosophy, Religion and much else besides, and critical questioning of the teacher was not practised. There were important distinctions by gender, age, and knowledge. Of these, knowledge was the most important. Indigenous societies globally were guided and, sometimes, ruled by select old people who had passed through all stages of education within that community. In Aboriginal Australia, for example, their power was based on their knowledge of ceremonies of the Law and, through them, the rule of the Law in Aboriginal life was absolute.

Relatedness

Martin (2007, p. 18) uses the term 'relatedness' to explain this powerful shaper of the new being and says of this:

The goal is to prepare for change so that it expands one's autonomy, agency and relatedness and does not diminish or limit this autonomy, agency and relatedness. This must occur as coming amongst others in relatedness, so as not to silence, displace or make them invisible. It is an experience that many Aboriginal peoples have been denied through the ongoing experiences of colonialism compounded by racism.

(p. 18)

For Ainu Japanese families, as distinct from the mainstream Japanese families, only one Ainu family – that is, a couple and their children – lived in a house. When one of the children married, they left the parents' home – usually in age order – and took up residence in a new house near their (or their spouse's) parents' house. When a child was born, s/he was called by a 'dirty' name referencing excrement or using similar insults because Ainu believed that this protected children from evil. After several years, if the child survived, she or he

Image 2.2 Ainu in front of a house in 1877.
Source: Hokkaido University Library Northern Studies Collection.

was named, taking into consideration their characters (Ainu Museum, 2018; Kayano, 2000).

Autonomy and belonging

As this new Ainu being became older, they got to learn by watching others, being encouraged to try out things and discouraged if there was danger. There was no expectation on the young person to do the task or activity until they, themselves, felt they had the expertise to carry out the activity. Muir and Bohr (2014) found:

> The concept of autonomy was honored by Aboriginal people from Canada, Australia and the United States as well. Sheperd (2008) found that Aboriginal parents from Canada more often than Euro-Canadian mothers, allowed their children to decide how much to explore their environment. The Inuit in Canada also viewed autonomy and independence as vital to parent and child interactions and as such, Inuit parents looked for indications from their children to guide their own responses (McShane et al., 2009). Australian Aboriginal children also traditionally self-directed their skill development, including relatively dangerous activities like knife handling and climbing trees (Kruske, Belton, Wardaguga & Narjic, 2012) and this early independence was encouraged for children by setting few limits (Nelson & Allison, 2000).
>
> (p. 70)

As such, each young being was treated as autonomous as well as in relation to others others. As shown in Image 2.3, the young person was part of the family, learning among the family about their world while at the same time being extended a level of autonomy.

In the Australian context, Muir and Bohr (2014) argue that 'Aboriginal cultures may understand developmental milestones differently (allowing each young person) to have their own path for development of milestones' (p. 74). Hamilton (1981) wrote an insightful text about Aboriginal child-rearing in North-Central Arnhem Land, Australia, that discusses this level of personhood and autonomy which extended to very young people in that community. Her study was a rare example of the sort of information that is needed in this field of education for teachers to understand Aboriginal child-rearing practices of relevance to the local community of their school. Not all communities share these practices, but some are similar across the globe among Indigenous Peoples. Insufficient research has been conducted to provide a comprehensive picture.

Each Indigenous young person is extended the autonomy to suit themselves about how much or how little they engage with any activity. Older people

Image 2.3 Drawings of an Aboriginal feast and Aboriginal mothers.
Source: Wood, 1870, p.759 of v.2.

rely on this process as a way of determining the interests of the young person without too much interference from them. Christie (1986) observes:

> All normal children, by the time they go to school for the first time, have already learnt to speak their mother tongue, have learnt who they are and where they fit into their family or community, and have learnt a vast range of behaviors which are appropriate (and inappropriate) for members of their culture. They have learnt all these through the informal process of socialization which affects all members of every culture throughout their lives. In traditional Aboriginal society, for example, hunting and food preparation skills, the traditional law, patterns of land ownership and important stories from the past, were all learnt informally in the daily life of the family.
> (p. 40)

Mastery learning and approximation

The Indigenous approach to education was firmly grounded in mastery learning principles. This way of achieving subject mastery is demonstrated in the next two images, showing important pedagogical moments. In Image 2.4, the master is fishing while at the same time demonstrating the technique of fishing such that the action was effective in catching a fish.

Image 2.5 demonstrates how the young people, having watched the mastery of the older person spearing fish, practise on their own and with their peers.

The children do not expect older people to be there watching them. They expect to work it out together and then come back to the older group, now

Image 2.4 Example of mastery.
Source: McCarthy, 1957, p. 13.

34 Chizu Sato and Zane M. Diamond

Image 2.5 Example of mastery learning and approximation.
Source: McCarthy, 1957, p. 12.

able to demonstrate their ability. In this self-motivation to practise a skill, there is ample evidence of the joy of learning that continues into the contemporary era. Going out bush, being 'on country', and learning from knowledgeable Elders are still cause for great excitement and anticipation. This joy of learning that motivates the children towards mastery learning and its practices of copying and approximation provides an important insight into a pedagogical approach that might best work in the mainstream classroom as well. Giving students time and space to practise approximate learning as part of the process of eventually achieving mastery has a sound pedagogical history across all civilisations. The process builds confidence and, while challenging, is rewarding to the learner once the skill has been learnt or improved.

In the following examples, it is possible to gain a glimpse of what are now being called informal learning spaces by examining old digital images. Such early stylised drawings capture some of the key elements of informal learning. A British missionary, John Batchelor, who arrived in Hokkaido in 1877, wrote about Ainu culture and language, observing that 'the first and chief duties taught to the children were obedience to parents, a careful regard to their elder brother, and reverence for the old men of their village' (1901, p. 254). He also noted that 'the men attended to the education of the boys, and the women

Indigenous education history 35

Image 2.6 Deer hunting.
Source: Nishikawa, n.d.

looked after the girls of a family' (p. 254). If the child was a boy, he learnt hunting using bow and arrow in a play, wood carving, courtesy, and words of prayer (Ainu Museum, 2018).

Shigeru Kayano, the first Ainu member of the Japanese Diet, said that when he looked back on his childhood, he remembered he was taken everywhere by his father to learn everything (Kayano, 2000). If a girl, she learnt patterns of kimonos from drawings inspired by the sand of a river or from the ashes in a furnace. She also learnt sewing, weaving, extracting fibres from tree bark, and cooking. In most cases, when the girl reached a certain age, she started to tattoo the back of her hands and around her mouth (Ainu Museum, 2018). Batchelor (1901) wrote: 'nor have I yet been able to get any simple, direct, sensible reason as to how the custom arose, or why it is kept up' (p. 20). But 'when the tattoo is finished all men know she is either a betrothed or married woman' (p. 24). Regarding the education of a girl, Kayano (2000) mentioned that his grandmother taught his elder sister what a girl should know, since, in most cases, the education of a girl is the role of the grandmother. His grandmother taught his sister that the first priority for women was watching out for fire because the houses were thatched and could catch fire easily, and the second was sewing.

Image 2.7 Grass weaving.
Source: Nishikawa, n.d.

There are similar stories in Australia that reflect the power and joy of learning within the context of one's family and community, in mother tongue, as these images reflect.

As Image 2.8 shows, in New South Wales, young people accompanied their parents or other relatives in daily life, watching and learning as they were able. If able, they would undertake particular tasks such as carrying the live coals that would be used to start the fire again at the next stopping place. It was important that the non-Indigenous young person understood the importance of keeping the coals live, of not burning themselves, and of being responsible. Such a job would not be allowed of someone who had not achieved some level of mastery because of the importance attached to keeping the coals alight.

There were myriad skills that young people needed, together with learning language, history, culture, geography, as well as, and in particular, food and other resource locations. Knowledge of things such as rope making for hunting, sewing skills for clothes making, fire-making for preparing food, and fishing are shown in these archival photos, which display how each young being was properly enculturated into their family, community, and region in recognisable ways of belonging.

Indigenous education history 37

Image 2.8 A New South Wales Family.
Source: Hunter, 1793, v2. Frontis.

Image 2.9 Learning fire mastery.
Source: McCarthy, 1957, p.106.

Image 2.10 Ropemaking mastery.
Source: McCarthy, 1957, p.93.

Without these knowledge markers, a young person would not be able to grow up as a spiritually, emotionally, and physically developed adult with adult responsibilities.

Mastery learning has been discussed in the Western context for some time. Building on early work in psychology (Washburn, 1922) and the pedagogies for learning (Block, 1971; Morrison, 1926), Bloom (1971) made the claim that '[m]ost students (perhaps 90 per cent) can master what we teach' (p. 48). He went on to summarise the key variables for mastery learning strategies as: aptitude for a particular kind of learning; quality of instruction; ability to understand instruction; perseverance; and time allowed for learning. He argued that 'if students are normally distributed with respect to aptitude, but the kind and quality of instruction and learning time allowed are made appropriate to the characteristics and needs of each learner, the majority of students will achieve subject mastery' (p. 50).

We are clearly limited in our ability to understand the full picture of how people educated their young before the period of colonisation by the British Crown in Australia, but there are strong and enduring traces of these aspects of Indigenous teaching and learning continuing into the present. These will be discussed more fully in later sections of this chapter and taken up again in Chapter 6.

Given the dearth of accurate information available to educators about Indigenous teaching and learning approaches, in the early 1980s, Harris (1984) proposed the need for more carefully examining the impact of Indigenous culture on students' learning styles. In the Australian context, while stressing the need not to stereotype Aboriginal students, he, like many others, were arguing that culture does have an impact on the approach to teaching and learning. Bell (1988) summarises the more general observations of Harris to present five aspects of teaching and learning that suggest Indigenous enculturation is present (in distinction to the Western classroom culture). While such lists should be regarded as possibilities rather than clear-cut learning styles, the similarity of findings across Australia and other Indigenous contexts over the years suggests that these are enduring aspects on a continuum. These are: learning by observation, imitation, and role play; personal trial and error; learning in real-life activities; context-specific learning; and person orientation. While neither Harris nor Bell included mastery learning, Bloom's (1971) ideas brought together with those of Harris and Bell can inform teaching practice in the Indigenous learning context.

Imperial and colonial schooling of Indigenous children: 1800s–1900s

Imperial and colonial education were, by definition, grounded in deficit thinking. Given the longer history of colonial education and the encompassing colonial mindset that informed government policy and practices in Australia, this section will focus predominantly on Australia. Even so, the underlying deficit approach to Indigenous Peoples is common across settler-colonial societies whether under imperial or colonial power.

Following Harris (1984), Christie (1986) observes that, '[i]n a sense, formal education can be seen to have developed in response to the needs of a newly complex and ever-expanding culture of technology and capital' (p. 40). At its foundation, what is understood as the formal or Western education system was commonly exported from imperial centres to their colonies in order to establish an educated class of colonial administrators. Indigenous and other local communities were rarely considered in the early days of the establishment of these systems in colonies such as the Malay Peninsula, the Americas, Papua New Guinea, Canada, New Zealand, India, or Australia. Over time, the occupying powers decided to establish schools for Indigenous populations. Australia was no exception. Embedded in this new formal teaching and learning context was, what Ma Rhea has referred to as, the 'colonial mindset' (2015a, 2015b). The groundwork for the colonial mindset was established over 200 years ago and there is convincing evidence of the enduring rhizomic nature of its legacy on the current provision of education services to Indigenous Australian people.

In late 1814, the fifth governor of North South Wales (NSW), Major General Lachlan Macquarie (1814), issued a proclamation on improving the lives of Aboriginal people:

> With a View, therefore, to effect the Civilization of the Aborigines of New South Wales, and to render their Habits more domesticated and industrious, His Excellency the Governor, as well from Motives of Humanity as of that Policy which affords a reasonable Hope of producing such an improvement in their Condition as may eventually contribute to render them not only more happy in themselves, but also in some Degree useful to the Community, has determined to institute a School for the Education of the Native Children of both Sexes, and to assign a Portion of land for the Occupancy and Cultivation of adult Natives, under such Rules and Regulations as appear to him likely to answer the desired Objects; and which are now published for general Information.

The full version contains 15 points containing ideas and assumptions that would still be argued to be relevant today by those persuaded by the colonial mindset. Of note, civilisation was the explicit goal (point 4); keeping children away from their families was another (point 14); and that Indigenous non-Indigenous young people were coerced into a type of schooling that has not changed very much in 200 years (points 8, 11, and 14). Given what was discussed earlier about teaching and learning approaches in Aboriginal families and communities, and the aspects of autonomy and relatedness, it must have been a horrifying experience for these Indigenous young people to be so blatantly 'civilised', denied access to family, and under coercion. Even though this first Native Institution with its 'experimentation' was deemed a failure, the intention to civilise and tame remained the goal of the formal schooling of Indigenous children. Fletcher (1989) contended that by 1850s there was nothing that had not previously been tried by the state and by the churches in relation to Indigenous education.

Even so, despite this coercive formal education approach, Indigenous People began, from the early days, to make sense of this new intrusion into their lives. Individuals with interest and talents for this new system began to engage and succeed. In this section, a few individuals will be discussed as example of the way Indigenous People have used their approach to informal learning to survive and succeed in the imposed, formal form.

The practices of settler-colonialism were not confined to Australia. In 1869, the Meiji government renamed the colonised island of Ezochi, calling it Hokkaido, and transformed it into a state-owned land. The government encouraged immigration from the mainland (Honshū) and land was given to the non-Ainu settlers, who were called Wajin. While the settlers in Japan were from another Japanese cultural group and the Australian settlers were from England and other European nations, the impact on the Indigenous communities in each case was similar. As the colonial frontier expanded across the Australian landmass, missions, reserves, and schools were established to deal

Image 2.11 Learning formal education.
Source: Robinson & Baglin, 1968, p.104.

with the displacement of Indigenous Peoples as their estates were taken from them, access to their sources of food and water denied them, and people began starving. In some places, there was more concern shown by the colonists than others. Similar stories emerge from the history of the occupation of Ainu lands.

Yorta Yorta and Ainu as examples of early formal schooling

Unlike in Japan, where only the Ainu have so far been recognised as being Indigenous, many Aboriginal nations have been recognised in Australia. In order to compare elements of Australian and Japanese Indigenous experiences, we have focused here on the Yorta Yorta People and their experience of Western education. Their Indigenous history of education is shared with many other Indigenous Peoples of Australia into the modern era, and some Yorta Yorta became involved in national advocacy for Australia's recognition of the distinctiveness of the Indigenous claim well prior to Australia's endorsement of UNDRIP. These two examples, Ainu and Yorta Yorta, when read in parallel during the same historical period, provide a unique snapshot of the stark similarities in approach taken by both imperial and colonial powers in the formal education of Indigenous students.

With respect to education for Ainu, Karino (2006) reports that a *kari-gakkō* (Provisional School) was opened on the site of *Zōjyō-ji* Temple in Tokyo to provide education for the *Kaitaku-shi* (Hokkaido Development Commission). This is recognised as the first attempt to provide Ainu with systematic education. Why did Ainu students have to attend the Hokkaido development commission school? The first aim of the school was to educate students who would contribute to the development of Hokkaido in the near future. This is closely related to the reason why the government had to develop the land of Hokkaido; arguably, a major reason for the Ainu assimilation policy was tension over north border issues with Russia arising in the later Edo era that concerned the newly established Meiji government. The Japanese government was intent on convincing foreign counterparts that Hokkaido was part of Japan where Japanese residents, including Japanised Ainu, lived (Karino, 2006). However, the idea of making Ainu attend formal schooling was implemented too quickly, so that the recruitment of Ainu students did not go well. Up to the time when this school was moved to Sapporo in 1875, only 36 Ainu students had attended, against a target of 100. Ainu students were brought all the way from Hokkaido to learn Japanese language and customs; that is, to assimilate them into a part of the newly established nation-state (Karino, 2006). In addition to the motivation of keeping foreign threats at bay, there was also a view among mainstream Japanese society that the Ainu were people who were inferior and needed to be civilised (Karino, 2006). This provides comprehensive evidence for what we term deficit education (see also Glossary). It was believed by the central Japanese government and its Education Ministry that Tokyo, rather than Hokkaido, was a more conducive place to change Ainu language and customs into Japanese ones (Ogawa, 1997).

Image 2.12 Opening ceremony of a new *Tsuishikari kyōiku-sho* school building.
Source: Hokkaido University Library Northern Studies Collection.

In addition to attempts to develop the feeling of 'Japaneseness' in Ainu People, educational provision was made for Ainu living in Hokkaido. In 1877, a *Kyōiku-sho* (education place) was started in *Tsuishikari* by the *Kaitaku-shi* (Development Commission) (Ogawa, 1997). *Tsuishikari* was a place where Ainu in Sakhalin known as *Karafuto* Ainu and the Kurils known as *Chishima* Ainu were forced to move to and settled in.

In the Yorta Yorta region of Australia, the first written records about their experiences of formal education come from the Maloga Mission that was established in 1874 by Daniel and Janet Matthews. They set up a school for Yorta Yorta on the *Dhungala* Murray River. In his diary, Matthews writes of a young Yorta Yorta (cited in Cato, 1976):

> 6 Aug. Maloga. The boy, Billy Cooper, shows great aptitude for learning. He has acquired a knowledge of the Alphabet, capital and small letters, in three days and then taught Bobby – capitals only – in one day.
>
> (p. 51)

Image 2.13 William Cooper.
[Portrait of] William Cooper (nee McCrae)

Image 2.14 Sarah Cooper.
[Portrait of] Sarah Cooper (nee McCrae)

Born and educated at Maloga Mission, Mr. William Cooper (1860–1941) went on to become an influential leader whose contributions are well-remembered among the Yorta Yorta Peoples (Attwood & Markus, 2004). Particularly poignant is his 'Letter from an Educated Black' which he introduces with:

> I am sending you the enclosed which I have compiled to give the aboriginal mind on the problem of the Native race. I will be glad if you will consider this because I feel very disappointed from time to time with the public statements by White men, made with all good intention, no doubt, but which, written from the point of view of the white man, does not reflect the opinions of natives.
>
> (Cooper quoted in Attwood & Markus, 2004, p. 90)

By 1881, a special Aboriginal Reserve had been established, named Cummeragunja Reserve. By 1888, all the residents and their teacher had moved from Maloga Mission to the Reserve. Here, the Yorta Yorta aimed for self-sufficiency, using the skills they had learnt from their work on local farms and the knowledge they had been taught by Thomas James. They farmed sheep and cattle, had a productive food garden, and sold wool and dairy products.

Ainu schools increased mainly in south Hokkaido to 'protect' Ainu children. The education system for Ainu was established by Article 9 of the Hokkaido *Kyū-dojin hogo-hō* (*Hokkaido Former Aboriginal Protection Act* [1899]) (Meiji 32)

Indigenous education history   45

Image 2.15 Cummeragunja school, c. 1800s.

Source: NSW Department of Education; NRS 15051, Photographic Collection. NRS-15051-1-10-[546]-3.

Image 2.16 Cummeragunja Aboriginal School, c. 1938.

Source: NSW Department of Education; NRS 15051, Photographic Collection. NRS-15051-1-10-[546]-6.

and *Kyū-dojin jidō kyōiku-kitei* (*Regulations for the Education of Former Aboriginal Children* [1901]). By 1910, 25 schools had been set up, and the enrolment rate for Ainu children rose to over 90 per cent in the 1910s (Ogawa, 1997). Many researchers argue that the policy relating to the Ainu, particularly with regard to education, denied their language and culture and contributed to assimilation.

The Ainu schools were abolished in line with the abolition of the *Kyū-dojin jidō kyōiku-kitei* in 1922 and the elimination of Article 9 of the *Hokkaido Former Aboriginal Protection Act* in 1937. Hence Ainu children were expected to attend the mainstream Japanese education system.

First-wave Indigenous activism in formal education

Ainu activism was evident as early as the 1910s, when peasant and labour movements occurred nationwide during and after the First World War. Political movements that aimed to restore Ainu rights and demand their independence appeared in bulletins, novels, and poems. Against this backdrop, the Ainu Association of Hokkaido (led initially by the Hokkaido government) was established in 1930 to improve the life of the Ainu and remove discrimination against them (Seki et al., 2006). After the Second World War, in 1946, the Ainu Association of Hokkaido was legally incorporated to promote independent activities by the Ainu. The association made an attempt to restore Ainu rights, eventually proposing a new law to the Hokkaido and Japanese governments.

There is scant research focusing on how Ainu understood formal education and how they tell their history of this period, particularly the powerful impact of imperial government education policies. After Japan's Meiji government enacted the *Koseki-hō* (*Family Register Act [1871]*), Ainu were included in the *heimin* (commoner class) and later called *Kyū-dojin* (former Aboriginals). In fact, the *Hokkaido Former Aboriginal Protection Act* (1899) would remain in force for almost a hundred years, and this may well have caused the persistent sense of discrimination felt among the Ainu.

In the late 1960s, the Buraku issue (relating to descendants of 'outcasts' excluded from the Japanese caste system during the Edo period [1603–1868]) was used for reference in discussing whether the problems faced by the Ainu were class- or ethnicity-related. In the context of education in Hokkaido, the Ainu's problems were once regarded as working-class issues that called for education drawing on the Buraku liberation movement, which strived to combat discrimination. After some trial and error, the problems faced by the Ainu finally came to be regarded as ethnic in nature simply because the effort to remove discrimination through education had proved far from successful. Other changes occurred in the early 1970s; for example, two major political parties, the Japan Communist Party and the Social Democratic Party of Japan, worked to restore Ainu rights, while, in educational settings, the term '*Ainu People*' came to be used rather than '*Ainu Japanese*'. Once Ainu issues were treated not as class issues but as ethnic issues, Ainu culture was recognised as unique, and Ainu ethnic differences attracted more attention (Yoneda, 1996).

In Japan, mainstream Japanese learning about the Ainu at the beginning was characterised as the education to remove misunderstanding of the Ainu, which spread widely within Hokkaido in the 1970s. In the 1980s, Japan was influenced by the shifting international policy landscape such that the learning about the Ainu came to be promoted more from an Indigenous Rights viewpoint even though formal recognition of the Ainu claim did not occur until Japan endorsed UNDRIP. In parallel, as the idea of multicultural education developed through the 1980s and the 1990s in terms of respecting minority culture and living with minorities, again the claims of Ainu People to be educated about their culture remained in the mainstream debates within Japanese education circles.

Before UNDRIP, in 1984, the Ainu Association of Hokkaido (then the Utari Association of Hokkaido) created the *Draft Law Concerning the Ainu People* (1984) (General Assembly of the Ainu Association of Hokkaido) (*Draft Law*), which included provisions for: (1) implementing a comprehensive education for Ainu children; (2) Ainu language learning in the education of Ainu children; and (3) taking action to eliminate discrimination against the Ainu in both school education and community education (Hokkaido Utari Association, 1984). From a present-day point of view, the underlying idea is in line with the concepts enshrined within UNDRIP (Maeda, 2019); however, no actual law ever materialised.

This might not have been the first time that they were disappointed at the government's policy. Ogawa's (2013) view is interesting: among Ainu polices, education policy had a different meaning for Ainu who had received education. Ogawa studied Sakhalin Ainu students who learnt at the *Tsuishikari* Ainu school in the Meiji era and argues that Sakhalin Ainu came to let their children receive education by proactively changing their way of thinking to recast their lives in a new place because they had no choice. He states, further, that earlier research often claimed that Ainu did not understand the significance of education but, in fact, they did understand and asked for education that they believed would help them build new lives, even in the restricted and difficult circumstances they faced. However, the government obviously did not take their needs seriously, which served only to disappoint them.

Ogawa (1997) also studied Ainu teachers who taught at Ainu schools, although there are no sound statistical materials about them. He concludes that Ainu teachers' desires for proper education for Ainu was not taken or reflected well in the policies. He concludes that Ainu teachers' desire to provide proper education for Ainu was not adopted or properly reflected in the policies.

In Australia, a group of Indigenous People began to emerge as leaders post-1900 when Australia became a federation of states governed under a federal system with both national- and state-level elections. While still formally under the rule of the English monarchy, Australia began as a nation. By doing so, it was believed that the *sui generis* rights (see the Glossary) of Indigenous Peoples

Image 2.17 The 'Day of Mourning' Aboriginal meeting, 26 January 1938.
Source: HORNER2.J03.BW-N04642_12.

of Australia had been extinguished, first by the claim of the English Crown and then by the formation of the nation of Australia, each with their legal structures that claimed to have taken territorial control of the landmass of Australia and some surrounding islands.

Indigenous Peoples in general and Ainu People and Yorta Yorta People as examples, did not accept these claims but were, at that time, not yet able to stop the attempts to extinguish their claims. Seeing opportunities to be educated in the ways of the settlers and colonisers, Yorta Yorta leaders seized the chance to use education to their advantage. Respected in their families and communities as holders of important cultural knowledge, they were also schooled in the ways of the English settlers and were able to navigate the political landscape in persuasive and powerful ways, impacts that continue into the present day. Two of many other noteworthy people came from the Yorta Yorta People: Pastor Sir Doug Nicholls (1906–1988) and Hyllus Maris (1934–1986).

William Cooper's nephew, Pastor Sir Doug Nicholls was born and educated at Cummeragunja Mission. Reflecting the discussion earlier in this chapter about ancestral approaches to socialisation, education, and the joy of learning, he brought his 'pre-contact' education theories to the task of mission and state-controlled education.

Late in his life, at the opening of Worawa College in March 1983, Sir Nicholls shared this important wisdom:

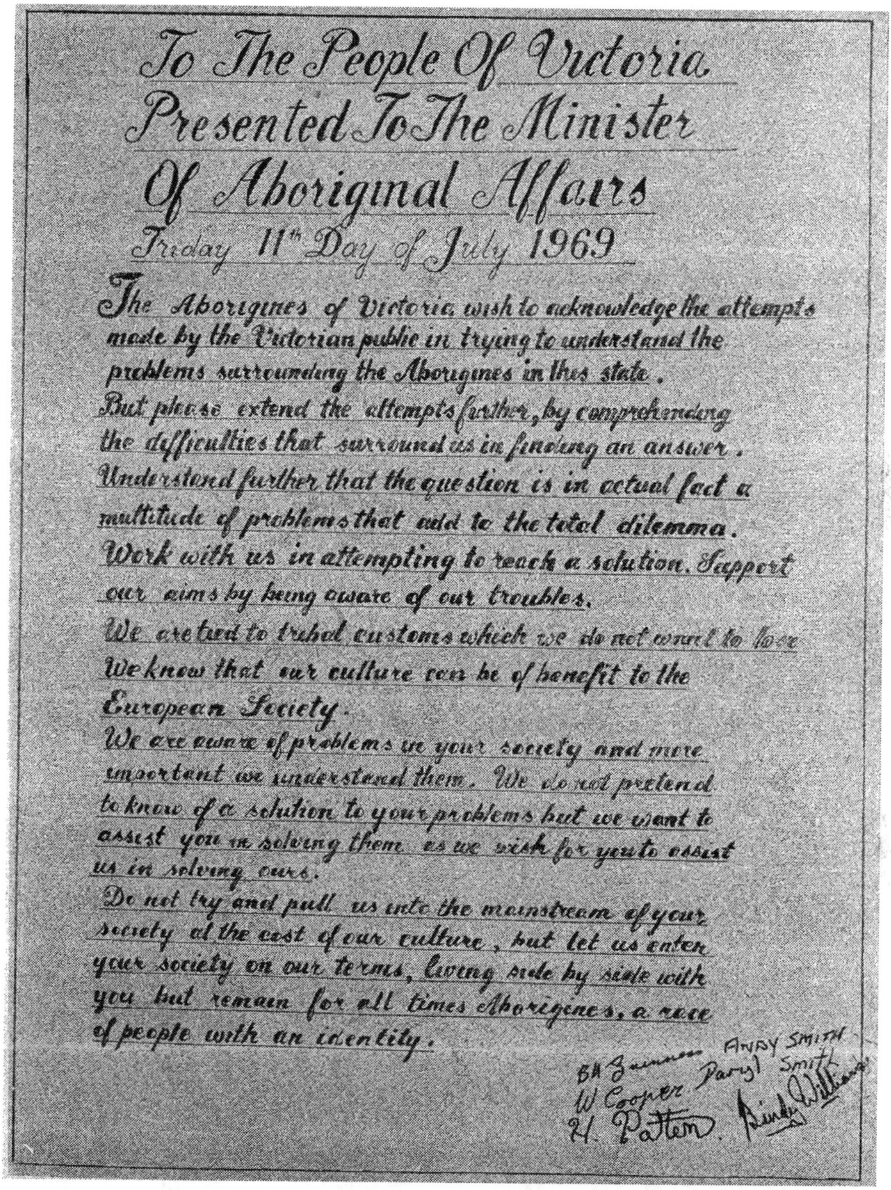

> **To The People Of Victoria**
> **Presented To The Minister**
> **Of Aboriginal Affairs**
> **Friday 11th Day of July 1969**
>
> The Aborigines of Victoria wish to acknowledge the attempts made by the Victorian public in trying to understand the problems surrounding the Aborigines in this state.
> But please extend the attempts further, by comprehending the difficulties that surround us in finding an answer.
> Understand further that the question is in actual fact a multitude of problems that add to the total dilemma.
> Work with us in attempting to reach a solution. Support our aims by being aware of our troubles.
> We are tied to tribal customs which we do not want to lose. We know that our culture can be of benefit to the European Society.
> We are aware of problems in your society and more important we understand them. We do not pretend to know of a solution to your problems but we want to assist you in solving them, as we wish for you to assist us in solving ours.
> Do not try and pull us into the mainstream of your society at the cost of our culture, but let us enter your society on our terms, living side by side with you but remain for all times Aborigines, a race of people with an identity.
>
> BA Gamner Anay Smith
> W Cooper Parcyl Smith
> H. Patten Lindy Williams

Image 2.18 Petition by the Victorian Aboriginal people presented by Doug Nicholls to the Minister of Aboriginal Affairs Ray Meagher.
Source: JACKOMOS.A12.BW-N05340_08.

Aboriginal children must be educated in the way of our people. They must learn their history, about their great ancestors, the language and the law.

They must also be educated in the way of the society in which they live in the very best of what it has to offer, so they can truly be a part, not only of Australia's past, but also its present and future.

(Nicholls, 1983)

Born on Cummeragunja Aboriginal Reserve in 1934, Hyllus Maris lived at Cummeragunja before walking off the Reserve with 200 other people because of the gross mismanagement and brutality that had been institutionalised at Cummeragunja by the NSW Aboriginal Protection Board. As recorded by the Victorian Department of Premier and Cabinet, she was inducted into the Victorian Honour Roll of Women in 2001.[1] And now to the important underlying thread of this chapter, which is narrating the Indigenous history of education, Hyllus Maris went on to establish Worawa Aboriginal College, the first independent Aboriginal school in Victoria, that opened in 1983, a school that continues into the present.

Pastor Sir Doug Nicholls and Hyllus Maris, like many other Aboriginal activists, were involved in the Federal Council for the Advancement of

Image 2.19 Hyllus Maris.
Source: Briggs Family album.

Aborigines and Torres Strait Islanders (FCAATSI). Both were particularly keen to promote the rights of Indigenous Peoples in education.

Indigenous People had started to become successful in formal education, developing the skills and knowledge to launch successful political campaigns for the recognition of their rights. Slowly, a movement swelled for Aboriginal representation in politics. At the time, Aboriginal people were not yet recognised as full citizens of Australia; Aboriginal people were, in effect, considered in the same category as flora and fauna. The referendum on that matter would not occur for another nine years at this stage. Aborigines had no voting rights and no political representation. In effect, the rights of Indigenous People were akin to those of a sub-18-year-old White person. Policies were developed to manage and otherwise deal with 'them'. The period between 1958 and 1967 was a very important one for Aboriginal politics, which started to craft a political voice that could engage with the national government of Australia and begin to influence policies. In particular, the proper education of Indigenous People became an important aspect of the growing agenda pursued by FCAATSI leaders.

The year 1967 was a watershed for the recognition of Indigenous People, their rights, and, in particular, their right to education. Up until the referendum, the federal government had no way to legislate for the needs of the Indigenous citizens of Australia. People mistakenly understand that the 1967 referendum gave Aboriginal people the vote but, in fact, the Indigenous Referendum of 1967 was about giving the Australian government the power to legislate for Indigenous People.

The success of the referendum (a rare occurrence in Australian political history) heralded increasing attention being paid to the education of Indigenous children. In 1975, the Commonwealth Schools Commission established a standing committee to advise them on Aboriginal education. The committee was selected by Indigenous People from across Australia and there was representation from each state and territory. Facing a significant challenge in an era when Indigenous children were still not allowed to attend certain schools, they discussed and advised across the range of issues facing metropolitan, rural, and remote communities in the provision of education and properly trained teachers. This committee became known as the Aboriginal Education Consultative Group (AECG). In 1980, the National Aboriginal Education Committee (NAEC) which was formed from the AECG crafted the first Indigenous education policy to be written by Indigenous People rather than the education administrators of the colonial bureaucracy (Fletcher 1989; Partington 1998).

In summary, despite the quite different contexts, what is known of Indigenous Peoples' histories of the commencement of imposed schooling on their children for both Ainu and Yorta Yorta were extremely disruptive to pre-contact socialisation processes that had been handed down ancestrally. Suddenly and coercively, Indigenous Peoples of Japan and Australia had to enter a new formal system where the joy of learning was stripped away from them, disconnected from the reason to learn and often dealt with poorly and cruelly. There are

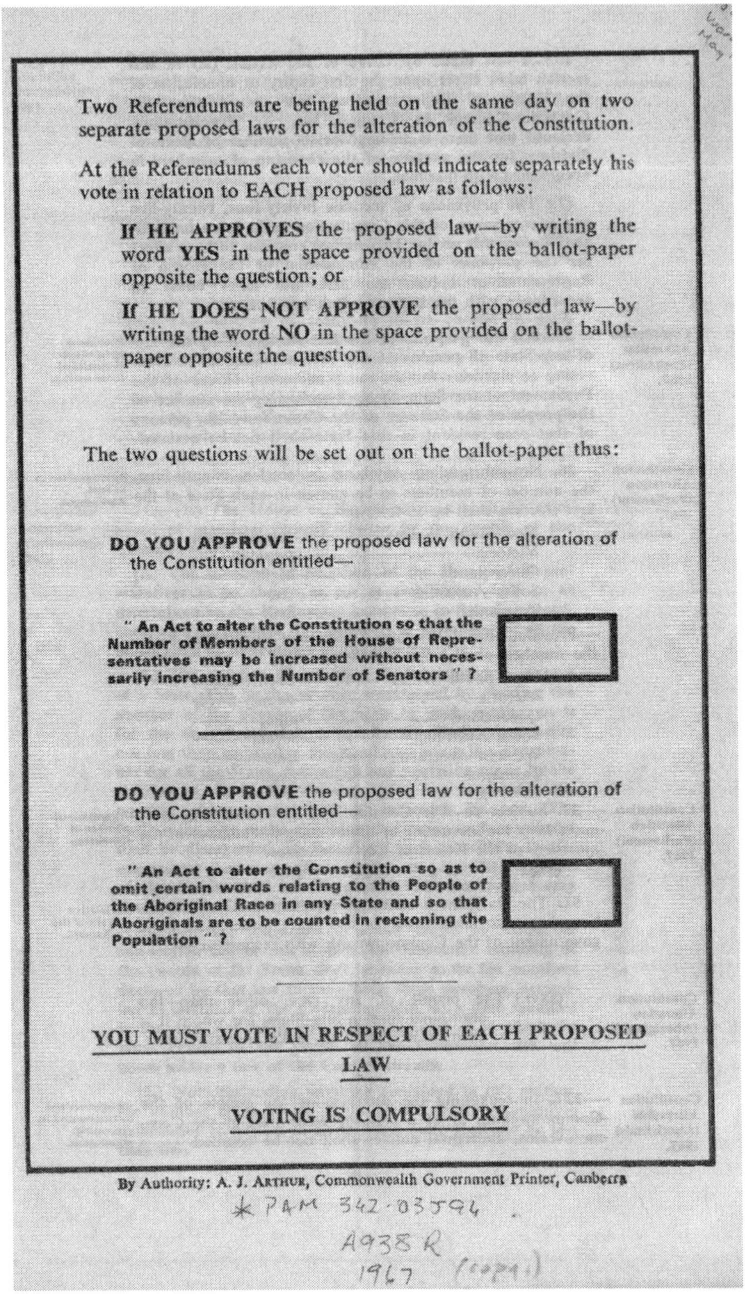

Two Referendums are being held on the same day on two separate proposed laws for the alteration of the Constitution.

At the Referendums each voter should indicate separately his vote in relation to EACH proposed law as follows:

If HE APPROVES the proposed law—by writing the word YES in the space provided on the ballot-paper opposite the question; or

If HE DOES NOT APPROVE the proposed law—by writing the word NO in the space provided on the ballot-paper opposite the question.

The two questions will be set out on the ballot-paper thus:

DO YOU APPROVE the proposed law for the alteration of the Constitution entitled—

" An Act to alter the Constitution so that the Number of Members of the House of Representatives may be increased without necessarily increasing the Number of Senators " ?

DO YOU APPROVE the proposed law for the alteration of the Constitution entitled—

" An Act to alter the Constitution so as to omit certain words relating to the People of the Aboriginal Race in any State and so that Aboriginals are to be counted in reckoning the Population " ?

YOU MUST VOTE IN RESPECT OF EACH PROPOSED LAW

VOTING IS COMPULSORY

By Authority: A. J. ARTHUR, Commonwealth Government Printer, Canberra

Image 2.20 Ballot paper 1967 Referendum.
Source: Commonwealth Electoral Office, 1967.

stories of surviving and adapting for both communities but the resonance of learning to country had been all but destroyed. The wave to change this situation began to arise for both Ainu and Yorta Yorta as they became more successful in the formal education system and were able to advocate for their rights. After many years of struggle and appeal to non-Indigenous policymakers, politicians, and educators, the nations of Japan and Australia began to formulate Indigenous Education policies that better reflected the aspirations of Indigenous People. Even so, the translation of policy aspiration to classroom practice continued to rely on the willingness and confidence of the teacher rather than being a required professional practice.

Second Wave – 1988–2009: tensions between multicultural education and national identity in Indigenous education moving towards UNDRIP

Tensions between internationalisation and national identity in Indigenous Education

Through the 1980s and 1990s, Ainu-related learning also developed as a form of multicultural education addressing the issues of respect for minority cultures and living with minorities. As noted earlier, Ainu issues came to be treated as ethnic issues rather than class issues, and Ainu culture was taught in relation to education on understanding different cultures. Within this context, multicultural education classes tended to set the Ainu culture of the past alongside contemporary Japanese culture to discuss modern-day multiculturalism, which was logically inconsistent (Yoneda, 1996). However, this kind of inconsistency was observed elsewhere in education in the 1990s. For example, the Japanese discourse on internationalisation that developed in an educational context from the 1980s was coupled with a nationalistic view of cultural identity.

One of the challenges in teaching about Ainu culture through multicultural education relates to Sato's (2007) observations concerning weaknesses in Japanese teaching about culture during the 1990s. Sato noted that the teachers' view of culture was found to be static and, hence, they were often tempted to interpret culture as emerging from a single mould and to formalise it as, for example, 'Japanese Culture', 'British Culture', and so on. Given that the teachers approached the subject in terms of a single 'Ainu culture', the more time they gave to promoting understanding of the differences – especially when they contrasted Ainu culture with Japanese culture – the more stereotyped the resulting impressions of the cultures tended to be (Sato, 2007).

Nonetheless, the 1997 *Ainu Cultural Promotion Act* definitely contributed to the promotion of Ainu culture. Behind the establishment of the act, we must not forget the efforts of Ainu People themselves, represented by the first Ainu to become a member of the Japanese Diet in 1994, Shigeru Kayano.

Image 2.21 Shigeru Kayano's first attendance at the Diet.
Source: Hokkaido Shimbun Press, 1994.

Another problem, however, is that teaching about Ainu culture in schools has posed a challenge to many Japanese teachers. Indeed, without understanding and respect for the fact that the Ainu are Indigenous People and have multi-layered identities as the result of a long history of discrimination, there can be no multi-symbiosis (Science Council of Japan, 2011). As described in Chapter 9, the Ainu had to wait another ten years, until the adoption of UNDRIP in 2007, for the next wave of advancement in their rights.

Policy-level developments in Indigenous education

The Australian Commonwealth Government and Aboriginal people across Australia recognised the issues facing Indigenous children at school. By 1991, after an exhaustive Royal Commission into Aboriginal Deaths in Custody

(Johnston, 1991), it was the raft of education-related measures that were recommended which emphasised the frustration and anger felt by Indigenous People as their education aspirations were being continually thwarted by local education systems (Dodson, Johnston, O'Dea, Wootten, & Wyvill, 1991, Chapter 33). Indigenous People were saying clearly to the government that they wanted an education system that supported their aspirations for the inclusion of their cultures, histories, languages, and lifeways and that they also had high expectations of Indigenous students to achieve in the traditional Western school subjects.

In the publication of its rationale, aims and objectives in Aboriginal Education, the NAEC (reproduced in full in Dodson et al., 1991) observed in 1980 that:

> Since 1788 the Aborigines of Australia have been subjected in varying degrees to an education system which has aimed to rationalise their dispossession from the land, deprecate their culture and, in general, endeavour to make the Indigenous People of this country lose their own rich cultural background and think, act and hold the same values as middle-class Europeans.
>
> (p. 1)

In Australia, in 1988, Paul Hughes led the Aboriginal Education Policy Task Force and recommended a national policy to address inequities and problems in Indigenous education. At this stage, Indigenous People were still central to the development of the policy and the findings of what became known as the *Hughes Report* that formed the basis of the new National Aboriginal and Torres Strait Islander Education Policy (Hughes, 1995). This policy built on the work done by the NAEC in its foundational document of 1980 (Royal Commission into Aboriginal Deaths in Custody & Johnston, 1991, pp. 115–118, Appendix V). The new National Aboriginal and Torres Strait Islander Education Policy (NATSIEP) was adopted in 1989 by a body known as the Australian Education Council and it contained an agreed 21 national goals for Indigenous Education (DEST, 2002). It remains a cornerstone policy document into 2020.

As Buckskin (2009) observed, Aboriginal and Torres Strait Islander people have had 'little decision-making power' (p. 84). Policy about the education of Indigenous children has been framed with a colonial mindset and most provisions were developed to make the administration of Indigenous education easy for the teachers and educations system (Ma Rhea, 2015b), and the measures suggest that Aboriginal students often do not receive an education that meets their needs (Partington & Beresford, 2012). Despite a high-water mark in policy making in Australia in 1989 with the National Aboriginal and Torres Strait Islander Education Policy noted in a review of Indigenous Education undertaken in 2000 (Taskforce on Indigenous Education & Greer [Chair], 2000), our analysis suggests that the general policymaking effort has been directed to the same goals as were initially established by the colonial administrative class under Macquarie. The ongoing focus of Australia's Indigenous Education policy efforts towards improving reading, writing and mathematics maintains echoes of the 15-point Macquarie Plan (point 11). While policies did begin to shift after the referendum in 1967 and researchers began to understand better what supported academic achievement for Indigenous students (Eckermann 1988), with the 1989 collaboration bringing forward a number of approaches supported nationally by Aboriginal education experts, the delivery of services and the evaluation of their quality has been firmly in the hands of state and territory education systems.

Curriculum-level changes

Since the Ainu did not write their history, pre-early modern Ainu cultural history seen by Ainu themselves is lacking. Some materials regarding Ainu culture written by *Wajin* appeared in the latter half of pre-early modern time. Most of the studies of Ainu People were based predominantly on written materials, such as diaries and records made by explorers, *Shogunate* officials, delegates sent to *Ezochi* while it was a territory under direct control of the Edo Bakufu (Naganuma et al., 2011). One famous figure of the explorers was Takeshiro Matsuura, who renamed Ezochi as Hokkaido. He travelled six times to Hokkaido over the course of 13 years, the last three times as a *Shogunate* official, and he wrote 151 reports about people's life, customs, population, folklore, name of places, journey, history, geography, and so on. Many popular guidebooks and maps were published based on his reports (Takeshiro Matsuura Memorial, n.d.).

Partly because of the troubles between the Ainu and some researchers, which predominantly occurred after the Meiji era, apart from touristic interest in Ainu culture, the Ainu have not been paid much attention in terms of academic interest. Not many research studies of Ainu People and their lifeways have been produced and their education has not been a focus in academic research until quite recently. This is especially so with respect to research being conducted by Ainu scholars. But a new generation is now emerging to take up the challenge.

As Yoneda (1996) notes, there were *Wanjin* schoolteachers who paid attention to Ainu children but they rarely took Ainu cultural elements into their educational activities. And it was not until the 1960s, when the needs for combatting discrimination against Ainu through education, was voiced. At the beginning of the 1970s, the movement that the history of interaction between Ainu and *Wajin* should be properly included in school textbooks grew. The quest for such education was primarily for the purpose of correcting misunderstanding concerning the Ainu, and some schoolteachers made efforts to develop their own materials for such education. This led to major administrative action (Yoneda, 1996). For example, the Hokkaido Government Board of Education set up a research council for Ainu education and began to develop supplementary materials to teach about the Ainu in 1973. The Hokkaido Government Board of Education published teachers' handbook for teaching about Ainu

Image 2.22 Takeshiro Matsuura in 1877.
Source: Hokkaido University Library Northern Studies Collection.

history and culture in 1984 to distribute to all the elementary and junior high schools all over Hokkaido and for high schools in 1992 (Shimizu, 2000). Since 1982, the Sapporo City Education Board has held workshops for teachers who teach children who have different cultural backgrounds and has developed teaching materials for education about the Ainu.

One of the big challenges for Japanese teacher education is how to incorporate learning about Indigenous Peoples in the Course of Study, which is the national curriculum standard. The content of school textbooks significantly influences the image of the Ainu. The first appearance of Ainu in elementary school textbooks after the Second World War was in 1961 for Social Studies

Image 2.23 A junior high school teacher demonstrates methods for teaching students about Ainu culture at a teacher workshop.

Source: City of Sapporo, 2018.

(Takegahara, 1993). The Ainu was mentioned in the history of the northern area of Japan, as 'merely serve(ing) to adorn explanations on the history of Hokkaido' (Takegahara, 1993, p. 289). However, a proliferation of research on Ainu People in the 1970s and a push by the Ainu to preserve their culture coincided with a new approach to teaching materials concerning Ainu culture and history in Hokkaido, as discussed earlier; though Takegahara (1993) analysed elementary Social Studies textbooks used from April 1992 and found that most had not changed much and were limited in the time covered and content. He noted that 'no headway has been made in the area of textbooks, where inadequate descriptions contribute to discrimination and prejudice against the Ainu' (p. 288).

The study of Indigenous Australian people began in anthropology departments in the 1890s. History texts rarely included Aboriginal content beyond an introductory chapter. Stanner and Sheils (1963) argued that much of the material that was taught, even into the 1960s, contained 'extraordinary misconceptions in proof of fanciful notions concerning the origin, history and character' of Aboriginal culture and lifeways (pp. xiv–xv). The emergence of Australian Indigenous Studies as a discrete area of research was significantly

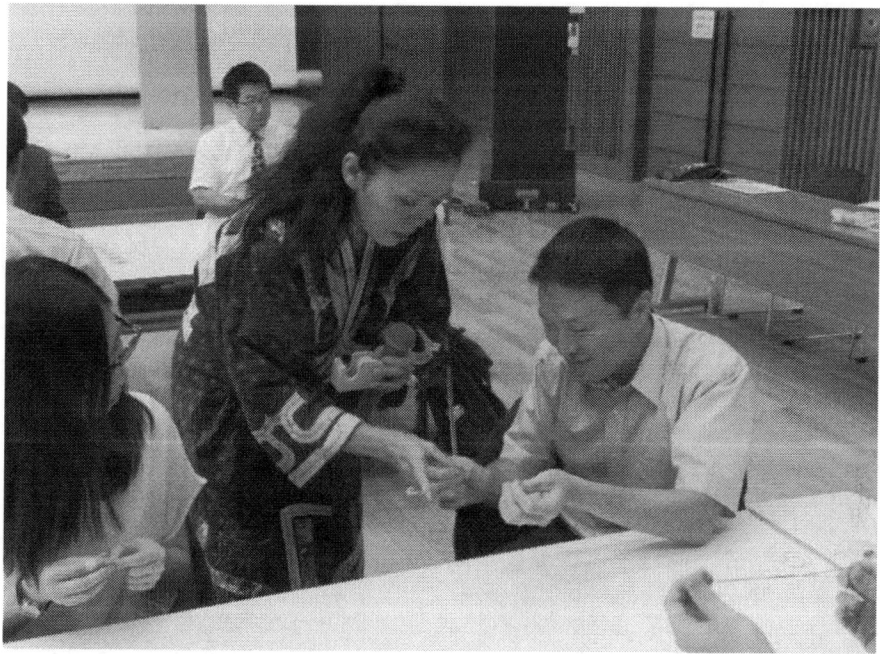

Image 2.24 School teachers making a strap decorated with traditional Ainu patterns at a teacher workshop.

Source: City of Sapporo, 2018.

shaped at a meeting chaired by W. E. H. Stanner on 15 May 1961 (Stanner & Sheils, 1963, p. 1). Significantly, as in the case of Ainu People, no Aboriginal person was involved and, in these early years of academic development of the field, Indigenous lifeways translated and abstracted into formal, codified knowledge by non-Indigenous academic researchers and other academics. The first Aboriginal person to be part of this work was admitted in 1970 (AIATSIS, 2018).

From these early beginnings, every university began to develop a subject called Aboriginal Studies (later Indigenous Studies) that became a standard feature of an Australian liberal arts education. Only recently has discussion emerged about how to teach Indigenous content, who should teach it, and for what purpose it should be taught. Ma Rhea and Russell (2012) argued that Indigenous Education in teacher education programs at universities draw on two interrelated but separate bodies of knowledge when considering the needs of Indigenous students. Their analysis suggested:

> The first comes from their professional, technical knowledge base, Indigenous Education as method. This is about pedagogical approaches, curriculum developments and assessment issues around the learning needs

of Indigenous students and how to teach non-Indigenous students about Indigenous society. The second knowledge base is found in Australian Indigenous Studies. Lecturers in Indigenous Education ideally draw on the broad canvass of expert knowledge about Indigenous cultures, identities, politics and history in order to ensure that the university training and ongoing development needs of their professionals has the capacity to understand the aspirations and needs of their Indigenous students and clients. They also ideally draw on what is known about Indigenous educational philosophy and methods of teaching and learning also including western education traditions in their pedagogical approach.

(Ma Rhea & Russell, 2012, p. 20)

Progressive two-way learning and both-way learning are ideas that developed during the 1980s and 1990s under the guidance of scholars such as Yunupiŋu (1994), Marika-Munuŋgiritj (1999), and Harris (1990). Harris, together with Hughes and Teasdale, argued that learning about the Aboriginal and Torres Strait Islander world and the Western world is a two-way process. In the face of continued failure by non-Indigenous teachers to create learning spaces where traditionally oriented Aboriginal children could learn in the Western way without losing their cultural identity, Aboriginal and Torres Strait Islander thinkers, such as Dr Yunupiŋu (1994) and Dr Marika (1999), began theorising how it might be possible for 'both-ways' learning to occur. As we have shown through examples in this chapter, their "Both Ways' approach asks all teachers to consider that Aboriginal people have access to complex educational philosophy that has evolved over millennium and that only in partnership will there be a culturally safe space created for the non-Indigenous young Aboriginal and Torres Strait Islander learner.

Conclusion

This chapter provided an overview of the Indigenous history of education in Japan and Australia. Drawing on examples of the development of formal schooling for Japanese Ainu and Australian Yorta Yorta People, it has described the development of ideas of how teaching and learning might best be undertaken in the modern world to ensure that the rights of Indigenous People are respected and that they receive the very best of education in their culture and in Western education.

How can teachers and teacher educators demonstrate the very best of Japanese and Australian society? How can they demonstrate the best of the profession in a way that moves Japanese and Australian Indigenous Peoples into a future that is Indigenous but is also part of the new post-imperial time? We have argued, in this chapter, that we cannot leave this only to Indigenous People to do, but that it must be Indigenous People who guide the future, rights-based education agenda.

In Japan, Shigeru Kayano asked a question in the Ainu language at the Diet simply because he wanted to let everybody know that there was another ethnic group living in Japan. For him, language is 'everything' for people, and his conviction paved the way to the *Ainu Cultural Promotion Act* of 1997 and beyond into the post-UNDRIP era. In Australia, the words spoken by Pastor Douglas Nicholls are echoed in the 1980 NAEC document and built on in the 1989 21-point agenda. In Chapter 6, we examine the schooling of Indigenous Australian and Japanese students and the preparation of teachers after UNDRIP, an international agreement that has had a profound impact on addressing the future needs and aspirations of Indigenous children and non-Indigenous young adults in Australia and Japan.

Note

1 *Hyllus Maris (1934–1986): A visionary with a passion for education*. Retrieved from www.dpc.vic.gov.au/index.php/aboriginal-affairs/projects-and-programs/leadership/victorian-aboriginal-honour-roll/victorian-aboriginal-honour-roll-2013-inductees/hyllus-maris-1934--1986

References

AIATSIS. (2018). *Our history*. Retrieved 31 May 2020 fromRetrieved 31 May 2020 fromhttps://aiatsis.gov.au/about-us/our-history

Ainu Museum. (Ed.). (1997). *Ueda Toshi no uepeker* [Uepeker by Toshi Ueda]. Sapporo, Japan: Hokkaido Kikanshi Insatsu-jo.

Ainu Museum. (Ed.). (2018). *Ainu bunka no kisochishiki* [Fundamental aspects of Ainu culture]. Chiba, Japan: Sofū-kan.

Ainu Association of Hokkaido. (2017). *Ainu minzoku no gaisetsu – Hokkaido Ainu Kyōkai no katsudo o fukume* [Overview of the Ainu: History of the Ainu Association of Hokkaido]. Retrieved 31 July 2019 from www.ainu-assn.or.jp/public/files/1d05c1d d9ceb9cf70478cd757622d3075a2c94b7.pdf.

Attwood, B., & Markus, A. (2004). *Thinking black: William Cooper and Australian Aborigines' league*. Canberra, ACT: Aboriginal Studies Press.

Batchelor, J. (1901). *The Ainu and their folk-lore*. London: Religious Tract Society.

Bell, H. (1988). An overview of some aboriginal teaching and learning strategies in traditionally oriented communities [online]. *Aboriginal Child at School, 16*(3), 3–23.

Block, J. H. (1971). Introduction to mastery learning: Theory and practice. In Block J. H. (Ed.). *Mastery learning: Theory and practice* (pp. 2–13). New York: Holt, Reinhart, and Winston,.

Bloom, B. S. (1971). Mastery learning. In Block, J. H. (Ed.). *Mastery learning: Theory and practice* (pp. 47–63). New York: Holt, Reinhart, and Winston.

Bloom, B. S. (1987). A response to Slavin's mastery learning reconsidered. *Review of Educational Research, 57*(4) (Winter), 507–508.

Bourke, C. J. (1976). Aboriginal education in Victoria: Evaluation of an innovatory emphasis. *Aboriginal Child at School, 4*, 1–26.

Buckskin, P. (2009). 'Hawke and Ryan: An acceleration of Indigenous education policy'. In Bloustien, G., Mackinnon, A., & Comber, B. (Eds.). *The Hawke Legacy* (pp. 83–95). Adelaide: Wakefield Press.

Burney, L., Lester, J., & Riley, L. (1993). School/classroom strategies for teaching aboriginal children [online]. *Aboriginal Child at School, 11*(1): 28–31.

Cato, N. (1976). *Mister Maloga: Daniel Matthews and his mission, Murray river, 1864–1902.* St. Lucia, Queensland: University of Queensland Press.

Christie, M. J. (1986). Formal education and Aboriginal children [online]. *Aboriginal Child at School, 14*(2): 40–44.

City of Sapporo. (2018). *Sapporo-shi minzoku kyōiku ni kansuru kenshūkai – Ainu minzoku kyōiku ni kansuru kyōin kenshū* [Workshops for Sapporo city teachers on the education of the Ainu community]. Retrieved 31 July 2019 from www.city.sapporo.jp/kyoiku/top/education/ainu/ainu_minzoku.html.

Craven, R. (Ed.). (1999) *Teaching Aboriginal studies.* Sydney: Allen & Unwin.

Department of Education, Science, and Training (DEST). (2002). *National report to parliament on Indigenous education and training.* Canberra: Australian Government.

Dodson, P., Johnston, E., O'Dea, D. J., Wootten, H., & Wyvill, L. F. (1991). *Royal commission into Aboriginal deaths in custody: Recommendations* (Vol. 5). Canberra, Australia: AGPS. Retrieved 31 May 2020 from www.austlii.edu.au/au/other/IndigLRes/rciadic/national/vol5/

Eckermann, A. K. (1988). Learning styles, classroom management, teacher characteristics and rural-urban Aboriginal people: Some thoughts [online]. *Aboriginal Child at School, 16*(1): 3–19.

Fletcher, J. (1989). Clean, clad, and courteous: A history of Aboriginal education in New South Wales. Carlton: J. Fletcher.

Hamilton, A. (1981). *Nature and nurture: Aboriginal child-rearing in North-Central Arnhem land.* Canberra: Australian Institute of Aboriginal Studies.

Harris, S. (1984). Aboriginal learning styles and formal schooling [online]. *Aboriginal Child at School, 12*(4), 3–23.

Harris, S. (1990). *Two-way Aboriginal schooling: Education and cultural survival.* Canberra, Australia: Aboriginal Studies Press.

Hokkaido Utari Association. (1984). Ainu minzoku ni kansuru hōritsu-an [Draft law concerning the Ainu community]. In Ainu Association of Hokkaido (Ed.). *Ainu minzoku no gaisetsu – Hokkaido Ainu Kyōkai no katsudō o fukume* [Overview of the Ainu: History of the Ainu Association of Hokkaido] (2017 ed.). Retrieved 31 May 2020 from www.ainu-assn.or.jp/public/files/1d05c1dd9ceb9cf70478cd757622d3075a2c94b7.pdf.

Hughes, P. (1995). A national strategy for the education of Aboriginal and Torres Strait Islander peoples 1996–2002. Ministerial Council on Education, Employment, Training and Youth Affairs. Retrieved 31 May 2020 from www.educationcouncil.edu.au/site/DefaultSite/filesystem/documents/Reports%20and%20publications/Publications/Cultural%20inclusion%20and%20ATSI/National%20Strategy%20for%20the%20Education%20of%20Aboriginal%20and%20Torres%20Strait%20Islander%20Peoples%201996-2002.pdf

Hunter, J. (1793). *An historical journal of the transactions at Port Jackson and Norfolk Island: With the discoveries which have been made in New South Wales and in the Southern Ocean since the publication of Phillip's voyage, compiled from the official papers; including* the journals of Governors Phillip and King, and of Lieut. Ball; and the voyages from the first sailing of the Sirius in 1787, to the return ... to England in 1792. London, England: John Stockdale.

Johnston, E. (1991). *National report of royal commission into Aboriginal deaths in custody: Overview and recommendations.* Canberra: AGPS.

Karino, Y. (2006). Kaitakushi kari-gakkō ni okeru Ainu kyōiku [Educating the Ainu community in provisional schools by development commissioners]. In Meiji-ishin-shi, G. (Ed.). *Meiji-ishin no chiiki to minshū* [Communities and their populace during the Meiji restoration] (pp. 157–176). Tokyo, Japan: Yoshikawa Kōbun-kan.

Kayano, S. (1988). *Kamuiyukara to mukashi-banashi* [Kamuy yukar (deity epics) and folktales]. Tokyo, Japan: Shogaku-kan.

Kayano, S. (2000). *Ainu saijiki: Nibutani no kurashi to kokoro* [Annual events held by the Ainu: The life and spirit of Nibutani]. Tokyo, Japan: Heibon-sha.

Ma Rhea, Z. (2015a). Leading and managing Indigenous education in the postcolonial world. London, England: Routledge.

Ma Rhea, Z. (2015b). Unthinking the 200-year-old colonial mindset: Indigenist perspectives on leading and managing Indigenous education. *International Education Journal: Comparative Perspectives, 14*(2), 90–100.

Ma Rhea, Z., & Russell, L. (2012). The invisible hand of pedagogy in Australian Indigenous studies and Indigenous education. *Australian Journal of Indigenous Education, 41*(1), 18–25. doi:10.1017/jie.2012.4

McCarthy, F. D. (1957). *Australia's aborigines: Their life and culture.* Melbourne, Victoria: Colorgravure.

Macquarie, L. (1814). 'Establishment of the native institution 1814'. NRS 1046 [SZ759, pages 11–14; Reel 6038]. Retrieved 31 May 2020 from www.records.nsw.gov.au/state-archives/digital-gallery/lachlan-macquarie-visionary-and-builder/public-notices/full-transcript-establishment-of-the-native-institution-1814.

Maeda, K. (2019). *Ōsutoraria senjūminzoku no shutai keisei to daigaku kaihō* [Autonomy development and higher education of the Australian indigenous community]. Tokyo, Japan: Akashi-shoten.

Marika-Munuŋgiritj, R. (1999). *1998 Wentworth lecture.* Retrieved 31 May 2020 from https://aiatsis.gov.au/publications/presentations/marika

Martin, K. (2007). Ma(r)king tracks and reconceptualising Aboriginal early childhood education: An Aboriginal Australian perspective. *Childrens Issues, 11*(1): 15–20.

Morrison, H. C. (1926). *The practice of teaching in the secondary school.* Chicago: University of Chicago Press.

Muir, N., & Bohr, Y. (2014). Contemporary practice of traditional Aboriginal child rearing: A review. *First Peoples Child and Family Review, 9*(1): 66–79.

Naganuma, T., Koshida, K., Emori, S., Tabata, H., Ikeda, T., & Miura, Y. (2011). *Hokkaido no rekishi: Kodai, Chūsei, Kinsei-hen* [The history of Hokkaido during the ancient, middle, and early modern eras] (Vol. 1). Sapporo, Japan: Hokkaido Shimbun Press.

Nicholls, D. (1983). *Worawa Aboriginal college opening address.* Retrieved 31 May 2020 from www.worawa.vic.edu.au/our-school/education/

Ogawa, M. (1997). *Kindai Ainu kyōikuseido-shi kenkyū* [A study of the history of the modern education system for the Ainu population]. Sapporo, Japan: Hokkaido University Press.

Ogawa, M. (2013). Tsuishikari gakkō no rekishi: Hokkaido ni kyōsei-iju saserareta Karafuto Ainu no kyōiku-shi [History of Tsuishikari School: Viewpoint of forcibly relocated Sakhalin Ainu children]. *Japanese Journal of Educational Research, 80*, 309–321.

Okuda, O. (1996). Reskishi kenkyū no shiryō toshite no Ainu kōtō bungei [Ainu oral lore as material for historical research]. *Bulletin of the Hokkaido Ainu Culture Research Center, 2*, 19–31.

Parbury, N. (1987). *Survival: A history of Aboriginal life in NSW.* Sydney: NSW Department of Aboriginal Affairs.

Partington, G. (1998) 'In those days it was that rough'; Aboriginal and Torres Strait Islander history and education. In Partington, G. (Ed.). *Perspectives on Aboriginal and Torres Strait Islander education* (pp. 27–54). Katoomba: Social Science Press, 1998.

Partington, G., & Beresford, Q. (2012). The context of Aboriginal education. In Beresford, Q., Partington, G., & Gower, G. (Eds.). *Reform and resistance in Aboriginal education* (Fully revised edition) (pp. 35–84). Western Australia: UWA.

Price, K. (2012). 'Aboriginal and Torres Strait Islander studies in the classroom'. In Price, K. (Ed.). *Aboriginal and Torres Strait Islander education: An introduction for the teaching profession.* Port Melbourne: Cambridge University Press, 151–163.

Price, K. (Ed.). (2015). Aboriginal and Torres Strait Islander education: An introduction for the teaching profession (Second edition). Melbourne, Australia: Cambridge University Press.

Reconciliation Australia. (2013). *Yirrkala celebrates 40 years of bilingual education.* Retrieved 31 May 2020 from www.reconciliation.org.au/yirrkala-celebrates-40-years-of-bilingual-education/#

Robinson, R., & Baglin, D. (1968). *The Australian Aboriginal in colour.* Sydney, NSW: Reed.

Royal Commission into Aboriginal Deaths in Custody, & Johnston, E. C. (1991). *National report: Overview and recommendations.* (Report No. 0644144076). Canberra, ACT: Australian Govt. Pub. Service.

Sarra, C. (2011). *Strong and smart: Towards a pedagogy of emancipation.* London and New York: Routledge.

Sato, C. (2007). Learning from weaknesses in teaching about culture: The case study of a Japanese school abroad. *Intercultural Education, 18*(5): 445–453.

Science Council of Japan. (2011). *Hōkoku – Ainu seisaku no arikata to kokuminteki-rikai* [Report: Future Ainu policy and the public understanding of the Ainu]. Retrieved 31 May 2020 from www.scj.go.jp/ja/info/kohyo/pdf/kohyo-21-h133-1.pdf.

Seki, H., Kuwabara, M., Oba, Y., & Takahashi, A. (2006). *Hokkaido no rekishi – Kindai, Gendai-hen* [Modern history of Hokkaido] (Volume 2). Sapporo, Japan: Hokkaido Shimbun Press.

Shimizu, T. (2000). Gakkō kyōiku ni okeru Ainu minzoku kyōiku no genjō ni kansuru chōsa [Survey on the current education of the Ainu people in school]. *Hekichi Kyoiku Kenkyu, 55*, 79–87.

Stanner, W. E. H., & Sheils, H. (1963). *Australian aboriginal studies: A symposium of papers presented at the 1961 research conference.* Melbourne, Australia: Oxford University Press.

Strong, S. M. (2011). *Ainu spirits singing: The living world of Chiri Yukie's Ainu Shin'yōshū.* Honolulu: University of Hawai'i Press.

Takegahara, Y. (1993). The Ainu in the new textbooks for Social Studies. In Loos, N., & Osanai, T. (Eds.). *Indigenous minorities and education: Australian and Japanese perspectives of their Indigenous peoples, the Ainu, Aborigines and Torres Strait Islanders* (pp. 288–297). Tokyo, Japan: Sanyusha.

Takeshirō Matsuura Memorial. (n.d.). *Samazama na kao o motsu bakumatsu no ijin* [The many faces of people during the Edo period]. Retrieved 31 May 2020 from https://takeshiro.net/about.

Taskforce on Indigenous Education, & Greer (Chair), A. (2000). *Report of MCEETYA taskforce on Indigenous education.* Canberra, Australia: AGPS

United Nations. (2007). *United Nations Declaration on the Rights of Indigenous Peoples.* Retrieved 31 May 2020 fromwww.un.org/development/desa/indigenouspeoples/wp-content/uploads/sites/19/2018/11/UNDRIP_E_web.pdf

Washburn, M. F. (1922). Introspection as an objective method. *Psychological Review, 29,* 89–112. Retrieved 31 May 2020 fromhttps://psychclassics.yorku.ca/Washburn/

Yoneda, Y. (1996). Gakkō kyōiku ni okeru 'Ainu bunka' no kyōzai-ka no mondaiten ni tsuite [Teaching 'Ainu culture' at school: Problems and controversies]. *Bulletin of the Hokkaido Ainu Culture Research Center, 2,* 123–148.

Yunupiŋu, M. (1994). *Yothu Yindi: Finding balance.* London, England: Sage Publications.

Chapter 3

The place of Indigenous Peoples in multicultural education

Policies, debates, and practices in Australia and Japan

Kaori Okano

Introduction

Indigenous peoples are often included among the culturally and linguistically diverse (CALD) peoples in modern nation states. All CALD peoples have distinctive histories which led to their marginalisation in mainstream societies. These histories include colonisation, which resulted in dispossession of and forced transportation from their land; enslavement; refugees fleeing oppression; and migrants seeking better lives elsewhere. In response to the transnational movement of people in the second half of the 20th century, the term 'multiculturalism' began to be widely used in policy and debates. Indigenous issues were drawn into the discussion within the context of multiculturalism – though in differing degrees across the globe. In some countries, Indigenous peoples were vocal and asserted their special status as the original inhabitants of the land who had been displaced by the coloniser, arguing they were distinct from other CALD minoritised peoples.

In this chapter, I use the definition of Indigenous peoples as stated in the 2007 *UN Declaration on the Rights of Indigenous Peoples* (UNDRIP):

> On an individual basis, an Indigenous person is one who belongs to these Indigenous populations through self-identification as Indigenous (group consciousness) and is recognized and accepted by these populations as one of its members (acceptance by the group). This preserves for these communities the sovereign right and power to decide who belongs to them, without external interference.
>
> (United Nations, 2007)

Multiculturalism has diverse understandings. It can denote: (1) a demographic description of a community; (2) the ideology that ethnic and cultural diversity be valued, celebrated and productive (often promoted by government and organisations); (3) government and institutional policies (or programmes) to promote the above-mentioned ideology; and (4) lived experiences of (1) and (3), or outcomes of the policies (Gloemraad,

Korteweg, & Yurdakul, 2008; Koopmans, 2013, p. 120). I will look at multiculturalism in all these aspects.

This chapter demonstrates that Australian Indigenous peoples have been more assertive of their special status among CALD minoritised groups than their Japanese counterparts and considers why that is so. Australia has adopted a national policy on multicultural education since the mid-1970s in order to facilitate the integration of increasing numbers of migrants (Ma Rhea, 2018). Simultaneously, Indigenous people have asserted their unique position as the First Nations people. To this day, debates on Indigenous education have continued separately from those on multiculturalism in education. By contrast, Japan does not have a national-level government policy on multicultural education or Indigenous education, continuing to adopt simple equality principles and leaving relevant local governments, schools, and NGOs to respond to local needs. There has been alliance among 'involuntary minority groups', namely, Buraku People (Japanese nationals who are descendants of a feudal outcaste population), Zainichi Koreans (descendants of former colonial subjects), and Indigenous peoples based on shared suffering caused by marginalisation resulting from state policies. Two decades after the first arrival of migrants from South America and Asia, there is also inter-group collaborative interaction between these recent migrants and Zainichi Koreans based on their shared experience of marginalisation as a result of not being Japanese citizens. Discussions about Indigenous Ainu education have been peripheral.

In writing this chapter, I am aware that my positionality influences my scholarship. I am a non-Indigenous, non-White migrant female in White-dominant Australia who has experienced institutional racism and unconscious bias as a secondary school teacher, a university lecturer, and a parent of two mixed heritage children. I am aware that my contribution as a non-Indigenous scholar to studies of Indigenous people may be seen as problematic. My chapter presents a comparative analysis and does not intend to offer advice as such.

I begin by examining how Indigenous education has been addressed in multicultural education policies and debates in Australia and Japan. I then explore why Indigenous Ainu have not been assertive about their special status in multicultural education, examine the inter-group panethnic alliance among involuntary minority groups in Japan, and explore potential directions for the future.

Australia's case: The place of Indigenous peoples

Recent scholars have suggested that there are five eras that characterise Australian policies for educating Indigenous peoples: (1) protection; (2) assimilation; (3) integration; (4) self-determination; and (5) normalisation (Patrick & Moodie, 2016, p. 167). The initial government policy of protecting Indigenous people began in the early 19th century with the appointment of 'Aboriginal protectors' and provided segregated education for Indigenous children with a high level of control over their lives. The policy shifted to assimilationist schooling to integrate the children into the mainstream Anglo-Australian society (Gray & Beresford, 2008), with the ultimate form of this approach being the removal of Indigenous children from their families. As is the case with policies regarding minoritised groups elsewhere, the assimilationist policies were still based on the early 20th-century social Darwinist idea that Anglo-White culture and practices were superior, and Indigenous children would benefit from assimilating into the mainstream; in this process, Indigenous children would learn to internalise the dominant culture and reject their own.

There have been numerous government policy documents since a 1967 referendum which resulted in the constitutional recognition of Indigenous people as Australian citizens. The years leading to the referendum saw a shift to an integrationist approach, which recognised the human right to maintain one's own culture (Patrick & Moodie, 2016). A minister for Aboriginal Affairs was appointed in 1968. The Federal Department of Aboriginal Affairs was established in 1972. Among the government policy documents produced over the period from the referendum to 1995 were the *Education for Aborigines* (National-Aboriginal Consultative-Group, 1975), the *Report of the Aboriginal Education Policy Task* (Hughes, 1988), and the *National Review of Education for Aboriginal and Torres Strait Islander Peoples* (Yunupiŋu, 1995). They variously advocated greater Indigenous participation in decision making, self-determination, Indigenous rights to retain their traditional life styles and have their culture recognised officially, and government commitment to achieving equity in educational outcomes (Schwab, 1995).

Around the same time in the 1970s and 1980s, there was growing concern about the way that Australia was conducting its immigration policies and, from a number of inquiries and debates (see Appendix), there emerged an approach to multiculturalism in state and federal government policy initiatives. Koleth (2010), in her report to inform Australian parliamentarians about the development of Australia's multicultural policies, found:

> Echoing developments in other immigrant-receiving countries, notably Canada, by the late 1970s there was a growing acceptance of broader expressions of cultural diversity or 'multiculturalism' within Australian society. Over time the term 'multiculturalism' has come to refer to the demographic reality of cultural diversity, a set of policies and policy orientations, as well as a concept which articulates a normative ideal or ideals about society.
>
> (Koleth, 2010, p. 2)

Early policy approaches aimed to address the needs of the large numbers of migrants from Europe by abandoning the assimilationist policies. Because schools are the responsibility of state and territory governments, the Australian government worked together with state and territory ministers of education to develop multicultural education approaches that advocated celebration of cultural diversity, equal value of all cultures, and the pursuit of human rights for all. In multiculturalism debates, Australian Indigenous peoples asserted their special place as First Nations people, having the original relation with the land, and did not actively seek to be a part of this nationwide movement (Hickling-Hudson, 2003). Governments continued to operate separate departments for Indigenous peoples and for multicultural affairs.

By the late 1980s, the focus in Indigenous education shifted to achieving equity in educational outcomes by closing the gap between Indigenous and non-Indigenous children. The 1989 Commonwealth-State National Aboriginal Education Policy proposed the goal of achieving equity by the year 2000. Since 1995, there have been many more reviews on Indigenous education (see, e.g., Patrick & Moodie, 2016, p. 173). Since the introduction of that policy, various Commonwealth government reports on Indigenous education highlight that, while there have been improvements, equity has, thus far, not been achieved and that a number of government educational reforms for Indigenous students have largely been failures (Altman, Biddle, & Hunter, 2009; Beresford, Partington, & Gower, 2012; Gray & Beresford, 2008; Patrick & Moodie, 2016; Vass, 2012). There is a new concern that the current policy focus on closing the gap in pursuit of equitable outcomes has become more emphasised than self-determination (Patrick & Moodie, 2016, pp. 167, 179).

In 2019, Mr Ken Wyatt became the first Indigenous cabinet minister when appointed as minister for Aboriginal Australians. He announced that he would develop a consensus option for constitutional recognition of Indigenous Australians to be proposed for the referendum in this parliamentary term (*The Age*, 2019). In July 2019, the Commonwealth government established the National Indigenous Australian Agency (NIAA) to replace the Indigenous Affairs Group within the department of the prime minister and cabinet. However, an idea of including an Indigenous voice in the constitution did not receive consensus support in parliament.

Japan's case: The place of Indigenous Ainu People

Compared to Australia, where immigrants are the majority and Indigenous peoples have struggled to have their aspirations and needs recognised, Japan is ethnically more homogenous; but, as a modern nation state, it has always been multi-ethnic. In order to picture Japan's contemporary multicultural landscape, it is helpful to consider four groups of CALD people, although the group boundaries are contentious, as is the case elsewhere, because of mixed ancestry (Okano & Tsuneyoshi, 2011). The groups are: (1) Indigenous peoples (Ainu and Okinawan); (2) Buraku People (descendants of the pre-modern outcaste population); (3) so-called Zainichi descendants of subjects from former colonies (Taiwan, the Korean Peninsula, Northeast China); and (4) so-called 'newcomer' migrants (including guest workers and their descendants) who have arrived from Asia and Latin America since the late 1980s. While an accurate figure for how many people comprise each of these groups is not available – since the Japanese government has not collected such data – I estimate that approximately 5–7 per cent of Japan's 127 million population are members of cultural minorities, with the Ainu constituting less than 0.5 per cent of the population (see Table 3.1).

Table 3.1 Estimated population of minority groups in Japan

Minority groups	Japanese citizens	Non-Japanese citizens living in Japan (2016)
Ainu (Indigenous)	Exact number unknown (24,000 self-categorised in Hokkaido; 300,000 in Japan)	
Okinawan	Exact number unknown (1.37 million in Okinawa Prefecture; 300,000 in other parts of Japan)	
Amerasians in Okinawa	Exact number unknown	
People of *Buraku* descent	Exact number unknown (estimated 1.5–3 million)	
Ethnic Chinese	Exact number unknown (88,123 naturalised 1972–2003; 55,708 children of Chinese–Japanese marriages 1986–2005)	677,571 (2016)
Ethnic Koreans	Exact number unknown (320,232 naturalised 1952–2008; 263,996 Korean–Japanese marriages 1955–2007; 133,253 children of Korean–Japanese marriages 1985–2007)	490,190 (2016)
Registered foreigners, excluding Chinese and Koreans		1,139,627 (2016) (including 176,284 Brazilians and 237,103 Filipinos)
Naturalised Japanese citizens	Exact number unknown (133,684 in 1952–2008, excluding ethnic Chinese and Koreans)	
Children of mixed descent where one parent is a Japanese citizen	Exact number unknown	
Japanese returnees	Exact number unknown (12,000 returned in 2008)	
Sub-totals	Exact number unknown (3.95–5.70 million or more)	2,307,388 (2016)
Estimated total	**6.24–8.00 million or more**	

Sources: Japan-Hōmu-shō, 2017; Okano & Tsuneyoshi, 2011.

The formation of the modern nation state of Japan in the mid-19th century included the colonisation of Indigenous peoples in Hokkaido (the northern most island of the Japanese archipelago) and in the Ryūkyū islands (now Okinawa prefecture). The Indigenous peoples became imperial subjects. Hokkaido is rich in minerals, forestry, and fisheries. The Tokyo government created the Development Commission (1869) to manage the development of Hokkaido – then regarded as terra nullius – and encouraged migration of mainland Japanese to clear forest areas for agricultural land. The Indigenous Ainu People were forced to leave the places where they had resided and work as labourers for the mainlander immigrants. The *Hokkaido Former Aboriginal Protection Act* (1899) (Meiji 32) was based on the social Darwinist view of race widely accepted at the time and expected the Ainu People to become farmers and assimilate into the mainstream Japanese society as productive imperial subjects.

The national government used the system of schooling to assimilate Ainu so that they could contribute to Japan's modernisation project. Their policy from 1901 to 1937 was to provide segregated schooling for Ainu children with a rudimentary curriculum suitable for their destinations in the adult world, following the North American practice at the time (Abe, 2008; Takegahara, 2010) and similar to the initial Australian policy towards Indigenous education. From 1937, Ainu children were required to attend co-educational schools with the majority Japanese children. For many Ainu children, co-educational schools were the first place they encountered racial discrimination and marginalisation, which led them to internalise the dominant Japanese view of their traditional culture and language in order to survive. As Japanese imperial subjects, Indigenous people were subject to military conscription and to paying tax. Ainu activism began in the 1920s, when activists started using the Japanese literacy and knowledge gained in mainstream schooling. This led to the creation of the first significant Ainu organisation, the Ainu Association, later renamed the Utari Association.

After the Second World War, the association prioritised welfare measures to improve living conditions. Recognising that Ainu living conditions, employment, and education levels lagged behind non-Ainu, the Hokkaido government implemented the Utari Special Welfare Project in 1961. In order to close the continuing gap, it implemented further welfare measures and continued to renew the project. These welfare measures resembled the ten-year 'Special Measures for Regional Improvement' for Buraku People. These measures prioritised educational achievement and provided scholarships. The gap in the retention rate to Year 10 and Year 12 became smaller but continued to exist at the higher education level (Okano, 2013).

Ainu activism took another turn in the 1970s. Encouraged by left-leaning university student movements and the Buraku and human rights activism in the 1970s, young Ainu activists became more assertive concerning their Ainu identity and, unsatisfied with the existing Utari Association, created new organisations such as the Ainu Liberation League and an urban-centred Tokyo Utari Association. The new activists were inspired by the success of the Buraku Liberation League and its uncompromising strategies (Siddle, 1996). The new activists gained support from the Japan Socialist Party and the Japan Communist Party, which made their activism more visible. Local teacher unions and local education boards in Hokkaido, the Research Association for Ainu Education, and individual teachers raised issues with the existing schooling practices, such as the depiction of Ainu in school textbooks and teacher training that failed to include Ainu perspectives. The association produced guidebooks for teachers in teaching Ainu history (Ueno, 2001) and the Hokkaido Senior High School Teachers Union developed teaching materials about Ainu and Japan's other minorities (Suefuji, 2009). In the 1980s, Ainu education activists began to align with other minoritised groups and human rights education activists based on a common experience of marginalisation in schools and a shared concern for minority children by, for example, attending Buraku organisation's meetings (Siddle, 1996). Ainu activists also began to engage with global Indigenous people's activism by attending the World Conference of Indigenous People. Not only was this conference boosting but it also enabled Ainu People to challenge their marginalisation and oppression at home in the global arena by referring to international covenants (Sjoberg, 2006).

The gap in educational participation between Ainu and non-Ainu children has declined over the post-war years, with the gap in retention to post-compulsory schooling (Year 9) becoming very small by 1999. There is still a significant difference in the entry rate to tertiary education, although the gap is also narrowing. In 2017, 95 per cent of Ainu students went on to university, compared with 98.8 per cent of the surveyed communities as a whole in Hokkaido (see Table 3.2). In the same year, 33.3 per cent of Ainu students went on to university, compared with 45.8 per cent of the surveyed communities as a whole in Hokkaido (see Table 3.3). Nevertheless, Ainu students in senior high schools and higher education are still less likely to complete these courses than non-Ainu children. In 2009, one in five Ainu university students left before completing their degrees (Nozaki, 2010). In order to improve the

Table 3.2 Retention of Ainu children to upper secondary school compared with that for the surveyed communities as a whole, 1972–2017

Year	1972	1979	1986	1993	1999	2006	2013	2017
Ainu (%)	41.5	69.3	78.4	87.4	95.2	93.5	92.6	95.0
The surveyed communities as a whole (%)	78.2	90.6	94.0	96.3	97.0	98.3	98.6	98.8

Source: Hokkaidō-chō, Kankyōseikatsu-bu (2017). *Heisei 29-nen Hokkaidō Ainu seikatsu jittai chōsa hōkokusho* [2017 Report of the Survey on the Actual Living Conditions of the Hokkaido Ainu]. Sapporo, Japan: Hokkaidō-chō.

Table 3.3 Retention of Ainu children to university compared with that for the surveyed communities as a whole, 1979–2017

Year	1979	1986	1993	1999	2006	2013	2017
Ainu (%)	3.8	8.1	11.8	16.1	17.4	25.8	33.3
The surveyed communities as a whole (%)	31.1	27.4	27.5	34.5	38.5	43.0	45.8

Source: Hokkaido-Kankyōseikatsu-bu (2017). *Heisei 29-nen Hokkaido Ainu seikatsu jittai chōsa hōkokusho* [2017 Report of the Survey on the Actual Living Conditions of the Hokkaido Ainu]. Sapporo, Japan: Hokkaidō-chō.

Ainu graduation rate, some universities have instituted programmes that are culturally responsive to the Ainu students, such as Sapporo University's Urespa Project (Maeda & Okano, 2013; see also Chapter 11, this edition).

There have not been clear national policies on Indigenous education in Japan as that in Australia. Indigenous Ainu education remains a local matter. Initiatives are developed by individual schools, by local education boards, and by local teachers' unions (Okano, 2013, pp. 14–16). The Foundation for Research and Promotion of Ainu Culture, established after the 1997 *New Ainu Cultural Promotion Act* (*Act on the Promotion of Ainu Culture and Dissemination and Enlightenment of Knowledge About Ainu Tradition, etc.* [Act No. 52 of 1997]), also created supplementary teaching materials for primary and middle school students in 2001, which were revised in 2008 (Okano, 2013, pp. 14–16). The official parliamentary recognition of Ainu as an Indigenous people of Japan came in 2008. The *New Ainu Policy Promotion Act* (*Act on Promoting Measures to Realize a Society in Which the Pride of the Ainu People Is Respected* [Act No. 16 of 2019]) replaced the 1997 *Ainu Cultural Promotion Act* and expanded its scope beyond culture promotion but does not mention self-determination and collective Indigenous rights as advocated in UNDRIP (United Nations, 2007). The national government's reluctance to embrace the Indigenous rights as advocated in UNDRIP (United Nations, 2007) has been a disappointment for many (Higashimura, 2016; Maruyama, 2016; Uemura & Gayman, 2018).

Indigenous people, panethnic identities, and strategies

The history described earlier shows that, in both nations, the state utilised schooling to assimilate Indigenous peoples into the mainstream, that this policy resulted in marginalisation and intergenerational cumulative disadvantage of Indigenous peoples materially and socially, and that it devalued the Indigenous view of the social world, their cultures, and ways of life. In both Australia and Japan, Indigenous languages are endangered as a result of the state's active discouragement of their use. However, there are important differences in the approaches of the two nations.

The Ainu have not asserted their distinctiveness as an Indigenous people in the debates on multiculturalism to the same extent as the Australian Indigenous peoples have. Discussion of Indigenous peoples have often been part of those about CALD minoritised groups and multicultural symbiosis. There is no government minister or body specialising in issues of Indigenous peoples, as there are in Australia. In Australia, there is a strong view that Indigenous Australians should not be treated as just another minoritised cultural group in multicultural Australia and that they should be recognised as a special group, as the only culture that emerged and developed within the Australian continent before the arrival of colonisers in the late 18th century (Hickling-Hudson, 2003, p. 384). Colonisation meant dispossession of land, culture, language, and exploitation in their own land – a cumulative marginalisation that continues to this day. Indeed, compared to other ethnic minority groups, Indigenous Australians experience a significantly higher level of disadvantage in terms of educational achievement, employment, and health impacts.

White Australians pursue reconciliation with Indigenous Australians in order to resolve the past sufferings and move forward, but Indigenous Australians are seeking constitutional recognition, recognition of sovereignty, and the right to self-determination that have not yet been recognised as part of the 'Reconciliation package' being offered by non-Indigenous Australians (see Chapter 12, this edition).

Why have the Ainu been unassertive regarding their special Indigenous status? One reason may be the relatively small number of Ainu People and Okinawan peoples. To draw upon estimates (see Table 3.1), along with Okinawans, Ainu comprise only about 1 per cent of the Japanese population, whereas Australian Indigenous people make up around 3 per cent of the national population. A second reason for Ainu unassertiveness may be that the gap in educational achievement and beyond has narrowed to the extent that material differences are no longer as clearly visible as they used to be. For example, by 1999, Ainu children's retention rate to post-compulsory schooling reached 95.2 per cent compared to the whole community rate of 97 per cent, while retention to university is 16 per cent compared to 34 per cent in the same year (see Tables 3.2 and Table 3.3). In 2017, the respective figures were 95 per cent and 98.8 per cent for retention to post-compulsory schooling, and 33.3 per cent and 45.8 per cent for retention to university (Hokkaido-kankyōseikatsu-bu, 2017). This contrasts with the glaring inequalities experienced by the Australian Indigenous population, which see federal and state governments advocating 'Closing the Gap' as a major policy.

A third reason may be that Japan has minorities other than Indigenous Ainu and Okinawans which have been created by state policies: Zainichi Koreans and Buraku People. The existence of Zainichi Koreans is a direct result of Japan's colonisation of the Korean Peninsula from 1910 to 1945. They were brought to Japan as forced labourers or reluctantly migrated after their lands were confiscated by the Japanese army and exploited as a cheap workforce in Japanese mines, construction, and tunnel building. By the end of the war, approximately 2.5 million Korean former imperial subjects were residents in Japan. Although many returned to Korea, those who remained became 'foreigners' in 1951 when Japan regained sovereignty. Buraku People are descendants of a feudal outcaste population. Although the pre-modern institution was abolished in mid-19th century, Buraku People continued to face discrimination in employment and relationships.

It is this common experience of state-institutionalised marginalisation shared by Ainu, Okinawans, Zainichi Koreans, and Buraku People that differentiates them from migrants who have arrived in Japan in pursuit of better life chances since the 1980s. Ogbu and Simons (1998) argue that Indigenous peoples, Zainichi Koreans, and Buraku People are 'involuntary minorities' who were forced into minority positions and have internalised their positions through intergenerational marginalisation, while the migrants who arrived since the 1980s are 'voluntary minorities' who still saw the possibility of upward mobility. Within this collective group of involuntary minorities, there are differences, including in citizenship: Buraku People and Indigenous People hold citizenship while Zainichi Koreans continue to be 'foreign nationals'. The involuntary minority groups' shared experiences and perspectives are likely to have encouraged intergroup interaction, alignment, and solidarity in challenging their marginalisation and pursuing their human rights. The early focus in Ainu schooling centred on improving their educational outcomes and life chances in mainstream society rather than cultural maintenance; other involuntary minority groups shared this focus.

There is continuity from Buraku activism, to Zainichi Korean activism, and then to new migrant activism at a local level (Okano, 2011, pp. 105–109). Ainu activism has also benefitted from this. Buraku People led grass-roots mobilisation for human rights in the 1920s, and formed the Buraku Liberation League (BLL) in the post-war period, which adopted strategies to denounce discriminatory employers, organisations, and individuals aligned with opposition political parties to force change. The BLL, with the cooperation of teachers' unions, promoted human rights education at schools and local education boards, particularly in localities with large numbers of minority students. Both Zainichi Korean and Ainu activist groups were inspired by the BLL's successful campaigns. In the 1980s, Ainu activists increasingly connected with other minority human rights movements in Japan, for example, attending Buraku meetings (Siddle, 1996).

More recently, an alliance developed between involuntary minority, Zainichi Koreans, and voluntary migrants. The National Association for Research into the Education of Resident Koreans in Japan (*Zenkoku Zainichi Chôsenjin Kyôiku Kenkyūkyôgikai*) is a grass-roots activist and professional group formed by educational practitioners engaged in school-based ethnic Korean classes that began organising research conferences in 1979. When some members proposed that the association include migrant education as its focus in light of many papers being presented on the topic, other members opposed it on the grounds that new migrants' concerns fundamentally differed from those of the association. However, some years later, the association changed its name, by replacing 'Koreans' with 'foreign residents'. In so doing, it signalled the organisation's inclusive position in relation to all children with 'foreign' roots (Okano, 2011, p. 120).

The inter-ethnic alliances have been observed elsewhere and are described by the term 'panethnicity' (Okamoto & Mora, 2014). It refers to different ethnic groups working as a collective and inclusive group, cooperating in organising and building institutions and identities across ethnic boundaries (Okamoto & Mora, 2014). This boundary adjustment could result from a collective reaction to an imperial colonising government decision to place multiple groups into one, or from the pursuit to forge a collective identity of marginalisation by minority groups. It involves creating a common social category or identity among multiple ethnic groups. In Hawaii, for example, a panethnic identity began to emerge in 1920 when exploited non-White workers from different ethnic groups (Indigenous peoples, Asians, and others) employed by White bosses joined together to strike for improved working conditions (Moniz, 2008, p. 10). During 1931 and 1932, this inter-ethnic movement expanded in a collective challenge to an allegation of sexual assault against a White woman. It became stronger again during the Second World War with the influx of a large number of White military soldiers from mainland (Moniz, 2008, p. 11).

In contemporary Japan, there is a panethnic identity or category of involuntary minorities as a result of the state's deliberate policies, including Indigenous peoples (Ainu and Okinawans), Zainichi Koreans, and Buraku People. Ainu People do not assert their special place as an Indigenous people, to the same extent as their Australian counterparts, and do not enjoy political and institutional agencies specifically established to cater for them. In contrast, in Australia, there are government departments and education policies and guidelines specifically focused on Indigenous peoples, in addition to those in relation to other non-Anglo-White and non-White ethnic migrants and refugees. It is likely that conditions in Japan have been more conducive to fostering a panethnic identity, since Indigenous peoples are not the only involuntary groups among ethnic minorities, and since the human rights activism was first launched by Buraku People, to be followed by Zainichi Koreans.

It is not difficult to understand Indigenous arguments to assert their special place in multicultural education. Critics argue that multiculturalism is a 'gloss' that provides a way for those benefiting from existing inequitable power relations to sooth their conscience, by promoting the illusion of diversity and social justice (e.g., Moniz, 2008, pp. 3–4). Multicultural education campaigns offer what look like a legitimate means for maintaining the existing inequity. This is demonstrated by the continued marginalisation that Indigenous children experience at schools which claim to be advancing multicultural education. In the different context of Japan, Ainu People may be seeing it as advantageous for them to be part of the larger multicultural symbiosis education activism. Other more powerful, long-existing involuntary minorities (Buraku People and then Zainichi Koreans) initiated civil activism against discrimination and oppression, and Indigenous activism has benefitted from their success. Given the relatively small Ainu population, they may be considering that their interests are better served by locating themselves among the CALD minorities and promoting inclusive panethnic identity.

Conclusions

Indigenous peoples do not currently have a voice in the constitutions of Japan or Australia. This chapter argues that Australian Indigenous peoples have assertively pursued special status as the original inhabitants of the land and that various government departments and bodies now focus on Indigenous education issues. Ainu people, in contrast, have not asserted their special Indigenous status among CALD-minoritised peoples in Japan, with few government institutions responsible specifically for Ainu people. Instead, Ainu have developed panethnic alliance with CALD minoritised groups. I have suggested that this is due to historical circumstances, current levels of disadvantage comparable to other minorities, and strategic reasons.

References

Abe, Y. (2008). *Ainu minzoku nitotteno kyōiku*. Kaihō Kyōiku [Education for the Ainu people], October issue.
Altman, J. C., Biddle, N., & Hunter, B. H. (2009). Prospects in 'closing the gap' for socioeconomic outcomes for Indigenous Australians? *Australian Economic History Review*, 49(3), 225–251.
Beresford, Q., Partington, G., & Gower, G. (Eds.). (2012). *Reform and resistance in Aboriginal education*. Perth, Australia: University of Western Australia Press.
Gloemraad, I., Korteweg, A., & Yurdakul, G. (2008). Citizenship and immigration: Multiculturalism, assimilation, and challenges to the nation-state. *Annual Review of Sociology*, 34, 153–179.
Gray, J., & Beresford, Q. (2008). A 'formidable challenge': Australia's quest for equity in Indigenous education. *Australian Journal of Education*, 52(2), 197–223.
Hickling-Hudson, A. (2003). Multicultural education and the postcolonial turn. *Policy Future in Education*, 1(2), 381–401.
Higashimura, T. (2016). Ainu seisaku no bunseki wakugumi: kyōseisareta 'kyōsei' no kōzō [Analytical framework of the Ainu policy: Structure of forced 'co-existence']. *Kokusai Kaihatsu kenkyū Foram* [Forum of international development studies], 47(8), 1–16.
Hokkaido-Kankyōseikatsu-bu. (2017). *Heisei 29-nen Hokkaido Ainu seikatu jittai chōsa hōkokusho* [2017 Report of the survey on the actual living conditions of the Hokkaido Ainu]. Sapporo, Japan: Hokkaido-chō.
Hughes, P. (1988). *Report of the Aboriginal education policy task force*. Canberra, Australia: Commonwealth of Australia.

Japan-Hōmu-shō. (2017). *Heisei-28nen 6gatsumatsu genzai niokeru zairyūgaikokujin ni tsuite* [Foreign national residents in Japan June 2016]. Tokyo: Japan-Hōmu-shō. Retrieved 31 May 2020 from www.moj.go.jp/nyuukokukanri/kouhou/nyuukokukanri04_00060.html

Koleth, E. (2010). *Multiculturalism: A review of Australian policy statements and recent debates in Australia and overseas.* (6 2010–11). Canberra, Australia: Parliament of Australia. Retrieved 31 May 2020 from www.aph.gov.au/About_Parliament/Parliamentary_Departments/Parliamentary_Library/pubs/rp/rp1011/11rp06

Koopmans, R. (2013). Multiculturalism and immigration: A contested field in cross-national comparison. *Annual Review of Sociology, 39,* 147–169.

Maeda, K., & Okano, K. H. (2013). Connecting Indigenous Ainu, university and local industry through the Urespa project. *The International Education Journal: Comparative Perspectives, 12*(1), 45–60.

Ma Rhea, Z. (2018). Teaching and learning for multicultural societies: Reimagining pedagogical content knowledge. *Journal of International Education* (Nihon Kokusaikyoiku Gakkai Kiyo), *24,* 87–98.

Maruyama, H. (2016). Sekai kijun no Ainu seisaku o motomete [Seeking Ainu policy of a global standard]. *Jinken to Buraku Mondai* [Human Rights and Buraku Issues], *881,* February, 7–17.

Moniz, J. A. S. (2008). Recovering the space for Indigenous self-determination: Multicultural education in colonized Hawai'i. *International Journal of Multicultural Education, 10*(2), 1–19.

National-Aboriginal Consultative-Group. (1975). *Education for Aborigines: Report to the school commission by the Aboriginal consultative group.* Canberra, Australia: National-Aboriginal Consultative-Group.

Nozaki, T. (2010). Kyōiku fubyōdō no jittai to kyōiku ishiki [The realities of educational inequality and educational aspirations]. In T. Sanai (Ed.), *Gendai Ainu no seikatsu to ishiki: 2008 nen Hokkaido Ainu minzoku seikatsu jittai chōsa hōkokusho* [Lives and views of Hokkaio Ainu people in 2008] (Hokkaido-Daigaku-Ainu-Senjūmin-Kenkyū-Sentā) (pp. 59–73). Sapporo, Japan: Hokkaido-Daigaku-Ainu-Senjūmin-Kenkyū-Sentā.

Ogbu, J., & Simons, H. D. (1998). Voluntary and involuntary minorities: A cultural-ecological theory of school performance with some implications for education. *Anthropology and Education Quarterly, 29*(2), 155–188.

Okamoto, D., & Mora, G. C. (2014). Panethnicity. *Annual Review of Sociology, 40,* 219–239.

Okano, K. H. (2011). Ethnic Koreans in Japanese schools: Shifting boundaries and collaboration with other groups. In R. Tsuneyoshi, K. H. Okano, & S. Boocock (Eds.). *Minorities and education in multicultural Japan: An interactive perspective* (pp. 100–125). London, England: Routledge.

Okano, K. H. (2013). Indigenous Ainu and education in Japan: Social justice and culturally responsive schooling. In R. Craven, G. Bodkin-Andrews, & J. Mooney (Eds.). *Indigenous peoples: Education and equity* (pp. 3–25). Charlotte, NC: Information Age Publishing.

Okano, K. H. & Tsuneyoshi, R. (2011). Introduction: An interactive perspective for understanding minorities and education in Japan. In R. Tsuneyoshi, K. H. Okano, & S. Boocock (Eds.). *Minorities and education in Japan: An interactive perspective* (pp. 1–26). London, England: Routledge.

Patrick, R., & Moodie, N. (2016). Indigenous education policy discourses in Australia: Rethinking the 'problem'. In T. Barkatsas & A. Bertram (Eds.). *Global learning in the 21st century* (pp. 165–184): Rotterdam, The Netherlands: Sense Publishers.

Schwab, R. G. (1995). *Twenty years of policy recommendations for Indigenous education: Overview and research implications.* Canberra, Australia: Centre for Aboriginal Economic Policy Research, Australian National University.

Siddle, R. (1996). *Race, resistance and the Ainu of Japan.* New York: Routledge.

Sjöberg, K. (2006). Redefining the past, taking charge of the present, appropriating the future: The Hokkaido Ainu case. In B. Sautman (Ed.), *Cultural genocide and Asian state peripheries* (pp. 39–62). New York: Palgrave Macmillan.

Suefuji, M. (2009). Nihon ni okeru tabunka kyōsei kyōiku no genjō to kadai: Ainu minzoku ni chūmokushite [Realities and challenges in Japan's cultural symbiosis education: A focus on the Ainu people]. *Shakai Kankyōronkyū, 1,* 19–32.

Takegahara, Y. (2010). *Kyōiku no nakano Ainu minzoku: Kindai nihon Ainu kyōikushi* [The Ainu in education: Modern history of Ainu education]. Tokyo: Shakaihyōronsha.

Uemura, H., & Gayman, J. (2018). Rethinking Japan's constitution from the perspective of the Ainu Ryūkyū peoples. *The Asia-Pacific Journal: Japan Focus, 16*(5), 1–18.

Ueno, M. (2001). Ainu minzoku o meguru kyōiku ni kansuru ichi kōsatsu [A study of education of the Ainu People]. *Waseda Daigaku Daigakuin Kyōikugakukenkyūka Kiyō Bessatsu* [Bulletin of the Graduate School of Education of Waseda University, Separate Volume], *9*(1), 45–56.

United Nations. (2007). *United Nations declaration on the rights of Indigenous peoples.* Retrieved 31 May 2020 from www.un.org/development/desa/indigenouspeoples/wp-content/uploads/sites/19/2018/11/UNDRIP_E_web.pdf

Vass, G. (2012). So, what is wrong with Indigenous education? Perspective, position and power beyond a deficit discourse. *Australian Journal of Indigenous Education, 41*(2), 85–96.

Wyatt, K. (2019). Walk with me, Australia: Ken Wyatt's historic pledge for Indigenous recognition. Opinion. 10 July, *The Age.*

Yunupiŋu, M. (1995). *Final report of the national review of education for Aboriginal and Torres Strait Islander peoples.* Canberra, Australia: Department of Employment, Education and Training, Commonwealth of Australia.

Chapter 4

Higher education in Japan and the history of Ainu demands

Koji Maeda

Introduction

This chapter examines whether higher education in Japan before the 2007 proclamation of the *United Nations Declaration on the Rights of Indigenous Peoples* (UNDRIP) (United Nations, 2007) included consideration of the special needs of Japan's Indigenous Ainu people. I consider the direction of university reform in Japan after a 1991 University Council report (University Council Report, 1991, p. 5) that aimed to improve university education in what is termed the 'third wave' of educational reform. In particular, I examine higher education reform in Japan from the perspective of equity and fairness of institutional arrangements for the Ainu, who face disadvantages in their access to higher education.

Trow (1976) foreshadowed that universities of the modern age needed to examine their student selection criteria and the educational opportunities they provided to the population, as well as the educational function served by universities. In 1991, following a report by the University Council, universities in Japan undertook substantial reform. The University Council was tasked by the Minister of Education to research and investigate basic matters and make recommendations concerning universities and technical colleges (Kyōiku roppō henshū iin-kai-hen, 1991, p. 60). The reforms eased regulations on universities and gave them greater discretion, such as enabling individual universities to restructure their institutions according to their needs and goals. The era marked a shift from mass higher education to universal higher education. According to the FY2006 School Basic Survey (preliminary results) announced by the Ministry of Education, Culture, Sports, Science and Technology on 3 August 2006, the undergraduate university and junior college entrance rate (including those who failed to enter a university immediately after high school graduation) has reached 53.7 per cent (Monbu kagaku-shō [Ministry of Education, Culture, Sports, Science and Technology], 2006). According to Trow, when the entrance rate exceeds 50 per cent, it signifies the transition from the mass-type that aims for equal opportunity in education to the universal-type that acknowledges universal participation in higher education by diverse population groups (Trow, 1976, pp. 194–195). When entering the universal type of system, it has been argued that inequality of opportunity for higher education due to race, ethnicity, social standards, or gender can be corrected, and access to higher education shifts to accepting groups of people with diverse and different attributes who were considered to be at a disadvantage. An active measure (quota system) is carried out aiming for a ratio of such groups in the higher education population to equal the structure of the national population.

Some universities in Japan broadened their student selection criteria, giving special consideration to citizens returning from China, and some universities reformed their entrance exams in the face of the declining population of 18-year-olds. However, there was no systematic rethinking of university education from the perspective of social equality and fairness. Those who truly needed assistance, such as Indigenous students, were not guaranteed the chance for higher education. Indeed, in Japan, the only institution with Indigenous quotas for the Ainu, Okinawan, and Ryūkyūan people is Shikokugakuin University.

In 1984, the General Assembly of the Ainu Association of Hokkaidô put forward the *Draft Law Concerning the Ainu People* (*Draft Law*), which included recommendations for what should be included in the government's higher education policy. I examine the recommendations in the *Draft Law* within the context of Japan's endorsement of the UNDRIP (United Nations, 2007; Advisory Council for Future Ainu Policy [ACFAP], 2009; see also Chapter 11, this edition) and other laws passed by the Japanese government.

Background

There are three reasons for examining access to higher education for the Ainu people. The *Act on the Promotion of Ainu Culture and Dissemination and Enlightenment of Knowledge About Ainu Tradition, etc.* (Act No. 52 of 1997) (*Ainu Cultural Promotion Act*) states:

> Article 1 Purpose of this Act
>
> [I]n view of the situation in which the Ainu tradition and their culture, which is the source of pride of Ainu people (is) to realise a society in which the pride of the Ainu people as an ethnic group is respected and thereby to contribute to the development of diverse culture of Japan by promoting the measures for the Ainu culture and dissemination and enlightenment of knowledge of the people about Ainu tradition, etc.
>
> (Author's translation)

First, the Act replaced the *Hokkaido Former Aboriginal Protection Act (1899)* (Meiji 32) and was considered as a revolutionary advance in the Japanese legal system. However, the Act does not make direct provisions to support higher education for the Ainu although it was expressly designed to be the main means to promote their culture. In reality, policies to assimilate Ainu within the non-Indigenous Japanese society continued via the Japanese educational system.

Second, in 1996 the Chief Cabinet Secretary's private advisory body of experts on the future of the Utari, known as *Utari taisaku no arikata nikansuru yūshikisha kondan-kai* [Advisory Council for Future Utari[1] Policy] submitted a report which stated:

> [I]t would be desirable to consider fostering researchers from the Ainu people by nurturing and supporting young researchers through grants and other means. Further, it is also important to increase the educational opportunities for the Ainu with the understanding of higher education institutions … and train instructors, establish permanent Ainu language courses, and have systematic Ainu language education from the introductory level through instructor training to improve Ainu language education. Also desirable are instructor training and the development of teaching materials and support for voluntary initiatives of higher education institutions and improving existing Ainu language classes.
>
> (*Utari taisaku no arikata nikansuru yūshikisha kondan-kai*, 1996, Author's translation, p. 9)

In spite of this recommendation concerning the need for special higher education initiatives for the Ainu, the new *Ainu Cultural Promotion Act* did not provide for special higher education consideration for the Ainu.

Third, a 1993 *Hokkaido Utari seikatsu jittai chōsa hōkoku-sho* [Survey of Hokkaido Utari Living Conditions] (*Hokkaido seikatsu fukushi-bu*, 1994, pp. 9–23), which covered 75 municipalities, 7,328 households, and 23,830 people, in the Ainu areas (where the Ainu live) of Hokkaido, found that 11.8 per cent of high school graduates went on to university (including junior college), up from 3.7 per cent from the previous survey in 1986. However, there was still a large gap between 27.5 per cent of university-goers rate for the municipalities overall including the Ainu areas. However, according to a Ministry of Education, Culture, Sports, Science, and Technology survey, as of 1994, the advancement rate to universities including junior colleges was 43.3 per cent (Monbu kagaku-shō, 1994) reaching the 'universal access stage' (Trow, 1976) which highlights participation in higher education by a diverse constituency ('educational security for all'). Under universal access, proactive measures (equality of outcomes as a group, i.e., quotas), are put in place so that all imbalances regarding advancement opportunities stemming from race, ethnicity, social hierarchy, and gender are redressed, and the shares of these groups in the higher education population are the same as the population overall. This entails the application of affirmative action (preferential treatment of minorities).

The *Ainu Cultural Promotion Act*

In December 1995, Japan ratified the *International Convention on the Elimination of All Forms of Racial Discrimination*, becoming the 146th country to do so, 20 years after Australia and 30 years since its adoption by the General Assembly of the UN. In practical terms, the convention supersedes individual countries' laws other than their constitutions – on coming into effect, laws that contravened the convention becoming invalid; this requirement is supported by Article 98-2 of the 1947 *Japanese Constitution*, which stipulates that '[t]he treaties concluded by Japan and established laws of nations shall be faithfully observed'. Article 1 of the *International Convention on the Elimination of All Forms of Racial Discrimination* prohibits discrimination 'based on race, colour, descent, or national or ethnic origin'.

Upon ratification, Japan's first step was the need to abolish discriminatory laws, such as the *Hokkaido Former Aboriginal Protection Act (1899)* (Meiji 32), the objective of which was to assimilate the Ainu into the non-Indigenous Japanese mainstream. The *Act on the Promotion of Ainu Culture and Dissemination and Enlightenment of Knowledge About Ainu Tradition, etc.* (Act No. 52 of 1997) (*Ainu Cultural Promotion Act*) replaced the 1899 Act, establishing the right recognition of Ainu as an independent and Indigenous people.

Several parties were involved in the formulation of the Act. The Advisory Council submitted a report calling for the enactment of new legislation in April 1996. In May of that year, representatives of the director general level for relevant ministries formed a forum to determine Ainu policies and investigate policy directions (Yomiuri Shimbun, 1996, p. 2). The Ainu leader, Kayano, who was elected as the first Ainu member of the Diet (Parliament). He is also presumed to have played an important role in the drafting of the *Ainu Cultural Promotion Act*.

The Act is one sign of progress towards the restoration of Ainu rights in Japan. Although it has value enabling the maintenance and development of traditional Ainu culture, it does not incorporate all the rights advanced by the UN convention. Furthermore, it has no provisions to provide a legal basis for the 'right to self-determination', particularly the right to participate in social decision making on matters that affect them – a right derived from the right to self-determination. Part of this discourse is the right to establish higher education arrangements that respect the independence of the Ainu people. Such a right was already written into the 1984 *Draft Law* and has been the focus of various discourses of the Ainu *ekashi* elders.

Higher education requirements of the Ainu

In reality, the new *Ainu Cultural Promotion Act* was not what the Ainu people had hoped would replace the discriminatory *Hokkaido Former Aboriginal Protection*

Act (1899). In terms of higher education requirements, the *Draft Law* had five provisions:

1. Take comprehensive educational measures for Ainu children
2. Systematically introduce Ainu language learning into education programmes for Ainu children
3. Implement measures in general school education and social education for the purpose of totally eliminating discrimination against the Ainu people
4. Create classes in university education programmes dealing with the Ainu language, Ainu cultures, Ainu history, etc.; recruit high-quality Ainu human resources as the faculty responsible for said classes in the positions of professor, assistant professor, lecturer, etc. without being caught up in existing rules and regulations; enable special cases with regard to the admission and attendance of Ainu youth in order to assist them to engage in research activities in respective fields
5. Set up a national research institution, which has as its main purpose researching the Ainu language as well as the preservation of Ainu cultures, in which Ainu people are expected to proactively participate as researchers. The ideas of Ainu people have not been reflected in past research. Japanese people have been doing research on Ainu people on their own, which is fundamentally wrong. Such a research style has to be changed.

(Hokkaidō Ainu Kyōkai, 2017, pp. 13–14)

The *Draft Law* includes policies for the Ainu people and provisions that form the basis for the execution of the policies. Several align with Articles 14 and 15-2 of the UNDRIP (United Nations, 2007) which sets a global standard in this area. Provision 2 of the *Draft Law* concerns the opportunity for the Ainu people to learn the Ainu language as their mother tongue. This is an important requirement to ensure Indigenous identity formation as provided in Article 14-1 of the declaration. Though not enshrined in legislation, some institutions do provide Ainu language classes: Hokkaido's *Saru-gun Biratori-cho Nibutani* Elementary School and Chitose City *Suehiro* Elementary School.

Even ignoring the *Draft Law*, the 1996 Advisory Council also recommended:

> [I]t is important to train instructors, establish permanent Ainu language courses, and have systematic Ainu language education from the introductory level through instructor training to improve Ainu language education. Also desirable are instructor training and the development of teaching materials and support for voluntary initiatives of higher education institutions.
>
> (*Utari taisaku no arikata nikansuru yūshikisha kondan-kai*, 1996, p.9)

This advice was also not heeded. The new *Ainu Cultural Promotion Act*, promulgated the following year, went no further than to state that the country's responsibility was:

> [T]o foster those who can carry on the Ainu culture, enhance public relations activities regarding Ainu tradition, and promote research activities and other policies that further Ainu culture, as well as endeavor to take necessary advice and put in place measures so local governments can implement policies to promote Ainu culture.
>
> (Art. 3)

The Act avoids specifying how opportunities for learning the Ainu language and culture in a systematic and ongoing manner will be positioned in the educational process.

Provision 3 of the *Draft Law* includes content similar to the intent of 14-2 of UNDRIP (United Nations, 2007) regarding 'the right to all levels and forms of education of the State without discrimination' (see also, Chapter 11, this edition). From the viewpoint of creating mutual understanding between different cultures, this highlights the importance of systematic educational activities to spread appropriate understanding and recognition of the Ainu. The Advisory Council recognised the need to train professionals such as school teachers engaged in education as follows: 'The production and distribution of teaching materials that can be used in teacher education and training through the classroom is desirable' (*Utari taisaku no arikata nikansuru yūshikisha kondankai*, 1996, p. 11). This is partly because, as shown in Tables 4.1. and 4.2, from a Hokkaido department of environment and lifestyle report from 1999, in reality the Ainu people face a great deal of the inherent discrimination in school education. However, the *Ainu Culture Promotion Act* does not reflect such Advisory Council recommendations.

Table 4.1 The actual nature and extent of discrimination: Survey of 715 Ainu (aged 15 years or older)

Have you experienced any kind of discrimination in the past 6–7 years?

Categories	Yes	% of respondents
1. Experienced discrimination	89	12.4
2. Observed discriminations to someone else	112	15.7
3. Never experienced	346	48.4
4. Do not have any idea	127	17.8
5. Survey nonresponse/no answer	41	5.7

Source: Hokkaido kankyō seikatsu-bu [Department of environment and life], Hokkaido Prefect. Govt, 1999, *Heisei 11-nen Hokkaido Utari seikatsu iittai chōsa-hōkoku-sho*. [The 11th year of Heisei era Hokkaido Utari report on actual living condition survey of Hokkaido Utari], p. 44.

Table 4.2 Situation in which discrimination takes place: Survey of 201 Ainu (aged 15 years or older)

Where have you experienced the discrimination?

Categories	Number of respondents*	% of respondents
1. While seeking employment	15	7.5
2. At the workplace	19	9.5
3. In the case of marriage	51	25.4
4. In school/educational institution	93	46.3
5. In the case of affair/relationship	19	9.5
6. From the administration (at national/prefectural/municipal level)	3	1.5
7. Others	32	15.9

Source: Hokkaido kankyō seikatsu-bu [Department of environment and life], Hokkaido Prefect. Govt, 1999, *Heisei 11-nen Hokkaido Utari seikatsu iittai chōsa-hōkoku-sho*. [The 11th year of Heisei era Hokkaido Utari report on actual living condition survey of Hokkaido Utari], p. 44.

* Multiple answers.

Sections in Article 4 of the *Draft Law* also highlight the need to develop higher education systems that incorporate the value systems of Indigenous peoples, thus raising the issue of affirmative action in higher education policy, which requires the teaching of the Ainu language and Ainu culture. At present, in the Kanto area, only some national and private universities teach the Ainu language, including Chiba University, Gakushuin University, and Waseda University. In Hokkaidô, only Hokkaidô University of Education Iwamizawa Campus, Hokkai Gakuen University, and Sapporo Junior College provide classes that are primarily focused on Ainu (*Kantō utari-kai shinpojiumu* [language and culture], 1993, p. 14). The latter half of provision 4 of the *Draft* Law states: 'We should not be bound by existing regulations but should appoint as class teachers Ainu outstanding in their respective fields as professors, assistant professors, and lecturers, and make special exceptions for the entry and attendance of the Ainu'. The provision's wording points to the need to train Ainu experts involved in decision making and in essence support Ainu self-determination.

Nakano (2014, p. 45) notes that the training, hiring, and placement of teachers from among their ranks is the starting point for the education of Indigenous peoples by Indigenous peoples. This is premised on creating opportunities for children to advance to secondary and higher education. From the perspective of his specialty in international human rights law, he argues for the importance of training Indigenous teachers. This is in line with the international convention, *Indigenous and Tribal Peoples Convention* (*ILO 169*), which came into force in 1991. Recommendation no. 104 of *ILO 169* states:

> Teachers working among the populations concerned should have training in anthropological and psychological techniques, which will enable them

to adapt their work to the cultural characteristics of these populations. These teachers should, as far as possible, be recruited from among such populations.

Educational systems and institutions to train those involved in creating communities that maintain and pass on traditional Ainu culture, such as Ainu curators and teachers with Ainu roots, should also aim at professional development and capacity building to nurture legal and medical professionals and researchers with Ainu origins.

Ekashi elder, Yuji Shimizu (2000, p. 34), representative of the Ethnic Minorities roundtable conference, points out the need to establish a teacher training university that would primarily target primary and secondary school teachers interested in obtaining a comprehensive and correct understanding of Ainu history and culture. From an Ainu woman's perspective, Shimazaki (2014, pp. 74–75) advocates for Ainu women participation in policymaking through activities in the political and public arenas, to restore their rights and achieve independence. She sees the establishment of training programmes to foster female Ainu leaders as an important issue and advocates for policies to expand the potential for the empowerment of Ainu women. Kawamura Shinritsu Eoripakku Ainu take on the discourse of Shigeru Kayano Nibutani Ainu Museum director Shiro Kanayo who argues that lawyers of Ainu descent are needed. He talks of the urgent necessity for legal training for the Ainu in response to frequent human rights violations and land rights issues (Senjūmin-zoku no 10 nen shimin renraku-kai, 1997, p. 5). This is a logical progression from the perspective that self-determination entails using one's own people to solve one's own legal issues. It is noteworthy that Shimizu, Shimazaki, Kawamura, and Kayano all have similar demands regarding the need for Indigenous-led professional and leadership training from an Ainu perspective (see also Chapter 10, this edition).

Provisions 4 of the *Draft Law* goes on to discuss the need for special exceptions for Ainu university entry and lecture attendance. It argues for special university entry quotas for the Ainu to express self-determination and promotes affirmative action for the Ainu. In 1995, Shikokugakuin University set affirmative action quotas and has special admission arrangements for members of minority groups subject to discrimination; those who are aware of their Ainu, Uchinanchu Okinawan, or Ryūkyūan origin are eligible to apply (Shikokugakuindaigaku, 2018). These arrangements provide a rare case where ethnicity is considered as part of entry requirements.

Nomoto (2014, pp. 9–10) argues that research into Indigenous education should begin with a critical analysis of the colonialist methods and the characteristics of existing research, employing Tuhiwai Smith's (2012, pp. 309–313) decolonial research methodology to point out the need to train Indigenous people as Indigenous education researchers. The recognition of a need for decolonial research methodologies is stated in provision 5 of the *Draft Law*. Ainu people should participate proactively as researchers, either leading research activities or conducting joint research and writing joint reports on findings. Considering that, to date, most researchers have been *Wajin*, and research has been carried out in the absence of Indigenous people, it is necessary to explore and examine ways in which research can play a role in building mutual relationships where both Indigenous and non-Indigenous people share questions and work together to solve them.

Conclusion

At roughly the same time as Japan promulgated the new *Ainu Cultural Promotion Act*, Australia embarked on university reform under a federal government policy document titled 'A Fair Chance for All: Higher Education That's Within Everyone's Reach' (Department of Employment, Education and Training & National Board of Employment, Education and Training, 1990, pp. 23–26). Australia implemented systematic policy support for Indigenous peoples and other minorities to participate in higher education. Selection criteria in Australian universities were vastly different to those in Japan. Japan was also searching for ways to diversify access to university education and promoted the acceptance of mature age students in regular university courses and other selection methods, including entry via the admissions office and special skills and qualifications other than academic ability as part of the evaluation criteria. Many universities reconsidered entrance examinations.

This chapter argues that neither the Advisory Council recommendations nor the new *Ainu Cultural Promotion Act* provides the directions to ensure higher education rights will promote the Ainu people's self-determination as intended by the *Draft Law* and, indeed, relevant international laws. There is still a considerable gap in understanding between the claims of the Ainu people and the Japanese government's proposals and actions. Chapter 11 in this edition goes on to examine the Japanese government's policy directions and university initiatives after the ratification of the UNDRIP (United Nations, 2007), whether they address imbalances in higher education due to the distinctive ethnic attributes of the Ainu and whether it is possible to build an Ainu-led higher education system in response to the provisions indicated in Article 3 of the *Draft Law*, and demands of the Ainu regarding education.

Note

1 The Hokkaido Ainu Association has used the name 'Utari' as the name of the association since 1960, which means 'brotherhood', because there is a sense of rejection to the ethnic designation of 'Ainu' (Mainichi Shimbun, 2008, p. 22).

References

Daigaku shingi-kai [University Council]. (1991). *Daigaku kyōiku no kaizen nitsuite* [About improvement of the university education]. Tokyo, Japan: Daigaku shingi-kai Tōshin (University Council Report).

Department of Employment, Education and Training, & National Board of Employment, Education and Training. (1990). *A fair chance for all: National and institutional planning for equity in higher education*. A discussion paper, February, Australia.
Hokkaidō Ainu Kyōkai [Ainu Association of Hokkaido] (Ed.). (2017). Ainu minzoku no gaisetsu – Hokkaido Ainu Kyōkai no katsudo o fukume [Overview of the Ainu: History of the Hokkaido Ainu Association of Hokkaido]. Retrieved 31 May 2020 from www.ainu-assn.or.jp/public/files/1d05c1dd9ceb9cf70478cd757622d307 5a2c94b7.pdf
Hokkaidō seikatsu fukushi-bu [Hokkaido life welfare part]. (1994). *Hokkaidō utari seikatsu jittai chōsa hōkoku-sho* [A 1993 survey of Hokkaido Utari living conditions].
International Labour Organization (ILO). (1989). *C169 – Indigenous and tribal peoples convention, 1989 (No. 169)*. Retrieved 31 May 2020 from www.ilo.org/dyn/normlex/en/f?p=NORMLEXPUB:12100:0::NO:12100:P12100_INSTRUMENT_ID:312314:NO*Kantō utari-kai shinpojiumu* [Kantō Utarikai symposium]. (1993). *Ainu minzoku to kyōkasho — mōhitotsu no kyōkashomondai* [Ainu people and textbooks: Another textbook problem].
Kyōiku roppō henshū iin-kai-hen [Commentary editorial committee of the six acts of education] (Eds.). (1991). *Kaisetsu kyōiku roppō* [Commentary six acts of education], Tokyo, Japan: Sanseidō.
Mainichi Shimbun [The Mainichi newspapers]. (2008). *Hokkaidō utari kyōkai* 'hokkaidō ainu kyōkai' ni meishō henkō he rainen shigatsu kara [Hokkaido Utari Association: Changed the name to 'Hokkaido Ainu Association' from April next year]. Hokkaido morning edition, 17 May, p. 22.
Monbu kagaku-shō [Ministry of Education, Culture, Sports, Science and Technology]. (1994). *Gakkō kihon chōsa nenji tōkei* [School basic survey annual statistics]. Retrieved 31 May 2020 from www.e-stat.go.jp/dbview?sid=0003147040
Monbu kagaku-shō [Ministry of Education, Culture, Sports, Science and Technology]. (2006). *Heisei 19 nendo gakkō kihon chōsa sokuhō nitsuite* [About FY2006 school basic survey (preliminary results)]. Retrieved 31 May 2020 from www.mext.go.jp/b_menu/toukei/001/07073002/001.htm
Nakano, I. (2014). ILO 169-gō jōyaku — senjūmin shuzoku-min no kenri hogo to kyōiku no yakuwari [ILO169 convention: The role of protection of the rights and education of Indigenous and tribal peoples], *Senshū Shōgaku Ronshū* [Commercial Review of Senshu University], 99(July), 37–51. Senshūdaigaku Gakkai. info:doi/10.34360/00001722.
Nomoto, H. (2014). Ainu minzoku senjūmin-zoku kyōiku kenkyū no kadai to tenbō [Introduction: Issues and prospective regarding research on the Ainu and Indigenous peoples' education]. In the Japan Society for the Study of Adult and Community Education (Ed.). *Ainu minzoku senjūmin-zoku kyōiku no genzai* [Current research on the of the Ainu and Indigenous peoples' education]. *Studies in Adult and Community Education*, No. 58. (pp. 8–25). Tokyo, Japan: Tōyōkan shuppan.
Senjūmin-zoku no 10 nen shimin renraku-kai [Indigenous 10-Year Citizens Liaison]. (1997). Ainu minzoku kara no iken hanron teigen (1) [Opinions, objections, and recommendations from the Ainu people (1)]: Ainu bunka no shinkō narabini ainu no dentō-tō nikansuru chishiki no fukyū oyobi keihatsu nikansuru hōritsu womegutte [On the act on the promotion of Ainu culture, and dissemination and enlightenment of knowledge about Ainu tradition, etc.], *Senjūmin-zoku no 10 nen News* [10 years of Indigenous peoples]. No. 37, September.

Shikokugakuindaigaku [Shikokugakuin University]. (2018). *Tokubetsu suisen nyūgaku senkō seido* [Special recommendation admissions]. Retrieved 31 May 2020 from file:///D:/abm.php_f=abm00001778.pdf&n=四国学院大学_tkb.pdf

Shimazaki, N. (2014). Ainu minzoku manabi no rekishi to kadai [The history of learning and issues of Ainu people's women]. In the Japan Society for the Study of Adult and Community Education (Ed.). *Ainu minzoku senjūmin-zoku kyōiku no genzai* [Current research on the of the Ainu and Indigenous peoples' education]. *Studies in Adult and Community Education*, No. 58 (pp. 66–79). Tokyo, Japan: Tōyōkan shuppan.

Shimizu, T. (2000). Gakkō kyōiku ni okeru Ainu minzoku kyōiku no genjō ni kansuru chōsa [Survey on the current education of the Ainu people in school]. *Hekichi Kyoiku Kenkyu, 55*, 79–87.

Trow, M. A. (1976). *Kougakureki Shakai no Daigaku—Erito kara Masu he* [The university in the highly educated society: From elite to mass higher education]. Ikuo Amano, I. & Kitamura, K. (Trans.). Tokyo, Japan: Tōkyōdaigaku shuppan-kai [Tokyo University Press].

Tuhiwai Smith, L. T. (2012). Decolonizing methodologies: Research and Indigenous peoples. London, England: Zed Books.

Retrieved 31 May 2020 fromUnited Nations. (1965/1969). *International convention on the elimination of all forms of racial discrimination*. Retrieved 31 May 2020 fromwww.ohchr.org/en/professionalinterest/pages/cerd.aspx

United Nations. (2007). *United Nations Declaration on the Rights of Indigenous Peoples*. Retrieved 31 May 2020 fromwww.un.org/development/desa/indigenouspeoples/wp-content/uploads/sites/19/2018/11/UNDRIP_E_web.pdf

Utari taisaku no arikata nikansuru yūshikisha kondan-kai [The chief cabinet secretary's private advisory body of experts on the future of the Utari]. (1996). *Hōkoku-sho* [Report]. Tokyo, Japan: Comprehensive Ainu Policy Office, Cabinet Secretariat, Government of Japan.

Yomiuri Shimbun [The Yomiuri newspapers]. (1996). *Ainu shinpō' ashibumi: tsūjō kokkai teishutsu hōshin tantō shōchō na o mitei* [Ainu new act footsteps: Policy to submit to the ordinary Diet, undecided by the ministry in charge]. Morning edition, 20 August, p. 2.

Chapter 5

Indigenous higher education in historical context in Australia

Leanne Holt

Introduction

The effect of colonisation/invasion on the education of Aboriginal peoples in Australia has been catastrophic:

> Since 1788, the Aborigines of Australia have been subjected in varying degrees to an education system which has aimed to rationalize their dispossession from the land, deprecate their culture and, in general, endeavour to make the indigenous people of this country lose their own rich cultural background and think, act and hold the same values as middle-class Europeans.
>
> (Albert 1978, p. 1)

It has only been in the past 45 years that Aboriginal and Torres Strait Islander People in Australia have achieved any viable form of progression in their education. Prior to this, government policies, practices and societal attitudes had resulted in the exclusion, discrimination and oppression of Aboriginal peoples. Aboriginal peoples received little or no formal education, being excluded from both traditional and contemporary education. Government policies concentrated purely on civilising Aboriginal people, who were regarded as savages, low-class and of limited intelligence (Parbury, 1991). Throughout history, federal and state government policies have created intergenerational disadvantage which has manifested itself in the long-term institutional inequality of educational outcomes between Aboriginal and non-Aboriginal peoples that is evident today. It is, therefore, no surprise that the first Aboriginal undergraduate graduation within an Australian universitydid not occur until 1966, when Margaret Valadian graduated with a Bachelor of Social Studies from the University of Queensland and Charlie Perkins graduated from the University of Sydney with a Bachelor of Arts.

After the years of educational deprivation and exclusion

After nearly 200 years of educational deprivation and exclusion came a new era. Led by the newly elected Whitlam government, the Self-Determination Policy was introduced. This created a significant shift from policies of assimilation and integration to a policy that proposed new relationships with Aboriginal peoples, promoting self-control of their own culture, heritage, language and future direction (Maddison, 2009). Determined activists fighting for the rights of Aboriginal peoples made way for community-controlled organisations in health, education, land, culture and heritage. Strong principles of equality and access were also introduced by the then Labor government, with a proactive approach to initiating a better future for Aboriginal people through education.

Simultaneous to this movement, a comprehensive review was initiated, focusing on the distribution of funding between government and non-government schools. Although outside the scope of the review, the final *Schools in Australia* report (Karmel Report, 1973) made a number of significant observations, highlighting the realities of education for Aboriginal children. Inconsistencies in school conditions for Aboriginal children, particularly those in large schools, were recorded. The report claims that for Aboriginal children:

> Schooling should offer a means of redress for the economic and political disadvantages of their background rather than a compounding of them … the problems of prejudice may exacerbate those of poverty.
>
> (p. 48)

The report strongly recommended that a special study be commissioned. The recommendation stated that the study should explore opportunities to identify and develop a coordinated policy for Aboriginal education, encompassing all levels of education from early childhood to higher education. The special study was undertaken by the Aboriginal Consultative Group in 1975, premising the study with the foundations that:

> We see education as the most important strategy for achieving realistic self-determination for the Aboriginal people of Australia. We do not see education as a method of producing an anglicized Aborigine but rather as an instrument for creating an informed community with intellectual and technological skills, in harmony with our own cultural values and identity. We wish to be Aboriginal citizens in a changing Australia.
>
> (Aboriginal Consultative Group, 1975, p. 3)

The report of the special study, *Education for Aborigines: Report to the Schools Commission* (Aboriginal Consultative Group, 1975), determined that Aboriginal peoples have unique cultural values and perspectives that unite and identify them as separate to non-Aboriginal people. It reinforced that Aboriginal identity be respected and fostered throughout educational experiences. It was deemed that an integral part of this process needed to be the inclusion of Indigenous peoples in decision making, particularly at the senior levels, which required the allocation of resources essential to ensuring appropriate training and development, including at a higher education level. The first recommendation of the report would, therefore, be vital to the future of Aboriginal education policy in Australia, with the recommendation calling for a separate statutory funding body to be established, called the National Aboriginal Education Committee (NAEC).

National Aboriginal Education Committee

Established in 1977, NAEC was responsible for providing advice and expertise to the Minister for Education. The Chairperson of NAEC, a senior public servant, led an all Aboriginal and Torres Strait Islander committee that represented all levels of education from early childhood to higher education. To respond to the ideas and aspirations of local communities, Aboriginal and Torres Strait Islander Education Advisory Committees were also established in every state and territory to ensure a continuum of relevant input into agendas and strategies at the national level.

State education committees played a vital role in bringing the Aboriginal community together and collaborating with the NAEC to ensure all states and territories were given a voice in developing a national agenda. It was an exciting time for Aboriginal communities; at last they were having a voice in determining their own futures and that of generations to come. The NAEC entrenched the principle of community accountability. This state and national collaboration model provided the NAEC with Aboriginal voices that stretched across states, territories and related regions.

In 1979, NAEC undertook extensive research and consultation project to develop a submission to the National Inquiry into Teacher Education (NITE). Contrasting with previous studies, this research responded to the needs of Aboriginal peoples from their own perspectives as opposed to the existing challenges in Aboriginal education that often resulted in a deficit view (Hughes & Willmot, 1979). The resultant paper from the research (Hughes & Willmot, 1979) was called *The Education and Employment of Aboriginal and Torres Strait Islander Teachers* (EEATSIT). The outcomes of EEATSIT and the subsequent submission to the NITE (Hughes & Willmot, 1979) resulted in strong future directives, particularly relating to Aboriginal and Torres Strait Islander higher education through what would become the 1,000 Aboriginal Teachers by 1990 initiative.

Recognising the geographic, cultural, social and economic diversity across Australian Aboriginal and Torres Strait Islander communities, a societal framework was developed for the EEASTIT research that ensured recognition of the diverse cultural groups across Australia. The framework grouped Aboriginal communities into four and examined Aboriginal education and teacher training within each group:

> **Category 1:** traditionally oriented communities consisting of people who have the greatest degree of geographic and social separation from the rest of Australian society, though usually retaining some degree of economic connection.
>
> **Category 2:** rural communities living in reserve situations who also have considerable social and geographical separation from the rest of Australian society but are not as traditionally oriented as Category 1 people.
>
> **Category 3:** urban communities who are highly geographically and economically embedded in non-Indigenous society but, because of their community organisation have considerable social separation.
>
> **Category 4:** urban dispersed communities who are highly socially, economically and geographically embedded in non-Indigenous Australian society.
>
> (Hughes & Willmot, 1982, p. 46)

The EEATSIT report concluded that the employment of Aboriginal teachers provided a means for Aboriginal people to achieve social and economic equality. However, achieving this was challenging because at the current rate there would only be approximately 400 Aboriginal teacher graduates over the next decade, whereas 5,000 graduates would be required if parity with non-Aboriginal teachers was to be achieved. The EEATSIT report, therefore, made two major recommendations. First, graduate 1,000 Aboriginal and Torres Strait Islander teachers by 1990, producing a sufficient number of Aboriginal and Torres Strait Islander teachers to provide a positive impact on the educational outcomes of Aboriginal children in the classroom and Aboriginal communities more generally. The aspiration was:

> these teachers will make their greatest contribution through the multiplier effect. From their children will come the economists, engineers, doctors, politicians, journalists and public servants of the future. In one generation Aboriginal society will have produced its managerial and political head and, more importantly, an intellectual arm that will be able to contribute to the shaping of Australia's destiny.
>
> (Hughes & Willmot 1982, p. 49)

Second, the report recommended that Aboriginal teachers be prepared to teach non-Aboriginal students, thus contributing to both societies. Furthermore, preparing teachers, generally, to be relevant to the Aboriginal geographic locations of traditional, regional, rural, remote and urban areas was seen as critical for developing successful relationships with communities. Failure to incorporate education about Aboriginal societies and perspectives would result in the continued privilege of Western knowledges in schools which would be detrimental to Aboriginal communities.

In establishing the foundations for the future of Aboriginal and Torres Strait Islander education, NAEC developed the first Aboriginal education policy document titled, *Philosophy, aims and policy guidelines for Aboriginal and Torres Strait Islander education* (1985). Providing a philosophical viewpoint, the policy defined aims for the future of Aboriginal education from early childhood through to higher education. At the core of the policy document were the following principles: education is key to an ongoing existence for Aboriginal peoples; educational practices must consider Aboriginal epistemologies; the acquisition of academic and technological skills should occur in conjunction with cultural identity and values; knowledge and understanding relating to the history and perspectives of Aboriginal peoples as traditional custodians of the land is needed by all Australians; cross-cultural programmes promoting the value of cultural diversity and the uniqueness of Aboriginal culture are needed to enable respectful and productive relationships between Aboriginal and non-Aboriginal people; Aboriginal peoples need to be involved in policy development and decision making; and Aboriginal peoples need to be employed across professions and service delivery (NAEC, 1980).

NAEC identified that, within Aboriginal and Torres Strait Islander higher education, Aboriginal peoples achieving qualifications across a broad range of professions was of the utmost importance, particularly in the areas of health, education, law and business administration. Further, NAEC identified that Aboriginal employment needed to be a focus within universities and the then colleges of advanced education, with these institutions setting up employment targets to create ongoing positions across all areas of the university, recruiting membership on university councils and committees as well as establishing Aboriginal advisory committees for consultation and collaboration. Further universities should introduce 'special programmes' and provide appropriate resources for Aboriginal programmes and courses, including teaching facilities and administrative assistance as a part of the usual operations of the institution. In addition, NAEC stated that it was imperative that universities incorporate or move towards Aboriginal control of 'special programme' as a compulsory component of the funding stipulations provided by governments (NAEC, 1980, p. 22).

Funding for Aboriginal and Torres Strait Islander education

On 8 July 1983, the Commonwealth Education Commission requested that NAEC conduct a review on the education of Aboriginal students for input to funding guidelines for 1984. The request stated:

> The Government wishes the Commission to give special consideration to measures that might be taken with existing programmes, or through new initiatives, to improving educational outcomes for Aboriginal children. It is concerned about both the quality of educational experience of Aborigines and their low participation rates in the higher levels of secondary schooling and tertiary education. The Government asks the Commission to review these matters in co-operation with the National Aboriginal Education Committee, the States and non-government school authorities, and Aboriginal communities and to report to the Government as early in 1984 as is practicable.
>
> (NAEC, 1984, p. vii)

The report titled, *Funding Priorities in Aboriginal and Torres Strait Islander Education* (NAEC, 1984, p. xi), was tabled in July 1984 and proposed the implementation of an Aboriginal Education Programme that comprised four components:

1 An Aboriginal education recurrent grants programme
2 A language and cultural studies programme
3 An Aboriginal education development programme
4 A scheme for teachers in Aboriginal community schools

The Aboriginal Education Programme aimed to provide targeted support towards increasing the outcomes of Aboriginal education. It was noted at the time of the report that there were no programmes offered by the Commission that directly targeted Aboriginal people. Instead, Aboriginal people needed to compete against other groups, such as ethnic communities, to access funding or resources within an already limited scheme.

Previous to the NAEC being established, the Commonwealth funding distributed to the states was based on applications from the state, largely influenced by the state's interests and resources in Aboriginal education. The NAEC initially had been delegated the role of an adviser to the Commonwealth on Aboriginal education, however, over time, was appointed the role as principal adviser to the Minister for Education with its level of influence increasing in determining government policy development and funding allocations. The focus was to provide a more equitable solution to distributing monies to the states from the Commonwealth. State committees and other stakeholders would nominate programmes within their state or territory that required funding along with justifications and priorities. The NAEC would assess all submitted proposals, prioritising the programmes to be funded, and determine the amounts based on the national pool of funds available. The recommendations for Aboriginal education funding distribution would then be made by NAEC to the Commonwealth. This process allowed for not only the funding of Aboriginal education centres within universities but also of special initiatives such as an Aboriginal Medical School at the University of Newcastle.

Participation of Aboriginal and Torres Strait Islander peoples within higher education

The 1,000 Aboriginal and Torres Strait Islander teachers by 1990 became a major policy initiative for the Labor Party–led Australian government in 1983. Increasing the participation of Aboriginal and Torres Strait Islander peoples in higher education was recognised as a significant factor in the success of the initiative. From 1977 to 1982, the number of qualified Aboriginal teachers grew from 72 to 220. As already noted, it was anticipated that the success of the 1,000 Aboriginal Teachers initiative would increase Aboriginal student educational outcomes as well as overcome other issues, such as Aboriginal student attendance rates, and, further contribute to the economic and social advancement of Aboriginal communities by empowering students to continue to engage in education. As Hughes and Willmot (1982) pointed out:

> While white Australians may open their social and political arms to their black brothers, their economic sorting machine is certain to steer Aboriginals to the lower end of the employment spectrum. Such a process is linked with education, not so much in the effect that education has upon economic mobility, but through the educational barriers that prevent access to employment.
>
> (p. 22)

The 1,000 Aboriginal Teachers by 1990 initiative stimulated a shared vision for Aboriginal and Torres Strait Islander peoples, government and higher education institutions. It placed an emphasis on the development of Enclaves as major resources to ensure access, retention and success of Aboriginal students to teaching courses and other disciplines within a higher education environment. Enclave programmes had already been introduced in a few higher education institutions, providing access pathways and additional support in a culturally appropriate setting for Aboriginal students enrolled in courses. The NAEC (1985) believed that these programmes should be embedded into the structures of the institution and not structured as a short-term programme or strategy. In addition, NAEC (1985) suggested that the enclave programmes should include personal and academic support covering tutoring, counselling, cultural programmes and a culturally safe space. NAEC noted that success would be greater if: an Aboriginal student officer was appointed; bridging programmes were introduced; research centres for Aboriginal student research were developed; and teaching programmes and education programmes were introduced in communities (NAEC, 1985, p. 29). The NAEC also sent a strong message out that Aboriginal Studies should be available to all students across all levels of education, including higher education, as an integral part of their learning and understanding. The preference would be that the development and teaching of Aboriginal Studies be led by Aboriginal people to ensure appropriate content and resources, understanding and sensitivities. Aboriginal Studies was defined as:

> [H]istory, cultures, languages and lifestyles of Aboriginal and Torres Strait Islander peoples, before and after colonization. The study involves understanding issues that are central to Aboriginal and Torres Strait Islander contemporary society, and their relevance to the total Australian community.
>
> (NAEC, 1985, p. 30)

In 1985, Jordan and Howard conducted a study to inform policy making and funding decisions in relation to Aboriginal higher education support. Although teacher training programmes for Aboriginal peoples commenced in the mid-1970s, only three institutions – Western Australia CAE (now known as Edith Cowan University), Townsville CAE (now known as James Cook University) and the South Australian Institute of Technology (now known as University of South Australia) – offered such courses. The teacher training programmes were primarily supported by enclaves and Jordan and Howard found that enclaves played a significant role in attracting, retaining and graduating Aboriginal teacher education students, highlighting the importance of special Aboriginal and Torres Strait Islander spaces for achieving the target of 1,000 teachers by 1990. In mid-1980s the Australian government made the decision to amalgamate CAEs with universities, which resulted in programmes such as teacher education and nursing programmes moving from diplomas to undergraduate programmes. In line with this movement the enclaves and support systems automatically became part of the university structures.

The Commonwealth government allocated funding that would be used to negotiate with all higher education institutions across Australia to encourage the adoption of enclave programmes or Student Support Systems. This funding was named Indigenous Support Program (ISP) and was legislated through the *Higher Education Student Support Act 2003* (Cth). With this funding, Aboriginal people came knocking on the door of universities asking permission to enter, money in hand. The ISP funding, for many years, became the sole source of funding for Aboriginal and Torres Strait Islander spaces. In some instances, this practice still continues today under the Indigenous Student Success Program.

Special entry programmes were a key strategy for enclaves in the attraction of Aboriginal and Torres Strait Islander peoples. Poor educational outcomes within the school system meant that most Aboriginal and Torres Strait Islander peoples were not receiving a Year 12 certificate and, given the very small numbers of Aboriginal peoples graduating from higher education programmes, there was a lack of awareness and aspiration to study. The special entry programmes were initially focused on mature-aged students and considered other personal attributes that would contribute to success in higher education in addition to academic qualifications. Special arrangements were also considered, such as extended completion time, academic preparation programmes and tutoring (Jordan & Howard, 1985). Once special entry programmes were introduced, it became obvious that further support services would be required to ensure Aboriginal students succeeded in 'foreign' tertiary learning environments. This space would contribute to students feeling a 'sense of belonging' in a Western learning environment that was not necessarily conducive to their own experiences and environments.

NAEC (1986) determined that a minimum of ten Aboriginal and Torres Strait Islander students needed to be enrolled for an enclave to be effective. Studying together as a cohort was seen to make students feel more at ease in an 'alien' environment as well as provide peer support and encouragement, bringing together a range of backgrounds and experiences that would complement the support provided by the enclave. Also important was engagement of Aboriginal students with non-Aboriginal students and staff to increase awareness and interaction with Aboriginal perspectives and experiences.

The Jordan and Howard (1985) report proposed renaming the Aboriginal support systems from Enclaves to simply 'support systems' or services to remove the restrictions placed on services provided by an enclave and the need to identify a name conducive to future growth. The 1,000 Aboriginal and Torres Strait Islander Teachers by 1990 initiative had set the ball rolling and the introduction of Enclaves and Support Systems/Services across Australian universities had resulted in significant increases to Aboriginal student enrolments from 85 when Enclaves were first introduced in the mid-to-late 1970s to 551 at the beginning of 1984.

By the start of 1986, 799 Aboriginal and Torres Strait Islander students were enrolled in higher education programmes with 617 retained at the end of the year. NAEC's (1986) *Policy Statement on Tertiary Education for Aboriginal and Torres Strait* focused on expanding attraction to more disciplines, notably Medicine and Law, because of the length of time it would take to make an impact on these professions. By 1983, it had only seven Aboriginal graduates in Law and two in Medicine (NAEC, 1986, p. 13). Enclaves were once more highlighted as crucial to the success of Aboriginal students across all disciplines and institutions were encouraged to allocate funding over and above their funded quota as well as implement bridging programmes for Aboriginal peoples to gain access to university.

In 1996, the Australian government agreed to fund Aboriginal Research Centres of Excellence at a number of universities. As a consequence, more Aboriginal and Torres Strait Islander senior appointments were made. The centres created a network to enable sharing of experiences and practice and provide mentoring and peer support in navigating the higher education environments and related policies.

National Aboriginal Education Policy

In 1989, a Taskforce led by Paul Hughes was appointed by the Department of Education, Employment and Training to make recommendations on how to guide the development and funding of a national Aboriginal Education Policy to lead Aboriginal and Torres Strait Islander education into the future. The work of NAEC, in collaboration with state and territory Aboriginal Advisory Committees, strongly contributed to the work of the Taskforce. The Taskforce (Hughes, 1988) stated that the apparently significant increase in Aboriginal student numbers over the past 20 years was from a low base and, while Aboriginal and Torres Strait Islander peoples placed a high level of importance on education, there continued to be substantial barriers to Aboriginal participation and success through the education system. Causes included:

> Racial discrimination which serves to exacerbate the educational disadvantage faced by many Aboriginal people;
> Social and cultural alienation which is experienced both in local communities and in schooling;
> Economic disadvantage and poorer living standards which inhibit Aboriginal participation and impede successful completion of an education;
> Geographical isolation ...;
> Lack of co-ordination among services at various levels of government which effectively isolates many Aboriginal people from available education programmes.
>
> (Hughes, 1988, p. 16)

The Taskforce recommended:

> To achieve equity in the provision of education to all Aboriginal children, young people and adults by the year 2000;
> To assist Aboriginal parents and communities to be fully involved in the planning and provision of education for themselves and their children;
> To achieve parity in participation rates by Aboriginal people with those of other Australians in all stages of education;
> To achieve positive educational outcomes for Aboriginal people in schooling and tertiary education; and
> To improve the provision of education services across the nation at the local level.
>
> (Hughes, 1988, pp. 16–17)

The Taskforce report resulted in the formulation of the *National Aboriginal and Torres Strait Islander Education Joint Policy Statement* (Commonwealth Department of Education, 1989), a cooperative effort among Commonwealth, state and territory governments. The policy, the foundations of which are still active today, is utilised as an evaluative framework across all levels of education.

Overall, the 1980s was a period when Aboriginal people began, for the first time, to genuinely influence decision making at the national level. Nevertheless, self-determination had not yet been achieved.

A collective voice for Indigenous higher education: The *Coolangatta Statement*

The *Coolangatta Statement on Indigenous Peoples' Rights in Education* (*Coolangatta Statement*) was initiated at the 1993 *World Indigenous Peoples Conference on Education* (WIPCE) held at Wollongong, Australia, with the final document presented in Hilo, Hawaii, in 1999. The *Coolangatta Statement* brings the voices of Indigenous peoples from across the world together to represent their various knowledges, experiences and aspirations. It continues to be a living document that speaks to reform and transformational education for Indigenous peoples, responding to the continued failure of Western education systems to meet the holistic educational needs of Indigenous peoples globally. The Coolangatta Statement sets out the struggles of Indigenous peoples to:

> [A]ccess education that acknowledges, respects and promotes the right of Indigenous peoples to be Indigenous – a right that embraces Indigenous people's language, culture, traditions and spirituality.
>
> (Coolangatta Statement 1999)

The *Coolangatta Statement* draws together international human rights statements and documents that represent self-determination in Indigenous rights to education, land, knowledges, language and culture. At the centre of all such documents and statements is the human right to be Indigenous that must underpin the future of Indigenous education. The statement calls for the need to action, the right to self-determination through education and the fundamental need to embrace Indigenous 'culture, knowledge and wisdom' for the benefit of Indigenous communities and individuals within a contemporary landscape (*Coolangatta Statement*, 1999).

National Aboriginal and Torres Strait Islander higher education advisory committees

At the same time as the *Coolangatta Statement* was being formulated, the need for a national Aboriginal and Torres Strait Islander network was being discussed by Aboriginal and Torres Strait Islander scholars across the sector. In the 1990s, Aboriginal and Torres Strait Islander support systems/service centres had expanded to incorporate Indigenous learning and teaching, developing Indigenous courses and programmes and, in some cases, Indigenous research centres were being introduced as the appointment of Aboriginal and Torres Strait Islander academics increased. This led to higher education sector's recognition of the importance of Indigenous research and the need for empowerment of Indigenous communities through research.

In 1994, the Indigenous Australian Higher Education Association (IAHEA) was established, chaired by Professor Colin Bourke, the first Aboriginal person to hold a senior position within a university. Bourke led the inaugural Faculty of Aboriginal and Torres Strait Islander Studies at the University of South Australia and, at the time of his retirement, was acting Deputy Vice-Chancellor. During his career he was also the first Aboriginal Principal in Victoria, the first Aboriginal Assistant Secretary, and the first Chairperson of the Victorian Aboriginal Education Consultative Group. Following Colin's leadership, Errol West – previous Chair of the NAEC – held the Chair position followed by Jill Millroy from 1996 to 1999. At this time the IAHEA transitioned to the National Indigenous Higher Education Network (NIHEN).

Over the years, NIHEN grew its membership and was becoming recognised for its advocacy of Aboriginal and Torres Strait Islander access, scholarship and research within higher education. The attraction was that NIHEN membership was inclusive of any Aboriginal and Torres Strait Islander person working within Australian universities and the committee was independent of individual universities and allowed a collective voice towards the advancement of Aboriginal and Torres Strait Islander higher education. The Chairs of NIHEN were Berice Anning and Gary Thomas.

In 2004, the Minister for Education, Science and Training appointed the Indigenous Higher Education Advisory Council (IHEAC). Unlike NIHEN, membership was through a government selection process, and the roles and responsibilities as defined were to provide advice to the minister and the Australian government on selected agendas related to Aboriginal and Torres Strait Islander higher education, research and research training. In 2012, the council was renamed the Aboriginal and Torres Strait Islander Higher Education Advisory Council. This council produced reports, made recommendations and plans with the aim of increasing the Indigenous workforce; increasing Indigenous participation in business and STEM (science, technology, engineering and maths) disciplines; encouraging whole-of-university approaches; and cultural competency within universities. The council was terminated in 2015 (Department of Education, 2019).

In 2015, NIHEN became incorporated and was renamed the National Aboriginal and Torres Strait Islander Higher Education Consortium (NATSIHEC). Incorporation enabled the organisation to build on its significant work of 20 years and strengthen its membership. NATSIHEC became a key adviser to the Minister for Education and Training (Cth) for Aboriginal and Torres Strait Islander higher education, in effect replacing the terminated Aboriginal and Torres Strait Islander Advisory Council. NATSIHEC continues to be an influential voice within higher education, forming strong collaborations with peak government and professional bodies related to learning and teaching; research; student and community engagement; international engagement; and workforce (NATSIHEC, 2019). The chairs of NATSIHEC to date have been Professor Peter Buckskin, Distinguished Professor Aileen Moreton-Robinson – the first Indigenous Distinguished Professor appointed in Australia – and Dr Leanne Holt (author of this chapter).

Review of Australian higher education

In 2008, the Minister for Education (Cth) commissioned a review of Australian higher education to determine educational needs to support the Australian community and economy into the future. The final report made 46 recommendations, including the need for the Australian government to regularly review the effectiveness of measures to improve higher education access and outcomes for Indigenous people in consultation with the IHEAC (Bradley, Noonan, Nugent & Scales, 2008). This was the precursor that motivated the Behrendt report (2012) that responded directly to this recommendation (see Chapter 10).

The Bradley report highlighted three groups deemed extremely under-represented: students from low socio-economic backgrounds; students from regional and remote areas; and Indigenous students. The report noted that increasing opportunities for these groups to access and complete higher education would significantly increase their success in finding, which would then have benefits to broader communities and societies. The report confirmed that Australia's history had excluded these groups from education including higher education, resulting in lower educational attainment and lack of exposure to higher education, affecting appropriate knowledge to guide aspirational career goals. Furthermore, given these challenges, higher levels of support are required to achieve success once such students enrol in higher education, including mentoring, financial and academic assistance.

Indigenous student outcomes and Indigenous knowledges were key considerations in the Bradley report, with the committee noting that the access rates to higher education had declined from 2001 to 2007, participation rates only slightly improving and success rates drastically below those of non-Indigenous students. The report recommended immediate action that would enable Indigenous students to achieve their highest potential, with universities to provide an environment that is conducive to the success of Indigenous students, cultural competency training and the delivery of a curriculum that values Indigenous knowledges and understandings. The unique knowledge and experiences of Indigenous staff and students were considered integral to developing this curriculum and would also contribute to research and scholarship (Bradley et al., 2008, p. 32). IHEAC's report to the Bradley review quoted:

Indigenous people do not come empty handed to Australia's higher education system but bring significant strengths, both in knowledge capital and human capital that enriches higher education in Australia. The recognition of Indigenous peoples' contribution as needs is critical to the full Indigenous engagement in higher education.

(p. 32)

The review suggested that to improve outcomes for Indigenous higher education, as well as other under-represented groups, there needed to be concentration on creating a greater awareness of higher education, provide programmes that build aspirations to participate in higher education and increasing educational attainments at school level as well as continued financial support. Even though the review explored the broader Australian higher education structures and systems, its focus on Indigenous higher education provided an important platform for future investigations, actions and programmes.

National and international priorities

Closing the gap

In 2008, the Commonwealth government introduced a major strategy for increasing the outcomes of Aboriginal and Torres Strait Islander peoples, titled *Closing the Gap* (Department of the Prime Minister and Cabinet, 2019). The strategy aimed to decrease the disadvantage of Aboriginal and Torres Strait Islander peoples, particularly in relation to life expectancy, infant mortality, access to early childhood education and achievement and outcomes in broader education and employment. Within education, the government committed to, at the very least, halving the gap between Indigenous and non-Indigenous students in Year 12 attainment by 2020 and increasing the number of students transitioning to university. The government also committed to halving the gap in literacy and numeracy within ten years (Department of the Prime Minister and Cabinet, 2019, p. 58). Unfortunately, the 2019 report that assessed the progress of the *Close the Gap* target noted that there continues to be disparity in Year 12 attainment rates and areas for improvement include increasing the quality of teacher training, as well as increasing the number of qualified Aboriginal and Torres Strait Islander teachers.

In 2011, the More Aboriginal and Torres Strait Islander Teachers Initiative (MATSITI) was launched. It was funded by the Commonwealth government to continue the work of the earlier '1,000 Aboriginal Teachers by 1990' programme. Like the earlier programme, MATSITI aimed to increase the number of Aboriginal and Torres Strait Islander teachers within schools but with a greater emphasis on mentoring and development opportunities, also focusing on retaining the teachers within schools. MATSITI developed a comprehensive five-year plan focusing on attraction and retention, as well as strategies to enhance professional and leadership capabilities so that experienced Aboriginal and Torres Strait Islander teachers could contribute to the ongoing development of early career teachers (MATSITI, 2019).

The Commonwealth government is currently working on a *Close the Gap Refresh* campaign that seeks to move beyond deficit objectives to a more strength-based approach (Department of the Prime Minister and Cabinet, 2019). However, the complications that continue to challenge Aboriginal and Torres Strait Islander higher education students are:

> Lack of educational aspirations being encouraged at school level, with the majority of students still being first in family to attend university;
>
> (Craven, 2004)

> Financial challenges;
>
> (Universities Australia, 2013)

> Unstable social, cultural and emotional wellbeing, based on past political agendas that continue to have devastating impacts on individuals and communities;
>
> (Dudgeon, et al., 2014)

> Achieving a 'sense of belonging' within a Western university environment, with students commonly suffering from the 'imposter syndrome' feeling that they don't fit;
>
> (Liddle, 2016)

> Lack of recognition of Indigenous knowledges and experiences that have the potential to value-add to all student experiences;
>
> (Behrendt, et al., 2012)

> Racism and discrimination creating hostile environments that impact the experiences of Aboriginal and Torres Strait Islander students and staff; and
>
> (Bodkin-Andrews & Carlson, 2016)

> Inadequate funding and resourcing of Aboriginal and Torres Strait Islander higher education within institutions.
>
> (Behrendt, et al., 2012)

These current challenges are compounded by the presence of minimal numbers of Aboriginal and Torres Strait Islander leaders across the academy and the ability of universities to provide an environment that is conducive to Aboriginal and Torres Strait Islander success. For many years, Aboriginal and Torres Strait Islander People continue to survive in a racist environment; whether conscious or unconscious, Aboriginal and Torres Strait Islander peoples are discriminated against and disadvantaged within the academy (Bodkin-Andrews & Carlson, 2016). Yet the discomfort of bringing this reality to life is compounded by the ongoing silence of the non-Indigenous majority that exists across the academy, even to the point that the uttering of the word 'racism' is deemed uncourteous and disruptive. These environments continue to have detrimental impacts on Aboriginal and Torres Strait Islander students, staff, communities as well as the work, opportunities and well-being of Aboriginal and Torres Strait Islander people.

United Nations Declaration on the Rights of Indigenous Peoples

Responding to national and international human rights movements in the 1960s and 1970s, which advocated against the violence, exclusion and discrimination of Indigenous peoples worldwide, the UN General Assembly adopted the UNDRIP (United Nations, 2007) with the support of 144 states. Australia, along with New Zealand, Canada and the United States, refused to sign the document at the time but subsequently endorsed it in 2009 (Human Rights Commission, 2019).

In the initial period of the UNDRIP's development, the UN initiated the annual meeting of the UN Permanent Forum for Indigenous Issues (UNPFII). UNPFII held its first meeting in 2000 with a focus on providing advice to the Economic and Social Council. In 2001, a special rapporteur on the rights of Indigenous peoples was appointed to investigate violations against the human rights and freedoms of Indigenous peoples internationally. The UNDRIP focuses on the development and advancement of Indigenous peoples and communities around the world, targeting issues related to the human rights of Indigenous peoples, including to education. Significantly, Article 14.1 states:

> Indigenous peoples have the right to establish and control their educational systems and institutions providing education in their own languages, in a manner appropriate to their cultural methods of teaching and learning.
> (United Nations, 2007)

This international movement enshrined within UNDRIP is significant for Aboriginal and Torres Strait Islander peoples who have the oldest living culture in the world and who have never ceded sovereignty over their land. Aboriginal and Torres Strait Islanders have embraced all aspects of their surroundings and interconnected them to their cultural identity, understandings and view of the world. Yet, the Australian government continues to be challenged by the implementation of these international standards. In spite of the enormous amount of the work of organisations such as the NAEC or NATSIHEC, the closest we have come to an Indigenous-controlled education institution is through the recognition of the Batchelor Institute as an educational institution that focuses on education for Aboriginal and Torres Strait Islander peoples through Indigenous ways of knowing and Indigenous leadership.

The Batchelor Institute, from its small beginnings in the early 1970s, focused on purely teacher education programmes. It became a dual sector provider in 1982, delivering both vocational and higher education programmes. It was the first of its kind in Australia and was led and governed by Aboriginal and Torres Strait Islander peoples. In 2003, the Institute became recognised by the government as a Table A provider, the same as other public universities in Australia. The Institute is unique in that it is guided by Aboriginal values, beliefs, philosophies and aspirations, though contextualised within a Western educational system (Huijser, Ober, O' Sullivan, McRae-Williams, & Elvin, 2015). Appropriately, the Institute's approach and philosophy is coined 'Both Ways'. The Batchelor Institute is significant to the history of Indigenous higher education in Australia. It gives Australia's Indigenous people hope that one day, in the future, the Institute will become the first Aboriginal and Torres Strait Islander university, recognised alongside other Australian universities for its students, learning and teaching, and research outcomes from an Indigenous perspective.

Conclusions

Asserting the voices of Aboriginal and Torres Strait Islander peoples on the advancement of their own education was an important milestone in contemporary Australian history. For 40 years, Aboriginal and Torres Strait Islander Peoples struggled to advance their higher education, challenging a system that has and continues to have low expectations of Australia's Indigenous people: as students; as academics and professionals; and as leaders (both parties are not recognised as having equal shared knowledges). A paradigm shift is required to move beyond an equity relationship to recognition of the unique knowledges, experiences and aspirations as an asset that value-adds to the academic and cultural dimensions of Australian universities.

Higher education is vital to the economic, social and cultural advancement of Aboriginal and Torres Strait Islander communities. This reality drives Aboriginal resilience in leadership and practice now and into the future. Acknowledgement needs to be given to the Aboriginal and Torres Strait Islander men and women who have been passionate and determined in their leadership in ensuring Aboriginal and Torres Strait Islander peoples have appropriate access and opportunities within higher education.

The true essence of Aboriginal education is the right of Aboriginal people to imagine their own 'dreaming' and to have access to the skills, knowledge and wisdom to help to not only define this 'dreaming' but also to capture it and to make it happen (Robert Morgan in Holt, 2016).

References

Aboriginal Consultative Group. (1975). *Education for Aborigines: Report to the schools commission by the Aboriginal consultative group.* June 1975. (064293312X). Canberra, Australia: Australian Government

Albert, S. (1978). Education of Aborigines criticised. *Northern Territory Teachers Federation Newsletter, 3*(7), 4.

Behrendt, L., Griew, R., & Larkin, R. (2012). *Review of higher education access and outcomes for Aboriginal and Torres Strait Islander people – Final report.* Canberra, Australia: Commonwealth of Australia.

Bodkin-Andrews, G., & Carlson, B. (2016). The legacy of racism and Indigenous Australian identity within education. *Journal of Race, Ethnicity, and Education, 19*(4), 784–807.

Bradley, D., Noonan, P., Nugent, H., & Scales, B. (2008). *Review of the Australian higher education.* Canberra, Australia: Department of Education, Employment and Workplace Relations (DEEWR).

Commonwealth Department of Education. (1989). *Cabinet submission 6577: National Aboriginal and Torres Strait Islander education policy* – Decisions 12855/ER and 13063. National Archives of Australia, Series A14039, Item 31430749.

Coolangatta Statement on Indigenous Peoples' Rights in Education. (1999). Hawai'I, HI: World Indigenous Peoples Conference on Education.

Craven, R. (2004). The challenge for counsellors: Understanding and addressing Indigenous secondary students' aspirations, self-concepts and barriers to achieving aspirations. *Journal of Psychologists and Counsellors in Schools. 14*(1), 16–33.

Department of Education. (2019). *Indigenous higher education advisory council.* Retrieved 31 May 2020 from https://docs.education.gov.au/documents/indigenous-higher-education-advisory-council-0

Department of the Prime Minister and Cabinet. (2019). *Close the gap report 2018.* Retrieved 31 May 2020 from https://ctgreport.pmc.gov.au/education

Dudgeon, W., Wright, M., Paradies, Y., Garvey, D., & Walker, I. (2014). Aboriginal social, cultural and historical contexts. In N. Purdie, P. Dudgeon, & R. Walker (Eds.). *Working together: Aboriginal and Torres Strait Islander mental health and wellbeing principles and practice* (pp. 1–24). Canberra, Australia: Commonwealth of Australia.

Holt, L. (2016). *Development of Aboriginal education policy in Australia: Voices of the NAEC.* Unpublished PhD thesis. Newcastle, Australia: University of Newcastle.

Hughes, P. (1988). *Report of the Aboriginal education policy task force.* Canberra, Australia: Department of Education.

Hughes, P., & Willmot, E. (1979). *Report to the NAEC: The education and employment of Aboriginal and Torres Strait Islander teachers.* Canberra, Australia: National Aboriginal Education Committee.

Hughes, P., & Willmot, E. (1982). 1,000 Aboriginal Teachers by 1990 Revisited. In J. Sherwood (Ed.). *Aboriginal education: Issues and innovations* (pp. 45–49). Perth, Australia: Creative Research.

Huijser, H., Ober, R., O'Sullivan, S., McRae-Williams, E., & Elvin, R. (Eds.) (2015). *Finding common ground: Narratives, provocations and reflections from the 40-year celebration of Batchelor Institute.* Batchelor, Australia: Batchelor Press.

Human Rights Commission. (2019). *United Nations Declaration on the Rights of Indigenous Peoples.* Retrieved 31 May 2020 from www.un.org/development/desa/indigenouspeoples/declaration-on-the-rights-of-indigenous-peoples.html

Jordan, D. F., & Howard, S. M. (1985). *Support systems for Aboriginal students in higher education institutions.* Adelaide, Australia: Tertiary Education Authority of South Australia.

Karmel, P. (1973). *Report of the interim committee of the Australian schools commission.* Canberra, Australia: Australian Government Publishing Service.

Liddle, C. (2016). First Peoples: Aboriginal and Torres Strait Islander participation in higher education. In A. Harvey, C. Burnheim, & M. Brett, M. (Eds.). *Student equity in Australian higher education: Twenty-five years of a fair chance for all* (pp. 53–68). Singapore: Springer.

Maddison, S. (2009). *Black politics: Inside the complexity of Aboriginal political culture.* Crows Nest, Australia: Allen & Unwin.

MATSITI. (2019). *More Aboriginal and Torres Strait Islander teachers initiative.* Retrieved 31 May 2020 from www.matsiti.edu.au

National Aboriginal Education Committee. (1980). *Rationale, aims and objectives in Aboriginal education.* Canberra, Australia: Department of Education.

National Aboriginal Education Committee. (1984). *Funding priorities in Aboriginal and Torres Strait Islander education: First report of the working party on Aboriginal and Torres Strait Islander education.* Canberra, Australia: NAEC and Commonwealth Schools Commission.

National Aboriginal Education Committee. (1985). *Philosophy, aims and policy guidelines for Aboriginal and Torres Strait Islander education.* Canberra, Australia: Australian Government Publishing Service.

National Aboriginal Education Committee. (1986). *Policy statement on teacher education for Aborigines and Torres Strait Islanders.* Canberra, Australia: Australian Government Publishing Service.

National Aboriginal Education Committee Working Party on Racism in Higher Education. (1989). *Combating racism in tertiary institutions.* Adelaide, Australia: Gillingham Printers.

National Aboriginal and Torres Strait Islander Higher Education Consortium (NATSIHEC). (2019). *About NATSIHEC.* Retrieved 31 May 2020 from http://natsihec.edu.au/about/

Parbury, N. (1991). *Survival: A history of Aboriginal life in New South Wales.* Surry Hills, Australia: New South Wales Department of Aboriginal Affairs.

United Nations. (2007). *United Nations Declaration on the Rights of Indigenous Peoples.* Retrieved 31 May 2020 from www.un.org/development/desa/indigenouspeoples/wp-content/uploads/sites/19/2018/11/UNDRIP_E_web.pdf

Universities Australia. (2013). *University student finances in 2012 – A study of the financial circumstances of domestic and international students in Australia's Universities.* Canberra, Australia: Universities Australia.

Part II

After UNDRIP

Japanese and Australian responses and possibilities

Chapter 6

Challenges and responses to UNDRIP in Australian and Japanese Indigenous education

Zane M. Diamond and Chizu Sato

Introduction: The impact of UNDRIP on the provision of education services in Japan and Australia

From deficit approaches through to assimilation and then to inclusion, it was not until Australia and Japan endorsed the *United Nations Declaration on the Rights of Indigenous Peoples* (UNDRIP) that the policy context has begun to reflect the aspirations of Indigenous Peoples. In Chapter 2, we suggested that Indigenous People have always developed teaching and learning styles that have been fit for their purpose of socialising children into Indigenous lifeways. As some of the oldest living cultures on the planet, progress and sustainable continuity attest to the effectiveness of these methods. During the imperial colonising periods, through to the more recent period of nation building in both countries, ways of teaching and learning that had been developed for other purposes, in other times, for other socio-political contexts in other geo-locations were transplanted and imposed on the Indigenous Peoples of Australia and Japan. In this era of disruption, the transition beyond the coercive aspects of imperial and colonial mindset into an as yet unknown post-imperial future has begun a process in both Japan and Australia whereby the methods of teaching and learning employed by Indigenous Peoples to communicate about their lifeways are undergoing a time of re-emergence.

Authors such as Kitchen, Hodson and Raynor (2013), Price (2012), Sarra (2011), and Thaman (2013) all argue that the capacity of schools to disrupt or maintain societal expectations about Indigenous education is centrally in the hands of principals and teachers. Even so, the education system continues to rely on information about Indigenous lifeways that has depended heavily on the codification work undertaken by non-Indigenous academics. This has been especially problematic for the formal education system because teacher educators and schoolteachers rely on this knowledge for the content of their curriculum. Two interrelated aspects are examined in this chapter, drawing on examples from Japan and Australia. The first aspect is about the mainstream formal schooling system and the policy, curriculum and pedagogy changes that have occurred since UNDRIP in Australia and Japan. The second is about how teacher education is responding post-UNDRIP to the training of pre-service teachers to have the professional skills, knowledge and understanding to engage with the aspirations of *UNDRIP*.

Post-UNDRIP schooling changes: Japan and Australia

Although we cannot say that a rights-based approach is enough to promote understanding of Indigenous lifeways in either society, UNDRIP has had a strong impact on reminding governments and, in particular, education ministries to consider the role of education for Indigenous Peoples. For example, many Ainu people still feel they are discriminated against, according to the country-wide questionnaire survey conducted by the Comprehensive Ainu Policy Office in Cabinet Secretariat (2016). Of 705 respondents, 72.1 per cent felt that there was discrimination or prejudice against the Ainu, and 78 per cent thought the reason behind such discrimination was insufficient understanding of Ainu history. Indeed, the Advisory Council for Future Ainu Policy (ACFAP) pointed out, in its 2009 report, that the government's modernisation policies seriously damaged Ainu culture, causing various disparities between Ainu and other Japanese in terms of living conditions and education.

In both Australia and Japan, education is recognised as playing a central role in changing the manner in which Indigenous Peoples are educated and how non-Indigenous People are taught about Indigenous lifeways. Anderson and Ma Rhea (2018) argue that, because of the adoption of UNDRIP, both nations are obliged to consider taking a rights-based approach to Indigenous education. They identify the need to have a clear pathway from policy to teacher practice in the classroom that has practical first steps for teachers, teacher educators and researchers to begin their journey towards understanding, respecting and approaching Indigenous education. They observe that acting now and:

> [B]y beginning on this journey that teachers, teacher educators and researchers will be able to contribute to a field of teacher practice that is still in its formative period. Unlike many other aspects of the teaching profession, the field of Indigenous Education is undergoing a transformation from a colonial to a rights-based approach. As yet, there is only a small but significant body of Indigenous education expertise that informs this new approach and we hope that the readers of this chapter will be part of these new approaches, informing both pedagogy and curriculum.
> (Anderson & Ma Rhea, 2018, p. 228)

Policy level changes

A major change in the formal school education sector can be observed in response to UNDRIP. In Japan, the House of Representatives and the House of Councilors of the Diet unanimously adopted the *Resolution to Recognize the Ainu as an Indigenous People* on 6 June 2008. The following month, the ACFAP was established, which included a recognised Ainu leader as a council member. After a year, the council published a proposal for future Ainu policy in which education policy was discussed under the heading 'Promotion of the public understanding' (Advisory Council for Future Ainu Policy, 2009). The challenges to be addressed in the educational context were: (1) few references to the Ainu existed in official courses of study; nearly all references were limited to history classes as part of lower-secondary Social Studies; (2) the content and length of textbook descriptions varied by publisher; (3) use of materials supplementary to the standard textbooks was very limited outside Hokkaido; (4) teachers were unsure how to teach the history of Ainu and what materials to use. In addition to its recommendations regarding these challenges, the council proposed that the research findings of academics be used to improve educational programmes on Ainu history and culture and the methods by which they were taught.

The Science Council of Japan (2011), a leading organisation within the Japanese scientific community, also published a report to promote understanding of the Ainu. The report stated that many measures could be taken to promote such understanding but the central vehicle of change would be to embrace content relating to the Ainu in education. It further argued that such education should be provided at all levels from elementary to high school and that it should be clearly prescribed in courses of study.

Curriculum changes

In Japan, the law requires school textbooks to be approved by the Ministry of Education, Culture, Sports, Science and Technology (MEXT). Most textbooks are created by private publishers, who are expected to show creativity in their production. These books are supposed to undergo an official examination by the Textbook Approval Research Council based on textbook examination standards and the relevant course of study. During the process of examination, the council sometimes requests publisher revise some content. Here we offer the example of discussions regarding the revision of two secondary history textbooks produced by the same publisher, one approved in 2010 and the other in 2014.

The textbook approved in 2010 states that the Meiji government enacted the *Hokkaido Former Aboriginal Protection Act* and 'took' land from the Ainu. However, the same publisher's textbook approved in 2014 for the same subject states that the Meiji government 'gave' the Ainu land. The publisher had changed the wording. The official course of study for secondary history at that time mentioned only that Ainu people should be dealt with as a people who conducted trade with Japan's northern regions, so specific explanations and descriptions of the Ainu depended on the publishers (Asahi Shimbun Digital, 2016). Despite 'taking' being the opposite of 'giving' and the fact that textbooks require detailed, balanced presentation, both versions were approved by MEXT, showing how deeply rooted this issue is.

Even so, one of the significant changes after UNDRIP is that, starting from the new course of study to be implemented for lower-secondary schools in 2021, teachers have to teach Ainu culture in addition to the history of Ainu trading. Indeed, MEXT has started to include the Ainu in school curricula not only as a form of cultural education but also as a way to learn about human rights issues. In elementary school textbooks, references to the Ainu increased from 8 references across three subjects, including Social Studies and Japanese, in 2013, to 13 references across five subjects in 2019 (Nippon Hosō Kyōkai Sapporo, July 2019).

In addition, the government has held several seminars concerning school textbooks on the Ainu in preparation for new textbooks for the new school subject. At the seminars, specialists provided briefings on Ainu history, culture, language, life and so on and shared that information with the textbook publishers to promote a proper understanding of the Ainu.

In Australia, the newly launched Australian Curriculum (ACARA, 2018) includes three cross-curriculum priorities (CCP) that, while not considered to be key learning areas, are supposed to be addressed by teachers and teacher educators across all 'established' cognate areas from Foundation to Year 10 (F-10) (ACARA, 2016 [2019]). One of the three cross-curriculum priorities is the study of Indigenous histories, languages and cultures, something that has been a policy preoccupation for the Australian government since colonisation (see also Chapter 2, this edition).

Only recently have discussions emerge about how to teach Indigenous content, who should teach it and for what purpose is it being taught. Ma Rhea and Russell (2012b) argued that Indigenous Education, in the training of their students at universities and in their ongoing professional development programmes, have needed to draw on two interrelated but separate bodies of knowledge when considering the needs of Indigenous students and clients. Their analysis suggested:

> The first comes from their professional, technical knowledge base, Indigenous Education as method. This is about pedagogical approaches, curriculum developments and assessment issues around the learning needs of Indigenous students and how to teach non-Indigenous students about Indigenous society. The second knowledge base is found in Australian Indigenous Studies.
>
> (Ma Rhea & Russell, 2012b, p. 20)

Analysis of the new Australian curriculum shows that there is very little guidance for teacher educators and teachers about how and where to include Indigenous content as a cross-curriculum priority, often appearing only in an elaboration of a particular aspect. As a total proportion of the knowledge 'real estate' reflected within the Australian Curriculum, topics about Indigenous lifeways continues to be dominated by the key learning areas. This is surprising when the Australian Curriculum 'sets the expectations for what all young Australians should be taught' (ACARA, 2018, para. 2). Some state and territory curricula have adopted more guidance for teachers in some learning areas but other subjects still do not include Indigenous perspectives. The question of how much content is enough is highly political and reflects the preferences of Ministers of Education and the broader majority Australian society.

Pedagogical challenges

In terms of teaching and learning strategies, as discussed in Chapter 2, Anderson and Ma Rhea (2018) argue for the need for teachers and academics to indigenise their pedagogy, not simply focus on the curriculum aspects of teaching. As discussed in Chapter 2, Aboriginal youngsters in Australia are socialised and given permission to wait until they feel they have internal mastery of something before they are prepared to demonstrate it. If a teacher pressures a child to demonstrate something before they are ready, which is a very common practice in the formal school classroom as a pedagogy, the teacher will find the child will back off and shut down. This is certainly not the case all the time. But it is something a teacher needs to keep in mind.

Similarly, if a teacher demonstrates relatedness and mastery, what they will find is that Aboriginal students will watch the teacher incredibly closely. They will start to mimic what the teacher is doing. They will learn by the mastery of the teacher to approximate that mastery themselves. This is an important pedagogical point about the influence of Indigenous approaches to teaching and learning on how young beings will relate to a teacher (relatedness), the scope of potential in pedagogy to recognise their autonomy, and will also demonstrate understanding that Indigenous People have of approaches to educating their young prior to colonisation, practices that have been maintained into the present.

Contemporary best practice example

Arguably, given the intentions and aspirations of the rights-based approach to education embedded in UNDRIP, the best policies and strategies should be developed by Indigenous education experts in collaboration with formal education systems. Such emerging examples have proven to be the most effective in recognising Aboriginal peoples' desire for their children to be educated in both ways of education. Lois Peeler (2017), sister of Hyllus Maris, provides one such example with the contemporary work being undertaken at Worawa Aboriginal College.

The work continues the visionary initiatives of Hyllus Maris (introduced in Chapter 2, this edition), who established a school in 1983 that was

Image 6.1 Presentation Day 2019 at Worawa Aboriginal College.
Source: Worawa Aboriginal College.

Aboriginal-controlled but worked within the requirements of the Victorian education system (Peeler, 2017). Post-UNDRIP, this school provides evidence of a sustainable, systemically compatible, successful school. The challenge facing education systems is to replicate this approach in a manner that is scalable while preserving the successful elements of this school.

The current principal of Worawa Aboriginal College, Lois Peeler, explains that the students need three things for a good future:

- pride and confidence in themselves and in culture
- strong education, especially in literacy and numeracy, but in all the main areas of school
- a safe, fit and healthy life-style (Peeler, 2019).

At Worawa Aboriginal College, the students are supported in culture, education and well-being and the college is led by Indigenous People.

Teacher education responses to UNDRIP

Anderson and Ma Rhea (2018, p. 207) argue, post-UNDRIP, that:

> The next critical step in the development of education surely needs to be the recognition of the importance of holistic education that brings the

Image 6.2 Dr Lois Peeler AM, executive director, Worawa Aboriginal College.
Photographer: Kate Baker.

child's world into the classroom in a respectful and culturally appropriate way. Such an approach would, by its principles, better meet the needs of not only Indigenous learners but all learners in Australian classrooms.

(p. 207)

Education of teachers who would teach perspectives of Indigenous lifeways is an important issue to be considered. Since the end of the Second World War, all teacher education programmes in Japan are provided at the university level and any national, public or private university can be equally involved in teacher education if their teacher education programmes are approved by the MEXT. As of 1 April 2019, 606 of a total 756 universities (80.2%) provided teacher education programmes at undergraduate level, which is the major route to the teaching profession.

One of the national, large, teacher education institutions offering students courses on Ainu history, culture and language is the Hokkaido University of Education (HUE). HUE has five campuses within Hokkaido with 5,055 undergraduate students enrolled in 2019 (HUE, n.d.a). Since many of the students are from Hokkaido, they have already learned about the Ainu before entering university. The courses on Ainu culture and language are included in the teacher education programme under the cluster of local area studies courses (HUE, n.d.b). Yasuyuki Tamai, a professor working at one of the HUE campuses, Kushiro Campus, explains the university's practice of teaching student teachers how to develop curricula using local materials (Tamai, 2013).

Image 6.3 University students visiting a museum to learn about the Ainu. Courtesy of Yasuyuki Tamai.

Although Kushiro is located in eastern Hokkaido, a depopulated rural area, there are local museums related to the Ainu, such as the Kussharo Kotan Ainu Folklore Museum (*Kussharo Kotan Ainu Minzoku Shiryōkan*) and the Ainu Folklore Museum (*Ainu Seikatsu Kinenkan*), among others. As Tamai observes, although teachers' professional knowledge and skills should be developed throughout their teaching lives, they do not always know about local museums. Instructors at HUE, therefore, guide their students to these museums and teach them how to incorporate local reference materials into school curricula.

Japanese classrooms are becoming increasingly diverse in practice, however, and living with various minorities in a multicultural society remains high on the policy agenda. This means there is a large gap that needs to be bridged between what is learning during teacher education and actual teaching in the classroom. Although Japan has no professional standards for teachers, the core curriculum for the teacher education programme was set in 2017 to provide common standards for some teacher education programme subjects. However, teaching in culturally diverse classrooms is mentioned only with regard to children with special educational needs, such as those whose first language is not Japanese. But teacher education has been slowly changing to accommodate new learning needs stemming from the revision of school curriculum after the UNDRIP.

As discussed, the mandatory teaching content of teacher education programmes in Japan was reviewed after almost 20 years, and the *Education*

Image 6.4 University students learning about the history of the Ainu at a museum. Courtesy of Yasuyuki Tamai.

Personnel Certification Act was amended in 2017. The Act was enacted in 1949 following the Second World War and drastically changed the country's teacher education system, bringing it in line with the new school education system. Since then, the Act has regulated teacher education programmes nationwide. The amendment to the teacher education system aimed to: (1) provide professional knowledge and skills that were better integrated than previously; (2) respond to rapid social changes; and (3) clarify the content of teacher education (MEXT, 2019). Subsequently, a core curriculum was introduced to set the mandatory teaching content of teacher education programmes nationwide. Thus, all teacher education programmes had to be revamped and re-approved in April 2019. The core curriculum is intended to unify the content of teacher education and secure a certain level of standardisation. Nevertheless, each university can create subjects customised to meet their own contexts in response to the new 'Course of Study', which will be introduced into elementary schools from 2020 and secondary schools from 2021. For example, Otani University, a private university with a long history in Kyoto, organised a subject called 'Together with Ainu People' for both elementary and secondary teacher education based on the university's Buddhism spirit (Otani University, 2019).

Individual instructors may, however, not create a special subject on Ainu teacher education programmes but incorporate discussion of Ainu topics in subjects such as 'Teaching Methods in Social Studies', 'Theory and Practice of Moral Education', 'Special Activities', and 'Seminar for Teaching Professions'. Although greater incorporation of Ainu issues is not prevalent so far, it may increase because of the recent considerable attention to the Ainu, created by the *Act on Promoting Measures to Realize a Society in Which the Pride of the Ainu People Is Respected* (Act No. 16 of 2019) (*Ainu Policy Promotion Act*).

As discussed in Chapter 2, prior to UNDRIP, there had been sustained advocacy undertaken by generations of Indigenous education experts to change the international policy landscape regarding the recognised rights of Indigenous Peoples in education. At the same time as Australia was considering whether to endorse UNDRIP, the *Melbourne Declaration on the Educational Goals for Young Australians* – the '*Melbourne Declaration*' (MCEETYA, 2008) – began a renewed effort to incorporate Indigenous histories and cultures into the Australian Curriculum. Influenced by the *Melbourne Declaration*, there are now, within that Australian schooling system, two guiding frameworks for changing the ways that teachers educate Indigenous children and young adults and educate non-Indigenous children and young adults about Indigenous lifeways. The first is the Australian Professional Standards for Teachers (APST) (Education Council, 2011 [2018]). The 'Standards' as they are now known have two specific focus areas – 1.4 and 2.4 – that require teachers at the graduate level to demonstrate skills, knowledge and understanding about Aboriginal and Torres Strait Islander education and lifeways. The other is the Australian Curriculum and its state and territory variations that guide teachers in the development of curriculum to include Aboriginal and Torres Strait Islander content into their work (ACARA, 2016 [2019]).

Chapter 7 will examine teacher education more closely, providing a case study of one approach to the development of these ideas within teacher education. Why is this important?

If a teacher or a teacher educator does not know the early imperial colonial history and the early schooling history of Indigenous People, it will be hard for them to understand the attitude held by local Indigenous People to current schooling. As was discussed in earlier chapters, care needs to be taken when developing curriculum materials for use by teachers and teacher educators. For example, it is best to develop a relationship with knowledgeable Indigenous People before a researcher or curriculum writer begins asking about the history of schooling in the local area.

Conclusion

Taking Australia and Japan as case examples, we have argued that UNDRIP has had an impact at the policy level and, to some extent, in the development of curriculum materials and the inclusion of perspectives on Indigenous lifeways within curriculum. Many challenges remain, particularly in the integration of pedagogical approaches with mainstream education theory and in undertaking the necessary research to provide empirical evidence to support the work.

Here we propose preliminary steps that need to be considered in order to review education from a new perspective that is emerging as a result of the challenges to the more coercive elements of the imperial and colonial education projects, following in part the endorsement of the UNDRIP by both countries. It is not possible, in this chapter, to cover 60,000 years of Indigenous lifeways and examine how to develop pedagogy and curriculum to meet modern needs. Even so, our research has found that there are a number of steps that education systems, teachers and teacher educators can take that are respectful to Indigenous learners in the classroom and are also able to provide accurate perspectives to non-Indigenous learners about Indigenous lifeways.

We note that, because Japan and Australia have endorsed the UNDRIP, in particular the relevant articles of interest to us, Articles 13 and 14 which focus on the education rights of Indigenous Peoples, the countries' education systems are beginning to evidence changes towards the education of Indigenous Peoples in policy, curriculum content and, to a more limited extent, pedagogical approaches.

We acknowledge an emerging critical element of success in this work, that is, education systems are forming education partnerships with knowledgeable Indigenous People who are also experts in education. Such partnerships will facilitate finding, planning and teaching positive, accurate examples of Indigenous contribution to Japanese and Australian societies. If teachers and academics are able to find reliable information and good resources on the web, how they plan their curriculum to include Indigenous perspectives will flow into their teaching practice. As Takegahara (1993, p. 292) pointed out: 'If official textbooks fail to even mention them, children will be given the impression that there is nothing of value to be learned about the Ainu'. We note that this has been changing rapidly since the advent of UNDRIP and that the education sector is now recognising, for example, the importance of presenting Ainu culture and history in teaching materials (i.e., school textbooks). The recently updated Australian Curriculum (ACARA, 2018) embeds Indigenous perspectives across the key learning areas and through a specific cross-curriculum priority to guide teachers in the development of the taught curriculum and its planning.

We also note that, post-UNDRIP, Indigenous People in both countries have increased their advocacy work to highlight the importance of including correct information about Indigenous People in Japan and Australia and we suggest that the voices and viewpoints of Indigenous People must be presented in Australian and Japanese school and pre-service teacher classrooms.

There is a significant gap in the technical aspects of pedagogy with respect to teaching Indigenous learners and teaching non-Indigenous children about Indigenous histories, languages and lifeways. We believe that, in both Japan and

Australia, this pedagogical work will be the future work to be undertaken as the education of Indigenous children responds to global developments.

References

Advisory Council for Future Ainu Policy. (2009). *Final report, provisional translation*. Retrieved 31 May 2020 from www.kantei.go.jp/jp/singi/ainu/dai10/siryou1_en.pdf.

Anderson, P. J., & Ma Rhea, Z. (2018). Rights-based Indigenous education in Australia: Evidence-based policy to pedagogy. In Barnes, M., Gindidis, M., & Phillipson, S. (Eds.). *Evidence-based learning and teaching: A look into Australian classrooms* (pp. 205–216). London and New York: Routledge.

Asahi Shimbun Digital. (2016). *Ainu minzoku kara tochi toriageta ataeta: kyōkasho kijyutsu henkō* [School textbook revision: Was land taken from or given to the Ainu?]. Retrieved 31 May 2020 from https://digital.asahi.com/articles/ASJ1N45K8J1NIIPE00R.html

Australian Curriculum, Assessment and Reporting Authority (ACARA). (2016/2019). *Cross-curriculum priorities*. Retrieved 31 May 2020 fromwww.acara.edu.au/curriculum/cross-curriculum-priorities

Australian Curriculum, Assessment and Reporting Authority (ACARA). (2018). *Australian curriculum*. Retrieved 31 May 2020 from www.australiancurriculum.edu.au/

Australian Human Rights Commission (AHRC). (2009). *United we stand – Support for United Nations Indigenous Rights Declaration a watershed moment for Australia*. Canberra, Australia: Australian Human Rights Commission. Retrieved 31 May 2020 from www.humanrights.gov.au/about/news/media-releases/2009-media-release-united-we-stand-support-united-nations-indigenous

Comprehensive Ainu Policy Office in Cabinet Secretariat. (2016). *Kokumin no Ainu ni taisuru rikaido ni tsuite no ishiki-chōsa* [Survey of the public understanding of the Ainu: A report]. Retrieved 31 May 2020 fromwww.kantei.go.jp/jp/singi/ainusuishin/pdf/rikaido_houkoku160322.pdf

Education Council. (2011/2018). *Australian professional standards for teachers*. Carlton, Victoria, Australia: Education Services Australia. Retrieved 31 May 2020 from www.aitsl.edu.au/docs/default-source/national-policy-framework/australian-professional-standards-for-teachers.pdf?sfvrsn=5800f33c_64

Freer, J. (2018). Teaching respect to support reconciliation. *Journal of International Education* (Nihon Kokusaikyoiku Gakkai Kiyo), *24*, 118–126.

Hokkaido University of Education (HUE). (n.d.a). *About the university: Student enrollment*. Retrieved 31 May 2020 from www.hokkyodai.ac.jp/eng/about/student_enrolment.html.

Hokkaido University of Education (HUE). (n.d.b). *Kyōin-yōsei katei ni tsuite* [Teacher training programme]. Retrieved 31 May 2020 from www.hokkyodai.ac.jp/faculty/intro/summary/teacher_annai.html.

Kitchen, J., Hodson, J., & Raynor, M. (2013). Indigenous teacher education as cultural brokerage: A university/first nations partnership to prepare Nishnawbe Aski teachers. *International Education Journal: Comparative Perspectives*, *12*(1), 119–134.

Ma Rhea, Z. (2018).Teaching and learning for multicultural societies: Reimagining pedagogical content knowledge. *Journal of International Education* [Nihon Kokusaikyoiku Gakkai Kiyo], *24*, 87–98.

Ma Rhea, Z., & Russell, L. (2012). The invisible hand of pedagogy in Australian Indigenous studies and Indigenous education. *Australian Journal of Indigenous Education*, *41*(1), 18–25. doi:10.1017/jie.2012.4

MCEETYA. (2008). *Melbourne declaration on educational goals for young Australians*. Melbourne, Australia: Australian Government. Retrieved 31 May 2020 from www.curriculum.edu.au/verve/_resources/National_Declaration_on_the_Educational_Goals_for_Young_Australians.pdf

Ministry of Education, Culture, Sports, Science and Technology of Japan. (MEXT) (March 2019). *Heisei sanjū-ichi nendo kara atarashii kyōshokukatei ga hajimarimasu* [New teacher education programmes starting in 2019]. Retrieved 31 May 2020 fromwww.mext.go.jp/a_menu/shotou/kyoin/1414533.htm.

Nippon Hōsō Kyōkai Sapporo. (2019). *Rainen shigatsu kara no shōgakkō kyōkasho ni Ainu minzoku no kijyutsu ga fueru* [Addition of further descriptions of the Ainu people in elementary school textbooks from April next year]. Retrieved 31 May 2020 from www.nhk.or.jp/sapporo/articles/slug-nebdc00e31b3e#top.

Otani University. (2019). *Gakubu – shikaku no shutoku* [Undergraduate programmes: Acquisition of qualifications]. Retrieved 31 May 2020 from www.otani.ac.jp/faculty/nab3mq000006fi5n-att/nab3mq000006fi7o.pdf.

Peeler, L. (2017). *Hyllus Maris: A visionary with a passion for education*. Retrieved 31 May 2020 from www.worawa.vic.edu.au/2017/01/hyllus-maris-visionary-passion-education/

Peeler, L. (2019). *Principal's welcome*. Retrieved 31 May 2020 from www.worawa.vic.edu.au/our-school/principals-welcome/

Price, K. (2012). Aboriginal and Torres Strait Islander studies in the classroom. In K. Price (Ed.). (2012). *Aboriginal and Torres Strait Islander education: An introduction for the teaching profession* (pp. 151–163). Port Melbourne, Melbourne: Cambridge University Press.

Sarra, C. (2011). *Strong and smart: Towards a pedagogy of emancipation*. London, England: Routledge.

Science Council of Japan. (2011). *Hōkoku – Ainu seisaku no arikata to kokuminteki-rikai* [Report: Future Ainu policy and the public understanding of the Ainu]. Retrieved 31 May 2020 from www.scj.go.jp/ja/info/kohyo/pdf/kohyo-21-h133-1.pdf.

Takegahara, Y. (1993). The Ainu in the new textbooks for social studies. In N. Loos & T. Osanai (Eds.). *Indigenous minorities and education: Australian and Japanese perspectives of their Indigenous peoples, the Ainu, Aborigines and Torres Strait Islanders* (pp. 288–297). Tokyo, Japan: Sanyusha.

Tamai, Y. (2013). *Hokkaido no hekichi no chiiki-sei o ikashita chiiki-kyōzai kaihatsu to karikyuramu kaihatsu no hitsuyōsei* [The need for local teaching materials and curriculum development utilizing regionality in remote areas of Hokkaido]. *Hekichi Kyōiku Kenkyū*, *68*, 1–12.

Thaman, K. H. (2013). Quality teachers for Indigenous students: An imperative for the twenty first century. *International Education Journal: Comparative Perspectives*, *12*(1), 98–118.

United Nations. (2007). *United Nations Declaration on the Rights of Indigenous Peoples*. Retrieved 31 May 2020 fromwww.un.org/development/desa/indigenouspeoples/wp-content/uploads/sites/19/2018/11/UNDRIP_E_web.pdf

Chapter 7

Embracing and resisting Indigenist perspectives in Australian pre-service teacher education

Peter J. Anderson, Zane M. Diamond, and Jeane F. Diamond

Australian teacher professionalisation in Indigenous pedagogy and curriculum

The nature and purpose of higher education is something that is never static. It is constantly evolving as it meets the needs of society. However, one area where there appears to be a high level of inertia is in the Aboriginal and Torres Strait Islander education space, particularly the areas of curriculum and pedagogy. Starkly absent is a consistent and credible content about Aboriginal and Torres Strait Islander lifeways in pre-service education. This is despite countless federal and state government initiatives and efforts by organisations such as Universities Australia that, in 2011, developed the *Indigenous cultural competency framework* (Universities Australia, 2017). This framework is directed by five guiding principles. The second principle states that 'All graduates of Australian universities will have the knowledge and skills necessary to interact in a culturally competent way with Indigenous communities' (Universities Australia, 2017, p. 9). The framework has provided a place marker for the inclusion of Aboriginal and Torres Strait Islander lifeways across the Australian higher education landscape, with varying degrees of success.

In parallel with these developments in the higher education sector, the Australian Institute of Teaching and School Leadership (AITSL) has been working to address the chronic lack of skills, knowledge, and understanding demonstrated by primary and secondary teachers in Aboriginal and Torres Strait Islander matters. Australian teachers currently must demonstrate competence in seven professional standards known as the Australian Professional Standards for Teachers (APST). Each standard has focus areas and descriptors that:

> [I]dentify the components of quality teaching at each career stage. They constitute agreed characteristics of the complex process of teaching. An effective teacher is able to integrate and apply knowledge, practice and professional engagement as outlined in the descriptors to create teaching environments in which learning is valued.
>
> (Education Council, 2011/2018, p. 6)

Table 7.1 Focus Area 1.4: Strategies for teaching Aboriginal and Torres Strait Islander students

Graduate	Proficient	Highly Accomplished	Lead
Demonstrate broad knowledge and understanding of the impact of culture, cultural identity, and linguistic background on the education of students from Aboriginal and Torres Strait Islander backgrounds	Design and implement effective teaching strategies that are responsive to the local community and cultural setting, linguistic background, and histories of Aboriginal and Torres Strait Islander students	Provide advice and support colleagues in the implementation of effective teaching strategies for Aboriginal and Torres Strait Islander students using knowledge of and support from community representatives	Develop teaching programmes that support equitable and ongoing participation of Aboriginal and Torres Strait Islander students by engaging in collaborative relationships with community representatives and parents/carers

Source: Education Council (2011/2018, p. 11).

Two specific focus areas, 1.4 and 2.4, have put the spotlight on the lack of skills, knowledge, and understanding of pre-service and practising teachers and have placed an expectation on university-level pre-service teacher education programmes to ensure that graduates are, at a minimum, able to demonstrate broad knowledge and understanding of each Focus Area. Focus Area 1.4 is one of the six focus areas in the section title: Professional Knowledge Standard *1: Know students and how they learn*. The expectation is that the newly graduated teacher will be able to 'Demonstrate broad knowledge and understanding of the impact of culture, cultural identity, and linguistic background on the education of students from Aboriginal and Torres Strait Islander backgrounds' (Education Council, 2011/2018, p. 11). As can be seen in Table 7.1, it is expected that teachers will increase their skills, knowledge, and understanding of this focus area during their career.

In Focus Area 2.4, the expectation is that the newly graduated teacher will be able to 'Demonstrate broad knowledge of, understanding of and respect for Aboriginal and Torres Strait Islander histories, cultures and languages' (AITSL, 2011, p. 13). Table 7.2 provides a guide for teachers about how they can demonstrate an increase in their skills, knowledge, and understanding of this Focus Area during their career.

This renewed focus about the lifeways of Indigenous Peoples and the teaching and learning approaches towards the education of Indigenous children and of non-Indigenous children about Indigenous lifeways has left teachers and the academics responsible for pre-service teacher education unprepared for the expectations about their skills, knowledge, and understanding of the field.

Table 7.2 Focus Area 2.4: Understand and respect Aboriginal and Torres Strait Islander people to promote reconciliation between Indigenous and non-Indigenous Australians

Graduate	Proficient	Highly Accomplished	Lead
Demonstrate broad knowledge of, understanding of, and respect for Aboriginal and Torres Strait Islander histories, cultures, and languages	Provide opportunities for students to develop understanding of and respect for Aboriginal and Torres Strait Islander histories, cultures, and languages	Support colleagues with providing opportunities for students to develop understanding of and respect for Aboriginal and Torres Strait Islander histories, cultures, and languages	Lead initiatives to assist colleagues with opportunities for students to develop understanding of and respect for Aboriginal and Torres Strait Islander histories, cultures, and languages

Source: Education Council, 2011/2018, p. 13.

Our research about teacher preparedness for these two focus areas (Ma Rhea, Anderson, & Atkinson, 2012; White, Ma Rhea, Anderson, & Atkinson, 2012) showed that, in the absence of appropriate education, unprepared teachers draw on questionable *ad hoc* and, often, culturally inappropriate knowledge learnt formally or informally in the past. We came to recognise a strong aspect of this as being the deficit approach to the education of Indigenous children, where the child or young adult learner is not regarded as having anything to bring into the classroom rather than the teacher needing to consider their own lack of understanding of the issues involved (also, see 'Deficit thinking in education' in the Glossary, this edition).

We also found that, in some cases, Indigenous content is covered begrudgingly as a 'tick the box' exercise in political correctness. As was examined closely in Chapters 1 and 2 (this edition), Indigenous Peoples and their lifeways are founded in ancestry, ethnicity, and socialisation into a community and, as such, the lifeways of Indigenous Peoples are not a sociological category but rather are the lived experiences of millions of Indigenous people over time. We argue that education faces a systemic crisis which we directly attribute to the absence of sufficient numbers of Aboriginal and Torres Strait Islander expert knowledge holders engaged in policy formulation, pedagogical leadership, curriculum design, and as recognised Lead or Highly Accomplished Teachers in schools.

The current teaching profession received little preparation for the expectations of Focus Area 1.4 or 2.4. As Ma Rhea and Russell (2012) argued, most schools and faculties of education responsible for preparing pre-service teachers drew on curriculum content developed in Indigenous Studies and often left the teaching of Indigenous content to the staff from other faculties. Sustained research carried out over a number of years by Anderson and

Ma Rhea demonstrates that post the *United Nations Declaration on the Rights of Indigenous People* (UNDRIP), there continues to be a strong deficit colonial imperial mindset that shapes approaches to APST Focus Area 1.4 in both policy and practice. Over time, it has been identified that there is a significant lack of research about the technical aspects of pedagogy, curriculum development, and assessment approaches when examining the field of Indigenous Education, which is in stark contrast to the field of Education generally (Anderson & Ma Rhea, 2018). This is particularly true of remote Indigenous school communities that continue to suffer greater educational disadvantage including higher teacher turnover, low retention rates, less community confidence in the benefits of education, limited cultural facilities in the community, lack of employment opportunities for school completers, and a less relevant curriculum (Lamb, Glover, & Walstab, 2014). The significance of these issues is that they lead to lower levels of education attainment and less opportunity for Aboriginal and Torres Strait Islander students to attend post-secondary and university education (Pont et al., 2013, p. 6).

In parallel, Moreton-Robinson and colleagues (2012) were commissioned to conduct a desktop audit of all universities' pre-service teacher training and review the Australian and international literatures appropriate to this area of study. They found that there is a pattern within the Australian, Canadian, and US literature showing a separation and imbalance between Indigenous content and the transfer of effective teaching skills in pre-service teacher education; there is a lack of empirical evidence in the literature to substantiate the claims being made for the transformative effect of Indigenous Studies; there is a paucity of Australian and international Indigenous education literature analysing the impact of racism on Indigenous educational outcomes; the majority of universities, mindful of commercial and marketing imperatives, restricted information regarding unit content in order to entice further contact with potential students; there is clearly a drive to embed Indigenous content within core pre-service teacher education subjects; and, the provision of Indigenous elective courses across institutions is clearly inconsistent (Moreton-Robinson et al., 2012, pp. 4–5).

These findings resonated with those of our research and, importantly, focused on pre-service education. Arguably, it is pre-service teacher education programmes that will support new graduates to leave university with the skills, knowledge, and understanding to demonstrate Focus Areas 1.4 and 2.4 into the future. In this chapter, we discuss a specific case study at Monash University where the authors were the developers, leaders, and lecturers of units of study that were specifically designed to address the expectations of Focus Areas 1.4 and 2.4 arising from the findings of both research projects.

Conceptual framework

In this chapter, we first outline our conceptual approach to the work. We draw on an Indigenist, rights-based approach to develop the curriculum and our pedagogical approach to the task.

A rights-based approach

Our approach is underpinned by the acknowledgement that Australian Indigenous Peoples have never ceded their claim to sovereignty over their land and water resources. Their estates were forcibly taken from them through a declaration by the English Crown of sovereign domain. The application of English land law provides a key to re-thinking how we teach about and understand the lands and waterways that surround us. As Pearson (1997) so wryly observed:

> Of all the miserable cargo that ever left the shores of England for the Antipodes, there are three I celebrate as amongst the finest imports: that sublime game cricket, Earl Grey's tea, and the common law of England.
> (p. 150)

What does this mean for us as teacher educators living on large and small islands of Gondwana surrounded by the Great Southern, Pacific, and Indian Oceans on a landmass within the Asian region?

Since the early days of the most recent period of colonisation by British and European powers, the educational needs of Indigenous Peoples have been largely ignored at the expense of educating them to fit in with new colonial arrangements. The activities of teaching and learning, pedagogy, curriculum, and assessment have been geared to meet the needs of the settler colonial society. We note that the overarching approach to Indigenous Education has been the deficit model in which Indigenous students are somehow 'helped' to become successful in mainstream society. We use the ideas of deficit thinking in education to highlight education theories and practices that approach the learner as 'falling short, having a deficiency' rather than considering that it is the education system that might be failing the learner (see 'Deficit thinking in education' in the Glossary, this edition). We are not arguing against becoming successful but that Indigenous students are able to grow up 'both ways strong', being confident in both their Indigenous knowledge and their Western knowledge.

The fundamental shift that we have brought to this work is to move away from the deficit approach and ground our curriculum development work in a rights-based orientation. We begin with a discussion about agreed international instruments. We then provide an important perspective on the impact on on-going legal decisions in Australia concerning Indigenous land rights and other substantive matters impacting curriculum and pedagogy. We begin with *Universal Declaration of Human Rights*, which – as Mick Gooda (in Australian Human Rights Commission [AHRC], 2012, at 2:42), former Aboriginal and Torres Strait Islander Social Justice Commissioner, points out – applies to Indigenous Australians because they are human beings. In 2019, Aboriginal and Torres Strait Islander Social Justice Commissioner June Oscar AO launched the *Hear Us, See Us* exhibition at the UN Human Rights Council in Geneva, Switzerland (AHRC, 2019), embedding the aspirational aspects of UNDRIP into the fabric of the work of the AHRC in promoting the importance of formal, mainstream education as a vehicle for change. UNDRIP enshrines the right of Torres Strait Island and Aboriginal people to control their own education. For example, the AHRC (2010) explains Articles 13 and 14 in this way:

Our ways of being and knowing (article 13)

We have the right to revitalize, use, develop and pass on to future generations our ways of being and knowing. This includes:
- our histories and our oral traditions
- our languages and ways of communicating
- our ways of thinking about the world
- our names for communities, people and places.

Governments should take steps to make sure this right is protected. Governments should make sure there is a two-way understanding when dealing with our people, including that:
- we are able to understand what is being said by all parts of government
- governments are to make every effort to understand us in that process. When needed, interpreters are to be used to support this two-way understanding.

(p. 33)

Education (article 14)

We have the right to access the same standard of education as all other Australians.

We have the right to own and control our schools and educational institutions. We have the right to teach and learn in our own languages and in a way that is culturally appropriate. Governments should work with us to help those of us who are living away from their communities to learn culture and language. The right to education is especially important for children.

(p. 36)

From 2009, Anderson developed a process of continuous improvement based on Kotter's (2007; see also Kotter & Cohen, 2002; Collarbone, 2005) approach to support the evaluation of the suite of Indigenous Education units. From an organisational leadership perspective, he found Kotter's (2007) eight-step approach for leading a successful change to be a good way of identifying and beginning to understand the relationship between policy drivers, positive enablers of change, (Ford & Ford, 1995; Gellerman et al., 1990; Whelan-Berry & Somerville, 2010), and resistance to change (Piderit, 2000). We applied Kotter's principles in evaluating student responses to our teaching.

Between 2009 and 2017, we conducted a yearly retreat with all teaching staff, together with Indigenous and other education sector 'critical friends', to consider a range of evaluation data that would guide the changes we would then implement in the following year. Such data included: informal feedback from students in class and after class; student feedback to the discussion fora set up on Moodle; data from mid-semester formative feedback from students based on the same themes as used in the formal university-wide Student Evaluation of Teaching Units (SETU) survey. These data were used in conjunction with the feedback from tutors, sessional lecturers, and mentor teachers, together with the insights from Indigenous education experts. We regarded the engagement of Indigenous education experts with the teaching staff as being of paramount importance to the success of the suite of units in Indigenous Education. Representatives who have been involved include the Victorian Aboriginal Education Association Incorporated (VAEAI), the Department of Education Victoria, a member from the Toorong Marnong Committee (a consortium of the nine universities in Victoria, which is auspiced by the Victorian Vice Chancellors Committee), and education leaders of the Kulin Nations on which our campuses are located. The bringing together of such Indigenous Education experts to guide us ensured that relevant policy approaches as well as pedagogical, curriculum, and community needs were included at the core of curriculum development. Even so, the pre-service teachers sometimes rejected this approach for reasons we will explore later in the chapter.

Indigenist if not Indigenous

Our work also recognises that improvements to the education of pre-service teachers cannot be left to Indigenous people to do. Universities are staffed by teacher educators who are mostly non-Indigenous. In the past, it had been common to invite an Indigenous person to give a special lecture, but this approach rarely involves Indigenous people in the overall conceptualisation of the required teaching and learning outcomes. There are rarely assessment tasks attached to such 'guest lecture' spots and, therefore, although peripherally important to the overall education of the student, the content delivered by such 'guests' is not specified as part of the core learning outcomes. To understand the concept of 'expertise' in Indigenous education, it is absolutely necessary to conceptually differentiate between an individual's Indigeneity and their disciplinary knowledge.

There are very few Indigenous academics who specialise in the disciplinary field of Education, let alone have academic expertise in the field of 'Indigenous Education'. The majority of Indigenous academics in Australian universities specialise in other disciplines and fields. These academics are often invited as guest lecturers in order to fill a specific niche Indigenous gap in the curriculum. We note that there is a dire need for Indigenous people who are knowledgeable educators and who take an Indigenous rights perspective to be at the core of pre-service teacher education, based in faculties of Education. Furthermore, by extension, we also argue that academics, both Indigenous and non-Indigenous, need to develop Indigenous Education programmes of study to take an Indigenist perspective.

The concept of 'Indigenist' is used to describe Indigenous and non-Indigenous people who are committed to providing support for Indigenous rights and perspectives. The term 'Indigenist' implies a commitment to a pro-Indigenous worldview' (Ma Rhea, 2015, pp. 154–155). As part of our conceptual framework, we choose to use an Indigenist approach to our work as we have seen that such an approach helps pre-service teachers to develop Indigenist perspective, giving them an overarching framework for the required skills, knowledge, and understanding they need to make sensitive choices concerning resources, curriculum, and pedagogy. In turn, the Indigenist approach will help them to create culturally safe and respectful learning environments in line with the international undertakings of the Commonwealth Government of Australia and the global social justice community, as agreed by the United Nations concerning the education of Indigenous children.

Using a rights-based, Indigenist approach to evaluate resources and develop curricula

One of the biggest challenges is to teach pre-service teachers how to assess classroom resources, and an Indigenist, rights-based approach brings to the fore the core question of whose viewpoint is being presented and by whom. In our conceptualisation of the work, we considered that the voices and viewpoints of Aboriginal and Torres Strait Islander people should be presented to the students alongside views from non-Indigenous people. In both cases, we wanted to provide resources of the highest quality rather than items that are easily found in a Google search. Much of what has been available from Google has not been through the usual academic processes of legitimation that other curriculum materials have been subjected to. There is no Indigenous Education Association in Australia of similar calibre to other key learning subject associations such as Geography, Mathematics, and Literacy. Unlike such professional bodies that work to scrutinise and support teachers with up-to-date resources, in Indigenous Education, teachers and teacher educators are left to find their way through myriad resources. Unsurprisingly, they lack confidence to choose appropriate resources. The challenge facing us, the authors, was that this problem is significantly increased for pre-service teachers and their academic lecturers.

Since 2009, with the impact of UNDRIP and the willingness of schools to seek out culturally appropriate Indigenous materials, local Aboriginal Elders and Traditional Owners have been creating more classroom-ready materials, which they have made available in bookstores and online. This is making it increasingly easy for new teachers to find appropriate resources to use for teaching about Indigenous matters.

We recognise that it is crucial that the Indigenous people whose lifeways are being explored in the resources being offered have actually been consulted and have participated in the creation of the resource. The involvement of Aboriginal and Torres Strait Islander Peoples in the creation of educational resources about their lifeways is fundamental to Reconciliation (see Glossary and Chapter 12, this edition) as it disavows the 'expert' knowledge of outsiders speaking about 'the other', which was the model of early academic work from the time of the arrival of the British on Australian shores. The production and reproduction of the deficit perspective has been a legacy of the colonial education mindset as discussed in other chapters, and teachers and teacher educators will still draw on such materials because they have not changed the perspective from which they teach about Indigenous matters (see also, 'Deficit thinking in education' in Glossary, this edition).

Remembering the importance of putting the viewpoints and voices of Aboriginal people at the centre and forefront of any lesson, therefore, became crucial. One of the challenges for teachers when teaching about Aboriginal histories is to keep the focus on Aboriginal Peoples themselves. Another conundrum for teachers is that while they are to teach respect for Aboriginal and Torres Strait Islander lifeways they are *not* empowered to teach Indigenous cultures and languages. They are tasked with teaching *about* cultures and languages, which can often require a great deal of self-reflective restraint in an enthusiastic young teacher.

Furthermore, many scholars and entrepreneurs have made careers and businesses gathering information and artefacts about Aboriginal culture and selling them back to academia and other outlets. In doing so, it is rare that any Aboriginal or Torres Strait Islander individuals, families, or communities receive any benefit. No payment is generally made for sharing of knowledge or providing experience, and no acknowledgement is given for intellectual property. This model is another core element of the colonial mindset, one that the rights agenda in education is committed to eliminating from the curriculum. Therefore, in our conceptual framework, we emphasised to pre-service teachers that any resources they use, either for their own understanding or to present to pupils in their classrooms, should be created and controlled by Aboriginal people and Torres Strait Islanders themselves. The content must genuinely reflect the Indigenous Peoples being discussed and, therefore, if possible, it is also wise to verify the correspondence of locale between the owners of a resource and the information it contains. As this is often beyond the competence of pre-service teachers, they are advised to make use of websites and texts that have been validated by Aboriginal educationalists. As will be shown later, many students rejected this core element of our teaching philosophy, choosing instead to use culturally inappropriate Google-sourced resources as they do for their other subjects.

Towards an evidence-based Indigenist, rights-based pedagogical and curriculum design

Based on the findings of our research for AITSL (Ma Rhea, Anderson & Atkinson 2012), we began the process of developing the units of study. By 2013, we knew from responses of students that there was a need to build the confidence of these pre-service teachers. From the research and in discussion with Indigenous education experts throughout Australia, we designed topics of work to address *Focus Area 2.4: Protocols of Engagement, Language and Culture, Identity, History, Policies and Practices, and Aboriginal and Torres Strait Islander Societies.*

The students were to approach each topic using a theme: Rights, Language, or Celebration. In this way, we anticipated that there would be deeper engagement with each topic. We designed the second half of the topics for these units around specific elements that are known to affect successful learning outcomes for Indigenous students (Focus Area 1.4). The critical innovation we made was to move the focus away from deficit thinking that focused on what Indigenous students cannot do towards a focus on teacher responsibility for the skills, knowledge, and understanding to effectively engage with and teach Indigenous students. This led us to create new topics for the second half of the unit: Understanding Myself as a Culturally Competent Teacher; Understanding Learners and Learning; Developing Culturally Competent Curriculum; and Connecting through the Profession to Schools and Community.

An example of the Programme of Study shows how the Focus Areas could be addressed, with the first half engaging with the expectations of Focus Area 2.4 and then moving into Focus Area 1.4 for the rest of the semester.

Week 1: Introduction and Protocols of Engagement
Week 2: Culture and Language
Week 3: Identity
Week 4: History, Policies, and Practices
Week 5: Aboriginal and Torres Strait Societies
Mid-Semester Break
Week 6: No Class (Professional Experience)
Week 7: No Class (Professional Experience)
Week 8: Understanding Myself as a Culturally Competent Teacher
Week 9: Understanding Learners and Learning in Diverse Contexts
Week 10: Developing Culturally Responsive Pedagogy
Week 11: Critical Place-Based Learning and Curriculum
Week 12: Connecting through the Profession to Schools and Communities

Our idea was that we needed to provide the students with a strong foundation of accurate knowledge about the histories, cultures, and languages of Australia's Indigenous Peoples before we embarked on thinking about the teaching and learning context and its most effective pedagogies (the subject of Focus Area 1.4). In addition to teaching Indigenous students effectively, Focus Area 2.4 requires teachers to be able to respectfully communicate about Australian Indigenous lifeways without in any way teaching these subjects directly, because it is not their right to do so. Students coming into units on Indigenous Education know very little about Indigenous matters. Some are open, but most are cautious, fearful, and sometimes resentful of having to take an Indigenous Education unit. Many students express a fear that they do not want to offend anyone but have no confidence in this subject. There are some who refuse to come to class, engage online with hostile and aggressive comments, or come to class and take the role of the 'devil's advocate', often prefacing their comments with this moniker. We collected such data at the beginning of each semester and then asked the students to reflect on their learning at the end of each semester. Their achievements are surprising to them, even to those who were initially reluctant or hostile. They willingly report that they had not expected to learn as much as they did and many also reflect that they were appalled at how little they knew about the topic. This feedback parallels the research findings from the AITSL study of teachers undertaken by us (Ma Rhea et al., 2012). Our challenge has been to develop approaches to teaching and learning that will build pre-service student teacher confidence in their professional and personal skills, knowledge, and understanding.

To enable this, we thought we were creating a supportive but challenging online and face-to-face environment that motivated students to learn. Over five years, the official SETU feedback from students (examined more closely in the next section) seemed to show that what we were doing was less well-received even after we had developed a scaffolded approach to foster student development. Nonetheless, they reported that some activities they liked. For example, at the beginning of each semester, tutors asked all the students to write down what they knew about Indigenous Education and where they learnt it from. Tutors also asked them to write down what they knew about Indigenous lifeways and where they learnt it. The response to both activities was virtually nothing and that what they knew was outdated. From this, our approach was to begin building their content knowledge based on UNDRIP and APST: know the content and how to teach it, in particular Focus Area 2.4: 'Understand and respect Aboriginal and Torres Strait Islander people to promote reconciliation[1] between Indigenous and non-Indigenous Australians'.

The first half of the unit focused on developing their ability to source and recognise culturally appropriate teaching resources for the pupils they will be teaching in future in their professional lives. We directed them to credible sources, such as websites developed by Indigenous cultural knowledge holders and those developed by public organisations that partner with Indigenous experts (such as the Australian Institute for Aboriginal and Torres Strait Islander Studies and television broadcasters NITV, SBS, and ABC). We encouraged their curiosity and independence in learning, offering workshops and online activities that give them the confidence as future teachers to be able to source reliable teaching resources across the key learning areas. Through the processes of didactic and peer learning, some students gradually gained the confidence to share their newfound knowledge with their colleagues. They frequently also became curious to learn from knowledgeable Indigenous parents and education experts – something we encouraged in support of their personal and professional development. Unfortunately, some students found the same activities and opportunities very confronting, annoying, and unhelpful. Each semester we received feedback that was starkly polarised – as will be discussed more fully in the next section.

The following example provides an insight into how we offered effective and empathetic guidance and advice to students in our teaching approach. In Week 1, we had a topic about Protocols of Engagement. We encouraged students to investigate local Aboriginal forms of 'Welcome to Country' in the school area where they would be undertaking their Professional Experience. We asked them to find examples of local Welcomes to Country and for them to contact local knowledgeable Aboriginal education experts, together with bureaucrats at at local councils, Aboriginal art venues, and so on who could guide them in the topic. From this they learnt the differences between a Welcome to Country and an Acknowledgement of Country. They then chose a resource that they had found (usually a YouTube clip of one of the Traditional Owner Welcomes to Country) to use as the resource to teach about this at an age-appropriate level to their pupils in the classroom and a brief reflection on how they might teach in a culturally respectful way. Their response to this topic allowed us to give tangible guidance to the students by uploading explanatory podcasts and providing targeted resources to support individual learning. Unsolicited student comments support the effectiveness of this approach for some. For example, one second year primary student said:

> I am really enjoying this unit the way the weekly tasks are really helping deepen my knowledge of Indigenous Education ... Peter's online podcasts and fora are also building my confidence.

Another wrote:

> Zane was able to explain how education of Indigenous people and being culturally sensitive is extremely important in the further professional development of myself as a teacher. This in turn motivated me to critically analyse the varying aspects that affect not only Indigenous education but education as a whole.

The reverse is also true. One student said:

> In this subject I felt anxious and unmotivated to complete the tasks through the teachers comments from my assignments and in class. I didn't feel comfortable participating in the class for being scared to say something that may offend or cause confusion. I think that the class structure and the way the content is presented needs to be informational and not attacking us as students who are here to learn and not feel like in detention.

And another reported:

> I found this unit was very unclear of what was wanted from us. We got thrown into doing assignments without actually understanding what was wanted of us then the feedback we received was unclear/all negative. I suggest that tutors give a clear explanation of what is expected. Also, that feedback given is constructive.

This sort of poliarized messaging about our teaching was confronting almost every week of every semester, and very early on we decided to approach the task by making it a self-study of our professional practice. Over time, we realised that there were some common critical learning issues for the students that clearly conflicted with our pedagogical approaches.

An integrated participatory action research (PAR), self-study approach working with student feedback data

In order to address what we regard as a critical gap in research about the development of a programme of learning to address the expectations of the APSTs for Indigenous Education, in particular addressing Focus Areas 1.4 and 2.4, we undertook a critical self-study of our work together between 2013 and 2017. The methodology of 'self-study' has evolved over the past 30 years, emerging out of the field of Teacher Education (Hawley & Hostetler, 2017). We regarded this approach as well-suited to our context as they explain:

> The promise of self-study is improved educational practices through inquiry that leverages collaboration and context responsive design features for rich learning in and through practice.
> (Hawley & Hostetler, 2017, pp. 83–84)

In our practice and theorising of our work together as teacher educators with backgrounds in education (an Indigenous man and two non-Indigenous women – one born in Australia and one overseas), we wanted to capture our discussions and thinking in a way that could help us to not only understand and improve our work but also, in such a chapter, to invite readers into the 'behind the scenes' pedagogical thinking we employed to develop the teaching and learning programme for our students. We wanted to examine the potential of our engagement to navigate and understand what we wanted to do and, most important, how we could encourage our students to engage in the work. As discussed earlier, we employed an Indigenist rights-based approach to our pedagogical methodology to reflect the broader conceptual framing of the work.

Methods

Data collection

For this self-study, we adopted a narrative stance for both data collection and analysis (Creswell, 2015). Each teaching week, we undertook professional conversations about both curriculum and pedagogy and, from these conversations, we made mind maps together with notes taken during our reflection meetings. At the beginning of each semester, we would ask the students to 'butcher's paper' what they knew about Indigenous lifeways and Indigenous Education (anonymously), and at end of each semester we would ask them to repeat the task, adding comments on what they had learnt.

After teaching and marking had been completed, the teaching team would gather for a debriefing retreat to review the 'butcher's paper' feedback and student SETU feedback to incorporate these data into the development of the next semester of work. The end-of-semester retreats followed the Participatory Action Research (PAR) model of 'Think, Plan, Act, and Reflect' phases in a spiral (Reason & Bradbury, 2006; Wadsworth, 1993). Starting with reflection, we gathered our notes and conversations and collated and analysed the SETU and open feedback data (see next section). From our analysis, we would then move to a planning stage which, over the next semester, would involve the 'Act' phase, and later moving at the end of the next semester to a reflect phase again.

We also documented our experiences and thoughts over the period of four years from 2013 to 2017 at the retreats and weekly debriefing meetings and shared our reflections with one another. In preparation sessions for the following semester, we also 'butcher papered' some of these conversations, mapping thoughts, emotions, and connections as we grew our understanding of what we were trying to achieve. Using both our self-study data and student feedback, we tried to better understand the overarching patterns of response from students and to navigate improvements to the programme of work while avoiding having a defensive response to hostile feedback. Interestingly, the self-study element of this work enabled us to get a perspective on hostile and sometimes personally attacking comments within the context of what is difficult and complex work. As discussed, our self-study questions were both triggered and framed by our commitment to shift the pedagogical content knowledge of our students in the Indigenous Education space.

Data analysis

In our PAR conversations, informed by discussions about critical self-study and PAR (International Workshop on Participatory Action Research, 2006), we challenged each other to explore more deeply our assumptions and misunderstandings in the cultural interface that is Indigenous Education. We identified similarities and differences between our experiences. The main focus was to examine the evolution of our own thinking about how to develop a programme of study that would demonstrate that graduates could meet the expectations of Focus Areas 1.4 and 2.4, succeeding both in meeting the institutional demands of the task and preserving our commitment to use an Indigenist rights-based conceptual framework. We also triangulated our self-study data with SETU and open feedback data from students.

Descriptive statistical analysis was done on the SETU data over the years 2013–2017. We provide a detailed examination of one example of a 'Red Unit' requiring 'critical attention' in this chapter. To further examine these data and documents, we gathered all the various examples of content descriptions and guidance into a Word document that we then analysed using Leximancer, a software tool that performs a computer-aided content analysis and, thus, goes beyond a simple keyword search (Poser, Guenther, & Orlitzky, 2012; Smith & Humphreys, 2006, p. 262). Such software allows for the analysis of the semantic and contextual structure of selected data. Hence, we were able to gain a view of the semantic context of student feedback within these various data sources. Conceptually related concepts are grouped by a theme. As Smith and Leximancer (2018) note:

> Leximancer is a text analytics tool that can be used to analyse the content of collections of textual documents and to display the extracted information visually. The information is displayed by means of a conceptual map that provides a bird's eye view of the material, representing the main concepts contained within the text as well as information about how they are related.
>
> (p. 3)

With Leximancer, one can use different theme sizes which address the generality of the themes. In this chapter, to enable comparison across different data sources, we chose a theme size of 52 per cent. We display all concepts on the map (100 per cent visibility), which means all identified concepts are found on the map not just the most frequent ones.

Understanding student feedback data

We framed our self-study analysis each semester around the feedback from a total student enrolment of over 500 per year in the compulsory units. Not all students completed the SETU or open feedback sections each semester, so the data is more descriptive and indicative rather than representative in the statistical sense. The subjects included in our study were: the compulsory undergraduate unit, EDF2031 Indigenous Perspectives in Teaching and Learning; the more developed, graduate-focused unit EDF 4513, Indigenous and Traditional Education in a Post-colonial World; and the postgraduate elective unit, EDF5657 Indigenous Perspectives in Professional Practice.

Leximancer analysis identified that there were both strongly positive responses and strongly negative ones. The analysis of the student feedback generated conceptual maps with two positive and two negative key concepts (see Leximancer-generated concept maps). The positive key concepts were Aboriginal and Respect with which all the other concepts related strongly. The negative feedback focused on far more generic aspects clustered around the 'Student' key concept and the other revealed that they had a keen interest in knowing what was important in relation to other concepts being taught.

The key concepts identified by those students giving positive feedback focussed on 'Aboriginal' and 'Respect' as displayed in Figure 7.1. We identified these responses as 'Embracing' the teaching and learning that was occurring in the classroom. The key concepts identified by those students giving negative feedback focussed on 'Student' and 'Important' as displayed in Figure 7.2. We identified these responses as 'Resisting' the teaching and learning that was occurring in the classroom. Significantly, and an issue for our analysis using Leximancer, there were numerous messages across these data within the open student feedback marked as '**#redacted content#**' by the Faculty Associate Dean (Education) and we suspect that the picture could have been far more graphically 'hostile' had these comments also been included.

When comparing the key concepts of 'Aboriginal' and 'Student' (Figure 7.3), we noted that many of the same concepts were related to the word chosen by the student with some being able to embrace our pedagogical and content focus on Aboriginal matters while others transformed our approach into the more familiar 'Student' focus with Indigenous being one aspect.

We interpret this to suggest that the positive comments from students having a key focus on 'Aboriginal' were related to their ability to privilege the Indigenous student and Indigenous perspectives, thus shifting the overwhelmingly dominant approach that would be more familiar in a pre-service teacher education course, more likely to be represented by the graphic Figure 7.2 where the conceptual focus remained on the key word of 'Student'.

Discussion

The specific change we were seeking to address both pedagogically, and in the resources they chose, was for students to move from a colonial mindset towards an Indigenist one that would enable the provision of education to Indigenous children that respects Australia's commitment to the UNDRIP. It is crucial that these new teachers understand the implications for them as teachers into the future in Australian schools. In deciding to adopt this target for change, we implemented our self-study approach using PAR and found it useful as a frame for our continual improvement approach. We had two simple goals: first, for students to successfully progress through this unit of work in order for them to be effective teachers in the Indigenous domain, able to demonstrate a graduate

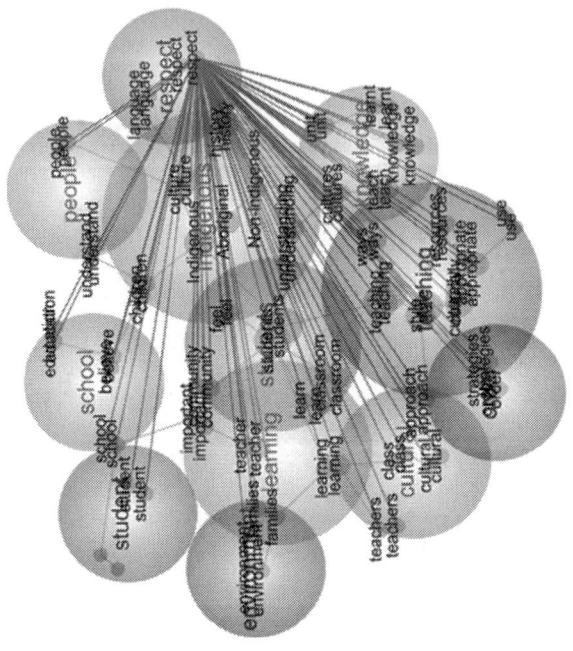

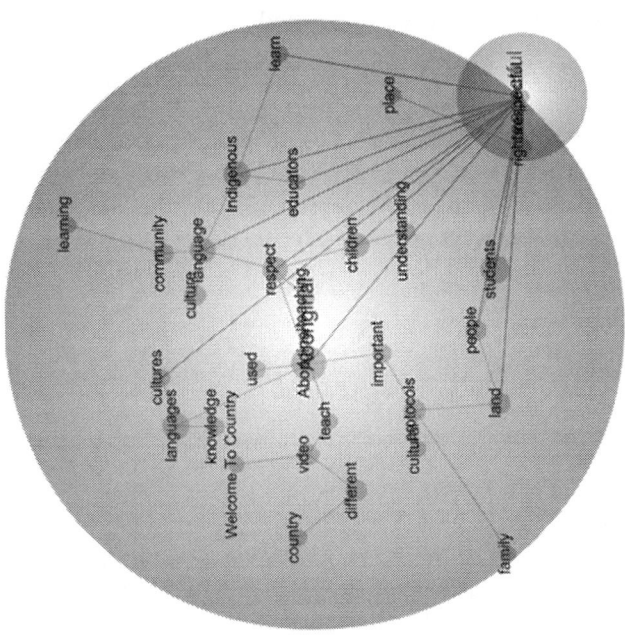

Figure 7.1 The 'Aboriginal' and 'respect' key concept maps.

Source: Authors.

Indigenist perspectives in teacher education 143

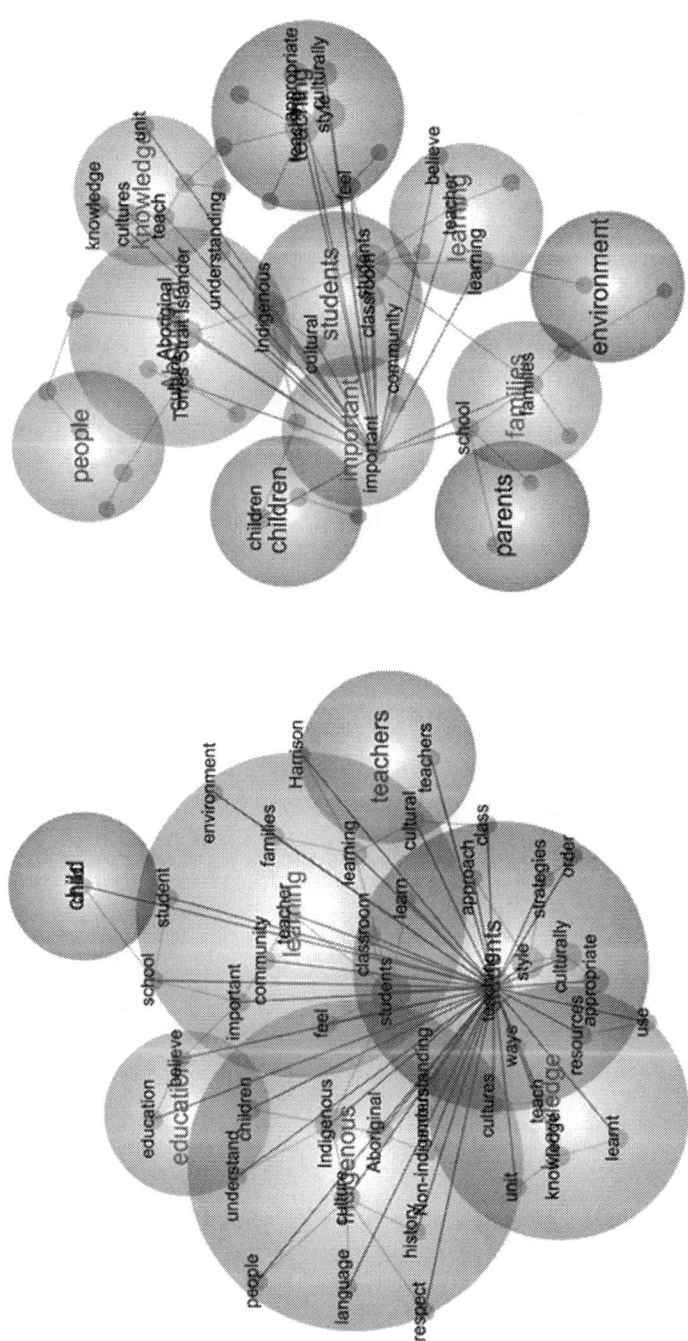

Figure 7.2 The 'student' and 'important' key concept maps.

Source: Authors

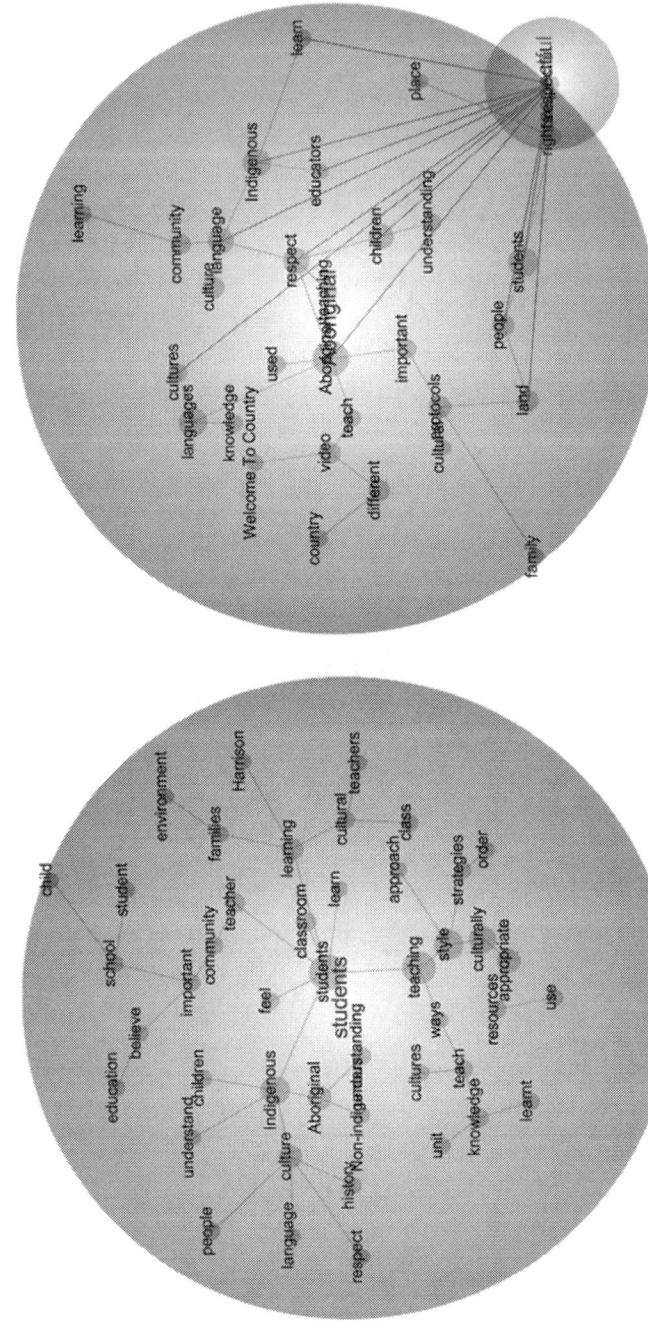

Figure 7.3 Difference of associated concepts with key word as 'Aboriginal' and 'student'.
Source: Authors.

level in the APST Focus Areas 1.4 and 2.4, in particular; and, second, for them to undertake the targeted change we had as the foundation for our teaching.

We employed evaluation strategies that would support change, using the data to guide our Think, Plan, Act, and Reflect approach. To inform ourselves on whether we are meeting our change target, we analysed their summative feedback. We could see from an analysis of their comments whether they understood or not the need for them to change the ways they had previously thought about Indigenous Education. Clearly, our approach was working for the 'Embracing' students, but we found that there was a consistently 'Resisting' group of students who rejected our rights-based approach, pedagogical methodology, and scaffolding of their learning. Our analysis suggested that they clearly wanted to remain within the teaching and learning paradigm fostered across their other units of study and, in their perception, supported by their social networks.

As can be seen in the example (see Table 7.3, n=50), the danger for us was that their negative summative feedback regularly took us into the 'Red Unit' category, as highlighted by the yellow-marked Median scores, the consequence of which was that the faculty's unit review processes regularly required us to produce a new plan to address the lack of satisfaction expressed by 49–51 per cent of the student group, even though their feedback was inconsistent between semesters and often contradictory. The constant demand for new plans also stopped us from being able to gain traction with evidence-based strategies that we were trying to embed.

Interestingly, while Leximancer analysis revealed clear differences between 'Embracers' and 'Resistors' in terms of the conceptual work of the unit, the summative SETU data caused us to repeatedly develop plans to improve our 'Instructions for Assessment' tasks and the 'Feedback that helped students to

Table 7.3 An example of SETU feedback: University-wide items (summary)

University-wide items	Responses	Median
The learning outcomes were clear to me	25	3.00
The instructions for the Assessment tasks were clear to me	24	2.17
The assessment in this unit allowed me to demonstrate the learning outcomes	25	3.08
The Feedback helped me achieve the Learning Outcomes for this unit	25	1.63
The Resources helped me achieve the Learning Outcomes for this unit	25	3.19
The Activities helped me achieve the Learning Outcomes for this unit	24	3.06
I attempted to engage in this unit to the best of my ability	25	4.08
Overall, I was satisfied with this unit	25	2.40

Source: Authors.

achieve the Learning Outcomes' of this unit in order to improve their 'Overall Satisfaction'.

Our strategy here was to improve our communication through our Unit Guide and online Moodle materials. Evaluation data suggested that even students who were not openly hostile did not have sufficient knowledge of the Indigenous world to be confident learners. We asked students in class after class and through online fora to tell us what they wanted to see in the Unit Guide and on Moodle that would help them to become confident learners. Their consistent message was 'clear communication'. We also recognised, as part of our overall change strategy, that people who do not feel confident will not easily learn anything new, so most of our work here was to gauge how to reduce student anxiety through clear, consistent communication.

To this end, each week, we met as a teaching team to reflect on the concerns and anxieties of the students (as expressed in class and online), something that only lessens once the marks for the first assignment have been received. Evidence that our PAR-inspired evaluation strategies to bring about change have been more successful than the consistently negative summative evaluation suggested each semester was that most students produced a wonderful final presentation that captured their sometimes-challenging learning journey.

Over the years of this research, our summative scores remained very negative even as we strove to improve on the aspects reported by students to be of concern. In considering the larger pool of data, it became clear to us that half of any student cohort did not want to make the conceptual transition on which we based our pedagogical methodology. In the same summative report, we received the following feedback:

> The content was interesting, doing lesson plans for assignment 1 were good as it is practical and helps me prepare for teaching. I found the protocols very helpful and the unit was great overall for my understanding of Aboriginal and Torres Strait Islander people.

And:

> [B]ig changes need to be made to this unit, i know i am one of many who are disappointed with this unit and the tutor's attitudes. I found them intimidating and was unable to feel they were approachable at all. we were not told how to pass the assignments, we were only told how we would fail, i had no idea what i was doing with the assignments because they were not clearly explained to us at all. the inconsistent marking for assignments does not make sense to me, many of my fellow colleagues and friends had such inconsistent marking for similar assignment responses. we just didn't know what we were doing wrong half the time as the feedback wasn't helpful either. i got a few great marks and the feedback was so negative i wondered how i got a good mark with the written feedback attached to it. felt the

unit was ¾ unfair overall, however the content was interesting, it was just the way it was delivered that needs to be improved.

Conclusions

As noted, we reflect that there is a dire need for Indigenous people who are knowledgeable educators who take an Indigenous rights perspective to be at the core of pre-service teacher education, based in faculties and schools of education. Furthermore, by extension, we argue that it is important for academics – both Indigenous and non-Indigenous – who are developing Indigenous Education programmes of study to take an Indigenist perspective. It is rare, in an Australian university, for Indigenous education experts to be centrally involved in the development of specialist units of study for pre-service teachers. We believe this will be a necessary ingredient in future.

We also have learnt that there is need for teacher educators to develop an Indigenist approach that recognises the rights of Indigenous Peoples to be centrally involved in the education of their children. There is a similar lack of knowledgeable non-Indigenous academics who are able to teach about the lifeways of Indigenous Peoples and, especially, Aboriginal and Torres Strait Islander Peoples' histories, languages, and cultures, and of culturally appropriate ways of teaching in the Indigenous education space.

The cognate area is severely undertheorised and lacking in sound empirical evidence (Anderson & Ma Rhea, 2018). The field of Indigenous Education requires more focused research to understand the most effective pedagogical methodologies to the scoping and sequencing of unfamiliar content (Focus Area 2.4) and of developing decolonial, Indigenist pedagogies (Focus Area 1.4). Until there is recognition at the government policy level of the need for sound, evidence-based approaches in Indigenous Education, the field will remain littered with diverse and conflicting opinions dressed up as 'good teaching'. Despite the guidance of UNDRIP, our research and analysis of student feedback demonstrates that resisting students fall easily into a deficit approach and are supported to do so under the banners of such theoretical trends as 'inclusivity', 'superdiversity', and 'identity'. The increased focus on improving the student experience that argues that Indigenous students must be 'school ready' does not automatically overcome 232 years of imperial and colonial education, and we argue that it will take some time to get schools and universities to be 'Indigenous' ready.

We have found, over the past years in this field, that without sound policy guidance based on empirical evidence, it will be difficult to undertake the fundamental changes that are required to prepare the new generation of teachers to move out of the deficit, colonial mindset towards an Indigenist, rights-based approach as advocated in this chapter. As a sector, we need to be encouraged to explore what a post-imperial, post-colonial provision of teacher training in the education of Indigenous students and young adults might look like. Until then, the consistent experiences we had of receiving hostile, resistant student feedback will continue. How is it possible for academics to take this sort of approach when their employing universities have an institutional aversion to poor student feedback?

Finally, we suggest that the methodology we adopted by undertaking a self-study PAR approach to our work has been beneficial and that Leximancer, because it assisted us to analyse the semantic and contextual structure of selected data, was able to help us understand complex and disparate student feedback and overcome our sometimes-defensive reactions to their hostility and personal attacks. For the 'Resistors', we can only hope that they are able to reflect on the ideas and concepts presented to them in their Indigenous Education specialist unit and, once in their classrooms, be able to understand the import of those lessons. For the 'Embracers', there was much to celebrate in their reported positive learning experiences and we continue to receive wonderful emails from them as they enter the profession and begin to forge their identities and professional practice as teachers.

Note

1   While beyond the scope of this chapter, we acknowledge the idea of Reconciliation to be a term rejected by many Indigenous people who say they have nothing to reconcile. This matter is discussed more fully in Chapter 12 (see Glossary).

References

Anderson, P. J., & Ma Rhea, Z. (2018). Rights-based Indigenous education in Australia: Evidence based policy to pedagogy. In M. Barnes, M. Gindidis, & S. Phillipson (Eds.). *Evidence-based learning and teaching: A look into Australian classrooms* (pp. 207–228). London, England: Routledge.

Australian Human Rights Commission (AHRC). (2010). *Community reference guide to the UN Declaration on the Rights of Indigenous Peoples.* Canberra, ACT: Australian Human Rights Commission. Retrieved 31 May 2020 fromwww.humanrights.gov.au/sites/default/files/document/publication/declaration_community_guide.pdf

Australian Human Rights Commission (AHRC) (Producer). (2012). *UN Declaration on the Rights of Indigenous Peoples.* [YouTube video] Retrieved 31 May 2020 fromwww.youtube.com/watch?v=bB2uZxekt-k

Australian Human Rights Commission (AHRC) (Producer). (2019). *See us hear us.* Retrieved 31 May 2020 from www.humanrights.gov.au/about/news/hear-us-see-us-exhibition

Collarbone, P. (2005). Policy forum: Government policy and performance of schools. *Australian Economic Review, 38*(1), 75–82.

Creswell, J. W. (2015). *Educational research: Planning, conducting, and evaluating quantitative and qualitative research.* Sydney, Australia: Pearson.

Education Council. (2011/2018). *Australian professional standards for teachers (APST).* Carlton, Victoria, Australia: Education Services Australia. Retrieved 31 May 2020 from www.aitsl.edu.au/docs/default-source/national-policy-framework/australian-professional-standards-for-teachers.pdf?sfvrsn=5800f33c_64

Ford, J. D., & Ford, L. W. (1995). The role of conversations in producing intentional change in organizations. *Academy of Management Review, 20*(3), 541–570.

Gellerman, W., Frankel, M. S., & Ladenson, R. F. (1990). *Values and ethics in organizational and human systems development: Responding to dilemmas in professional life*. San Francisco, CA: Jossey Bass.

Hawley, T. S., & Hostetler, A. L. (2017). Self-study as an emergent methodology in career and technical education, adult education and technology: An invitation to inquiry. *International Journal of Adult Vocational Education and Technology (IJAVET), 8*(2), 82–92. doi:10.4018/IJAVET.2017040107

International Workshop on Participatory Action Research. (2006). *Participatory action research, perceptions and practice*. Paper presented at the Research Initiatives, Bangladesh, Dhaka.

Kotter, J. (2007). Leading change, why transformations efforts fail. *Harvard Business Review* (January), *85*(1), 96–103.

Kotter, J. P., & Cohen, D. S. (2002). *The heart of change*. Boston, MA: Harvard Business Review Press.

Lamb, S., Glover, S., & Walstab, A. (2014). *Educational disadvantage and regional and rural schools*. Paper presented at the ACER Research Conference, Melbourne, Australia.

Ma Rhea, Z. (2015). *Leading and managing indigenous education in the postcolonial world*. London, England: Routledge.

Ma Rhea, Z., Anderson, P. J., & Atkinson, B. (2012). *National professional standards for teachers standards 1.4 and 2.4: Improving teaching in Aboriginal and Torres Strait Islander education*. Melbourne, Australia: Australian Institute for Teaching and School Leadership. Retrieved 31 May 2020 from www.aitsl.edu.au/tools-resources/resource/improving-teaching-in-aboriginal-and-torres-strait-islander-education-australian-professional-standards-for-teachers

Ma Rhea, Z., & Russell, L. (2012). The invisible hand of pedagogy in Australian indigenous studies and indigenous education. *Australian Journal of Indigenous Education, 41*(1), 18–25. doi:10.1017/jie.2012.4

Moreton-Robinson, A., Singh, D., Kolopenuk, J., & Robinson, A. (2012). *Learning the lessons? Pre-service teacher preparation for teaching Aboriginal and Torres Strait Islander students*. Melbourne, Australia: Australian Institute for Teaching and School Leadership. Retrieved 31 May 2020 fromwww.aitsl.edu.au/tools-resources/resource/learning-the-lessons-pre-service-teacher-preparation-for-teaching-aboriginal-and-torres-strait-islander-students

Pearson, N. (1997). The concept of native title at common law. In G. Yunupiŋu (Ed.). *Our land is our life, land rights – Past, present and future* (pp. 150–161). St Lucia, Australia: University of Queensland Press.

Piderit, S. K. (2000). Rethinking resistance and recognizing ambivalence: A multidimensional view of attitudes toward an organizational change. *Academy of Management Review, 25*(4), 783–794.

Pont, B., Toledo Figueroa, D., Zapata, J., & Fraccola, S. (2013). *Education policy outlook: Australia*. Paris, France: Organisation for Economic Co-operation and Development. Retrieved 31 May 2020 fromwww.oecd.org/education/EDUCATION%20POLICY%20OUTLOOK%20AUSTRALIA_EN.pdf

Poser, C., Guenther, E., & Orlitzky, M. (2012). Shades of green: Using computer-aided qualitative data analysis to explore different aspects of corporate environmental performance. *Zeitschrift für Planung und Unternehmenssteuerung, 22*(4), 413–450. doi:10.1007/s00187-011-0147-2

Reason, P. & Bradbury, H. (2006). *Handbook of action research*. London, England: Sage.

Smith, A. E., & Humphreys, M. S. (2006). Evaluation of unsupervised semantic mapping of natural language with Leximancer concept mapping. *Behavior Research Methods, 38*(2), 262. doi:10.3758/BF03192778

Smith, A. E., & Leximancer. (2018). Leximancer user guide 4.5. Retrieved 31 May 2020 from https://info.leximancer.com/tutorial-guides

United Nations. (2007). *United Nations Declaration on the Rights of Indigenous Peoples*. Retrieved 31 May 2020 from www.un.org/development/desa/indigenousPeoples/declaration-on-the-rights-of-indigenous-Peoples.html

Universities Australia. (2017). *Aboriginal and Torres Strait Islander education strategy 2017–2020*. Canberra, Australia. Retrieved 31 May 2020 from www.universitiesaustralia.edu.au/wp-content/uploads/2019/06/Indigenous-Strategy-v16-1.pdf

Wadsworth, Y., & Action Research Issues Association. (1993). What is participatory action research? Melbourne, Australia: Action Research Issues Association.

Whelan-Berry, K. S., & Somerville, K. A. (2010). Linking change drivers and the organizational change process: A review and synthesis. *Journal of Change Management, 10*(2), 175–193.

White, S., Ma Rhea, Z., Anderson, P. J., & Atkinson, B. (2012). *Design and development of a unit outline and content for professional learning units to support teachers in meeting Focus Areas 1.4 and 2.4*. Melbourne, Australia: Australian Institute for Teaching and School Leadership. Retrieved 31 May 2020 from www.aitsl.edu.au/tools-resources/resource/a-unit-outline-and-content-for-professional-learning-units-to-support-teachers-in-meeting-focus-areas-1.4-and-2.4

Chapter 8

Teacher education issues in Okinawa

Kengo Kakazu and Eisuke Saito

Introduction

Okinawa Prefecture is in the most southern part of Japan with a population of about 1.45 million. The area is about 2,281 km², the fourth smallest prefecture in Japan. The prefecture, once an independent country called the Ryūkyū Kingdom, prospered in times past through trade with neighbouring countries. In 1879, at the time of the Satsuma Domain, Japan invaded Okinawa and forced it to become a prefecture of Japan. After the Second World War, the prefecture remained under the rule of the US for 27 years.

The people in the prefecture have different cultural habits, languages, foods, political system, and music traditions from the majority Japanese population, which means that Okinawans are often treated as cultural others by the majority Japanese or, in other words, a minority group in Japan. Nevertheless, the Government of Japan does not recognise Okinawans as Indigenous people (Ministry of Foreign Affairs, 2014) and, therefore, the rights that would potentially be afforded to Okinawans under the 2007 *UN Declaration of the Rights of Indigenous People* (UNDRIP) have not been applied by the government (United Nations 2007; Advisory Council for Future Ainu Policy [ACFAP], 2009).

The term 'Indigenous people' refers to those who have continuously occupied their land and have an identity that is different from the prevailing majority stemming from the time of pre-invasion and pre-colonisation (Jacob, Liu, & Lee, 2015). Demonstrably, this is the case for Okinawans who have an ethnic identity that is distinct from the majority Japanese. Many second and third generations of Okinawan migrants in Hawaii still identify themselves as 'Okinawans' rather than 'Japanese' by choosing the item of 'Others' in reporting their backgrounds (Arakaki, 1998). In addition, 90 per cent of Okinawans in Japan distinguish themselves as *Uchi-nanchu*, which means 'Okinawans' in the Okinawan language rather than simply 'Japanese' (Lim, 2009).

The history of education in Okinawa can be divided into three stages. The first stage is the period when Imperial Japan invaded and colonised Okinawa before the Second World War (Kajimura, 2010). In that period the Okinawan language was banned in the classroom and use of standard Japanese was made mandatory in the school (Kajimura, 2010). The second stage was the period under the rule of the US, during which, again, the Okinawan language was banned for use in schools because of the expectation that Okinawa would become part of Japan again in future (Hasegawa, 2014). In both periods, 'dialect tablets' were hung around the necks of students who happened to speak the Okinawan language in the classrooms to encourage everyone to speak only the standard Japanese language (Asano, 1991). The intent of the use of the tablets, however, differed in the two periods (Fujisawa, 2005): in the former period, it meant oppression by the mainland, casting the Okinawan language as an inferior 'dialect'; in the latter, it was a form of self-adaptation by the Okinawan teachers.

In the third stage after integration, on 18 September 2013, the Okinawa Prefectural Government established the Day of *Shima-kutuba* Okinawan Language and the Okinawan language began to be used in the schools. In addition, the Okinawa Prefectural Government put forward a policy to promote the use of *Shima-kutuba* for the next generation (Okinawa Prefectural Government, 2013).

Current issues for teachers

There are three issues of interest concerning current-day teachers in Okinawa: (1) what are the lived experiences of teachers and student teachers? (2) what are the pedagogical matters?; and (3) what are the teacher education systems?

The first issue deals with the difficulties that teachers and student teachers have with teaching in the Okinawan language. Many teachers, because of the regimes which attempted to quash the Okinawa language, have lost familiarity with their mother tongue. As Moore (2019) explains, language is one of the critical keys to understand how a person sees themselves, even at a moral level. Without a sound knowledge of their own language, people can feel disconnected from their own ethnicities. With language, people will construct and re-construct deeper connection with their own communities and build up their identity as the Indigenous people (Moore, 2019). Indigenous teachers or student teachers who have a sound knowledge of their own language are likely to find the meaning and value their knowledge and learning as something embedded in their common and daily lives based on their cultures and worldviews (Veintie & Holm, 2010).

Second, pedagogically, presenting culturally appropriate teachings is largely dependent upon the language used. In many countries, despite a huge demand for cultural appropriateness in educational practices, actual practices tend to be conducted in the languages of the majorities, rather than those of the culture (Rogers, 2018). Indigenous education aims to break the pedagogical practices of colonisation and racism (Madden, 2015). To do so, four pedagogical approaches have been introduced into Indigenous teacher educational programmes: (1) appreciation of learning from Indigenous traditional pedagogical models; (2) pedagogy for decolonisation, which aims to deconstruct settlers' colonial intents behind contemporary, largely accepted pedagogical practices by the majorities and to centre the knowledge outlined by the Indigenous communities; (3) anti-racist education to debunk on-going colonial racism in the current educational practices; and (4) place-based education, introducing student teachers to the local places for reconciliation between the Indigenous communities and themselves (Madden, 2015). To quote an example, in Okinawa, there are a range of efforts to re-introduce cultural practices. For instance, there are attempts to introduce traditional dance arts called as 'Eisa' as a part of the local school curriculum (Watanabe, 2015). Eisa is a performance that aims to honour the spirits of the family ancestors and a petition for the health and safety of current family members. Youth organisations which have expertise in this dance are often invited to schools to teach Eisa to students through which the students learn more deeply about their localities.

The third question concerns the teacher education system. In the Okinawa Prefecture, higher education institution comprises seven universities, two junior colleges, one technical college, and one graduate university. Teacher education programmes are provided in six universities and one junior college, with primary teacher education programmes provided in two universities and one junior college and secondary teacher programmes provided in six universities. Two universities provide both primary and secondary teacher education programmes. The research outcomes presented here are based on the study conducted in Okinawa University. The university has five Indigenous Okinawan faculty members out of nine for primary teacher education programmes, and 11 out of 17 faculty members for secondary education programmes.

The teacher education system in Okinawa, in spite of an explicit statement recognising the needs of Indigenous students, tends to marginalise special Indigenous programmes (Chen, 2016). In part this is because of the relatively smaller number of Indigenous students at the universities, reducing the viability of such courses (Chen, 2016), and in part it is because the curriculum in large is nationally defined with a preference for teaching content in the majority's languages (Rogers, 2018). Such systemic issues are likely to cause teachers to be reluctant and apprehensive about changing their pedagogical practices, and, in turn, will influence the choices of student teachers (Rogers, 2018).

Given that colonisation by Japan has caused the Okinawa Prefecture to now be populated by majority Japanese (Chen, 2016; Côté, 2013; Madden, 2015), Indigenous – Okinawan – groups face explicit and implicit racism and prejudice and significant difficulties when advocating for their rights (Chen, 2016; Rogers, 2018), even in their own localities (Côté, 2013; Gera, 2015). It should be noted that Indigenous Okinawans suffered cultural challenges under the colonial rules of Japan and US (Arasaki, 2001; McCormack & Oka-Norimatsu, 2012; Miyagi, 2011), but the impact of migration on Okinawans is relatively new phenomenon from the early 2000s (Shibata, 2015). Okinawans struggle to have their voices heard at the national level even after reintegration into

Japan in 1972 (Arasaki, 2001; Kishimoto & Saito, 2019; McCormack & Oka-Norimatsu, 2012; Miyagi, 2011) because of the relatively small Okinawan population compared to the majority Japanese population – a problem found in other Asian countries too (Bertrand, 2014; Côté, 2013; Gera, 2015). However, because the islands of Okinawa are still occupied predominantly by Indigenous Okinawans, they provide a sense of group identity and belonging (Kelle, 2016). Thus, it is theoretically possible for Indigenous Okinawans to manage teacher education programmes to their own benefits as a quasi-autonomous, self-determination group (Åkermark, 2013).

Analytical framework

Comparative Institutional Analysis (CIA)

To study the research question, we used the Comparative Institutional Analysis (CIA) framework from microeconomics. CIA was originally developed to interrogate the neo-classical framework of mainstream economics, which seeks a singular equilibrium and, therefore, judges different patterns of economic practice as underdeveloped exceptionalities (Aoki, 2001). In CIA, an institution is the target of analysis. Some scholars define a institution as a set of socially shared beliefs held or, sometimes more critically, as the rules of the game played by actors about how to interact with each other to achieve their economic, political, and social goals (Aoki, 2010; Greif & Laitin, 2004; Hall & Taylor, 1996; Morgan, Campbell, Crouch, Pedersen, & Whitley, 2010). Others view the institution as a social structure designed to reduce the degree of uncertainty people face in their lives (North, 2005). Usefully for our analysis, some consider the institutionas helping to achieve a state of social equilibrium (Aoki, 2001, 2010).

However, equilibriums can shift (Aoki, 2010). The aim of CIA is to discuss such a shift of equilibrium and to develop theories on dynamic institutional changes. Many studies, though not all utilised CIA, employed mathematical analysis using game theory, but not necessarily always. It is possible to discuss institutions using CIA in a qualitative manner. Aoki himself provided a theoretical enquiry into the types of coordination in the nuclear power plant disasters at Three Mile Island, Chernobyl, and Fukushima based on open source documents (Aoki & Rothwell, 2013). CIA has been applied, using qualitative approaches, in the discipline of education in researching the strategies of university graduates in labour markets in Australia, Japan, and Vietnam (Saito & Pham, 2019) and in approaches of professional development activities (Saito, Khong, Hidayat, Hendayana, & Imansyah, 2020). The present study is also a qualitative study referring to the available literature.

The context of Okinawan teacher education

This section explains the context of teacher education in Okinawa, especially after the Second World War. The first subsection discusses the situation of re-commencement of teacher education after the war in the period 1945–1950. The discussion then turns to the development of the teacher education programme at the university levels from 1950 to 1972. The final subsection describes teacher educational tendencies after the 1972 reintegration of Okinawa with Japan.

Re-commencement of teacher education after the Second World War: 1945–1950

Before the end of Second World War, there was no university in Okinawa with the Okinawa Normal College being the only higher educational institution. After the Second World War, the US occupied and ruled Okinawa. The intent of the US was to remove the link between Indigenous Okinawans and the majority Japanese, enabling the Indigenous Okinawans to reclaim their own identities and policies (Kaminuma, 1962). The US recognised the fundamental difference between Indigenous Okinawans and the majority Japanese (Tamaki, 1987). The US established education policies to enable Okinawans to claim independence even before the ending of the war (Fujisawa, 2005). Especially, the US planned to develop technicians and engineers, which had not been an option for Okinawans in the pre-war period (Fujisawa, 2005) in addition to discouraging teacher education programme that emphasised imperialisation (Tamaki, 1987). In 1946, the US established the first education facility, the *Okinawan Bunkyō Gakkō* [Okinawa Teacher College] (Kano, 1999).

The college had three departments: (1) the normal department, which was in charge of teacher education for primary schools; (2) the foreign language department; and (3) the agriculture and forestry department (Kano, 1999). The main purpose of the college was to educate student teachers to address primary educational needs. Subjects taught at the college included: Education, Philosophy, English, Music, Okinawan Literature, and Physical Education. The teacher training period was up to six months (Kano, 1999). The faculty members of the college were predominantly those who used to teach in the normal college before the war, with the teaching content being much the same as in the past (Kano, 1999). Thus, the college inherited the programme developed by colonising (Kano, 1999; Teruya, 2010). Especially, the way of teaching was based on conventional one-way lecturing and there were no textbooks or materials (Kano, 1999). However, some faculty members taught student teachers topics that were based on the Okinawan values, with some faculty members even preparing their own textbooks that included Okinawan local histories (Kano, 1999).

Although the college served to address the increasing demands to supply the teachers in primary schools, there were questions about its contribution to the improvement of the quality in the actual classroom situations. The original intent of the college was to produce work-ready student teachers (Kano, 1999). In the four years before the college was merged with the University of the Ryūkyūs, it graduated 900 students (Takushi, 2005). However, there were concerns that the period of education provided may be insufficient to properly train teachers (Umene, 1953). In effect, the purpose of the college under the US rule did not lead to a reconstruction of education after the Second World War in Okinawa (Tamaki, 1979).

Development of teacher education programmes in universities: 1950–1972

The University of the Ryūkyūs (UR), into which the college was merged, was founded as the first university in Okinawa. The US established UR with the aim of establishing a 'university of Okinawa in Okinawa', heeding the increasingly strong public opinion that Okinawa should have its own university as well as implement the strategies held by the US to separate Okinawa from Japan (Okihara, 1972). Thus, all the costs of establishing and running the UR were borne by the US, as well as its jurisdiction. This pro-US nature of UR was reflected in various regulations and practices. For example, the condition of employment was that an employee must be neither against the policies of US occupation forces nor be a communist (Okihara, 1972). Also, student activists against US occupation were sanctioned (Okinawa University, 2008).

Several junior colleges were established as higher educational institutions in the 1950s and 1960s, many of which were upgraded to universities later. The Department of Education of UR was the leading institution producing student teachers but other junior colleges and universities also conducted teacher education programmes. At the UR's Department of Education, there were six divisions: Education, Psychology, Primary Education, Music, Health and Physical Education, and Technical Education (Okihara, 1972). The department combined the teacher education programme with the research into pedagogy and psychology in the belief that the combination would inform both research and practice mutually (Okihara, 1972). The Division of Primary Education was established for students who would teach at primary schools, and other divisions were established to prepare students to teach in secondary schools (Tamashiro, 1964).

Because of the urgent need for more teachers, especially to replace those teachers who had been killed in the war (Kinjo, 2014), the Government of the Ryūkyūs encouraged more private junior colleges to provide teacher education programmes. Okinawa Junior College (OJC) provided the programme for secondary school teachers and extended its primary school teacher programme to two years in 1959. Responding to the urgent need to supply teachers to remote islands outside Okinawa Island and into rural areas, the Government of the Ryūkyūs requested OJC to train those more likely to accept assignments to those islands (Kakazu, 1967; Okinawa University, 2008), recognising that graduates of UR were likely to work for the schools in the major cities (Okinawa University, 2008).

Teacher education programmes after reintegration since 1972

In this section, there will be discussions on (1) the meaning of reintegration of Okinawa in educational terms, (2) the increased tensions on the academic achievement issues, and (3) the efforts of universities to collaborate with the local boards of education (LBEs), as the distinctive characteristics of recent programmes. In 1972, Okinawa once more became part of Japan, and the prefecture's educational and socio-economic system needed to compete with the rest of the country (Asano, 1991). The Ministry of Education, Science, and Culture (now the Ministry of Education, Culture, Science, and Technology [MEXT]) directed Okinawa's educational facilities were to be brought 'up to the standards in the mainland' (see also Chapter 6, this edition). The integration of the Okinawan school system into the Japanese system signalled that the educational development of the Okinawans achieved since the end of the war under the US regime would be lost (Asano, 1991).

The direction of MEXT steered the attention of the Okinawan public away from the original in terms of the national average. Reintegration with Japan also meant that the Okinawan economy changed its orientation from agriculture to business (Asano, 1991). Thus, children were less likely to follow in the footsteps of their parents into agriculture but to choose other occupations upon completing school (Asano, 1991). In short order, Okinawan students also wanted to attend universities on the mainland with the view that the academic achievements of Okinawan students would be lower than the national average. In an attempt to increase the standard of academic achievement, local educational authorities were introduced, which continue their role to this day (Agarie, 1991; Asano, 1991; Kishimoto & Saito, 2019). The rate of stress leave is currently extremely high as a result of the pressure imposed on teachers by LBEs and the public to improve teaching standards to raise academic standard (Kishimoto & Saito, 2019).

Okinawa University: Building up the identity of the 'Okinawan' teacher

This subsection explains the recent initiatives by Okinawa University to reform teacher education and work closely with local educational authorities to encourage student teachers to learn from and serve in Okinawan schools. Okinawa University was established under US rules with an emphasis on independence: the university of Okinawans, by Okinawans, and for Okinawans (Kakazu, 1967). It was the first private university in Okinawa Prefecture, established in 1961, with OJC as a predecessor. At that time, in Okinawa, there was only one university: UR. The students of UR tended to be elitist and the opportunities for Okinawan people to receive university education were limited. An entrepreneur, Noboru Kakazu, decided to establish a private university for Okinawans. Interestingly, Kakazu thought of Okinawans as Japanese, despite the prefecture being under US military rule (Kakazu, 1967; Okinawa University, 2008) – a demonstration of the then 'adaptation' mindset.

Kakazu was also responsible for establishing Okinawa High School in 1957 and OJC in 1958. His aim was to develop Okinawan human resources and provide equal educational opportunities for everyone (Kakazu, 1967). The university was particularly attractive as a teaching educator, with 90.5 per cent of students enrolled in teacher education courses (Okinawa University, 2008). This fact demonstrates the magnitude of the contribution of Okinawa University, the first institution established by an Indigenous Okinawan for other ordinary Okinawans. In Okinawa University, even today, more than 90 per cent of students who take teacher education courses are Indigenous Okinawans who plan to work as teachers in Okinawa.

In recent years, Okinawa University has attracted the attention of educators from within and outside of Okinawa Prefecture with regard to collaboration. The Naha City Board of Education (NCBE) and schools in teacher education collaborate with the university, not necessarily with the aim of addressing Indigenous education but to encourage student teachers, the majority of whom are Indigenous Okinawans, to understand more about the needs of Indigenous students, teachers, and communities. Special programmes, such as visits to schools, have been designed to educate the student teachers concerning the challenges they will meet in classes (Kishimoto & Saito, 2019).

The first author of this chapter has been involved in developing the special programme and will now explain the three stages, precipitated by the role of the NCBE. NCBE is a unique local educational authority in that it promotes the use of the Okinawan languages, even in the simplest forms, such as greetings, in the schools. The previous mayor of Naha, Mr Takeshi Onaga, advocated 'all Okinawa beyond ideologies', which means an emphasis on the identity of Indigenous Okinawans should be given preference before differences in political ideologies. Mr Onaga began to advocate this idea when the Japanese government started, once again, to suppress Okinawa ethnicity, especially ignoring the pressures imposed upon Okinawans during the terms of the US military occupancy. Advocacy for using the Okinawan language, called *Haisai-Haitai Undo* [Hello Movement], has prevailed in official functions and events, including local assemblies or meetings of NCBE. The first author, therefore, realised the importance of recognising Indigenous identity and began using Okinawan languages in his classes, aiming to highlight to the Indigenous Okinawan student teachers the importance of the Okinawan language and honour their Indigenous identities.

First phase: Going first anyway. In Okinawa University, volunteer activities were conducted with one primary school and one lower secondary school where Okinawa University faculty members had connections. In April 2009, Okinawa University and NCBE exchanged an agreement on the 'School Support Volunteer', and Okinawa University Teaching Support Centre (OUTSC) began to dispatch students to the schools. The purpose of the agreement was to further develop activities for the teacher education curricula and to enrich the experiences of pupils at the schools of Naha city. The university students were expected to conduct their voluntary activities at the schools in ways that would not interfere with their studies in the university. The variety of volunteer activities included: supporting teachers in their teaching; assisting with the marking of home assignments submitted by their pupils; and even helping pupils with their home assignments after school. Although records were not kept at the time, estimates are that 90 per cent of the volunteers were Indigenous Okinawans. The length of time students were involved varied from student to student, from just a couple of months to nine months. The time of involvement in the schools also depended on each school; some students were at the schools in the morning, other students worked for several hours after school hours.

While the agreement between NCBE and Okinawa University was negotiated only around the student volunteer programme, the actual activities students engaged in largely depended on each school – types of activities, periods of involvement, and length of involvement. Without a more structured framework, the inevitable problems became the arbitrary participation of students, such as absenteeism before periodic university examinations, volunteer students being 'on holiday' over the university vacation periods and therefore not available to be in schools, and so forth. Some teachers were also hesitant about letting students into their classrooms, and sometimes there were mismatches in preferences of activities or aims between school principals, teachers, student teachers, and OUTSC. For example, principals of schools might not take into account the unwillingness of teachers to let students into their classrooms and only consider students' desire to be exposed to classroom situations.

Second phase: Accrediting volunteering activities. From 2011, in order to better organise 'school support volunteers' programme, NCBE and Okinawa University reviewed the contents of the agreement with the aim of making the collaboration between the local educational authorities and Okinawa University more institutionally sustainable and embedded. As a result, the organisations agreed on a necessity to accredit the volunteer activities as official courses in the teacher programme, namely 'Educational Volunteer Practice I' (EVPI) for the second year and 'Educational Volunteer Practice II' (EVPII) for the third year.

On the basis of such an agreement, coordination with schools became more strategic, that is, the schools provided more opportunities for student volunteers to work as teaching aides when the teachers conducted lessons. In other words, student volunteers were treated more like student teachers and not as volunteers tasked with small chores. The practices of volunteers in such schools became a foundation of further revisions of the programme and curriculum in the next phase, which sought to overcome two issues that became evident in running the accredited programme of school support volunteers: lack of (1) deep working relationships between the volunteers and receiving teachers in the schools; (2) systematic and consistent activities planned in the programmes in the schools.

With regard to the first issue, it became clear that despite original expectations, students were not given many opportunities to interact with pupils in the school with teachers being confused about how to support or mentor volunteer teachers. In fact, the concept of 'volunteer' was not clearly defined, nor were the expectations concerning school support of the programme or supervision of students. In addition, although the volunteer activities in the schools were accredited as EVPI and EVPII, there was no clear plan of what students were expected or supposed to experience in their assigned schools. Also, there was not a differentiation in the curriculum or expected goals between EVPI and EVPII. Therefore, some students experienced, for some years, the same activities that were not necessarily related to interaction with pupils in the schools, such as sweeping and cleaning of the school.

Third phase: Further systematisation. In 2014, NCBE and Okinawa University reviewed the agreement again and tried to change the status of student teachers from 'volunteers' to 'interns'. Their exposure in the schools as the interns was also included in the teacher programme, called 'Introduction to Teaching Internship' (ITI) in the second year and 'Practice of Teaching Internship' (PTI) in the third year. The ITI internship is conducted once a week with emphasis on providing learning support for pupils in the schools throughout the year. The PTI internship is also held each week, and the student teachers are required to teach lessons in teams with mentor teachers, followed by solo teaching experience for a short period, such as conducting a morning briefing session in each classroom before the classes start. In this programme, schools submit their plans for student teachers to NCBE and student teachers choose their preferred schools based on the plans.

The programme provides a valuable opportunity for student teachers and faculty members in charge of the programme to become familiar with the needs of Indigenous stakeholders. In the spirit of Article 14 of UNDRIP, the programme provides precious opportunities for the students and faculty members of Okinawa University to access the educational needs of Indigenous communities and deepen their understanding of the communities (United Nations, 2007).

Discussion

This section discusses the education programmes using the CIA framework compared with the existing literature and dividing the development of teacher education programmes in Okinawa into three modes after the Second World War: first, the programme up to 1972, which can be named as 'rehabilitation mode'; second, from 1972 till 2010s, termed the 'standardisation mode'; and,

Table 8.1 Comparisons of three modes on teacher education in Okinawa

	Rehabilitation mode	Standardisation mode	Localisation mode
Identities	Japanese under US rule	Japanese as part of Japanese territories	More emphasis on being Okinawans with characteristics different from the majority
Goals	Providing educational opportunities as in the majority areas Expanding the teacher educational programmes in multiple universities	Standardising the teacher education practices as part of Japanese territories	Familiarising the student teachers with local contexts and needs as Indigenous Okinawan teachers
Factors to cause shifts from the previous modes	US rules after the Second World War Increasing demands of teacher supplies	Demands for compliance with Japanese rules after reintegration	Demands for producing teachers with deeper knowledge on local needs Demands for more systematic collaboration for teacher education with LBEs

Source: Authors.

third, since 2010s, known as the 'localisation mode'. The main characteristics of each mode are shown in Table 8.1.

The localisation mode is based on the activities of the sole university, only Okinawa University at this stage. Nonetheless, this emerging and evolving mode has the possibility to be disseminated with other universities in Okinawa and local educational authorities. This is because, in Okinawa, there is a consortium between universities and local educational authorities, called 'The Council on Teacher Professional Development in the Okinawa Prefecture' (the Council). The Council is a base for the universities to demarcate the works of their neighbouring local educational authorities by region. In June 2015, there was a regular meeting to discuss partnership between the universities and local educational authorities and the case (localisation mode) was referred to as an innovative model when the first author attended the Council. Thus, this emerging mode can be considered as a possible guiding model on the partnership between the universities and the local educational authorities.

The history of Okinawa since the later part of the nineteenth century and to date has been dominated by the impositions of rules by their suzerains – Japan, the US, and now Japan again. The latest 'localisation mode' reflects the arguments in the political confrontations with Tokyo for the recognition of Okinawans as a separate people, along with a gradual promotion of movements towards recognition of the Okinawan language and cultural uniqueness, such as the 'Hello Movement' and 'Eisa'. The imposition of rules aimed at integrating Okinawans into the general Japanese community has motivated Okinawan leaders to increase their emphasis on reviving and developing their distinctive culture.

In other words, Okinawan educators and teacher educators have sought greater autonomous teacher education programmes in the 'localisation mode' since 2010s. This is a quiet but dramatic turn of events in terms of preferences and orientations of teacher education programmes. It signals that simply implementing efforts to catch up with majority Japanese programmes is insufficient and cannot solve the problems of poor standards. Okinawan teacher educators are now turning their attention towards investigating the deeply rooted issues in schools and among student teachers and managing them with the development of special measures through collaboration with local educational authorities and schools.

The rights under UNDRIP are not discussed in Okinawan teacher education or education in general because the Government of Japan does not recognise Okinawans as an Indigenous People. In addition, Okinawans, being the majority population in the Okinawa Prefecture, do not consider themselves as a minority. Nevertheless, the political confrontations with Tokyo and US have made Okinawans more aware of their distinctive ethnic identity. Should more political tensions arise, Okinawans may well seek more autonomy, using UNDRIP as a tool (United Nations, 2007).

As discussed in the introduction, three perspectives are utilised to frame our analysis: (1) lived experiences of teachers and student teachers; (2) pedagogical matters; and (3) teacher education systems.

From the perspective of teachers, the lived experiences of student teachers received greater attention from us than ethno-linguistic or ethno-cultural teachers (Moore, 2019; Veintie & Holm, 2010) in the teacher education programmes in Okinawa. Although some faculty members attempt to deal with local histories in the college as official units or subjects (Kano, 1999), more general scientific knowledge and theories have tended to be taught since the establishment of UR. In the case of the programmes by Okinawa University, the student teachers regularly participate in the daily lives of the schools in their localities and have more opportunities to reflect on their practices and interactions with the pupils and teachers in the host schools.

This kind of professional lived experiences is critical from the Indigenous perspective because teachers gain opportunities to understand the current contexts of the children, their parents, the teachers, and the schools in Okinawa, which are marginalised and anxious because of discriminatory practices and political tensions (Kishimoto & Saito, 2019). The sharing of these lived experiences is the beginning of Okinawan attempts to value education, culture, and languages of Indigenous Okinawan people, as advocated by UNDRIP (United Nations, 2007). At this stage, the trials are still at the initial stage of using some simple conversations in the teaching or official settings. However, Okinawan language is the basis of identity of Indigenous Okinawans (Okinawa Prefecture Government, 2013) and further exploration to develop curriculum, pedagogical approaches, and programmes of teacher education and collaboration should continue.

In terms of pedagogical matters, cultural appropriateness is not necessarily at the core of the curriculum, but student teachers have received more opportunities to place themselves in the real settings of Okinawan schools, especially in the case of Okinawa University programmes. Throughout the whole history of teacher education after the Second World War, the instructional language has been Japanese, not Okinawan. In this sense, the teacher education programmes in Okinawa were run in the language of the majority as recorded by Rogers (2018). Few of the approaches categorised by Madden (2015) have been incorporated into the mainstream pedagogical strategies: (1) appreciation of learning from Indigenous traditional pedagogical models; (2) pedagogy for decolonisation; (3) anti-racist education to debunk on-going colonial racism in the current educational practices; and (4) place-based education for reconciliation. There are also an increasing number of ethical questions concerning the student teachers and how they should conduct themselves as Okinawan teachers in Okinawa, especially if the living conditions of Okinawan children are challenging and tough (Arasaki, 2001; Kano, 2018; Kishimoto & Saito, 2019; McCormack & Oka-Norimatsu, 2012; Miyagi, 2011); if students understand the conditions and realities the schools are coping with, it would be expected that those student teachers who have chosen to work as professional teachers should be equipped with practical strategies based on deeper ethical missions.

A third impact is the lack of recognition of Indigenous status of Okinawans, partly because of the small number of Okinawans compared to the majority Japanese population (Chen, 2016), which influences the nationally defined curriculum that preferences the teaching of content in the majority's language (Rogers, 2018). Such systemic situations are likely to lead to a reluctance by current working teachers to change their pedagogical practices, thus influencing student teachers to do the same (Rogers, 2018).

The student intern programme run by Okinawa University, however, may provide an opportunity for further research and action on the use of the Okinawan language. The student teachers, having completed their internship, have an opportunity to inform university faculty concerning the realities facing the schools, who are likely to know the schools only in a limited way. The student teachers can function as antenna for faculty members, and their exposure and reflection can create a new space for research to produce theory and knowledge based on the realities of Okinawa. For example, in Naha city, the Okinawan language is used in various circumstances. Student teachers experience this effort to promote the speaking of Okinawan language and will note that the younger generations have difficulty speaking the Okinawan language (Okinawa Prefecture Government, 2013) and may support the demand of stakeholders that Okinawa University provide programmes to learn the Okinawan language. This can provide a new potential horizon to combine research and practice for a new Indigenousness of Okinawa.

To sum up, the case of Okinawa University suggests that (1) the development of teacher education programmes deepens the understanding of both student teachers and faculty members of the educational needs of Indigenous Okinawans; (2) some advanced stakeholders on the awareness of Indigenous identity, like NCBE, also helped the faculty members and student teachers realise the importance of Indigenous education; (3) it would help faculty members understand more about their missions to produce Indigenous teachers for Indigenous Okinawan students; and (4) Indigenous student teachers realise more about their responsibility to grow as Indigenous professional teachers. In other words, the teacher education programmes at Okinawa University show the potential to create the space for independence and self-awareness of Indigenous education for, of, and by Indigenous Okinawans, moving Okinawans out of the oppression of the Second World War and self-adaptation during the US rule.

Conclusions

This chapter discussed how the teacher education programmes evolved in Okinawa after the Second World War. The teacher education programmes were started at Okinawa Teacher College as a six-month programme for teachers directly after the war. Universities were then established to provide substantial programmes, with the establishment of the UR being particularly significant. Upon the reintegration of Okinawa with the rest of Japan, Japanese policies and regulations have been officially applied to the university programmes in Okinawa. However, the school context in Okinawa is very challenging, requiring schools, LBEs, and universities to work closely together to enhance teacher education programmes. Okinawa University, for example, provides regular and long-term opportunities for students to undergo internships in schools even before their practicum.

The evolution of the teacher education programmes in Okinawa does not reflect worldwide trends and discussions concerning Indigenous education, especially in terms of ethno-cultural or ethno-linguistic perspectives. Rather, the evolution has been a history of how to professionalise student teachers with reference to the challenging realities of schools in Okinawa. This is partly because Okinawans are in the process of national integration and reintegration with Japan and its educational system is catching up with the mainstream Japanese society and education, even though there is debate whether doing so is the right choice for Okinawans (Arasaki, 2001; Asano, 1991; Kishimoto & Saito,

2019; McCormack & Oka-Norimatsu, 2012). In other words, the efforts made by teacher educators so far can be considered as reducing 'Okinawanness' from teacher education programmes, with Okinawan school programmes becoming less and less different from that of other institutions in other prefectures in terms of curriculum or pedagogical approaches. Even the attempts by Okinawa University to enhance their teacher education programme can be considered as transferrable to other institutions in Japan.

However, there is a potential to change this situation as student teachers face the harsh realities of schooling in Okinawa and seek a more socially just education system that will positively impact the realities of Okinawan children. Okinawans are still the majority group in Okinawa and most student teachers are Okinawans, and thus there is potential for producing a space for teacher education for Okinawans that might, in some measure, reflect the aspirations of Indigenous peoples internationally as have been recognised in UNDRIP.

References

Advisory Council for Future Ainu Policy (ACFAP). (2009). *Final report*. Tokyo, Japan: Government of Japan (Provisional translation into English on 14 November 2011). Retrieved 31 May 2020 from www.kantei.go.jp/jp/singi/ainu/dai10/siryou1_en.pdf

Agarie, N. (1991). *Okinawa jin no ishiki kōzo* [The structure of consciousness of Okinawans]. Naha: Okinawa Times.

Åkermark, S. S. (2013). Internal self-determination and the role of territorial autonomy as a tool for the resolution of ethno-political disputes. *International Journal on Minority and Group Rights, 20*(1), 5–25.

Aoki, M. (2001). *Toward a comparative institutional analysis*. Cambridge, MA: MIT Press.

Aoki, M. (2010). *Corporations in evolving diversity: Cognition, governance, and institutions*. Oxford, England: Oxford University Press.

Aoki, M., & Rothwell, G. (2013). A comparative institutional analysis of the Fukushima nuclear disaster: Lessons and policy implications. *Energy Policy, 53*, 240–247. doi:10.1016/j.enpol.2012.10.058

Arakaki, M. (1998). Okinawa no kokoro 'Uchinanchu Spirit': Hawai ni okeru 'Uchinanchu' to iu syūtaisei ni tsuite no ichi kōsatu [Uchinanchu spirit: A discussion on the subjectivity of Okinawans in Hawai'i]. *The Annual Review of Migration Studies*, (4), 20–40.

Arasaki, M. (2001). *Gendai Nihon to Okinawa* [Contemporary Japan and Okinawa]. Tokyo, Japan: Yamakawa.

Asano, M. (1991). *Okinawa ken no kyōku shi* [History of education in Okinawa]. Tokyo, Japan: Shibunkaku Shuppan.

Bertrand, J. (2014). Autonomy and stability: The perils of implementation and 'divide-and-rule' tactics in Papua, Indonesia. *Nationalism and Ethnic Politics, 20*(2), 174–199. doi:10.1080/13537113.2014.909157

Chen, S. (2016). Dawning of hope: Practice of and reflections on Indigenous teacher education in Taiwan. *Policy Futures in Education, 14*(7), 943–955. doi:10.1177/1478210316656312

Côté, I. (2013). Internal migration and the politics of place: A comparative analysis of China and Indonesia. *Asian Ethnicity, 15*(1), 111–129. doi:10.1080/14631369.2013.830365

Fujisawa, K. (2005). *Okinawa/kyōiku kenryoku no gendaishi* [The modern history of Okinawa/educational authorities]. Tokyo, Japan: Syakaihyoronsya.

Gera, W. (2015). The politics of ethnic representation in Philippine bureaucracy. *Ethnic and Racial Studies, 39*(5), 858–877. doi:10.1080/01419870.2015.1080374

Greif, A., & Laitin, D. D. (2004). A theory of endogenous institutional change. *American Political Science Review, 98*(4), 633–652.

Hall, P. A., & Taylor, R. C. R. T. (1996). Political science and the three new institutionalisms. *Political Studies, 44*(5), 936–957.

Hasegawa, S. (2014). '*Sengo*' *Okinawa ni okeru 'hyōjungo' shidō* [Instruction of 'standard Japanese' in 'postwar' Okinawa]. *The Soai University Bulletin, 30*, 21–29.

Jacob, W. J., Liu, J., & Lee, C.-W. (2015). Policy debates and Indigenous education: The trialectic of language, culture, and identity. In W. J. Jacob, S. Y. Cheng, & M. Porter. (Eds.). *Indigenous education: Language, culture and identity* (pp. 39–61). The Netherlands: Springer.

Kajimura, M. (2010). Okinawa no hyōjungo kyōikushi kenkyū: Taishō ki no tsuzurikata kyōiku jissen wo chūshin ni [History of linguistic standardisation in Okinawa with particular emphasis on writing education during the Taisho period]. *Treatises on Language and Culture, 7*, 51–79.

Kakazu, N. (1967). *Okinawa no shigaku to sinkō* [Private educational institutions and their development]. Naha, Japan: Okinawa University.

Kaminuma, H. (1962). *Sengo Okinawa kyōiku syōshi: kyōiku minrippou seiritsu no katei*. [Postwar Okinawan education history: The process of educational legislation]. Tokyo, Japan: Nanpō dōhō engo kai.

Kano, H. (1999). *Sengo Okinawa kyōiku no kiseki. Naha* [Trajectories of education in postwar Okinawa]. Naha, Japan: Shuppan Sha.

Kano, H. (2018). Kodomo no manabi no ba to ibasho zukuri [The place for the children can learn and socialise: Through the learning support class in Nago City]. *Regional Studies, 21*, 77–86.

Kelle, F. L. (2016). To claim or not to claim? How territorial value shapes demands for self-determination. *Comparative Political Studies, 50*(7), 992–1020. doi:10.1177/0010414016666837

Kinjo, M. (2014). Yogawari to daigaku: sengo Okinawa ni okeru shiritsu kōtō kyōiku kikan no tōgō [Changing times and the establishment of universities: The consolidation of private higher educational institutions in postwar Okinawa]. *The Meio University Bulletin* (19), 85–95.

Kishimoto, K., & Saito, E. (2019). Okinawa as dystopia: Panoptic monitoring systems in schools. *International Journal of Comparative Education and Development, 21*(4), 251–264. doi:10.1108/ijced-10-2018-0040

Lim, J. C.-T. (2009). Okinawa jūmin no aidenthithi chōsa (2005–2007) [Survey of the self-identity of the Okinawan people (2005–2007)]. *Review of Policy Science and International Relations, 11*, 105–147.

Madden, B. (2015). Pedagogical pathways for Indigenous education with/in teacher education. *Teaching and Teacher Education, 51*(1), 1–15. doi:10.1016/j.tate.2015.05.005

McCormack, G., & Oka-Norimatsu, S. (2012). *Resistant islands: Okinawa confronts Japan and the United States*. Maryland, MD: Rowman & Littlefield.

Ministry of Foreign Affairs of Japan. (2014). *International covenants on civil and political rights. Concluding observations on the sixth periodic report of Japan*. Retrieved 31 May 2020 from www.mofa.go.jp/policy/human/cove_civil/cove_civil.html

Miyagi, H. (2011). Okinawa kara no hōkoku: beigun kichi no genjō to beihei ni yoru reipu jiken [A report from Okinawa: The current condition of US military bases and sexual crimes by US soldiers]. *Ritsumeikan Studies in Language and Culture, 23*(2), 179–182.

Moore, S. (2019). Language and identity in an Indigenous teacher education program. *International Journal of Circumpolar Health, 78*(2), 1–7. doi:10.1080/22423982.2018.1506213

Morgan, G., Campbell, J. L., Crouch, C., Pedersen, O. K., & Whitley, R. (2010). Introduction. In G. Morgan, C. Crouch, O. K. Pedersen, & R. Whitley. (Eds.). *The Oxford handbook of comparative institutional analysis*. Oxford, England: Oxford University Press. doi:10.1093/oxfordhb/9780199233762.003.0001

North, D. C. (2005). *Understanding the process of economic change*. Princeton, NJ: Princeton University Press.

Okihara, Y. (1972). *Okinawa no kyōiku* [Education in Okinawa]. Tokyo, Japan: Daiichihōki.

Okinawa Prefecture Government. (2013). *'Shima kutuba' hukyū suishin keikaku* [Plan of promoting universalisation of 'Ryūkyū language']. Naha, Japan: Okinawa Prefecture Government.

Okinawa University. (2008). *Chīsana daigaku no ōkina chōsen: Okinawa Daigaku 50 nen no kiseki* [Big attempts by a small university: The trajectory over 50 years by Okinawa University]. Tokyo, Japan: Kōbunken.

Rogers, J. (2018). Teaching the teachers: Re-educating Australian teachers in Indigenous education. In P. Whitinui. (Ed.). *Promising practices in Indigenous teacher education* (pp. 27–39). Singapore: Springer.

Saito, E., & Pham, T. (2019). A comparative institutional analysis on strategies that graduates use to show they are 'employable': A critical discussion on the cases of Australia, Japan, and Vietnam. *Higher Education Research and Development, 38*(2), 369–382.

Saito, E., Khong, T. D. H., Hidayat, A., Hendayana, S., & Imansyah, H. (2020). Typologies of lesson study coordination: A comparative institutional analysis. *Professional Development in Education, 46*(1), 65–81.

Shibata, K. (2015). Ijūsha no ukeire to chīki keishō no kadai: Ijū būmu ga tsuzuku okinawa-uraishigaki karano hōkoku [Issues of receiving migrants and succession of the localities: A report from Uraishigaki, Okinawa, with rising boom of migration]. *Urban Housing Sciences*, (89), 18–23. doi:10.11531/uhs.2015.89_18

Takushi, E. (2005). Okinawa ni miru kyōiku no shinkō [Educational development in Okinawa]. In JICA Okinawa Center. (Ed.). *Okinawa no kyōiku fukkō keiken to heiwa kōchiku* [Okinawan expereinces of their educational reconstruction and peace-building] (pp. 13–51). Naha, Japan: Japan International Cooperation Agency (JICA).

Tamaki, T. (1979). Senryōki no Okinawa niokeru kyōin yōsei to beikoku no kanyo: Shōwa 20nen kara Shōwa 27nen made [Teacher education in Okinawa under occupation and the intervention by US: From 1945 to 1952]. Paper presented at the Annual Conference of Japan Educational Research Association, Fukuoka, Japan.

Tamaki, T. (1987). *Okinawa senryō kyōiku seisaku to Amerika no kō kyōiku* [Okinawa occupation policies in education and American public education]. Tokyo, Japan: Toshindō.
Tamashiro, M. (1964). Kyōin yōsei daigaku/gakubu no mondaiten: Ryūdai kyōikugakubu wo chūshin ni [Problems of teacher training in the education department of Ryūkyūs University]. *Kenkyū Shūroku,* (7), 11–24.
Teruya, S. (2010). 'Ken bunka undō' no kikan to shite no 'Okinawa Kyōiku': 1923 nen kara 1933 nen made no shimen bunseki [The journal Okinawa education as 'the medium of cultural movement in the prefecture': An analysis on Okinawa education in the period from 1923 to 1933]. *Bulletin of Postgraduate School of Education,* Kyoto University (56), 293–305.
Umene, S. (1953). Ryūkyū no Kyōiku Kai [Educational trends in the Ryūkyūs]. *Japanese Journal of Educational Research, 20*(6), 75–80.
United Nations. (2007). *United Nations Declaration on the Rights of Indigenous Peoples.* Retrieved 31 May 2020 from www.un.org/development/desa/indigenouspeoples/wp-content/uploads/sites/19/2018/11/UNDRIP_E_web.pdf
Veintie, T., & Holm, G. (2010). The perceptions of knowledge and learning of Amazonian Indigenous teacher education students. *Ethnography and Education, 5*(3), 325–343. doi:10.1080/17457823.2010.511443
Watanabe, R. (2015). Gakkō taiiku ni okeru dansu kyōzai ni tuite: Fork dansu kyōzai wo jirei tosite [A study of dance educational materials in school physical education: The traditional Okinawa dance 'Eisa']. *Annual Report of the Faculty of Education, 49,* 169–176.

Chapter 9

Questioning current issues in the higher education sector for Japan's Ainu People

Jeffrey J. Gayman and Masayuki Ueno

Introduction

This chapter provides a snapshot of the current issues in the higher education sector for Japan's Ainu people through the lens of the two rights to education enshrined in Article 14 of the *United Nations Declaration on the Rights of Indigenous Peoples* (UNDRIP) (United Nations, 2007): the right of Indigenous Peoples to establishment and control of education through their own language and culture; and the right to access to education provided by the state.

The following pages juxtapose the historically constrained nature of education for the Ainu people, cultural promotion policies, and recent limited-scope Ainu Studies programmes with international standards of Indigenous education aimed at collective empowerment of Indigenous Peoples. We will be examining how, although isolated programmes contain germinal elements of these international trends, Ainu Indigenous education has a long way to go to catch up with international norms.

The *Merriam Webster Dictionary* (online) defines 'higher education' as 'education beyond the secondary level, especially, education provided by a college or university'. Higher education institutions include colleges, graduate schools, junior colleges, colleges of technology, and post-secondary courses in specialised training colleges. This chapter addresses these questions: 'What does higher education entail for Indigenous Peoples, why is it important for them, and how does higher education for Indigenous Peoples differ from that of education for non-Indigenous Peoples?' UNDRIP (United Nations, 2007) in and of itself does not provide standards per se via which higher education for Indigenous Peoples could be measured, but the principle of self-determination, enshrined in Article 3, is an indispensable lens for examining issues of education in general for Japan's Ainu people. In addition, Article 14 of UNDRIP states:

1. Indigenous Peoples have the right to establish and control their educational systems and institutions providing education in their own languages, in a manner appropriate to their cultural methods of teaching and learning.

2. Indigenous individuals, particularly children, have the right to all levels and forms of education of the State without discrimination.
3. States shall, in conjunction with indigenous Peoples, take effective measures, in order for indigenous individuals, particularly children, including those living outside their communities, to have access, when possible, to an education in their own culture and provided in their own language.

The fundamental rights addressed in Article 14 of (a) right to education and (b) right to control of educational systems providing education in the Ainu language and culture, provide an overarching framework from which to analyse higher education for the Ainu. Combined with the right to self-determination, they comprise the basic analytical parameters of this chapter.

Standards and frameworks of Indigenous education

In this section, standards and frameworks of Indigenous education will be introduced. In terms of standards, UNDRIP, Article 14, as well as Articles 13 and 15 which precede and follow it, provide only scant frameworks. In order to augment them, UNDRIP must be seen in light of the international Indigenous rights recovery movement (Niezen, 2003), which could be framed within other world trends, such as post-colonialism and post-imperialism.

Perhaps one of the most comprehensive guidelines for understanding Indigenous education yet to appear is the *Coolangatta Statement on the Rights of Indigenous People to Education* (Coolangatta Statement) (World Indigenous Peoples Conference on Education [WIPCE], 1993). Setting out Indigenous ducation as a process intricately interwoven with Indigenous Peoples' connection to land, shaped and supported by Indigenous languages, the *Coolangatta Statement* portrays education as a thoroughly cultural process embedded in the nests of the family and community, and juxtaposed against non-Indigenous educational systems, which are portrayed as having failed again and again to meet the needs and aspirations of Indigenous students.

Importantly, the *Coolangatta Statement* dovetails with the main tenet of UNDRIP as laid out in Article 3 by providing a comprehensive list of arenas in which the right to self-determination in Indigenous education 'is embodied', including curriculum, establishment, and control of educational institutions, incorporation of Elders into the education process, control of teacher training, priority in hiring decisions, and so on.

Scholarly reviews of research on programmes and initiatives of education for Indigenous students, such as in the work of Demmert and Towner (2003), congest the contents of the *Coolangatta Statement* into manageable rubrics with perhaps the most concise being contributed by Castagno and Brayboy's (2008) three element framework of self-determination, epistemology, and anti-racism. To paraphrase Castagno and Brayboy's rubric, education for Indigenous students must take into account and be responsive to the sophistication, depth, breadth, diversity of Indigenous worldviews, and epistemologies, and all of their manifestations in culture. These understandings must be reflected in and made available in praxis through the policy, measures, and infrastructures which will make Indigenous control of, establishment, and management of educational institutions and systems possible. Finally, Indigenous education must also take place in a framework which positions Indigenous students, families, and communities in a position of empowerment in relation to the surrounding society.

Importantly, it must be realised that none of the above guidelines and rubrics of Indigenous education involves a rejection per se of schooling in its entirety. This perspective is one reinforced by sections (a) and (b) of Article 14 of UNDRIP; that is, schooling is necessary for the stabilisation of Indigenous Peoples' lives, for the improvement of their living conditions, and for their empowerment as a people. In addition, Article 14(a) taken together with Article 14(b) is indispensable for guaranteeing the rights of Indigenous people to their language and culture, for the maintenance, transmission, and development of that language and culture, and for their existence as a people. In addition, while increasing Indigenous presence and Indigenous voice in the content and implementation of mainstream education leads to improvement of Indigenous self-esteem and, thereby, to improved academic performance, it contributes to societal recognition. These indexes can be applied not only to schooling but also to the phenomenon of higher education.

In these guidelines and rubrics of Indigenous education, mainstream knowledge systems are also recognised as a vital means for Indigenous Peoples to gain the knowledge and skills which will allow them to further their unique political and economic aspirations vis-à-vis the larger society. But, what exactly does higher education entail from an Indigenous standpoint?

Indigenous higher education

In their struggles to achieve increasing control over their own lives according to their own knowledge systems, values, and aspirations, Indigenous Peoples have consistently focused on the realm of higher education as a central vehicle of Indigenous empowerment (Champagne, 2015; see also Chapters 5 and 11, this edition). To the extent that post-secondary education provides the knowledge and skills necessary to engage in jobs needed in Indigenous country, capacity building is a crucial component of the economic goal of nation-building. In addition, realigning of norms and values in higher education institutions to Indigenous ones – the so-called Indigenising of the academy – is a vital ideological facet of the project of decolonisation (Smith, 2012). Indigenous Peoples throughout the world have become increasingly engaged in this struggle in the evolving process of creation of systems of Indigenous higher education (see also Chapters 5 and 10, this edition).

Japan is no exception to the process, but, in terms of readiness factors in the Ainu people's relation to mainstream society, it may be lagging behind other countries. In order to provide a standard against which the higher education for Japan's Ainu people may be juxtaposed, this section reviews the issues and conditions of Indigenous higher education and introduces policy structures established to support it in various locations throughout the world.

A number of models related to Indigenous education exist, from intercultural and bicultural universities to decolonising methodologies (Smith, 1997, Smith, 2012). Each of these models is not without its critics (Pérez-Aguilera & Figueroa-Helland, 2011). However, as many have pointed out (Barnhardt & Kawagley, 2005; Champagne, 2015; Stein, 1999), the restoration of cultural diversity to the hallowed halls of education, the market, and to systems of communication and governance poses a huge potential contribution to humanity. Critics of this stance tend to draw a hard line on the point of Indigenous self-determination, and critical theory has been criticised for being too conceptual and lacking an empirical base grounded in the realities of everyday life. A thorough review of the strong and weak points of each standpoint is beyond the scope of this paper; rather, the discussion indicates that any gradated set of indexes by which higher education for Japan's Ainu people might be evaluated must in itself be questioned.

Importantly, any distinction between (a) access to mainstream education and (b) the right to establish and control systems and institutions offering education through Indigenous languages and according to Indigenous cultural norms and protocols (i.e., Indigenising) potentially represents a false binary. This becomes very clear if one is to consider the advice of Vine Deloria to Indigenous students in the 1970s that they think seriously about the dangers of getting a mainstream education lest they should lose their Indigenousness (quoted in Pidgeon, 2008, p. 247). Indigenous Peoples throughout the world have responded to the dilemma of 'access' at the expense of 'Indigenising' by establishing their own higher education institutions, or by seeking to establish the presence and voice of local Indigenous communities in higher education (Ma Rhea, 2014).

One common trend in Indigenous higher education is for post-secondary educational institutions to arise organically out of local educational initiatives geared towards fulfilling local job training needs. Such institutions have tended to start as two-year colleges offering a smattering of associates degrees and to draw the majority of their student enrolment from nearby communities (Stein, 1999). Examples would be most of the Tribal Colleges in the US. Reliance on family and community networks to support Indigenous student persistence towards graduation has been featured as one of the strong points of this type of system (Brown, 2003). The opposite end of the spectrum is the Indigenous Studies concentrations often associated with prestigious educational institutions, such as the Harvard University Native American Program at Harvard University in the US. The struggles of melding two knowledge and value systems into one university founded upon mainstream norms and aspirations has frequently been addressed in research literature (e.g., Jennings, 2004).

Since the first version of the *Coolangatta Statement* was drafted (WIPCE, 1993), increasingly sophisticated standards for Indigenous higher education have been developed and, in some cases, implemented at the provincial, prefectural, and state level. For example, Rigney (2011), in a review of higher education for Indigenous Peoples in Australia, provides a comprehensive rubric based on a thoroughgoing analysis of higher education programmes for Australian Aboriginal and Torres Strait Islander Peoples at the University of Adelaide. Even in the argument of Pidgeon (2016) – who builds upon Kirkness and Barnhardt's (1991) Four Rs model – to list the important determinants of Indigenous student persistence (access and retention) in mainstream education, it is possible to discern a number of these standards.

The four essential characteristics of the Indigenous educational set-ups reviewed by Kirkness and Barnhardt (1991) of 'Respect, Relevance, Reciprocity and Relationships' (the four Rs) are important keywords, but must be tempered in usage through consideration of situationality. Obviously, within any one country, support structures for these programmes as well as degree of connection with local Indigenous communities will vary according to the type and nature of the programme. However, also crucially important to these rubrics are the pre-existing support systems for Indigenous education existing at the provincial and federal level. These can often be contingent upon sovereign or autonomous Tribal governance structures and resource rights based on federal recognition through treaties or other legal devices. The US established the *Tribal College Act* (Tribally Controlled Colleges and Universities Assistance Act of 1978 [25 U.S.C. 1801 et seq.]) to support Tribal Colleges through federal funding. Stein (1999) notes that amongst Tribal governance structures within the US, Tribal Advisory Councils possess exclusive rights of decision making concerning hirings. Pidgeon introduces the Indigenous Education Protocol for Colleges and Institutes developed by the College and Institutes Canada. Aboriginal and Torres Strait Islander Support Units at National Universities in Australia have been established by federal mandate. Granted the debatable nature of just how much Indigenous knowledge, which is primarily situational and experiential and only learnable in the bush (Berkes, 2008), can be brought into the urban academic setting,[1] programmes in Indigenous fisheries and forestries management available at Tribal Colleges in North America are grounded in the fisheries and forestries rights granted to Tribes on Reservations. In any event, degrees of incorporation of Indigeneity into higher education programmes is something which exists on a continuum, from piecemeal incorporation in the curriculum and/or limited support systems in mainstream institutions to fully Indigenous-established and Indigenous-controlled colleges and universities.

Education for Ainu people before UNDRIP

There are several obstructive factors that must be considered in developing an approach towards the higher education for Ainu people. The first factor is their economic poverty and its repetitive cycling over generations; the second is discrimination towards the Ainu in educational settings and, consequently, their avoidance of education; and the third is their weak motivation to advance to higher education. Ainu people have generally suffered from life in secluded regions, economic poverty, and its cycling over generations.

The second factor, discrimination, is an age-old issue for them. As Ainu children come to receive school education, they get bullied as an ethnic minority and begin to avoid school education. Consequently, in many cases, Ainu children fail to obtain academic skills and, accordingly, a precondition for their path towards higher education is lost (Ueno, 2014, p.130–131).

The third factor is the educational philosophy of the Ainu parent generation. Ainu people are placed in an inferior position socially and economically within broader Japanese society. Over 60 per cent of Ainu parents want their children to advance to higher education in order to change this situation (Hokkaido Life Environment Division, 2017, p. 21). However, Ainu parents themselves have had negative experiences in school education and their children do not have role models around them to lead them to success. This social gap in cultural capital is a crucial factor in their approach towards higher education (Ueno, 2015, pp. 37–38).

Ainu people started dispatching delegations to the United Nations in 1987 to attend the Working Group on Indigenous Populations (WGIP), involving themselves in the drafting of the *Declaration on the Rights of Indigenous Peoples*. Ainu people successfully made their presence as an Indigenous people of Japan felt in the international community, obtained information from other Indigenous Peoples around the world, and deepened their relationships with such Peoples, which then caused changes in the Ainu people themselves. With the International Year of the World's Indigenous People in 1993 and the changes in domestic situations thereafter, the Government of Japan passed the *Act on the Promotion of Ainu Culture and Dissemination and Enlightenment of Knowledge About Ainu Tradition, etc.* (Act No. 52 of 1997) (*Ainu Cultural Promotion Act* [ACPA]).

This law aimed to realise a society in which the pride as Ainu People was respected, mainly seeking the development and popularisation of Ainu cultures. The establishment of this law built a momentum to drastically change the awareness of Ainu People in Japanese society and the social consciousness towards them; academic studies on Ainu people were encouraged and advanced, and many Ainu-related study courses were created, particularly in universities in Hokkaido (Ueno, 2013, pp. 170–171). Teaching the history and cultures of Ainu People became common in school education as well, substantially changing the awareness of children. Further, frequent Ainu-related questions in the Japanese History subject of the National Centre Test caused children to recognise that the history of Ainu People was an indispensable part in the approach to higher education.

The self-affirmation of Ainu children was enhanced because they were less frequently bullied and their lifestyle improved. In association with the progress of the education and welfare policies by the Hokkaido government and the change in Ainu people's recognition, their university enrolment ratio began to increase in the 2000s. The improvement in educational environments for Ainu people occurred during the drafting process of the UNDRIP, affected by the International Year of the World's Indigenous People and subsequent International Decade of the World's Indigenous People, and eventually bolstered in the form of the establishment of ACPA. It can be said that such developments made a considerable impact on Japanese society and Ainu People's living environments.

Support for UNDRIP and its impact on Japan

However, since 2007, there has been no substantial change in the Ainu people's situation. In September of that year, UNDRIP was adopted internationally (United Nations, 2007). Then, partly because of the lobbying activities of the Ainu people, a *Diet Resolution to Recognize Ainu People as Indigenous People* was proposed in June of 2008 and subsequently approved by both Houses of the Diet. Even so, the Government of Japan endorsed it with reservations (Advisory Council for Future Ainu Policy [ACFAP], 2009).

With this, the Ainu people who had until then not been recognised even as an ethnic minority were recognised as an Indigenous People of Japan both in name and reality. Ainu people had long been hoping to be recognised as an Indigenous People by the Government of Japan. The Japanese government's endorsement of UNDRIP and its recognition of the Ainu People as an Indigenous People was probably precipitated by the advent of the G8 Summit (Lake Toya Summit) in June 2008 in Hokkaido, Japan, at which the government wanted to deliver a strong message to the world that it was proactively addressing the domestic issue of its Indigenous People.

However, there is a major contradiction: the Government of Japan put forth three conditions on its support of UNDRIP: (1) the prohibition of the exercise of the right to become independent and secede; (2) the disapproval of the human right to collective rights; and (3) harmonisation with and prioritisation given to public interests in exercising economic rights (Uemura, 2008, p. 64), meaning that Ainu People's right of self-determination, rights as an ethnic group, and economic rights were not admitted. In other words, while nominally recognising the Ainu People as an Indigenous People of Japan, the Government of Japan did not in actuality admit to Indigenous rights, because the government feared the Ainu People would pursue independence and act to acquire the right of self-government.

It would be safe to say that currently the Ainu People do not have such intentions at all; however, the government's concerns remain and, therefore, do not allow the Ainu People to enjoy their own educational, political, or economic rights. Granted, welfare policies, including the provision of student loans, have been implemented to increase the ratio of Ainu youth advancing to higher education, but these policies are only an extension of general educational policies and not measures specified as affirmative action for the Ainu People.

Consequently, the Ainu university-going student ratio has increased slowly, and many Ainu youth matriculate to universities specialising in the humanities such as provided at Tomakomai Komazawa University or Sapporo University where they can study Ainu culture. Few Ainu youth advance to universities outside Hokkaido or to sciences and technology departments of universities, which would impose upon them the economic burden of expensive school fees. However, after the passing of the *Ainu Cultural Promotion Act* (1997), educational content in public education regarding Ainu people began to be taught in detail because the national curriculum guideline states: 'the culture of the Ainu people who possess their own unique Indigenous language, religion, etc. must be addressed as well'. This development was a result of Japan's endorsement of UNDRIP and the subsequent *Diet Resolution to Recognize Ainu People as Indigenous People* (ACFAP, 2009).

The national curriculum guidelines embody the educational policies designed by the Government of Japan and direct the contents that Japanese people should learn. The implication of the guidelines is that Japanese people are to be taught the history and cultures of Ainu people in order to understand them but not deal with the Ainu People's right to their own Indigenous education, regarded as an Indigenous right by UNDRIP. The same applies to Ainu language education. Ainu language as an area of cultural learning even in higher education and as a language being used for the purpose of sightseeing in Hokkaido as a famous sightseeing destination is recommended, but neither the Government of Japan nor that of Hokkaido has any intention to establish and use the Ainu language as an official language. In fact, in 2009, a conservative Hokkaido politician, Onodera Masaru, in an invective against Ainu use of public funding which had been designated for a variety of Ainu cultural transmission activities (for more information, see lewallen, 2016), managed to force the cessation of funding for 10 out of the 14 previously existing Ainu Language Community Classrooms. In addition, Ainu language courses at public universities have neither increased in number nor changed in content since the adoption of UNDRIP. At the K-12 level, the education system for the Ainu has been precarious, with the same Onodera almost achieving a recall of the sole Supplementary Side-Reader materials available on the Ainu (Citizens' Support Association for the Ainu Side Reader, 2012).

In general, over the past decade, hate speech remarks fuelled by conservative backlashes have been the order of the day (lewallen, 2015), and lackadaisical attitudes towards these violations of human rights by professors employed at mainstream educational institutions in Ainu country (e.g., see Okawada and Winchester, 2015) have contributed little to the furthering of the Indigenising of the academy within universities in Hokkaido, as envisaged by Indigenous scholars globally. Overall, up to the time of the proclamation of the *Act on Promoting Measures to Realize a Society in Which the Pride of the Ainu People Is*

Respected, (Act No. 16 of 2019) (*Ainu Policy Promotion Act*), the Ainu situation was precarious, even in terms of cultural subsidies. How these issues will play out in the future depends on how the *Ainu Policy Promotion Act* (2019) is contextualised and put into action on the ground.

Current higher education for Ainu People

As discussed in Chapters 4 and 11 (this edition), the Hokkaido Ainu Association, as early as 1984, had prophetically envisioned trends in Indigenous higher education (Hokkaido Utari Association, 1984). They called for establishing special measures for the employment of Indigenous Elders and cultural bearers, as well as special enrolment systems. These systems would privilege the training of researchers with an Ainu ethnic background and increase the synergy between the content of higher education by establishing research centres devoted to the Ainu language and culture. In turn, the centres would empower Ainu culture through a thorough review of systems in place for the transmission of Ainu culture. In addition, the Association demanded the elimination of discrimination against the Ainu, a move which is in line with the elements of Indigenous epistemology, self-determination in education and research, and anti-racism propounded by Castagno and Brayboy (2008).

However, as explained in the previous section, the demands of the Hokkaido Ainu Association for structures which would enhance their economic and political autonomy have been consistently ignored by the Japanese and Hokkaido governments and, instead, replaced with arbitrary and authoritarian policies for 'cultural' promotion while the economic issues at the heart of low educational attainment have been dealt with almost exclusively through welfare support measures. In order to unpack this situation and in terms of positioning Japan in relation to the post-UNDRIP world, it is necessary to make a distinction between the spirit of post-imperialism embodied in the thoughts of academics who have been influential in the support of higher education for the Ainu People since before 2007 at the individual level and the actual developments which have been occurring on the ground in terms of collective rights.

As a general trend, the principles of Article 14 of UNDRIP have been honoured only with regard to Article 14(b), gaining access to education provided by the state, and only in a limited sense in terms of Article 14(a). In other words, establishment of programmes for education on the Ainu culture and, to some extent, language, have been achieved to a limited degree, but control of these programmes is still within mainstream Japanese hands. Furthermore, the programmes that are in place for group empowerment of the Ainu People are all occurring in private universities and are, thus, at the whims of the market economy. Contrary to the spirit of UNDRIP, the conclusion must be that there has been no change whatsoever to public university education for the Ainu since the endorsement of UNDRIP (ACFAP, 2009). In addition, there has been no change in public language policy since the endorsement of UNDRIP. Hence, it is not possible to talk about 'operationalisation of policy' in public higher education. Rather, efforts like those of the authors and those of a few other isolated supporters of the Ainu People have been made despite policy lacunas.

Certainly, as a trend in recent years, Ainu Studies has become common in the Humanities undergraduate programmes of universities in Hokkaido and elsewhere. Like Hokkaido University, some institutions providing university education understand that they are responsible for dealing with Ainu Studies as a subject of their research and education. Hokkaido University Centre for Ainu and Indigenous Studies (HUCAIS) was launched in 2007 as an affiliated facility where, besides undergraduate programmes, unique research and educational activities were to be carried out. Sapporo University established the Urespa Club for developing human resources knowledgeable about the language and culture of Ainu people, thus achieving outcomes in arenas other than academic research. This institution is also making proactive efforts to improve its scholarship scheme and to help students find their future career after graduation. In addition, Tomakomai Komazawa University and its Research Centre for Ainu and Pacific Cultures concurrently opened in 1998, providing substantial Ainu-related programmes and Hokkaido regional studies. However, it must be said that most of the currently offered courses place their importance on intercultural understanding of Ainu and, accordingly, their contents remain within the category of primarily Ainu language education and the understanding of Ainu history and cultures.

In most cases, support systems for Ainu youth in higher education are not those for the purpose of seeking the resolution of social issues that the Ainu People are facing or for pursuing the realisation of the Ainu People's own educational rights. If one were to take a cynical view, it could be said that they exist within rigid systems of categorisation of the Ainu People which have been stripped of contemporary political and social elements. Indeed, Ainu doctoral students are seeking academic training abroad because of the innocuous nature of the Japanese graduate school curriculum. At the very least, it would be desirable from now on for Hokkaido universities to introduce subjects for Ainu students in specialised fields through specialised courses that accord with the education aspirations of Ainu tertiary-level students while maintaining their current positioning on intercultural education in the liberal arts curriculum.

Specific programmes

In general, initiatives in the higher education sector for the Ainu People have been sparse and isolated and, in some cases, successful in producing college graduates due to dedicated actions by non-Ainu faculty who were able to support Ainu students. Approximately, a dozen universities throughout Japan, centred in the Kanto region and Hokkaido, offer courses on the Ainu language – mainly – and culture. While some, such as Chiba University, have long-standing programmes, others have been more sporadic in course offerings, with adjunct Ainu lecturers being hired for one season only to lose their job again in the next. Even at well-established institutions, such as Hokkaido University, there is not yet a consistent curriculum at the undergraduate level. Shikoku Gakuin University has introduced an affirmative action programme for Ainu students, but Shikoku is far removed geographically from the main Ainu population centres.

Nevertheless, local higher education institutions in Hokkaido have demonstrated considerable success in improving access and retention rates for local students of Ainu descent. The Hokkaido Culture specialisation at Komazawa Tomakomai University aided by several passionate faculty who actively recruit local Ainu youth from the Iburi and Hidaka districts, has produced a half-dozen graduates who are impassioned about living, practising, and transmitting their culture to their children and future generations. Four of the graduates have been hired by the Ainu Museum at Shiraoi. Sapporo University likewise has developed a unique student peer-support system for its Ainu students (Maeda & Okano, 2013 ; see also this edition, Chapter 11)

Staff dedicated to cultivating future Ainu researchers at Chiba and Hokkaido Universities have likewise played important roles in supporting young Ainu researchers, such as Kitahara (2018, 2019) and Ishihara (2018), who have subsequently been quite vocal on issues of Indigenous research methodologies and ethics (Ishihara, 2018; Kitahara, 2018, 2019). For example, Ishihara would have faced significant obstacles to using an autoethnographical approach for her PhD studies if it had not been for the support of senior, well-established Japanese faculty. Emergent Ainu PhD scholars, like their counterparts in universities internationally, face a cultural obligation to speak for their People when faced with discrimination or affront to their traditional cultural protocols. Ishihara, through her doctoral studies and auto-ethnographical account, included material she had written which was critical of the university's attitude towards the Ainu ancestral remains housed on campus. Such specific challenges to the authority of the university place Ainu students in a deeply difficult situation (see Chapter 10, this edition, for a similar discussion on Indigenous Australian university students and academics).

At the local level, the Cultural Bearers Training Initiative at the Ainu Museum, Shiraoi (Gayman, 2011; Ueno, 2018), has been successful in training future Ainu leaders and cultural bearers. Now in its tenth year of existence, the initiative trains cadres of four–six Ainu youth in the Ainu language, culture, history, and ethnology over an intensive three-year period. Notably, one faculty member responsible for curriculum development and Ainu language instruction, Professor Kitahara Jirōta, is Ainu, and trainees regularly attend Ainu events throughout the island as part of the programme's hands-on, experiential approach. On these points, the Cultural Bearer's Training Initiative at Shiraoi may be the closest approximation to Indigenous higher education initiatives abroad. On a similar note, although not yet an educational programme, Biratori Town has several cultural employment programmes in action, and has recently established a Crafts Education Centre which may provide it with the resources to create a small crafts- and language-centred community college (personal communication, Kimura Hidehiko). The town has also recently commenced a cultural exchange at the high-school level, which brought three Maori youth to Hokkaido for three months of study in 2018.

Ironically, scholars at Hokkaido University and elsewhere who were originally quite orthodox in their support of Ainu Indigenous rights have become increasingly conservative. Notably, the creation of the Urespa Club at Sapporo University, and of the HUCAIS, both coincide approximately with the adoption of UNDRIP (ACFAP, 2009). Interestingly, however, the tone of the academics at the HUCAIS, particularly those of the centre director over the past decade, have become increasingly pessimistic in terms of affirmative action.

According to the rationale of denying collective rights to the Ainu People and economic rights being harmonised with those of the general populace, affirmative action programmes such as those at Sapporo University, which HUCAIS scholars have supported wholeheartedly, are not to be allowed at public or national universities, such as Hokkaido University. Thus, while the Faculty of Letters of Hokkaido University recently established a graduate school Division of Ainu Research to be staffed by HUCAIS, it is open equally to members of Ainu and non-Ainu ethnicity. Likewise, the prospects for a university-spearheaded Ainu academic support system seem minimal, as do any policy or support measures which could be deemed to be providing concessions to the Ainu People as a collective.

Perhaps due to the no-collective rights stance being propagated by its scholar-supporters from Hokkaido University and their Ainu supporters in the major tourist centres, the content of the Urespa Programme has been markedly a-political. Similarly, the courses available in the newly founded Division of Ainu Research at the Hokkaido University Faculty of Letters are limited to conservative fields of Ainu Archaeology, Ainu Language and Literature, Ainu History, and Ainu Ethnology, while nothing is to be heard about courses in Ainu Leadership, Ainu Governance, or Ainu Law. Two positions on the Board of Directors at HUCAIS are reserved for Ainu leaders, but, again, with no research content being devoted to the issue of self-determination, the post seems a moot point.

The status of Indigenous education for Ainu People

In this chapter, we have confirmed that none of the elements which would allow for actualisation of UNDRIP Article 14(b) on self-determination or autonomy into public Ainu education has changed since Japan's endorsement of UNDRIP (ACFAP, 2009). Whatever tendencies towards collective empowerment are occurring in private education and efforts towards support of individual Ainu students at public universities are necessarily limited to the efforts of individual faculty. However, small-scale developments toward a set-up resembling that of Tribal Colleges in North America can be seen in the Cultural Bearers Initiative and in the efforts of Biratori Town.

Admittedly, the societal environment which has made the gains achieved possible was largely a result of the ACPA, which in turn was a product of the positive attitude towards Indigenous Peoples fostered by the then ongoing UN Decade of Indigenous Peoples. Ironically, even the 'rights to culture in the broad sense' approach, which might have created space for educational initiatives under the umbrella of 'culture' and which the centre scholars had been promulgating since Japan's ratification of UNDRIP in 2007, seem to have derailed during Diet deliberations regarding the new *Ainu Policy Promotion Act*. Despite vigorous objection from Ainu People's rights groups that the proposed new law does not recognise Ainu Indigenous rights, it was passed and implemented on 18 April 2019.

Minister Ishii of the Ministry of Land, Infrastructure, Transport and Tourism remarked in the Parliamentary debates:

> UNDRIP has no binding force of law, and only states that countries should recognize that the situation of indigenous people varies from country to country, and that the significance of national and regional particularities and various historical and cultural backgrounds should be taken into consideration. Not all of the content of the Declaration is something which should be implemented ...
>
> (Hokkaido Shimbun, 19 April 2019)

Recognition of language rights as intrinsic to culture, which would have fulfilled the conditions of UNDRIP Article 14(a), have been left out of the wording of the new law. Under its stipulations, Ainu People's resource rights have, unfortunately, been limited to collection of salmon and certain trees and plants 'for ceremonial purposes only'. Collective participation by the Ainu People in management of forestry, sea, or riverine resources, which might have been possible under the 'rights to culture in the broad sense' approach and which would have synergised well with the creation of new Ainu higher education majors, have now been obviated. The central principle of UNDRIP, self-determination, has thus been neatly surgically removed from the new *Ainu Policy Promotion Act*. To this extent, discussion of Ainu establishment and control of institutions and systems for education in the Ainu language and culture has become not a matter of policy but of the market and private education. All mechanisms which might have made the Indigenous education philosophy or practices listed in the first half of this chapter have been thus eliminated as possibilities in public education.

In spite of setbacks, the Ainu People's access to higher education has been on the increase. Although lacking in an element of continuity, it is now possible for graduates of the undergraduate programmes at Tomakomai Komazawa and Sapporo University, and the Masters programme at Sapporo University, to matriculate to more critical academic labs at Hokkaido University. As before the passage of UNDRIP, Ainu empowerment issues in Japan have been relegated to the realm of individual effort, the continuing denial of substantive collective rights limiting the target of the battle solely to elimination of discrimination against Ainu individuals.

Conclusions

From the perspective discussed, although the Government of Japan recognised the Ainu people as its Indigenous people, it never intended to admit any of their Indigenous rights. In the meantime, the *Ainu Policy Promotion Act* has been enacted as a domestic law in 2019. One main feature of this new law is a National Ainu Museum. Although not being a research institution based at a national university corporation, such as the National Museum of Ethology, this museum could become a case example encouraging distinctive ethnic education to the degree that it designs programmes for cultivating researchers engaging in Ainu research by closely collaborating with universities in Hokkaido and other institutions. In addition, the *Ainu Policy Promotion Act* designates respective local municipal governments as the implementing bodies for its policies. Since these municipal governments would initiate the educational policies for the Ainu People as an extension of university education in cooperation with universities and their equivalents, it can be said that higher education institutions such as universities have a duty to assume responsibility, based on their expert knowledge pertaining to laws and other matters, to provide feedback and advice on these educational policies.

A review of the law in five years has been mandated and an Addendum stipulating Ainu involvement attached. The future operational situations of this law must be supervised in order to judge its effectiveness. For the purpose of implementing the policies one by one, which will lead to the Indigenous rights of the Ainu People, it would be the best possible method at the moment to steadily negotiate with the Japanese and Hokkaido governments in accordance with this law. To the extent that students have been encouraged to take pride in their culture and heritage, an institution like an Ainu Community College, the Shiraoi Ainu Cultural Bearer's Training Initiative, or the Urespa programme contain inchoate elements of successful higher education programmes for Indigenous students in other countries. However, these authors feel there are limits to the degree of ideological transformation made possible by individual professors, when policy remains unchanged. Of course, the authors intend to maintain a critical stance but, at present, in terms of Indigenous empowerment through collective self-determination, the conclusion is that nothing has improved over the past 60 years. Perhaps external pressure from the conscientious international community will create leverage for Japan to more closely align its policies with international standards of support for Indigenous Peoples at the time of the review of the law in five years.

Note

1 The degree of congruence between Indigenous educational programmes which focus on Indigenous knowledge, such as Indigenous Forestry Management, and actual practices of Traditional Ecological Knowledge is an investigation which have been carried out by Langton and Ma Rhea (2005), but which is beyond the scope of this chapter.

References

Advisory Council for Future Ainu Policy (ACFAP). (2009). *Final report*. Tokyo, Japan: Government of Japan (Provisional translation into English on 14 November 2011). Retrieved 31 May 2020 from www.kantei.go.jp/jp/singi/ainu/dai10/siryou1_en.pdf

Barnhardt, R., & Kawagley, A. O. (2005). Indigenous knowledge systems and Alaska native ways of knowing. *Anthropology & Education Quarterly, 36*(1), 8–23.

Berkes, F. (2008). *Sacred ecology*. Second Edition. New York: Taylor and Francis

Brown, D. (2003). Tribal colleges: Playing a key role in the transition from secondary to postsecondary education for American Indian students. *Journal of American Indian Education, 42*(1), 36–45.

Castagno, A., & Brayboy, B. (2008). Culturally responsive schooling for Indigenous youth: A review of the literature. *Review of Educational Research, 78*(4), 941–993.

Champagne, D. W. (2015). Indigenous higher education. In W. J. Jacob, S. Y. Cheng, & M. Porter (Eds.). *Indigenous education: Language, culture and identity* (pp. 99–108). The Netherlands: Springer.

The Citizen's Support Association for the Ainu Side Reader (Ainu Minzoku Fukudokuhon Mondai o Kangaeru Kai). (2012). *Ainu Minzoku Fukudokuhon no Kakikae Mondai o Kangaeru Shimin no Tsudoi* [Materials booklet of the citizen's meeting on the problem of the revision of the Ainu side reader] (). Self-published.

Demmert, D., & Towner, J. (2003). A review of the research literature on the influences of culturally-based education on the academic performance of Native American students. Portland, OR: Northwest Regional Educational Laboratory.

Gayman, J. (2011). Ainu right to education and Ainu practice of 'education': Current situation and imminent issues in light of indigenous education rights and theory. *Intercultural Education, 22*(1), 15–28.

Hokkaido Life Environment Division. (2017). *Heisei 29-nen Hokkaido Ainu seikatu jittai chōsa hōkokusho* [2017 report of the survey on the actual living conditions of the Hokkaido Ainu]. Sapporo, Japan: Hokkaido Kankyō Seikatsu Bu.

Hokkaido Shimbun. (2019). Ainu Shinpōan Sangiin Kaketsu [New Ainu law passes Diet]. Evening Edition. 19 April.

Hokkaido Utari Association. (1984). Ainu minzoku ni kansuru hōritsu-an [Law proposal concerning the Ainu community]. In Ainu Association of Hokkaido (Ed.). *Ainu minzoku no gaisetsu – Hokkaido Ainu Kyōkai no katsudō o fukume* [Overview of the Ainu: History of the Hokkaido Ainu Association of Hokkaido] (2017 ed.). Retrieved 31 May 2020 from www.ainu-assn.or.jp/public/files/1d05c1dd9ceb9cf70478cd757 622d3075a2c94b7.pdf

Ishihara, M. (2018). *Chinmoku no ōto-esunogurafi: sairento Ainu no sabarutanka to posuto-coroniaru jyōkyō* [An autoethnography of silence: The subalternization and post-colonial situation of the 'Silent Ainu']. Unpublished PhD thesis. Hokkaido, Japan: Hokkaido University Faculty of Letters. Retrieved 31 May 2020 from http://hdl.handle.net/2115/72199

Jennings, M. (2004). Alaska native political leadership and higher education: One university, two universes. Lanham, MD: Altamira Press.

Kirkness, V. J., & Barnhardt, R. (1991). First Nations and higher education: The four Rs – Respect, relevance, reciprocity, responsibility. *Journal of American Indian Education, 30*(3), 1–15.

Kitahara, J. (2018). Ima Ainugaku to dou mukiau ka [Now, how should we proceed with Ainu studies]. *Transit, 34* (Winter), no pagination.

Kitahara, J. (2019). Daigaku o hiraku: Ainu gaku, Wajin gaku o mezasite [Opening the campus: In pursuit of Ainu studies, Japanese studies]. In Alternative Map Editing Group (Ed.). *Hokkaidō Daigaku Mou Hitotsu no Kyanpas Map: Kakusareta Fukei o Miru, Kesareta Koe o Kiku* [The alternative map to Hokkaido University: Seeing the hidden scenery, listening to the silenced voices] (pp. 185–191). Sapporo, Japan: Jyurōsha.

Langton, M., & Ma Rhea, Z. (2005). Traditional indigenous biodiversity-related knowledge. *Australian Academic & Research Libraries, 36*(2), 45–69.

lewallen, a.e. (2016). *The fabric of indigeneity: Ainu identity, gender, and settler colonialism in Japan.* Santa Fe, NM: University of New Mexico Press in Association with the School for Advanced Research Press.

lewallen, a.e. (2015). Human rights and cyber hate speech: The case of the Ainu. *FOCUS, 81,* September 2015. Retrieved 31 May 2020 from www.hurights.or.jp/archives/focus/section3/2015/09/-in-early-autumn-2014-two-hokkaido-politicians-engaged-in.html

Maeda, K., & Okano, K. H. (2013). Connecting indigenous Ainu, university and local industry in Japan: The Urespa project. *International Education Journal: Comparative Perspectives 12*(1), 45–60.

Ma Rhea, Z. (2014). Educational equality, equity, and sui generis rights in Australian higher education: Theorising the tensions and contradictions. In H. Zhang, P. W. K. Chan, & C. Boyle (Eds.). *Equality in education: Fairness and inclusion* (pp. 35–50). Rotterdam, The Netherlands: Sense Publishers.

Niezen, R. (2003). *The origins of indigenism: Human rights and the politics of identity.* Berkeley, CA: University of California Press.

Okawada, A., & Winchester, M. (2015). *Ainu minzoku hiteiron ni kōsuru* [No! to the denial of the Ainu people]. Tokyo: Kawadeshobōshinsha Publisher.

Pérez-Aguilera, D. A., & Figueroa-Helland, L. E. (2011). Beyond acculturation?: Political 'Change', Indigenous knowledges, and intercultural higher education in Mexico. *Journal for Critical Education Policy Studies, 9*(2), 268–296.

Pidgeon, M. (2016). More than a checklist: Meaningful Indigenous inclusion in higher education. *Social Inclusion, 4*(1), 77–91.

Pidgeon, M. (2008). Pushing against the margins: Indigenous theorizing of 'success' and retention in higher education. *Journal of College Student Retention Research, 10*(3), 339–360.

Rigney, L. I. (2011). Indigenous higher education reform and Indigenous knowledges. Report to the *Review of higher education access and outcomes for Aboriginal and Torres Strait Islander people,* Department of Education, Employment and Workplace Relations. Canberra, Australia. Retrieved 31 May 2020 from https://docs.education.gov.au/documents/indigenous-higher-education-reform-and-indigenous-knowledges

Smith, G. H. (1997). *The development of kaupapa Maori: Theory and praxis.* Unpublished PhD Thesis. Auckland, New Zealand: University of Auckland.

Smith, L. T. (2012). *Decolonizing methodologies.* Second Edition. London, England: Zed Books.

Stein, W. J. (1999). Tribal colleges: 1968–1998. In K. G. Swisher & J. Tippeconnic (Eds.). *Next steps: Research and practice to advance Indian education* (pp. 259–270). Retrieved 31 May 2020 from https://files.eric.ed.gov/fulltext/ED427913.pdf

Uemura, H. (2008). 'Senjyūmizoku no kenri ni kansuru kokurensengen' kakutoku heno nagai michinori [Long way toward acquisition of *UN Declaration on the Rights of Indigenous Peoples*]. Tokyo, Japan: International Peace Research Institute, Meiji Gakuin University. *PRIME, 27,* 53–68.

Ueno, M. (2018). Nihon ni okeru Ainu shidōsha yōsei no genjyō to kadai [The current situation and issues of training of Ainu specialists in Japan]. *Kokusai Kyōiku, 24,* 127–133.

Ueno, M. (2015). Hinkon ga kyouiku ni motarasu sedaikanrensa [Chain over generations brought about on education by poverty]. *Journal of Japan Association for the Study of Learning Society, 11,* 35–38.

Ueno, M. (2014). *Ainu Minzoku no gengo fukkō to rekishi kyōiku ni kansuru kenkyū* [Study on language reconstruction and history education of Ainu people]. Tokyo, Japan: Kazamashobō.

Ueno, M. (2013). Ainugakushu to minzokukyōikukikansetsuritu ni mukete [Toward Ainu study and establishment of ethnic education institution]. *Electrical Proceedings (No. 14) of Nihon University Graduate School of Social and Cultural Studies* (pp. 167–177). Retrieved 31 May 2020 from https://atlantic2.gssc.nihon-u.ac.jp/kiyou/pdf14/14-167-177-Ueno.pdf

United Nations. (2007). *United Nations Declaration on the Rights of Indigenous Peoples.* Retrieved 31 May 2020 from www.un.org/development/desa/indigenousPeoples/wp-content/uploads/sites/19/2018/11/UNDRIP_E_web.pdf

World Indigenous People's Conference on Education in Hawaii. (1999, August). *The Coolangatta Statement on Indigenous Peoples' Rights in Education.* Retrieved from http://press.anu.edu.au/wp-content/ uploads/2011/02ch.191.pdf

Legislation

Act on the Promotion of Ainu Culture and Dissemination and Enlightenment of Knowledge About Ainu Tradition, etc. (Act No. 52 of 1997) (*Ainu Cultural Promotion Act*) （アイヌ文化の振興並びにアイヌの伝統等に関する知識の普及及び啓発に関する法律 [アイヌ文化振興法]）

Act on Promoting Measures to Realize a Society in Which the Pride of the Ainu People Is Respected (Act No. 16 of 2019) (*Ainu Policy Promotion Act*) （アイヌの人々の誇りが尊重される社会を実現するための施策の推進に関する法律 [アイヌ政策推進法]）

Chapter 10

Stabilising and sustaining Indigenous leadership in Australian universities

Peter J. Anderson and Zane M. Diamond

Indigenous leadership in Australian universities

From the 1500s in Japan and 1800s in Australia, the education of Indigenous Peoples who live in these nations has been a complex matter. The international rights mechanism, the *United Nations Declaration on the Rights of Indigenous Peoples* (UNDRIP) (United Nations, 2007) challenges both nations to recognise the *sui generis* rights of Indigenous Peoples and, of particular interest in this chapter, the issues surrounding the leadership and management of higher education. Currently, both nations have embedded education systems built as part of their past imperial colonising projects to educate Indigenous populations to 'fit in' with imposed arrangements (see also Chapter 9, this edition).

In this chapter we examine the impact of UNDRIP on supporting the acceleration of Indigenous participation in Australia's universities. We approach the challenge for change from an Indigenist, rights and strengths base that includes Aboriginal leadership as one of the core necessary elements. This recognises the human rights of Indigenous Peoples as being fundamental to the 'public value' of the modern university (Moore, 1995) and gives specific recognition of Indigenous Peoples' distinctive economic, linguistic and cultural rights within complex, globalised, postcolonial and post-imperial universities (Rigney, 1999). The chapter builds on the outline of pre-UNDRIP history of Australian Aboriginal and Torres Strait Islander Peoples' participation in higher education provided by Holt in Chapter 5 in which she argues that Australian universities are lagging in their commitment to parity between Indigenous and non-Indigenous employment – which argues for 2.2 per cent of university employees to be Indigenous, in line with expectations of, and reporting requirements to, the Department of the Prime Minister and Cabinet in the Australian government (Australian Government, 2019; Australian Government, 2014; Larkin et al., 2018).

Bringing together the academic fields of educational leadership, educational administration and strategic change management, we observe that the leadership and management of universities as public service organisations requires a university to do more than simply educate a nation's citizens into the future.

Universities today offer education to an increasingly mobile international student body, thus needing to maintain and improve their international reputations in research and teaching, while also being responsive to national policy drivers as part of delivering public value to the communities they serve (Universities Australia, 2017). In previous research (Anderson & Atkinson, 2013; Anderson & Ma Rhea, 2018; Ma Rhea, 2015; Ma Rhea, Anderson, & Atkinson, 2012; White, Ma Rhea, Anderson, & Atkinson, 2012), we have argued that the enormity and complexity of the task of indigenising an entire education system demands simultaneously addressing community governance and leadership capacity building, offering culturally appropriate professional development and developing explicit approaches to the leadership and management of policy development in order to address the demands of total quality improvement of higher education with Indigenous leadership at its heart.

In this chapter, we problematise the concept of the leadership pipeline (Charan, Drotter, & Noel, 2001) for accelerating employment of Indigenous people in Australia's universities, exploring senior executive, administrative, professional and academic roles in Australian universities from the perspective of Aboriginal and Torres Strait Islander employees. Our particular, but not exclusive, interest is in how this highly specialised group of people are undertaking their leadership, managerial, intellectual and cultural roles. We argue that conventional organisational approaches practised by universities that assume a proper, functioning 'pipeline' into senior leadership, professional or academic, are unable to achieve the espoused Australian government targets for Indigenous employment growth. More important, such approaches fall short of ever being able to address the aspirations of Indigenous People because the required institutional reforms envisaged by such mechanisms as UNDRIP cannot be achieved by the traditional pipeline approach.

This chapter canvasses a number of key elements that will enable a more detailed examination of how universities can more quickly achieve parity between non-Indigenous and Indigenous cohorts in senior leadership, professional and academic positions.

Pathways of Indigenous education leaders into university leadership roles

There are three interrelated careers in higher education: senior leadership, professional and academic. Here we focus on Indigenous employment into these roles and examine each aspect according to the expected skill and knowledge requirements for each.

A person holding a senior leadership role is generally expected to hold a relevant PhD and be able to demonstrate substantive management experience, including responsibility for strategic planning, financial resources and budgets along with the management of complex staffing structures. They would hold, for example, outstanding interpersonal skills, an inclusive leadership style, thrive in an atmosphere of innovation and could demonstrate critical thinking along with creative and flexible responses in a challenging and continually evolving environment. They would also have proven ability to lead resourceful approaches to developing new external partnerships and funding opportunities.

An entry-level professional staff member, known in Australia by the classification of Higher Education Worker (HEW), is someone who holds qualifications in a relevant discipline and has the capacity to work in programme development and delivery and/or production within a large complex organisation. They would be able to demonstrate problem-solving skills and enjoy working collaboratively with a wide range of colleagues and stakeholders and consistently deliver on projects with the help of exceptional interpersonal, organisational and analytical skills. To gain promotion in this classification, they would be expected, increasingly, to be able to demonstrate a record of success as a strategic leader in their area of expertise and substantial management experience with diverse and highly skilled teams.

In Australia, the levels of classification for an academic appointment are Level A–Level E. Appointment to Level A (the entry level) will require, at least as a minimum, an Honours degree or higher qualifications, such as an extended professional degree or a three-year degree with a postgraduate diploma. In determining a candidate's experience relative to their qualifications, teaching experience, experience in research, experience outside higher education, creative achievement, professional contributions and/or contributions to technical achievement are taken into consideration. At the highest level, Professor (Level E), the person is expected to provide strategic direction and leadership for research and teaching and manage resources to promote and develop research activities, including significant external grants, strong research collaborations with government, industry and philanthropy, high-quality publications and strong doctoral completions.

While there is considerable discussion about the development of an Indigenous employment strategy at the policy level, the operationalisation of this has been substantially left to individual universities to develop. We argue that university leaders are doing this without drawing on an underpinning field of research and historical practice and are employing methods of trial and error with mixed results (Universities Australia, 2018). Moreton-Robinson, Walter, Singh and Kimber (2011) observed that it is clear that many universities demonstrated poor performance in increasing Indigenous access and participation through their customary business management practices. Larkin et al. (2018, p. 103) note that the *National Indigenous Higher Education Workforce Strategy*, developed by the Indigenous Higher Education Advisory Committee (IHEAC) and endorsed by Universities Australia (Indigenous Higher Education Advisory Committee (IHEAC) and Larkin, S. (Chair), 2011) provides a best-practice approach to improving the recruitment and retention of Indigenous people in the higher education sector. Key points are: Indigenous people should be actively involved in university governance and management; Indigenous staffing should be increased at all appointment levels and for academic staff, across a wider variety of academic fields; and universities should operate in partnership with their Indigenous communities and help disseminate culturally competent practices to the wider community (Universities Australia, 2011, p. 8).

Our analysis of the issues surrounding the ongoing challenges to achieving Indigenous employment parity in universities draws on rich sociological research that has: examined university work under neo-liberal pressure of performativity (Ball, 2000; Bernstein, 1996, 2000; Lazear, 2001; Sikes, 2001; Stillwaggon, 2008); the new public managerialism identified by Marginson (1993, 2000) within the higher education sector and the body of research about academic work (e.g., Anderson, Johnson, & Saha, 2002; Coaldrake & Stedman, 1999; McInnes, 1996, 1999, 2000); the concept of intellectual leadership (Macfarlane, 2012); and the associated identity work that depicts individuals as 'outsiders' or 'insiders' (Said, 1994).

The following sections examine two traditional pipelines being used to accelerate Indigenous leadership in Australian universities. The first to be examined is the leadership pipeline of government public service into senior university managerial roles. The second draws on the 'grow your own' strategy to build Indigenous professional and academic employment that mirrors the development of professional and academic leadership for non-Indigenous academics. These two approaches are common university leadership responses to the issue, where Aboriginal people will take up roles that are familiar to the university and help the university to achieve the performance metrics that are currently necessary for a university to secure its financial future in the face of government funding commitments.

Leadership pipeline

In this section, we examine the historical development of an Indigenous Australian administrative class to enable us to have a fuller discussion of the potential for acceleration of Indigenous leadership in universities (see also Chapter 5, this edition). Australia has a long colonial history that shaped the Australian government's provision of services to Aboriginal and Torres Strait Islander people. The mid-1970s heralded increased interest by the government to encourage Indigenous people enter the public service and help with this work. The report prepared by 'Nugget' Coombs remains a key document for understanding the history of this move and its complications. The Coombs Report (Royal Commission on Australian Government Administration [RCAGA] 1976) laid bare something that Indigenous Australians knew to be true, but which came as a surprise to many non-Indigenous people:

> It is only recently that it has become apparent (at least to white Australians) that a substantial proportion both of those Aboriginals whose pattern of life is predominantly based on Aboriginal tradition and of the urban and

fringe-dwelling part-Aboriginals, share a desire to preserve a separate identity – to salvage and restore a distinctive Aboriginal culture and to resist complete assimilation into the general Australian society. Furthermore, although they differ widely in the purposes for which they would use it, both groups seek significant authority in the determination of policies and the management of programs concerned with their affairs ... Political and official actions, on the other hand, have been handicapped by the persistence of attitudes based on now rejected policies of assimilation and 'protection', by a profound and widespread ignorance of Aboriginal attitudes and by a lack of experience in dealing with the problems of ethnic minorities.

(p. 335)

O'Donoghue (1997) observed:

Since 1967, when the Commonwealth took up its special responsibility towards indigenous Australians, the states and territories have been reluctant to provide for the special needs of indigenous people from within their own budgets. Instead, they have looked to the Commonwealth, and its specialist agency, to provide services and facilities that are their own proper responsibility and other Australians receive as a matter of course.

(p. 6)

Her view echoes the view of many Indigenous people up to the present and points to an urgent need to change the quality of engagement between education bureaucracies and the people they are supposed to serve. The preference of bureaucracies continues to be one of having consultative councils of Aboriginal people advising ministers and education administrators through executive means. Inevitably and unfortunately, such a preference, rather than ceding real governance and implementation responsibility to Indigenous people, will continue to generate conflicts and frustrations over implementation of the education agenda for Indigenous children. The Coombs Report (RCAGA, 1976) heralded this state of affairs, reporting that members of the National Aboriginal Consultative Council (NACC):

[C]omplain of their lack of real power and of the failure of the Minister and the Department to seek or follow their advice. At the same time, the Department believes that the Committee's advice is seriously heeded and influences departmental advice to ministers.

(p. 337)

Importantly, the Coombs Report (RCAGA, 1976) recognised that even though changes had been implemented:

They are, however, unlikely to satisfy legitimate Aboriginal aspirations until those employed in these processes include a substantially higher proportion of Aboriginals than at present at all levels of work and responsibility and until opportunities for Aboriginals in this and other governmental work are seen to correspond more closely with those open to other Australians.

(p. 342)

Important for our discussion, the Australian government remains the key funder of Indigenous services to education. The evidence from 2011–2018 demonstrates that the approach to Indigenous employment in the Australian federal government during the ensuing 35 years since the Coombs Report has not sufficiently changed the mindset of this massive organisation. Within the Education portfolio, for example, Ma Rhea (2015) observed that the 2012 report by the Australian Public Service Commission (APSC) shows that in 2011–2012, the Australian national education department responsible for aspects of Indigenous Education reported that, of the 48 Indigenous public servants who left the agency, 31.3 per cent resigned, 4.2 per cent retired and a worrying 54.2 per cent were retrenched. This was at a time when there was a strong focus on the employment of Indigenous Australians in the public service with a target set of 2.2 per cent by 2015.

In 2015, the Australian government adopted a new strategy: *Commonwealth Aboriginal and Torres Strait Islander Employment Strategy 2015–2018* (The Strategy) (Australian Government, 2015). Responsibility for implementing the Strategy lies with the APSC. The Strategy establishes a goal of increasing the representation of Indigenous employees across the Commonwealth public sector to 3 per cent by 2018. Launched in 2015 and expiring at the end of 2018, the Strategy focused on four key action areas:

- expand the range of Indigenous employment opportunities
- invest in developing the capability of Indigenous employees
- increase the representation of Indigenous employees in senior roles
- improve the awareness of Indigenous culture in the workplace.

An evaluation of the strategy, undertaken at the end of 2018 (*Inside Policy*, 2019), found both positive and negative outcomes. In the positive:

Indigenous representation as a percentage of all Commonwealth public sector employees, based on self-identification by Indigenous employees, increased from 2.2 percent in 2015 to 2.9 percent in 2018. Across APS agencies, Indigenous representation as a percentage of all APS employees increased from 3.5 percent in 2015 to 4.3 percent in 2018. Representation of Indigenous staff in senior roles increased from 2015 to 2018.

(*Inside Policy*, 2019, p. 7)

In the negative, the evaluation noted:

Indigenous ongoing employee engagements fluctuated between 2015 and 2018. Further, Indigenous ongoing employee separations grew as a proportion of all ongoing employee separations (3.6 percent to 5.4 percent). Taken together these changes mean that the Indigenous proportion of ongoing employee separations has increased faster than has the Indigenous proportion of total ongoing employee engagements. Also, the rate of Indigenous ongoing employee separations as a proportion of Indigenous ongoing employees has increased, while the rate of non-Indigenous ongoing employee separations as a proportion of non-Indigenous ongoing employees has decreased.

(*Inside Policy*, 2019, p. 7)

Given that the ongoing trend for the percentage of Indigenous employees is falling and, even more worryingly, falling through retrenchment, it is questionable how much Indigenous employees are able, by themselves, to influence the leadership and management of Indigenous services in Australia. Such a trend is particularly worrying for employment in higher education institutions with respect to the preservation and maintenance of Indigenous perspectives as endorsed by the Australian government in UNDRIP (Australian Human Rights Commission [AHRC], 2009). The *Inside Policy* (2019) evaluation findings should trigger serious consideration regarding the employment of Indigenous Australians in higher education institutions, because traditionally, Indigenous senior leaders have come from strong government administrative backgrounds.

As discussed in Chapter 5, the 2012 *Review of Higher Education Access and Outcomes for Aboriginal and Torres Strait Islander People: Final Report* (Behrendt Review), led by Indigenous Professor Larissa Behrendt provided a comprehensive study of Aboriginal and Torres Strait Islander higher education in Australia. The review made a number of recommendations for furthering the goal of accelerating Indigenous leadership in Australia's universities. The Panel recommended that the parity target for Indigenous employment

> be based on the proportion of the total population aged between 15 and 64 who are Aboriginal and Torres Strait Islander people. This means that the initial national parity target for would be 2.2% and revised in line with new population data following each national census.
>
> (ABS 2011)

In summary, the following has been applied in the Australian university setting to guide its work (Behrendt, Larkin, Griew, & Kelly, 2012):

> Recommendation 2: That universities use the population parity target identified by the Australian Government (2.2%) to set their own targets and timeframes for … for the proportion of the university general and academic staff to be Aboriginal or Torres Strait Islander people.
>
> (Behrendt et al., 2012, p. 17)

We interpret this to mean that universities should aim for at least 2.2 per cent of the senior leadership team of the university identify as Indigenous Australian.

> Recommendation 29: That universities develop strategies, informed by the National Indigenous Higher Education Workforce Strategy, to recruit, support and retain Aboriginal and Torres Strait Islander staff to meet the parity targets set by the Australian Government.
>
> Recommendation 30: That the Australian Government bring forward work to implement an Aboriginal and Torres Strait Islander researcher workforce plan under the national Research Workforce Strategy.
>
> Recommendation 31: That the Australian Government consider developing:
> - a funding program to provide additional scholarships at both the undergraduate and postgraduate level to support universities' ability to 'grow their own' Aboriginal and Torres Strait Islander academic staff
> - a 'top-up' funding program for positions for three years to support universities to attract new Aboriginal and Torres Strait Islander staff members to join the higher education sector.
>
> Recommendation 32: That universities continue to develop and implement a range of strategies to:
> - improve the cultural understanding and awareness of staff, students and researchers within their institution, including the provision of cultural competency training
> - increase the number of Aboriginal and Torres Strait Islander people in senior management positions
> - increase the number of Aboriginal and Torres Strait Islander people represented in the highest-level governance structures
> - increase accountability of faculty leaders and senior management for achieving parity targets and improved outcomes.
>
> (Behrendt et al., 2012, p. xxiv)

The report (Behrendt et al., 2012) observes that:

> Vice-Chancellors will need to lead from the top and, together with faculties, drive change in university culture and governance, so that there is shared responsibility for Aboriginal and Torres Strait Islander higher education outcomes across each university leadership. Improving Aboriginal and Torres Strait Islander higher education outcomes should be integral to the university's core business.
>
> The Panel believes that there should be greater representation of Aboriginal and Torres Strait Islander people in senior governance positions. The Vice-Chancellor and other senior university management should be responsible and accountable for delivering Aboriginal and Torres Strait

Islander student and staff success and this should be reflected in their performance arrangements.

The achievement of the parity targets is central to achievement of the Panel's vision and will require all of the above issues to be addressed and progress to be measured. The Panel believes that the most appropriate accountability mechanism for articulating strategies and measuring progress will be through the mission-based compacts between the universities and government. The Panel would like to see universities articulate their strategies for achieving the parity targets within their negotiations with government and for these to be recorded and reported on through the compacts. The government should consider adjusting reward payment structures to recognize those universities that exceed the targets through performance payments.

(p. 15)

As of 2019, the Australian government and universities generally are still struggling to address the issues raised in the *Behrendt Report*. It is true that, under the impetus of many reviews as discussed in Chapter 5 and earlier in this chapter, Australian universities are making significant new appointments of Aboriginal and Torres Strait Islander professors – increasingly at the level of Deputy or Pro-Vice-Chancellor. They have begun to form Indigenous governance committees to respond to new policy drivers linked to funding. Thus, the first annual report on the progress or change in universities (Universities Australia, 2018) noted:

At the time of the survey, 19 out of 39 universities had filled Indigenous senior executive positions. A majority of the remaining universities were undertaking recruitment processes in a bid to fill similar roles. Whilst surveys reported positive signs of collaboration across university faculties, schools and units, and diversification of responsibility, much of the heavy lifting continues to be done by the Indigenous centres or units of universities.

(p. 40)

Findings of our preliminary research undertaken for this chapter suggest that many of the Indigenous people taking up senior roles in Australian universities have moved across from senior roles in the federal, state or territory public service, where they have developed their administrative skills. If, indeed, highly skilled Indigenous senior leaders are simply moving between various government departments and universities, then it will not solve the problem of the need to increase the number of Indigenous employees in the public service generally. Anecdotally, there is the accusation that a common university practice of Vice-Chancellors is to rely on the advice of Indigenous academics who have been appointed into senior leadership roles, but little is known about whether these leaders have any professional expertise in Indigenous employment and its complexities, any expertise in workforce planning or have an understanding of the particular organisational culture of Australian universities, as distinct from the government public service. Larkin et al. (2018) reported on the discomfort reliance on single Indigenous voices causes:

> There is one senior staff member who is always called upon for advice and I find this to be a very dangerous situation for our university to be in, when they rely on only one Indigenous voice, and definitely does not encourage collaborative Indigenous advice and input.
>
> (Larkin et al., 2018, p. 129)

Every public service agency is searching for Indigenous people to fill a range of roles and there is significant danger that, under such pressures, it may become more persuasive to employ an Indigenous person because of their identification as Indigenous rather than because of their suitability for the role. Larkin et al. (2018, pp. 90–91) argue that there needs to be policy stability and a matrix of legislation, funding and reporting to rebalance this sector of employment. They observe:

> While it is obvious that legislative and best-practice drivers influence the institutional priority given to Indigenous employment, it is likely other factors are also involved. As Schofield et al. (2013) advised, there seems to be an ideological tension in Australian universities between prioritizing social justice and equity issues while also responding to marketisation demands as corporate producers of educational services in a global economy. Herein lies both a challenge and an opportunity for universities to embrace the unique contributions of Indigenous academics to the social and economic capital of Australia.
>
> (pp. 90–91)

In effect, the raft of reports and analysis of the higher education sector since Australia's endorsement of UNDRIP (AHRC, 2009) has influenced policy development across the sector but the translation from policy to practice has been challenging to achieve. Buckskin (2018, p. 13) summarises:

> The launch of Universities Australia's Indigenous Strategy 2017–2020 in March 2017 represented the first comprehensive national Aboriginal and Torres Strait Islander higher education strategy endorsed by universities across Australia and NATSIHEC (AC). Together, NATSIHEC (AC), the DET, the Department of the Prime Minister and Cabinet, and Universities Australia are committed to accelerating higher education outcomes for Aboriginal and Torres Strait Islander students, staff and communities, now and well into the future.

Asmar and Page (2018) drew attention to this aspect, noting that 'Indigenization is occurring within the top levels of university hierarchies, long considered bastions of ivory tower privilege' (p. 1681). We observe that many of these roles are being taken up by Indigenous managerial leaders, not those who are aspiring to sit in the intellectual 'ivory towers' of traditional academic leadership as suggested by Asmar and Page. Minthorn and Chavez (2015) explicitly critiqued Indigenous leadership in higher education in an edited collection that reflected the growing field of research being conducted by American Indian scholars. Even so, they note that most research has focused on the roles of Presidents of Tribal Colleges and Universities. With only a slowly emerging evidence-based and stable understanding of how to accelerate Indigenous senior leadership, many universities espouse the philosophy of 'growing your own'. While this holds potential, at least theoretically, it has proved to be more challenging in its operationalisation.

'Grow your own' strategy to build Indigenous academic and professional staff

There is scant research on the extent of Indigenous employment into Indigenous professional or academic employment, and in particular about those in senior leadership roles. Yet, as noted by Universities Australia (2018), 'many university employment plans refer to growing their own and for example developing and establishing a professional/technical intern and graduate employment program' (p. 58). The meta-analysis conducted by Larkin et al. (2018, pp. 88–89) confirmed that there is limited literature privileging Indigenous academics' experiences in the workplace. They point to work conducted in 2009 by Asmar, Mercier and Page (2009) concerning the unique workplace roles and pressures placed on Indigenous people within academia. They interviewed Indigenous academics and found that teaching was the 'dominant dimension' of their work. Nine years on, in 2018, Larkin et al. (2018, pp. 121–131) reported on a survey conducted of Indigenous staff in Australian universities and found 30 per cent of respondents had a higher education workforce classification and 70 per cent had an academic classification. This is somewhat the inverse of the current profile overall in universities (67.2–32.8 per cent respectively) but responses were in keeping with comparable data in our analysis. The Universities Australia (2018) report also found that:

> In 2017, a greater proportion of Indigenous staff were women, over 40 years old and in lower academic positions compared with non-Indigenous staff. This share has remained relatively unchanged since 2005.
>
> (p. 54)

Analysis of 2018 HEIMS data (Department of Employment and Training [DET], 2018)[1] shows there were 1,316 staff employed in Australian universities who identified as Indigenous: 419 (31.8 per cent) identified as male and 897 (68.2 per cent) identified as female; 316 (24.0 per cent) staff reported being in a 'Teaching Only' or 'Teaching and Research' function and 1,000 (76.0 per cent) staff with a 'Research Only' or an 'Other' function. In addition, 431 (32.8 per cent) identified as being in academic roles and 885 (67.2 per cent) as being in non-academic roles. Therefore, of the 431 people identifying as being in 'academic' roles, 315 are in traditional teaching or teaching and research roles. By extrapolation, we assume that some of the other 116 Indigenous staff are in senior leadership roles that are classified as academic. We also assume that some of the 1,000 who report being in the 'Other' classification and some of the 885 who report being 'non-academic' are in professional staff classifications, and some may also be in senior leadership roles that are classified as executive higher education professional staff. Though we have worked through these assumptions, what is most clear in our calculations is that the way such data are reported does not allow the fine-grained analysis that is needed in this sector. To meet the need for more fine-grained data for the employment of Indigenous people in higher education, Universities Australia has begun surveying universities annually so that it can develop a more targeted understanding of matters that need to be resolved and those that remain to be improved (Universities Australia, 2018).

Professional roles

There is little independently funded research that has been conducted about the nature of the work undertaken by Indigenous professional staff in Australian universities. Most of the data are from broader reporting by government and quasi-government agencies. Anecdotal reports reveal that most faculties and departments employ Indigenous professional staff at predominantly lower levels and, commonly, in fixed-term contract arrangements. Some Indigenous professional staff advance through the HEW levels to senior appointments and a few have moved into senior leadership roles in recent years, highlighting that:

> [R]ecent focus on spreading building senior Indigenous academic leadership (and Indigenous academic progression) within faculties and in supporting the career progression of Indigenous professional staff will also ensure that additional workload is distributed evenly and that capacity is built at all levels.
>
> (Universities Australia, 2018, p. 60)

Somewhat problematically, the Behrendt Review (2012) identified that professional staff may be targeted as a future supply pool of Indigenous academics. As Larkin et al. (2018, p. 88) note:

> The approach of targeting general duties staff is included under the umbrella term 'growing your own', which includes universities targeting promising

undergraduate Indigenous students (Behrendt et al., 2012, p. 140). For the most part, this strategy is based on the premise that the majority of Indigenous university employees in Australia are currently in general duty roles and could be an undervalued asset in increasing the Indigenous academic workforce. The Behrendt Review (2012, p.140) commented that 'growing your own' could be achieved through 'academic internships, time release and more flexible study leave provisions for their non-academic staff'.

(p. 88)

Like Larkin et al. (2018), we note the lack of an evidence base on which to develop such a strategy. This was something flagged for attention by Behrendt et al. (2012) when they reported that:

> Some Indigenous general duties staff are both casually employed as academics and HDR candidates. This places them in double disadvantage, in both workload and research, due to their general inability to access study leave.
>
> (p. 88)

As with the 'revolving door' simile used to describe the movement of highly skilled Indigenous administrative professionals between the public service and universities, there is also pressure on Indigenous professional staff to move into academic roles. Again, we argue that this is a flawed, unsustainable, and undesirable strategy as discussed in the next section.

Academic roles

The parity gap between Indigenous and non-Indigenous university staff is most problematic in academic roles. Despite numerous reporting mechanisms and university self-reporting, very little is known about the academic profession from an Indigenous academic perspective. Larkin et al. (2018, p. 93) report:

> Indigenous academics are poorly represented in the Australian academic workforce and that, nationally, percentages fall short of the parity target goal of 2.7%. For example, meeting the target in 2015 would have required a further 816 Indigenous academics to be employed. While the total number remains low, there is evidence of positive growth albeit at a much lower rate than for the non-Indigenous academic workforce. The numbers of Indigenous academics employed in individual universities demonstrates wide variance. Data show that some institutions employ no Indigenous academic staff and others more than 20 Indigenous academics.
>
> (p. 93)

A number of practices have evolved over time that enable administrators of public service institutions, such as universities, to have a 'pipeline' of potential employees to fill junior academic roles. In the case of the university, the requirements are well developed and universally recognised. At the outset, an early career academic (Level A) needs to have completed or nearly completed a PhD before being able to become employed. The Level A entry phase into academia is the time for a new academic that is often marked by deep and steep organisational learning. As Erlandson and Beach (2008) note:

> Tacit knowledge is not verbalized (and maybe is impossible to verbalize) and has, therefore, not been taught in universities. It is a situated knowledge that is only accessible when work is actually being carried out. This 'knowing-in- action' is a foundation for the action-related attitude that the experienced practitioner has and that Schön called 'reflection-in-action'.
>
> (p. 412)

In terms of the day-to-day work, this period in the career of a new academic is the time when they are brought into teaching teams to learn the required skills, knowledge and understanding of how to develop their lecture materials and the curriculum, navigating student needs and demands, dealing with negative student feedback, becoming aware of the larger institutional expectations about their teaching and research roles, developing small research projects that build on their PhD studies and becoming involved in large research projects under the tutelage of more senior academics who act as supervisors and mentors. Senior academics pass on their institutional, disciplinary cultural knowledge and values to their charges, in a master–apprentice model of mentorship, which has largely remained unchanged for centuries in the university system. The doctoral student socialisation is a common framework in which to view one's entry into the academic profession, with a growing body of literature examining it (Austin, 1990, 2002, 2009; Baird, 1992; Gardner, 2010).

Anderson (2014) undertook research about the impact of organisational culture of universities on academic values, focusing specifically on the traditional value of 'academic freedom'. All Indigenous academics with PhD qualifications were proactively invited to participate. Many who were approached to be involved in the initial study who were in senior leadership positions shared that they did not hold a PhD and were thereby excluded from the research. Their lack of a PhD caused us to think about the consequence of not holding a PhD in a leadership position in a university and as an aspect of Indigenous employment in senior leadership positions as requiring more research.

Of the few who did agree to participate, even fewer reported being mentored in the traditional master–apprentice model. From the available statistical data and qualitative survey responses from various studies as discussed earlier, our analysis for this chapter suggests that the traditional master–apprentice model, founded on having an available 'pipeline' of new and willing PhD-holding candidates is not working in terms of growing the Indigenous academic workforce. This gap has also been identified by Delugan (2010) and Johnson (2003). For example, in the most recent available data from the Universities Australia's (2018) first annual report on its Indigenous Strategy and in terms of Duties Classification, respondent universities (n=39) reported:

> In 2017, Indigenous academic staff were proportionally over-represented at below lecturer (Level A) (19.5 per cent, compared to 17.8 per cent for non-Indigenous) and lecturer (Level B) (37.3 per cent, compared to 30.5 per cent for non-Indigenous).
>
> In contrast, Indigenous academic staff were proportionally under-represented at senior lecturer (Level C) (17.8 per cent, compared to 23 per cent for non-Indigenous) and above senior lecturer (Level D and above) (25.4 per cent, compared to 28.7 per cent for non-Indigenous). Nonetheless, it is important to note that the share of Indigenous staff in senior academic roles – Level D and above – has doubled since 2005, from 12.1 per cent to 25.4 per cent.
>
> (p. 56)

In terms of population parity,

> In 2017, 423 Indigenous staff were employed in teaching or research function in Australian universities, representing 0.75 per cent of all staff employed in teaching or research function … the sector would need to employ an additional 128 Indigenous staff in teaching-only function, 453 in research-only function and 735 in teaching and research function in 2017.
>
> (Universities Australia, 2018, p. 57)

We conducted a meta-analysis of available data up to 2019 and we conclude that there are currently quite a few Indigenous academics in most Australian universities, many without PhDs, in untenured positions, employed as researchers on soft money from grants or as sessional lecturers. They appear to be predominantly employed in Faculties of Arts, Education or as quasi-academic administrators of Indigenous matters. Our analysis of available trend data from 2009 to 2018 (see Figure 10.1) shows negligible growth in Indigenous employment despite an almost continual policy focus and programme of work being undertaken.

For a number of reasons, both historical and external to the university, the work of an academic is both particular and marked by distinct organisational values. While there is 'demand' in terms of government policy pressure on

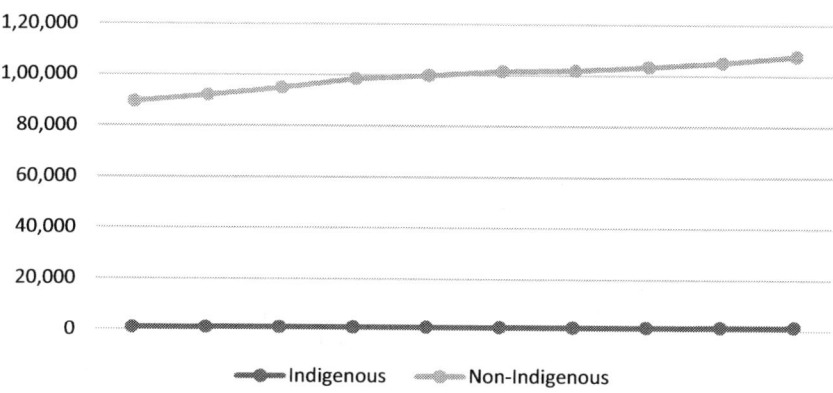

Figure 10.1 Indigenous and non-Indigenous academic employment trend data 2009–2018.
Source: Authors from HEIMS data, DET, 2018.

universities to accelerate the number of Indigenous academics in the sense of classic economic theory, there is only a very small supply and that too only in particular disciplines.

In terms of workforce planning and modelling, there appear to be a number of factors preventing the academic pipeline from functioning properly. First, analysis of relevant literature cited in the Behrendt Report by Australian Council for Education Research (ACER) (2011, p. 12) found that Indigenous academics are commonly expected to undertake significant student support beyond formal role expectations. Larkin et al. (2018, pp. 88–89) reported this aspect as being a significant and hidden dimension of Indigenous academic roles. The second burden identified by Asmar et al. (2009) was the requests from non-Indigenous academic colleagues for help on issues of pedagogical revision, research ethics support and community engagement, which further adds to Indigenous academic workloads.

The third significant institutional burden was reported by the National Tertiary Education Union (NTEU), which has undertaken a number of surveys of its Indigenous membership and documented common experiences of racial discrimination, cultural disrespect and lateral violence in their higher education workplace (NTEU, 2000, 2011, 2017). Confirming these findings, research by Page and Asmar (2004, 2008) and Bond (2014) found that the teaching of Indigenous Studies was mostly delivered by junior and mid-level Indigenous academics. Larkin (2014) focused broadly on the racialised construction and evaluation of Aboriginal bodies and work, which, in turn. builds on his work with Behrendt et al. (2012) examining the challenges of achieving a critical mass of Aboriginal and Torres Strait Islander academics in Australian universities. In more recent research, Larkin et al. (2018) cite feedback from

Indigenous academics who report continued high levels of racism and ignorance about Indigenous Australian lifeways, languages, histories and cultures:

> Indigenous interviewees believed that universities are built on traditional western notions of knowledge production and reproduction, and that the structures, practices and informal corporate culture of the university are inherently ethnocentric and/or racist.
>
> (p. 124)

This ongoing reporting of racism and ignorance has a strong negative impact on aspiring Indigenous academics and management professionals. We believe that these negative experiences are slowing down the 'grow your own' pipeline strategy and that many early career Indigenous academics are arguing for a complete overhaul of Australian universities as being a more beneficial strategy for them in terms of job security and long-term career prospects (Larkin, 2014; NTEU, 2017).

The lack of competitive remuneration for higher education employment compared to the wider public sector acts as an inhibitor for Indigenous higher education employment. Behrendt et al. (2012) identified that if the Australian government maintains its policy commitment to reaching parity in the Indigenous academic workforce, it must commit the funds to make these roles financially attractive. While recent focus on student experience in Australian universities is expecting all of the academic workforce to pay more attention to the quality of the student experience, as we have discussed earlier, the expectation placed on Indigenous academics, particularly those in junior roles, is an additional and demanding role that is not expected of non-Indigenous academics. In the reverse of the traditional master–apprentice model, it is common for senior non-Indigenous academics to rely on Indigenous colleagues for anything to do with Indigenous pedagogy, curriculum and assessment matters, even when the Indigenous academic might be Level A or on a sessional teaching contract.

Our meta-analysis of the available reports and data undertaken for this chapter suggests that a fifth – and possibly most significant proportion – of potential Indigenous academics are not being mentored into the university organisational culture in the traditional manner. In particular, we examined the potential of mentoring to develop the characteristics of Macfarlane's (2012) account of intellectual leadership – a concept informed by Bourdieu's (1989) definition:

> [A]n intellectual is a bi-dimensional being; someone who belongs to an autonomous field of intellectual study (such as an academic or scientist) and who uses their authority and competence as an expert to undertake political action that is 'carried out', outside the intellectual field proper.
>
> (p. 656)

Of significance, Anderson (2014) found that the different organisational cultures of Australian universities, as proposed by Marginson and Considine (2000, pp. 189–190) in their typology of universities as Sandstones, Gum Trees and UniTechs, appears to have significant influence over an individual academic's understanding of their academic work and of their educational philosophy. Anderson also found that this understanding was further shaped by the level of appointment, length of time at the institution, exposure to other university cultures and institutional research and teaching goals throughout the academic's career, including an individual's understanding of academic freedom.

Conclusions

In conclusion, given the analysis of current approaches to accelerating Indigenous leadership in Australian universities, many questions remain about how to radically change the discussion to address the 'real' issues. If the current use of the revolving door principle of hiring Indigenous staff into roles that are comparable to a previous role in another sector, job classification or faculty, then the overall growth of an Indigenous professional and academic university workforce will stagnate. At its most fundamental, the Australian Public Service pays more money to potential Indigenous aspirants to attract them into a professional public service role, the mentoring and training is well developed, and there are numerous opportunities for promotion. Junior academic roles, by comparison to the roles available at a similar level and skill requirement in the Australian Public Service, are very demanding, with opportunities for recognition, mentoring and promotion arising from within the master–apprentice model – a tradition that is largely unavailable to Indigenous academics and professional staff, the majority of whom are corralled into Indigenous-identified positions to meet the needs and expectations of the university and the Indigenous community.

The lack of integration of Indigenous staff into the university organisational culture has given rise to demands by Indigenous senior leaders for a completely different academy that would fit the cultural expectations of Indigenous staff. What emerges from research by the authors of the Minthorn and Chavez (2015) collection of essays concerning Indigenous leadership is emblematic of the emerging trend within the sector towards developing a model of Indigenous cultural leadership that puts it at odds with the traditional values and metrics of the modern university, moving the university system towards a future where the lifeways of the world's Indigenous Peoples are at the heart of the work. This approach resonates with aspirations reflected in UNDRIP and develops a series of propositions about the role of the modern university and the characteristics of those who are employed in these institutions: Who we are; What we strive to embody; What is known; What we do; and, Our context of leadership (Minthorn & Chavez, 2015).

We suggest that the fundamental challenge posed by Indigenous people to the modern university about its role and purpose will make it even more difficult for universities to maintain their traditional approaches, such as the pipeline and the master–apprentice models that do not appear to be sufficiently attractive to potential Indigenous employees.

We have identified that specific historical antecedents have created pipelines into both academic and professional elites in Australian universities and that these are not working for Indigenous people wishing to gain entry to higher education leadership positions. A third pipeline beyond the scope of this chapter – cultural leadership – emphasises cultural leadership and is attractive to Indigenous people because it is a clear demonstration of the aspirations of UNDRIP, operationalised in the Larkin et al. (2018) research and is supported by emerging data by Universities Australia (2018). However, this approach to the 'growing your own' pipeline puts aspiring Indigenous university leaders on a collision course with a number of competing values and performance expectations of Australian universities.

The question being asked of universities and of senior Indigenous academic and professional leaders and their non-Indigenous peers is how to accelerate the employment of Indigenous people into the university in the future in a manner that is cognisant of the issues while respectful of the constraints. Indigenous university staff across role classifications and levels have made clear that without there being a commitment by universities to significant structural change and organisational development, many Indigenous people do not see a career for themselves in the Australian higher education sector.

Note

1 We highlight that this may, or may not, represent accurate figures because some Indigenous Australians choose not to identify as Indigenous with their employer. It is also difficult from the HEIMS data to ascertain the classifications of senior leadership roles as being distinct from Professional or Academic roles because this depends on the way that each university classifies and reports such roles to the government.

References

Anderson, D., Johnson, R., & Saha, L. (2002). *Changes in academic work: Implications for universities of the changing age distribution and work roles of academic staff*. Canberra, Australia: Commonwealth of Australia.

Anderson, P. (2014). *Academic freedom: Examining its enactment as an organisational value in Australian universities*. Unpublished PhD thesis. Melbourne: Monash University.

Anderson, P. J., & Atkinson, B. (2013). Closing the gap: Using graduate attributes to improve Indigenous education. *The International Education Journal: Comparative Perspectives*, *12*(1), 135–145.

Anderson, P. J., & Ma Rhea, Z. (2018). Rights-based Indigenous education in Australia: Evidence based policy to pedagogy. In M. Barnes, M. Gindidis, & S.

Phillipson (Eds.). *Evidence-based learning and teaching: A look into Australian classrooms* (pp. 207–228). London, England: Routledge.

Asmar, C., Mercier, O. R., & Page, S. (2009). 'You do it from your core': Priorities, perceptions and practices of research among Indigenous academics in Australian and New Zealand universities. In A. Brew & L. Lucas (Eds.). *Academic research and researchers* (pp. 146–160). Maidenhead, England: Open University Press and McGraw-Hill.

Asmar, C., & Page, S. (2018). Pigeonholed, peripheral or pioneering? Findings from a national study of Indigenous Australian academics in the disciplines. *Studies in Higher Education, 43*(9). doi.org/10.1080/03075079.2017.1281240

Austin, A. E. (1990). Faculty cultures, faculty values. *New Directions for Institutional Research, 1990*(68), 61–74.

Austin, A. E. (2002). Preparing the next generation of faculty: Graduate school as socialization to the academic career. *Journal of Higher Education, 73*(1), 94–121.

Austin, A. E. (2009). Cognitive apprenticeship theory and its implications for doctoral education: A case example from a doctoral program in higher and adult education. *International Journal for Academic Development, 14*(3), 173–183.

Australian Bureau of Statistics (ABS). (2006). *Employment – Education and training industry in Australia*. Canberra, Australia: Statistical Subdivision Profile.

Australian Bureau of Statistics (ABS). (2011). *Census of population and housing: Characteristics of Aboriginal and Torres Strait Islander Australians: 2011* (cat. no. 2076.0). Retrieved 31 May 2020 fromwww.abs.gov.au/ausstats/abs@.nsf/Lookup/2076.0main+features302011

Australian Council for Education Research (ACER). (2011). 'Literature review relating to the current context and discourse of Indigenous tertiary education in Australia.' Australian Council for Educational Research, unpublished report to the Review of Higher Education Access and Outcomes for Aboriginal and Torres Strait Islander People, Department of Education, Employment and Workplace Relations, Canberra.

Australian Government. (2009). *Transforming Australia's higher education system*. Canberra, Australia: Department of Education, Employment and Workplace Relations.

Australian Government. (2014). *Indigenous employment in Australian government entities*, in Auditor-General Report No.33 of 2013–14. Canberra, Australia: Commonwealth of Australia. Retrieved 31 May 2020 from www.anao.gov.au/work/performance-audit/indigenous-employment-australian-government-entities

Australian Government. (2015). *Commonwealth Aboriginal and Torres Strait Islander employment strategy 2015–2018*. Canberra, Australia: Commonwealth of Australia. Retrieved 31 May 2020 from www.apsc.gov.au/sites/default/files/Commonwealth-Aboriginal-and-Torres-Strait-Islander-Employment-Strategy-r....pdf

Australian Government. (2019). *Higher education*. Canberra, Australia: Department of the Prime Minister and Cabinet. Retrieved 31 May 2020 from www.pmc.gov.au/indigenous affairs/education/higher-education

Australian Human Rights Commission (AHRC). (2009). *United we stand – Support for United Nations Indigenous Rights Declaration a watershed moment for Australia*. Canberra, Australia: Australian Human Rights Commission. Retrieved 31 May 2020 from www.humanrights.gov.au/about/news/media-releases/2009-media-release-united-we-stand-support-united-nations-indigenous

Baird, L. L (1992). *The stages of the doctoral career: Socialisation and its consequences*. Paper presented at the American Educational Research Association, San Francisco, CA.

Ball, S. J. (2000). Performativities and fabrications in the education economy: Towards the performative society. *Australian Educational Researcher, 17*(3), 1–24.

Behrendt, L., Larkin, S., Griew, R., & Kelly, P. (2012). *Review of Higher Education access and outcomes for Aboriginal and Torres Strait Islander people: Final report.* Canberra, Australia: Commonwealth of Australia.

Bernstein, B. (1996). *Pedagogy, symbolic control and identity: Theory, research, critique.* London, England: Taylor and Francis.

Bernstein, B. (2000). Official knowledge and pedagogic identities: The politics of recontextualising. In S. J. Ball (Ed.). *The sociology of education: Major themes.* London, England: Routledge Falmer.

Bond, C. (2014). When the object teaches: Indigenous academics in Australian universities, *Right Now, 14*. Retrieved 31 May 2020 from http://rightnow.org.au/opinion-3/when-the-object-teaches-indigenous-academics-in-australian-universities/

Bourdieu, P. (1989). The corporatism of the universal: The role of intellectuals in the modern world. *Telos, 81*(Fall), 99–110.

Bradley, D., Noonan, P., Nugent, H., & Scales, B. (2008). *Review of Australian higher education: Final report.* Canberra, Australia: Commonwealth of Australia.

Buckskin, P. (2018). Executive summary. In P. Buckskin & M. Tranthim-Fryer (Eds.). *Accelerating Indigenous higher education* (pp. 12–13). Adelaide, South Australia: NATSIHEC(AC).

Charan, R., Drotter, S. J., & Noel, J. L. (2001). *The leadership pipeline: How to build the leadership-powered company.* San Franscisco, CA: Jossey-Bass.

Coaldrake, P., & Stedman, L. (1999). *Academic work in the twenty-first century.* Canberra, Australia: Higher Education Division Department of Education, Training and Youth Affairs.

Delugan, R. (2010). Indigeneity across borders: Hemispheric migrations and cosmopolitan encounters. *American Ethnologist, 37*(1), 83–97. doi: 10.1111/j.1548-1425.2010.01243.x

Department of Education and Training (DET). (2018). *Indigenous staff 2018.* Higher Education Information Management Systems (HEIMS) data. Retrieved 31 May 2020 from https://docs.education.gov.au/node/51706

Erlandson, P., & Beach, D. (2008). The ambivalence of reflection – Re-reading Schön. *Reflective Practice, 9*(4), 409–421. doi: 10.1080/14623940802475843

Gardner, S. K. (2010). Faculty perspectives on doctoral student socialization in five disciplines. *International Journal of Doctoral Studies, 5*, 39–53.

Indigenous Higher education Advisory Committee (IHEAC), & Larkin, S. (2011). *National Indigenous higher education workforce strategy.* Canberra, Australia: Australian Government Department of Education, Employment and Workplace Relations. Retrieved 31 May 2020 from https://docs.education.gov.au/system/files/doc/other/nihews.pdf

Inside Policy. (2019). *An evaluation of the Commonwealth Aboriginal and Torres Strait Islander employment strategy.* Canberra, Australia: Commonwealth of Australia. Retrieved 31 May 2020 from www.apsc.gov.au/sites/default/files/apsc_catsies_evaluation_report_final.pdf

Johnson, E. P. (2003). Performance and/as pedagogy: Performing blackness in the classroom. In E. P. Johnson (Ed.). *Appropriating blackness: Performance and the politics of authenticity* (pp. 219–256). Durham, NC: Duke University Press.

Larkin, S., Ireland, S., MacGibon, L., Small, T., Butler, K., & Chatfield, T. (2018). Academic workforce. In P. Buckskin & M. Tranthim-Fryer (Eds.). *Accelerating Indigenous higher education* (pp. 90–155). Adelaide, Australia: National Aboriginal and Torres Strait Islander Higher Education Consortium AC (NATSIHEC).

Larkin, S. R. (2014). *Race matters: Indigenous employment in the Australian public service.* Unpublished PhD thesis. Brisbane, Queensland: Queensland University of Technology.

Lazear, E. P. (2001). *Paying teachers for performance: Incentives and selection.* Stanford, CA: Hoover Institution and Graduate School of Business, Stanford University. Retrieved 31 May 2020 from https://pdfs.semanticscholar.org/8733/1eac6d2bf5a46 2c7cc1a60035f6f52f8e1ab.pdf

Ma Rhea, Z. (2015). *Leading and managing Indigenous education in the postcolonial world.* London, England: Routledge.

Ma Rhea, Z., Anderson, P. J., & Atkinson, B. (2012). *National professional standards for teachers standards 1.4 and 2.4: Improving teaching in Aboriginal and Torres Strait Islander education.* Melbourne, Australia: Australian Institute for Teaching and School Leadership. Retrieved 31 May 2020 from www.aitsl.edu.au/tools-resources/ resource/improving-teaching-in-aboriginal-and-torres-strait-islander-education-australian-professional-standards-for-teachers

Macfarlane, B., & Society for Research into Higher Education. (2012). *Intellectual leadership in higher education: Renewing the role of the university professor.* Abingdon, England: Routledge Together with the Society for Research into Higher Education.

Marginson, S. (1993). *Education and public policy in Australia.* Melbourne, Australia: Cambridge University Press.

Marginson, S. (2000). Rethinking academic work in the global era. *Journal of Higher Education, 22*(1), 23–35.

Marginson, S., & Considine, M. (2000). *The enterprise university: Power, governance and reinvention in Australia.* Cambridge, England: Cambridge University Press.

McInnes, C. (1996). Change and diversity in the work patterns of Australian academics. *Higher Education Management, 8*(2), 105–116.

McInnes, C. (1999). *The work roles of academics in Australian universities.* Canberra, Australia: Department of Education, Training and Youth Affairs.

McInnes, C. (2000). Changing academic work roles: The everyday realities challenging quality in teaching. *Quality in Higher Education, 6*(2), 143–152.

Minthorn, R. S., & Chavez, A. F. (2015). *Indigenous leadership in higher education.* New York: Routledge.

Moore, M. H. (1995). *Creating public value: Strategic management in government.* Cambridge, MA: Harvard University Press.

Moreton-Robinson, A., Walter, M., Singh, D., & Kimber, M. (2011). On stony ground: Governance and Aboriginal and Torres Strait Islander participation in Australian universities. Report to the *Review of Higher Education Access and Outcomes for Aboriginal and Torres Strait Islander people.* Canberra, Australia: Department of Education, Employment and Workplace Relations.

National Tertiary Education Union. (2000). *Unhealthy places of learning: Working in Australian universities.* Melbourne, Australia: National Tertiary Education Union (NTEU).

National Tertiary Education Union. (2011). *NTEU submission to the Review of Higher Education Access and Outcomes for Aboriginal and Torres Strait Islander people.* Melbourne, Australia: National Tertiary Education Union (NTEU).

National Tertiary Education Union. (2017). *How secure do you feel?* Melbourne, Australia: National Tertiary Education Union (NTEU).

O'Donoghue, L. (1997). *Spann oration: The case for Indigenous rights: Reflecting on a contentious area of public administration.* Sydney, Australia: Institute of Public Administration, 12 August 1997, p. 4.

Page, S., & Asmar, C. (2004). Indigenous academic voices: Stories from the tertiary education frontline. *Higher Education Research and Development Society of Australasia* (HERDSA) *News, 26*(1) (April), 13–15.

Page, S., & Asmar, C. (2008). Beneath the teaching iceberg: Exposing the hidden support dimensions of Indigenous academic work. *The Australian Journal of Indigenous Education, 37*(S1), 109–117. doi:10.1375/S1326011100000442

Rigney, L. I. (1999). Internationalization of an Indigenous anticolonial cultural critique of research methodologies: A guide to Indigenist research methodology and its principles. *Wicazo sa Review, 14*(2), 109–121. doi: 10.2307/1409555

Royal Commission on Australian Government Administration, & Coombs, H. C. (1976). *Report: Royal commission on Australian government administration.* Canberra, Australia: Australian Government Publishing Service. Retrieved 31 May 2020 from https://apo.org.au/sites/default/files/resource-files/1976/08/apo-nid34221-1236056.pdf

Said, E. W. (1994). *Culture and imperialism* (1st Vintage Books edition). London, England: Vintage Books.

Sikes, P. (2001). Teachers' lives and teaching performance. In D. Gleeson & C. Husbands (Eds.). *The performing school: Managing teaching and learning in a performance culture* (pp. 86–100). London, England: Routledge Falmer.

Stillwaggon, J. (2008). Performing for the students: Teaching identity and the pedagogical relationship. *Journal of Philosophy of Education, 42*(1), 67–83.

United Nations. (2007). *United Nations Declaration on the Rights of Indigenous Peoples.* Retrieved 31 May 2020 from www.un.org/development/desa/indigenousPeoples/wp-content/uploads/sites/19/2018/11/UNDRIP_E_web.pdf

Universities Australia. (2011). *Guiding principles for developing Indigenous cultural competency in Australian universities.* Canberra, Australia. Retrieved 31 May 2020 from www.universitiesaustralia.edu.au/wp-content/uploads/2019/06/Guiding-Principles-for-Developing-Indigenous-Cultural-Competency-in-Australian-Universities.pdf

Universities Australia. (2017). *Aboriginal and Torres Strait Islander education strategy 2017–2020.* Canberra, Australia. Retrieved 31 May 2020 from www.universitiesaustralia.edu.au/wp-content/uploads/2019/06/Indigenous-Strategy-v16-1.pdf

Universities Australia. (2018). *Universities Australia Indigenous strategy: First annual report.* Canberra, Australia. Retrieved 31 May 2020 from https://apo.org.au/sites/default/files/resource-files/2019/02/apo-nid222106-1334871.pdf

White, S., Ma Rhea, Z., Anderson, P. J., & Atkinson, B. (2012). *Design and development of a unit outline and content for professional learning units to support teachers in meeting Focus Areas 1.4 and 2.4.* Melbourne, Australia: Australian Institute for Teaching and School Leadership. Retrieved 31 May 2020 from www.aitsl.edu.au/tools-resources/resource/a-unit-outline-and-content-for-professional-learning-units-to-support-teachers-in-meeting-focus-areas-1.4-and-2.4

Part III

Considering post-imperial Indigenous education in Japan and Australia

Chapter 11

The significance of building an Ainu-led higher education system and the empowerment of the Indigenous Ainu[1]

Koji Maeda and Kaori Okano

Introduction

The Ainu are an Indigenous people of Japan who were integrated into the newly created modern nation state of Japan in the mid-19th century. The Ainu share many experiences with other Indigenous peoples around the world, including internal colonisation, dispossession of their land, and exploitation as cheap labour, and remain marginalised to this day. It was only in 2008 that the Ainu gained official recognition from the government as Indigenous people. Ainu are physically almost indistinguishable from the majority Japanese and many pass as majority Wajin Japanese, despite their distinctive ethnic identity. Ainu people have gradually raised their retention rate to post-compulsory education to almost the national average, but a significant gap remains in retention to and completion of higher education.

It is important to note that the exact size of the Ainu population is unknown. Since the national census has never collected data on ethnic heritage among Japanese citizens, we can gain an indication only from local government data. The estimated population of self-identified Ainu people in Hokkaido was approximately 24,000 in 2006 (Hokkaido-chō-kankyōseisaku-bu, 2013); but Teruki Tsunemoto, the head of the Hokkaido University Centre for Ainu and Indigenous Studies, estimates that the real number is close to 50,000 (Tsunemoto, 2009). Many Ainu reside in cities outside Hokkaido, as implied by the existence of Ainu organisations in Tokyo. Tsunemoto (2009) estimates that Tokyo has 5,000 Ainu residents.

The absence of official data on the ethnic heritage of Japanese citizens is at least partially responsible for the lack of attention to Ainu people in the prevailing political and public discussion on multiculturalism in Japan. This lack has caused the public debate to frame Japan's ethnic diversity in the discourse of *zainichi gaikokujin* foreigners in Japan (Okano, 2012; Chapter 3, this edition). For example, when the media discuss increasing ethnic diversity, they list the number of registered foreign nationals and their nationalities. The public is constantly reminded of how many foreigners live in Japan but has little idea about the number of Ainu people.

The aim of this chapter is to examine how Ainu participation in higher education can be promoted and to discuss this in the context of the *United Nations Declaration on the Rights of Indigenous Peoples* (UNDRIP) (United Nations, 2007). We will use Sapporo University's *Urespa Project* as a case study. Under this project, the university offers scholarships to Ainu students – who then take a special course in Ainu Culture and History – and develop collaborations with private sector companies – in order to assist Ainu students' transition to employment. We can see the university's commitment to this collaborative approach in the project's name, 'Urespa', which means 'mutual nurturing' in the Ainu language.

We suggest that 'two-way mutual learning' signifies a challenge to the conventional approach to Ainu education, which has centred on the majority Wajin providing unidirectional assistance to the Ainu in order to achieve the national benchmarks. The 'mutual learning' approach (*sodateai* in Japanese, *urespa* in the Ainu language) stresses the creation of a nurturing environment in which both Ainu and non-Ainu students feel included and learn from one another. That such initiatives came from private universities rather than the national government is indicative of how Ainu education is perceived in Japan.

We begin with a brief description of Ainu social conditions in terms of employment and educational achievement. We then examine the Japanese government's deliberations on Ainu policies following UNDRIP, and the views by the main Ainu organisation. Our discussion will turn to how the relevant articles regarding Ainu education can be understood in the context of Ainu people in contemporary Japan. This chapter then presents Urespa Project as a case study and discusses future possibilities for university contributions to empowerment of Ainu and non-Ainu students.

Ainu people in Japanese schools: A history of assimilation and marginalisation

As discussed in Chapters 4 (this edition), the Ainu lived in the dense forests of Hokkaido prior to the arrival of mainlander Japanese from the south in the 13th century. Over the next 500 years, they traded with Wajin on an individual basis. When Japan emerged as a modern imperial state in the mid-19th century, it politically incorporated the Indigenous peoples of Hokkaido. Japan went on to colonise the Korean Peninsula and Taiwan, and people from those colonies also became imperial subjects, some of whom moved to mainland Japan. Imperial Japan, hence, had a multi-ethnic population (Lie, 2001; Oguma, 1998; Weiner, 1997).

The national government created the Development Commission in 1869 to oversee the development of Hokkaido, which the state regarded as *terra nullius*, and directed migration of mainland Japanese to the new land. Ainu people, who until then had depended for their livelihood on the forests and waterways, had no choice but to resettle and work as cheap labour for the immigrants.

Informed by the social Darwinist view of race that was prevalent at the time, the government enacted the *Hokkaido Former Aboriginal Protection Act* (1899) and expected that Ainu people would become small farmers and assimilate, becoming Japanese imperial subjects.

Imperial Japan lost its colonial territories as well as colonial subjects at the end of the Second World War. The post-war Japanese state created a single category of Japanese citizens, which included Indigenous Ainu and Okinawans, designating the remaining ethnic groupings 'foreign nationals', for example, former colonial subjects Koreans and Taiwanese living in Japan.

The modern system of state education has effectively forced Ainu children to abandon the language and culture of their parents, to learn to see the world in ways determined by mainstream Japanese and to conform to what has long been considered the 'Japanese way' (see Chapter 2 and 6, this edition). From the beginning, the imperial government considered schools a central instrument for Ainu assimilation, which then enabled Ainu people to contribute to Japan's modernisation project. Initially adopting a policy of segregated schooling, the government provided a simpler curriculum for Ainu children than that for Wajin children. In 1937, there was a switch to co-education of Ainu and Wajin, which imposed further damage on Ainu children in the form of routine bullying and discrimination at the hands of Wajin children. Schooling reinforced the then prevailing view of Ainu inferiority among all children. Schools became alienating and fearful places, which in turn encouraged many Ainu children to drop out. Even in the 1960s, the number of compulsory-age students with long-term school absences was high (Takegahara, 2010).

The Ainu have not been passive recipients of this discriminatory system. Ainu activism emerged in the 1920s and 1930s and led to the formation of *Ainu Kyōkai* (Hokkaido Ainu Association) in 1930, renamed *Utari Kyōkai* (Utari Association) in 1961. From the outset, the association saw welfare measures as central to solving the problems of Ainu people.

The association has widely been considered one of the largest and most influential organisations of Ainu people. The organisation's mission is to promote the social status and cultural maintenance of Ainu with the ultimate goal of establishing Ainu dignity. The association has actively implemented various programmes to improve Ainu people's living conditions, employment, and education, including the institution of loans, to research Ainu culture, and to promote interaction with other minority groups. The association is currently represented in the government committee to promote *Ainu seisaku suishinn kaigi* Ainu policies.

In 1961, the Utari Special Welfare Project was implemented to improve the living conditions and employment and education levels. When it was found that Ainu living conditions remained inferior to those of non-Ainu, another welfare package, the First Hokkaido Utari Welfare Measures, was implemented, at a cost of 12 billion yen (about US$11 million) over the period 1971–1980 (Siddle, 1996). The Utari Welfare Measures are still in place, having been renewed in 1981–1987, 1988–1994, 1995–2001, 2002–2008, 2009–2015, 2016–2020 (Hokkaido-kankyōseikatsu-bu, 2017). These special measures recognise that education is a key means for improving Ainu lives and providing financial assistance to Ainu children to attend upper secondary schools and tertiary institutions.

Influenced by Ainu activism, primary and secondary school teachers began to question the existing Ainu education practices. They produced a guidebook in 1982 titled 'Discussing minorities in Japan with students: The current situation and guides for teaching' (Hokkaido-kōtōgakkō-kyōshokuin-kumiai – Hokkaido High School Teachers Union, 1982). In 1983, a professional association of teachers, the Research Association for Ainu Education, was formed within the Hokkaido Education Board. The association produced two publications to guide teachers in the teaching of Ainu history in primary and middle school (1984) and senior high school (1991) (Ueno, 2001).

In the 1980s, Ainu activists started to connect with the global Indigenous rights movements by, for example, attending the 1981 Third World Conference of Indigenous People in Education, held in Australia in 1981, and the 1992 UN International Year of World Indigenous Peoples. Such global alliances not only fostered Ainu self-perceptions as an Indigenous people but also offered them a means to challenge domestic marginalisation by appealing to international covenants (Sjöberg, 1993).

Ainu children's school attendance has gradually risen to almost the level of national average in the past three decades, triggered in part by the Utari Welfare Measures. This is a general perception among teachers, confirmed by surveys conducted by the Hokkaido prefectural government (Hokkaido-chō-kankyōseikatsu-bu, 2006) and Hokkaido University's Centre for Ainu and Indigenous Studies (Onai, 2010). The post-compulsory retention rate of Ainu children (i.e., into upper secondary school) has almost caught up to that of the community standard, with 3.8 per cent gap remaining in 2017. However, there remains a significant difference in tertiary entry rates with 12.5 per cent gap, although 33.3 per cent of Ainu students went on to university (an increase from 25.5 per cent in 2013) (Hokkaido-kankyōseisaku-bu, 2017). Of Ainu under 30 years old, 95 per cent have completed 12 years of schooling; the figure falls with age, however (87 per cent of those 30–40 years old and 24 per cent of those over 70) (Nozaki, 2010). The older generations of Ainu have much lower levels of higher education.

Regarding completion rates, Ainu children are still more likely to leave senior school before graduating. In 2009, 13 per cent of Ainu senior high school students left before graduation, and this percentage is lower compared with the previous generations (Nozaki, 2010); in that year, one in five Ainu university students left before gaining a degree. The figure for those under 30 years old was 11 per cent, while for those aged 60–70 it was 59 per cent (Nozaki, 2010).

The majority of Ainu people aspire to further education. For example, 56 per cent of those under 30 wanted to go to university (Nozaki, 2010, p. 63).

Sixty-four per cent of Ainu parents want their children to attend university (i.e., post-secondary) and only 21 per cent aim for only upper secondary school (Nozaki, 2010). The most frequently stated reasons for giving up a desire to pursue further education are financial (78%), the need to obtain employment (25%), academic achievement (14%), and parental opposition (particularly in the case of girls – 11%). Studies reveal cycles of poverty in Ainu families over generations (see, e.g., Nakamura, 2008). The income gap between Ainu and other groups in Japan is still a problem: in 2006, average annual Ainu income was 3.69 million yen (US$28,000), compared to 4.06 million (US$37,000) for the average Hokkaido family and 5.8 million (US$46,000) for the average family nationally – although the gap has narrowed recently (Nakamura, 2008). Ainu are more likely to be receiving government living protection allowances (*seikatsuhogo*) provided for low-income families. In 2009, 5.2 per cent of Ainu in Hokkaido received this welfare payment, compared with 3.9 per cent of the Hokkaido population as a whole and 2.2 per cent nationally (Nakamura, 2010).

As noted, educational opportunities based on equality principle and affirmative action in terms of financial assistance and scholarships for Ainu children have been effective in reducing the achievement gap but insufficient to enable students to benefit more fully from schooling. This is because of: (1) the limited resources (economic, social, and cultural) of Ainu families to facilitate this process; (2) the experience of schooling of both Ainu and the majority Japanese children and negative interactions in the school grounds; and (3) the school culture, all of which centre on the dominant Japanese institutions and culture (Okano, 2013).

Contemporary Ainu policies and the impact of UNDRIP

The UNDRIP (United Nations, 2007) has had a significant impact on Japanese government policies concerning the Ainu. The process leading to UNDRIP began in 1982 when a study group on Indigenous peoples was established within the Committee on Human Rights. Of particular note is that representatives of Indigenous peoples of many countries participated in the study group, which created a transnational collaborative and cooperative relationship among Indigenous peoples globally. Although UNDRIP has no legally binding obligations, its impact has been significant in Japan. It has provided a normative framework for policies on Indigenous peoples and for multicultural and multi-ethnic societies. How the declaration has affected domestic policies on Indigenous peoples is of global interest; Japan's case provides an insightful example.

In 2008, for the first time, the Japanese government officially recognised the Ainu as an Indigenous people (Advisory Council for Future Ainu Policy [ACFAP], 2009).

Both houses of the parliament unanimously adopted the resolution to acknowledge the Ainu as 'an Indigenous people who have resided in the northern part of the Japanese archipelago, in particular, Hokkaido, and who maintain their own unique languages, religions and culture.

(House of Councillors, 2008)

Within one month of the passing of this resolution, the government established an expert study group on Ainu policies named *Ainu seisaku no arikata nikansuru yūshikisha kondankai* and began research and discussion towards the formulation of Ainu policies which would include education. The UN declaration was thus a trigger in opening a way for subsequent deliberations on Ainu policies (Maeda, 2011).

The study group presented a report in July 2009 and proposed future directions for Ainu policies. In December of the same year, the *Ainu Seisaku Sokushin Kaigi* (Committee to Promote Ainu Policies) was established with the cabinet secretary as its chairperson and began discussing concrete measures to address the July proposals. The committee was then divided into two groups with specific roles: one group to discuss multi-ethnic co-living and the other group to research the lives of Ainu people living outside Hokkaido. The latter group confirmed that Ainu people living outside Hokkaido were also relatively disadvantaged in terms of income and educational achievement.

Higher education has not been raised in reports prepared by any of the abovementioned study groups or the committee. This ignores the wishes expressed by the *Ainu-minzoku ni kansuru Hōritsu,* an Hokkaido Utari Association's draft proposal (Hokkaido-Utari-Kyōkai, 1988). The draft proposal argued for learning about Ainu culture and affirmative action for Ainu youths in higher education; universities to establish courses in Ainu culture and history; and teachers of such courses to be recruited from ethnic Ainu people who excel in these fields and appointed as professors, associate professors, and lecturers. Such appointments require a degree of flexibility in normal academic requirements and universities should provide special consideration for Ainu children so that they can enter universities and focus on their respective studies (Hokkaido Utari Kyōkai, 1988). This statement conveys the association's desire for tertiary-educated Ainu experts who can actively participate in decision making in Ainu matters, and ultimately pursue self-determination. In order to achieve this, they want universities and/or governments to provide a quota for Ainu applicants at universities.

To date, these initiatives have been received positively. For example, Shikoku Gakuin University began offering a special entry system in 1995, through a quota for minority students (including Ainu) for admission via school recommendation (instead of examinations). In 2010, Tomakomai Komazawa University (in Hokkaido) began offering a course in Hokkaido-Ainu culture in the Faculty of International Cultures. The former's focus was to enable Ainu student access to university while the latter assisted Ainu students in completing the course by offering scholarships and considering their ethnic background.

Other universities have offered subjects in Ainu language and culture and organised guest lectures by advisers from the *Ainu Bunka Shinkō Kenkyū Suishin Kikō* (Ainu Culture Promotion and Research Centre) under the Centre's scheme to send advisers on request. The Centre was established in Tokyo to implement the 1997 *Ainu no bunka no shinkō narabini Ainu no dentō nado ni kansuru chishiki no fukyū oyobi keihatsu ni kansuru hōritsu (Act on the Promotion of Ainu Culture and Dissemination and Enlightenment of Knowledge About Ainu Tradition, etc.* [Act No. 52 of 1997] (*Ainu Cultural Promotion Act).* These efforts, while providing the curriculum that enables both Ainu and the majority Wajin Japanese students to learn about Ainu Culture and History, remain initiatives of individual academics or universities rather than the result of a systematic effort to provide assistance for Ainu students on campus (see Chapter 9, this edition). The *Ainu Cultural Promotion Act* was replaced in April 2019 by the *Act on Promoting Measures to Realize a Society in Which the Pride of the Ainu People Is Respected* (Act No. 16 of 2019) (*Ainu Policy Promotion Act).* The legislation fails to offer concrete strategies to promote Ainu people's greater participation in higher education. It does not engender optimism about how this new legislation would actively contribute to Ainu engagement with university education, which is essential for advancing Ainu language and culture through schooling. Sapporo University's Urespa Project, which we will examine in detail in the section that follows, presents a new direction. It attempts to assist Ainu students through the university's institutionalised collaboration with the Ainu community and private sector corporations.

Collaboration advocated in UNDRIP

The UNDRIP (United Nations, 2007) touched on several aspects concerning education of Indigenous peoples: (1) access to schooling; (2) access to ethnic education; (3) special measures to remove discrimination; and (4) special measures to ensure unexploitative employment. The declaration emphasised the state's collaboration with Indigenous communities:

Article 14–2

Indigenous individuals, particularly children, have the right to all levels and forms of education of the State without discrimination.

Article 14–3

States shall, in conjunction with Indigenous peoples, take effective measures, in order for Indigenous individuals, particularly children, including those living outside their communities, to have access, when possible, to an education in their own culture and provided in their own language.

Article 15-2

States shall take effective measures, in consultation and cooperation with the Indigenous peoples concerned, to combat prejudice and eliminate discrimination and to promote tolerance, understanding and good relations among Indigenous peoples and all other segments of society.

Article 17-2

States shall in consultation and cooperation with Indigenous peoples take specific measures to protect Indigenous children from economic exploitation and from performing any work that is likely to be hazardous or to interfere with the child's education, or to be harmful to the child's health or physical, mental, spiritual, moral or social development, taking into account their special vulnerability and the importance of education for their empowerment.

There are several guidelines within these articles for designing concrete measures regarding the education of Indigenous peoples. First, the government should provide financial assistance in order to ensure Indigenous people's 'entitlement to education without discrimination', given that poverty has long prevented Indigenous children from receiving higher levels of education. Second, the government should provide education to promote intercultural understanding in order to eliminate ethnic discrimination. Third, the government should ensure that Indigenous people can learn their heritage language and culture in the way acceptable to them. Fourth, the government should implement special measures to provide the kind of learning that can empower Indigenous students. All these measures will be best achieved if a collaboration between the state and Indigenous peoples is fostered.

These guidelines are applicable to the Ainu in Japan. The government, with Ainu people, should promote social network based on 'mutual assistance', improve conditions of schooling that is inclusive of Ainu culture and history, and establish a system of schooling which potentially empowers Ainu. Ironically, however, it is private universities, rather than the national government, that have taken initiatives in this direction, on the strength of the greater degree of autonomy that private universities enjoy under the *Shiritsu gakkō hō Private School Act (1949)*. Sapporo University, which we study in the next section, is an example. Because 75 per cent of Japanese universities are private institutions, there is some optimism among Ainu activists that initiatives advocated by UNDRIP will be widely taken up – but this is a simplistic view to be explored later in the chapter.

The Urespa Project: 'Mutual nurturing'[2]

The Urespa Project began in Sapporo University's Faculty of Humanities in 2010. *Urespa* means 'mutual nurturing' in the Ainu language and reflects the Faculty mission: co-living and harmony. The project aims to produce potential Ainu leaders by providing scholarships to Ainu young people who demonstrate enthusiasm and capacity and by promoting their employment in local companies which support the project.

One of the key features of this project is a 'two-way mutual learning approach'. It aims to assist young Ainu people and concurrently educate the majority Japanese to respect and accept the 'differences' (Interviews with Yūko Honda, vice president, Sapporo University, and Hideyuki Kanazawa, associate professor, Hokkaido University, 22 February 2012). This approach is a departure from the prevailing trend of policies concerning minority groups whereby the majority offers one-way assistance to minority groups (Tsunemoto, 2011). Applicants must have participated in maintaining and developing the Ainu culture and demonstrate an enthusiasm for contributing to society. The university provides Ainu students with guidance and assistance in completing a curriculum specifically designed for Ainu students and consequently gaining post-graduation employment.

How then does the Urespa Project create a system of learning which enables Ainu students to acquire a commitment? How does the project try to realise a 'nurturing community' of mutual learning that is inclusive of Ainu culture? In the section that follows, we examine the specifics of the Urespa Project, its development, curriculum, learning strategies, and measures to assist students.

The project was initiated by Yūko Honda. She was born on mainland Japan and studied Anthropology at Hokkaido University before moving to Biratori-town Nibutani, where she lived among Ainu for the next 11 years. She worked with Shigeru Kayano, an Ainu elder, teaching the Ainu language to Ainu children and creating an Ainu language dictionary. Kayano was an Ainu activist, who became the first Ainu MP (as a Japan Socialist Party candidate) in 1994. Honda was the Dean of the Faculty of Cultural Studies when the Urespa Project started, and is now the vice president of the university. She recalls (Honda, 2011) what drove her to this project.

> The majority *Wajin* Japanese can maintain their mother tongue and own history without much effort. How many Ainu children are like that? There are very few Ainu children familiar with even one Ainu legend. They would have grown up in extraordinary environments, for example, having a family with an exceptional commitment to Ainu education, or having attended Ainu language courses. The vast majority of Ainu children have no opportunity to learn about their ethnic culture. The majority Wajin need to know that it is a 'privilege that they take for granted' and that their fellow Ainu should be entitled to have the same.
>
> (pp. 94–95)

Honda was keen to see Ainu people enjoy the same privilege that the majority Wajin children take for granted – to learn their own language and culture as part of their daily lives. She wanted the majority *Wajin* to recognise that the Ainu do not have such a simple privilege.

Under the Urespa Project, the university accepts a quota of young Ainu people and educates them to be future Ainu leaders, simultaneously working to create a model of 'multicultural co-living' within the university. The missions of the Urespa Project can be summed up as:

- To promote understanding of Ainu society and culture among Ainu and no-Ainu students through studying Ainu history and culture and being involved in activities to revitalise Ainu culture.
- To train leaders of Ainu people, and to provide the space for future social activities by creating a system of cooperative support with local companies and Indigenous communities.
- To construct mutually trustful relationships based on intercultural understanding and a model of multicultural community, and to promote this to the public.

(Sapporo-Daigaku, 2012)

The project consists of three pillars as discussed. The first is the Urespa scholarship for which Ainu students wishing to attend Sapporo University can apply. It covers four years of tuition fees and the entrance fee. In 2011, there were six recipients. Eligibility for the scholarship centres on Ainu ethnicity but, given the lack of official records of individual ethnic heritage among Japanese citizens, to be eligible for the scholarship, an applicant must satisfy one of the following conditions: (1) have a recommendation by the Hokkaido Ainu Association; (2) have a recommendation from an Ainu culture protection organisation endorsed by the national government; (3) demonstrate five years of involvement in a similar organisation that does not have official government endorsement and receive its recommendation; or (4) demonstrate Ainu heritage by such means as *koseki* family registration, if unable to satisfy one of the mentioned criteria (Interviews with Yūko Honda, vice president, Sapporo University, and Hideyuki Kanazawa, associate professor, Hokkaido University, 22 February 2012).

The second pillar of the Urespa Project is to create a 'mutual learning' environment where Ainu students learn to be leaders. Urespa scholarship holders are required to complete a Urespa special course as well as another major course. The Urespa special course includes Ainu language, Ainu culture, and traditions, and the history of Hokkaido and the Ainu (Sapporo-Daigaku, 2012). In addition, the students are required to play active roles in the university's Urespa Club.

The Urespa Club was originally set up in 2010 by Sapporo University to promote its Urespa Project. In 2013, it became a general incorporated association involving ordinary citizens outside the university and private companies. Since then, the club has expanded its activities to promote and publicise Ainu culture and issues across Japan and globally. It arranged fieldtrips to Taiwan, Hawaii, and Norway to study indigenous peoples and to engage in discussions with them (Sapporo-Daigaku-Ureshipa-Kurabu, 2019). In the club, students design and implement twice weekly study sessions on Ainu language, culture, and history, and festivals which present to the public the achievements of their learning; editing the club's newsletters; and organising excursions to local Ainu communities in order to promote interaction.

The club had 18 students in February 2012. Seven members were Ainu scholarship holders, and the rest comprised Ainu, *Wajin,* and international students. Twelve scholarships were issued in 2010 and 2011, but several recipients discontinued their course mid-way after struggling to combine study with earning a living; this occurred if they failed to gain financial assistance towards living expenses from the Hokkaido Ainu Association since the Urespa scholarships cover only tuition fees. Diaspora Ainu outside Hokkaido are not eligible for such assistance from the association and do not apply for scholarships.

The Urespa Club also approaches local primary schools to share learning about Ainu culture and environmental protection through such activities as Ainu dancing and Ainu language playing cards. It is expected that Ainu students' active engagement in learning through both mainstream courses and the Urespa Club will cause students to see the Ainu presence as a natural part of the Faculty, and encourage them to mix more with Ainu students (Honda, 2011).

The case of one Ainu scholarship student provides an insight into how the project can impact personal development. Akiko (a pseudonym) is a 38-year-old mature age student who was interviewed by one of the authors (Maeda). Akiko has excelled academically since her primary school days. When her primary school teachers told her to aim at university education, her mother regretfully responded that it was beyond the family's means. Akiko gave up the idea of going to university, went to vocational college, and became a skilled carpenter, coming second in Hokkaido's carpenters' competition. Akiko never revealed her Ainu heritage until interviewing for the scholarship. Her comments show how she is now negotiating her Ainu identity in the university setting:

> It has been demanding to keep up with university study. I know that I will not be able to speak the Ainu language without a commitment to study. I was mentally draining at the beginning, but now I feel better since I know my friends like Ainu people. I had never been able to reveal my Ainu identity before coming to university because of a fear of discrimination. But now I feel better about it and take it for granted to be living as an Ainu. I even forget to mention that I am Ainu when visited by people from other universities. Yes, studying at university was a challenge, but the most challenging is to accept my Ainu heritage and talk about it with others. I could

learn to do this because I came to trust that I'm supported by, and learn together with, others. We have mutual assistance here.
(Interview with a student, Akiko, 22 January 2012)

Akiko seems to have gained a positive self-image through the learning process based on *sodateai* mutual nurturing, which has resulted in her motivation for academic study and active participation in extra-curricular activities. Akiko was the top academic student in her last two years of study.

The third pillar of the Urespa Project is the university's active collaboration with private sector employers. To be more precise, the Urespa project aims to create a network of companies which support the project's missions on the grounds of *kigyō no shakaiteki sekinin* (corporate responsibility for society). Urespa companies are those that support the project's missions, gain membership of the project by paying annual fees, and participate in various project activities. These companies work with Urespa students and develop close collaborative relationships (Sapporo-Daigaku, 2012) and are currently considering plans to accept Urespa students as interns and provide quotas for new permanent positions. There were 33 registered companies as of November 2019 (Sapporo-Daigaku-Ureshipa-Kurabu, 2019). The companies already registered with the project include leading companies, such as Japan Railway Hokkaido, Fuji, Hokuyō Bank, Sapporo Breweries, and Nippon Travel Agency Hokkaido. Company presidents actively participate in Urespa-organised activities such as Urespa Fiesta (Honda, 2011, p. 97), and are involved in nurturing scholarship students.

Interviews with these companies reveal a strong sense of social responsibility in relation to their local communities. For example, Sapporo Beer, a prominent local company, is currently exploring the ways the Urespa Club can present their learning outcomes at a company annual event (Interview with Toshihiko Izumiyama and Hideki Obata, representatives of Sapporo Beer Corporation, 23 February 2012). Another prominent local company, Hokkaido Clean System Inc., believes in the benefit of discussing Indigenous issues through its involvement with the Urespa students because such discussions encourage critical thinking among employees (Interview with Managu Kuromiya and Tatsumi Nohiro, representatives of Hokkaido Clean System, 23 February 2012). The ultimate goal of the project is to expand the corporate network through invitations by Urespa company to other companies to join and to disseminate what Urespa does to the wider public.

Reliance on private university initiatives to promote tertiary education of Ainu students and partnership with private sector companies to empower young Ainu contrasts with initiatives in some other countries. For example, in Australia and Taiwan, the national governments play major roles in promoting the participation of Indigenous peoples in higher education. In Taiwan, for example, the national government has provided affirmative action programmes for Indigenous student admission to universities since 1987 by adding extra marks to their examination scores, through special entry schemes without entrance examinations, and by allowing institutions to increase their quota of students if they are Indigenous (Refworld-UNHCR, 2008). In Japan, the absence of concrete initiatives from the national government may be because the Ainu gained official recognition only in 2008 and more formally in 2019 under the *Ainu Policy Promotion Act*, and because the Japanese government has traditionally relied on the Hokkaido government to address Ainu.

Conclusions

We have examined how the Urespa Project addresses the following aspects of Ainu access to higher education: (1) access to schooling, enabling progression to higher education; (2) access to ethnic education; (3) special measures to remove discrimination; and (4) special measures to ensure unexploitative employment. These issues were raised in UNDRIP. Sapporo University offers scholarships to Ainu students who are required to take a special course in Ainu Culture and History as well as undertake mainstream courses. The university takes seriously the notion of collaboration, creates active partnerships with private sector companies and the Ainu community, and acts as an effective mediator between them. Such collaboration is expected to assist Ainu students' transition from university to the workforce. The commitment to a collaborative approach is apparent in the project's name 'Urespa', which means 'mutual nurturing' in the Ainu language.

We suggest that mutual learning signifies a challenge to the conventional approach to Ainu education, which has centred on the majority Japanese (including governments) providing one-way assistance to the Ainu to help them reach the majority children's educational achievement. By contrast, the mutual learning approach stresses a nurturing environment where both Ainu and non-Ainu students feel included and comfortable, and where each group assists the other's learning. This is particularly important for the Ainu students who have often felt isolated on campus.

Rather than waiting for national government leadership, private universities have taken initiatives to promote Ainu's participation in higher education, utilising the greater degree of institutional autonomy that private universities enjoy. Since three-quarters of Japanese universities are private, there is hope that the successful example of the Urespa Project will mean that such initiatives will be adopted elsewhere.

Notes

1 This is an updated and revised version of a paper published: Maeda, K., and Okano, K. H. (2013). Connecting indigenous Ainu, university and local industry in Japan: The Urespa project. *International Education Journal: Comparative Perspectives*,

12(1), 45–60. Republished here with permission. Original paper available at: https://openjournals.library.sydney.edu.au/index.php/IEJ/issue/view/632

2 We would like to acknowledge those who were interviewed for this study, in particular, students and staff members involved in the Urespa Project.

References

Advisory Council for Future Ainu Policy (ACFAP). (2009). *Final report.* Tokyo, Japan: Government of Japan (Provisional translation into English on 14 November 2011). Retrieved 31 May 2020 from www.kantei.go.jp/jp/singi/ainu/dai10/siryou1_en.pdf

Hokkaido-Utari-Kyōkai. (1988). Sankō shiryō: Ainu minzoku ni kansuru hōritsu (Hokkaido-Utari-Kyōkai An) [Reference: Hokkaido Utari Association's draft proposal for legislation on Ainu people]. *Ainu minzoku ni kansuru shinpō mondai ni tsuite: Shiryō hen* [Issues regarding new legislation on Ainu people]. Sapporo, Japan: Hokkaido-Utari-Kyōkai.

Hokkaido-chō-kankyōseisaku-bu. (2006). *Heisei 18-nendo Hokkaido Ainu seikatsu jittai chōsa hōkokusho* [Report on the 2006 survey on the lives of Hokkaido Ainu]. Retrieved 31 May 2020 from www.pref.hokkaido.lg.jp/ks/ass/grp/H18houkokusyo.pdf

Hokkaido-cho-kankyōseisaku-bu. (2013). *Keizaiteki shakaiteki chii no kōjō o hakarutameno sōgōteki sesaku no suishin.* [Promoting the measures to assess economic and social status]. Retrieved 31 May 2020 from www.pref.hokkaido.lg.jp/ks/ass/suisinhousaku.htm

Hokkaido-kankyōseisaku-bu. (2017). *Heisei 29-nen Hokkaido Ainu seikatu jittai chōsa hōkokusho* [2017 report of the survey on the actual living conditions of the Hokkaido Ainu]. Retrieved 31 May 2020 from www.pref.hokkaido.lg.jp/ks/ass/H29_ainu_living_conditions_survey_.pdf

Hokkaido-Kōtōgakkō-Kyōshokuin-Kumiai. (1982). *Seito to tomoni kangaeru nihon no shōsū minzoku: sono genjō to shidō no tebiki* [Discussing Japanese minorities issues with students: The realities and guidelines]. Sapporo, Japan: Hokkaido-Kōtōgakkō-Kyōshokuin-Kumiai (Hokkaido High School Teachers Union).

Honda, Y. (2011). Ainu no wakamoto tachi to Urespa purojekuto [Ainu youth and the Urespa project]. In Kaihō-shuppan-sha (Ed.). *Jinken Kīwādo* [Keywords for human rights] (pp. 94–97). Tokyo, Japan: Kaiho shuppansha.

House of Councillors (2008, June 6). Ainu minzoku o senjuminzoku to surukoto o motomeru ketsugi [Resolution to Recognize the Ainu as an Indigenous People]. Retrieved 31 May 2020 from www.sangiin.go.jp/japanese/gianjoho/ketsugi/169/080606-2.pdf

Lie, J. (2001). *Multiethnic Japan.* Cambridge, MA: Harvard University Press.

Maeda, K. (2011). *Senjūmin o meguru kyōiku seisaku no kadai to kokusai kyōikugaku no shiza* [Educational policies on Indigenous people from the pervective of international education]. In Nihon-kokusaikyōiku-gakkai-sōritsu-20-shūnenn-kinen-nenpō-henshūiinkai (Ed.). *Kokusai kyōgaku no tenkai to tabunka kyōsei* [International education and multicultural co-living] (pp. 9–21). Tokyo, Japan: Gakubunsha.

Nakamura, Y. (2008). Gendai Ainuminzoku no hinkon [Ainu people in poverty]. *Kyōiku Funkushi Kenkyū, 14,* 15–25.

Nakamura, Y. (2010). Shakaihoshō no genjitsu to kadai [The realities and challenges of social welfare]. In T. Onai (Ed.). *Gendai Ainu no seikatsu to ishiki: 2008 nen Hokkaido*

Ainu minzoku seikatsu jittai chōsa hōkokusho [Lives and views of Hokkaido Ainu pople] (pp. 49–58). Sapporo, Japan: Hokkaido Daigaku Ainu Senjūmin Kenkyū Sentā.

Nozaki, T. (2010). Kyōiku hubyōdō no jittai to kyōiku ishiki [The realities of educational inequality and aspirations]. In T. Onai (Ed.). *Gendai Ainu no seikatsu to ishiki: 2008 nen Hokkaido Ainu minzoku seikatsu jittai chōsa hōkokusho* [Lives and views of Hokkaido Ainu pople] (pp. 59–73). Sapporo, Japan: Hokkaido-Daigaku-Ainu-Senjūmin-Kenkyū-Sentā.

Oguma, E. (1998). *Nihonjin no kyōkai* [Boundaries of Japanese]. Tokyo, Japan: Shinyosha.

Okano, K. H. (2012). Language and citizenship in education: Migrant languages in government schools. In N. Gottlieb (Ed.). *Language and citizenship in Japan* (pp. 58–78). London, England: Routledge.

Okano, K. H. (2013). Indigenous Ainu and education in Japan: Social justice and culturally responsive schooling. In R. Craven, G. Bodkin-Andrews, & J. Mooney (Eds.). *Indigenous peoples: Education and equity* (pp. 3–25). Charlotte, NC: Information Age.

Onai, T. (Ed.). (2010). *Gendai Ainu no seikatsu to ishiki: 2008-nen Hokkaido Ainu minzoku seikatsu jittai chōsa hōkokusho* [Lives and views of Hokkaido Ainue people]. Sapporo, Japan: Hokkaido Daigaku Ainu Senjūmin Kenkyū Sentā.

Refworld-UNHCR. (2008). *World directory of minorities and Indigenous peoples – Taiwan: Indigenous peoples*. Retrieved 31 May 2020 from www.refworld.org/docid/49749c9fc.html

Sapporo-Daigaku. (2012). *Urespa Kurabu 2012*. Retrieved 31 May 2020 from www.sapporo-u.ac.jp/department/ureshipa/

Sapporo-Daigaku-Ureshipa-Kurabu. (2013). *Ureshipaorushipe: Ainu bunka de sodateau hibi* [Ureshipaorushipe: Mutual nurturing in the Ainu culture]. Sapporo, Japan: Sapporo Daigaku.

Sapporo-Daigaku-Ureshipa-Kurabu. (2019). *Ureshipaorushipe: Ainu bunka de sodateau hibi*. Sapporo: Sapporo Daigaku. Retrieved 31 May 2020 from www.urespa-club.com/index.html

Siddle, R. (1996). *Race, resistance and the Ainu of Japan*. New York: Routledge.

Sjöberg, K. (1993). *The return of the Ainu: Cultural mobilization and the practice of ethnicity in Japan*. Chur, Switzerland: Harwood Academic.

Takegahara, Y. (2010). *Kyōiku no nakano Ainu minzoku: Kindai nihon Ainu kyōikushi* [The Ainu in education: Modern history of Ainu education]. Tokyo, Japan: Shakaihyōronsha.

Tsunemoto, T. (2009). Ainu minzoku to daigaku kyōiku [Ainu people and university education]. *Hikaku Bunka Ronsō, 23*, 97–110.

Tsunemoto, T. (2011). *Ainu minzoku to kyōiku seisaku: Atarashii ainu seisaku no nagare no nakade* [Ainu people and educational policies: New Ainu policies]. Booklet (A publication of Sapporo Daigaku Fuzoku Sōgō Kenkyūsho) 4, 20–31.

Ueno, M. (2001). Ainu minzoku o meguru kyōiku ni kansuru ichi kōsatsu [A study of education of the Ainu people]. *Waseda Daigaku Daigakuin Kyōikugakukenkyūka Kiyō, 9*(1), 45–56.

United Nations. (2007). *United Nations Declaration on the Rights of Indigenous Peoples*. Retrieved 31 May 2020 from www.un.org/development/desa/indigenouspeoples/wp-content/uploads/sites/19/2018/11/UNDRIP_E_web.pdf

Weiner, M. (Ed.). (1997). *Japan's minorities: The illusion of homogeneity*. London, England: Routledge.

Legislation

Hokkaido Former Aboriginal Protection Act (1899) (Meiji 32)（北海道旧土人保護法）
Private School Act (1949)（私立学校法）
Act on the Promotion of Ainu Culture and Dissemination and Enlightenment of Knowledge About Ainu Tradition, etc. (Act No. 52 of 1997) (*Ainu Cultural Promotion Act*)（アイヌ文化の振興並びにアイヌの伝統等に関する知識の普及及び啓発に関する法律 [アイヌ文化振興法]）
Act on Promoting Measures to Realize a Society in Which the Pride of the Ainu People Is Respected (Act No. 16 of 2019) (*Ainu Policy Promotion Act*)（アイヌの人々の誇りが尊重される社会を実現するための施策の推進に関する法律 [アイヌ政策推進法]）

Chapter 12

The usefulness of the idea and concept of reconciliation for guiding Australian Indigenous higher education in the postcolonial, post-imperial world

Veronica Goerke and Peter J. Anderson

Cultural Warning
Please note: Aboriginal and Torres Strait Islander people are warned that this chapter includes names and references to people who are deceased.

Introduction

This chapter defines and unpacks the idea of 'reconciliation' and the related process of 'Reconciliation', as used in our assessment of its usefulness to achieve the aspirations of Australian Indigenous peoples in the Australian university. To do so, we first consider the definition of the word within the English language. The online *Oxford Dictionary*'s (2016) definition of reconciliation is 'the restoration of friendly relations' and 'the action of making one view or belief compatible with another'. Although there are numerous explanations for the origin of the word, this dictionary's first entries include several biblical allusions, all referring to the restoration of relationships between God and His people. James (2008) helpfully explains it is 'a never-concluding, often uncomfortable process of remaking or bringing together (from the Latin "reconcilare") of persons, practices and meanings in ongoing places of meeting (from the Latin "concilium")' (p. 117). Often referred to as the Father of Reconciliation in Australia, Patrick Dodson (2007) offered a supplementary explanation for the formal, political process of Reconciliation in Australia, which provides both a challenge and affirmation of the idea as being useful for institutions such as universities and for broader Australian political processes:

> Reconciliation gave Australia a doorway to a political settlement approach on how the modern Australian state could recognize the traditional ownership status of Indigenous people and unravel the historical layers of colonial legacy that continue to determine contemporary relationships

between Indigenous communities and Australian governments and other institutions.

(p. 21)

We have followed Sutton (2009, p. 247) in the usage of the lowercase 'reconciliation' to denote 'reconciliation' in the informal, often personal, state and the capitalised version of the word 'Reconciliation' to denote the formal political and bureaucratic processes associated with international, national, and local processes and, in this chapter, specifically referring to Australian universities (see Glossary). As summarised by one interviewee, who was a member of a university senior executive in a study by Goerke (2019):

> I think the way you described a small 'r' reconciliation and non-Indigenous and Indigenous people working together is in the long-term a key to moving way forward. The university is listening to our Indigenous students, our Indigenous colleagues and our Indigenous community about what they think. I think there's an onus on universities to lead the way. That's another part of that, not to be playing catch up. But we're [universities] certainly not leading the way in terms of proportions. But there are some success stories in some universities and some areas.
>
> (Interviewee #26)

However, there is no intention to indicate that 'reconciliation' and 'Reconciliation' are binary concepts. There are many instances in which these two states are so embedded or intertwined with each other that one cannot – should not – differentiate them. By itself, the definitional aspects of the idea of reconciliation are open to interpretation and it is useful, therefore, to give a brief overview of the idea of reconciliation in international perspective before moving on to a discussion about the concept of 'Reconciliation' as it has been understood in the Australian policy context.

The idea of reconciliation and the concept of Reconciliation

There is no definitive ontological explanation for the process of reconciliation – or the state of being reconciled – and there are many ways in which people have provided epistemological evidence of its presence, especially as a process. The formal concept of Reconciliation has been a vexed issue in Australia since it was first introduced as a national political social justice process during the 1980s. Before considering why this is so, it is helpful to briefly consider the idea of reconciliation in the international context.

International reconciliation narratives

The concept of reconciliation has been explored within peace studies (Morrison, 2011, p. 820) and is a critical component of the 'peace versus justice' debate, which centres on processes of Reconciliation as being part of the 'peace' that explains the ways in which 'societies emerging from political violence and repressive rule can address human rights abuses committed in the past' (Rodman, 2011, p. 824). The contemporary understanding of political Reconciliation can also be linked to attempts by Abraham Lincoln during the American Civil War to reconcile the North and the South (Rodman, 2011). This notion was further developed among older disciplines – such as Sociology, Philosophy, and Psychology – in which there appears to be an abundance of research and thinking about the idea of reconciliation and its related concept, Reconciliation. The South African Truth and Reconciliation Commission (TRC) and the Canadian TRC provide relevant examples of Reconciliation in national formalised environments that are similar to the Australian context. However, as Hattam, Atkinson, and Bishop (2012, p. 3) noted, the differences between the processes of Reconciliation in South Africa and Australia are vast. Significantly, for a background context for our discussion, Reconciliation in South Africa was instigated by a black majority leadership to try to peacefully address a recent history of horrific violence perpetrated by a white minority. In Australia, when the Council for Aboriginal Reconciliation (CAR) was formed to respond to similar injustices by the settler-colonials, it was a white population who held the majority power that defined and determined the 'Reconciliation' process.

The Canadian higher education perspective

The Canadian experience of political Reconciliation, especially, offers pertinent insights for the Australian university sector. For example, Smith (2017) explored aspects of reconciliation within Canadian higher education institutions and reflected on how he, as someone in a senior position, thought the idea of reconciliation should be understood, and how his workplace enacted Reconciliation and addressed changes that he felt were required for reconciliation to occur. He used statistics about Indigenous student engagement, such as retention figures, as well as its plans and campus activities. Smith's (2017, p. 73) final hopeful and realistic observation was that

> Reconciliation in the academy requires difficult conversations; there will be sceptics and opponents and there will be champions and allies. Fundamental change is difficult for any major societal institution, let alone one which can trace its history back 1,000 years.

The university-related Reconciliation Smith and others are referring to is occurring within the backdrop of a national reconciliation process. The Canadian TRC was established in 2008 as an outcome of the 1996 Report of the Royal Commission on Aboriginal Peoples. The 2015 TRC report (Truth and Reconciliation Commission of Canada, 2015b) called on the Canadian government to fully implement the *United Nations Declaration on the Rights of Indigenous Peoples* (UNDRIP); it also called on the education sector to engage especially with Article 14 of the UNDRIP regarding the rights of Indigenous peoples to determine and control their education.

Reconciliation Action Plans (RAPs) do not exist in Canada but, since 2015, Canadian universities have provided evidence of their response to the TRC recommendations in public reports and on their websites (Queen's University, 2019; University of Waterloo, 2019). Referring to the challenges of the 'indigenization' of the curriculum, Zinga (2018) noted some of the complexities of translating reconciliation in a Canadian university, asserting that 'reconciliation requires an examination and understanding of what has happened and how current structures, systems and attitudes/biases that are conscious or unconscious continue to uphold colonialism and Eurocentrism' (p. 2). First Nation Canadian scholars Sasakamoose and Pete (2015) argued that the amount of work they must do is so much more than that of the non-Indigenous peoples because they must constantly explain and justify their knowledges to their peers

> to address these absences [of knowledge and understanding from their university colleagues] in the university (and thus) we are compelled to work towards the re-centering of these knowledge systems and pedagogies to ensure our survival as Indigenous peoples in higher education.
>
> (p. 3)

Further, Indigenous people must do extra work to correct and educate their colleagues 'about culturally responsive practices in support of greater levels of Indigenization' (Sasakamoose & Pete, 2015, p. 11).

Australian narratives about reconciliation

Here we are providing only a brief snapshot of the historical context for the formal political story of Reconciliation in Australia. We have noted a few of the myriad of events deemed useful in providing some background to the idea of reconciliation in Australia and how it became a political process of social justice, in particular, how it has been operationalised in Australian universities.

Reconciliation – colonial understandings

There are some insights into the current challenges of reconciliation to be gained from observing the usage of the word 'reconciliation' in the documents of the early colonialists. Woodward (1974, p. 151) cited a letter written by Governor Arthur Phillip to Lord Sydney in 1788. The letter captures a version of reconciliation related to making some sort of relationship, albeit the expectation was that the First Peoples were expected to make all the concessions and live like the settlers: 'When I shall have time to mix more with them every means shall be used to reconcile them to live amongst us'. In another letter two years later, Phillip wrote:

> Not a native had come near the settlement for many months and it was absolutely necessary that we should attain their language, or teach them ours, that the means of redress might be pointed out to them if they are injured and to reconcile them by showing the many advantages they would enjoy by mixing with us.
> (Cited in Woodward, 1974, p. 151)

However, in Australia, it was not until the later decades of the 20th century that the idea of a formal, national conversation about the idea of reconciliation was presented by the government in the public arena.

Formal reconciliation—a concession on recognition and treaty

There are several significant moments in the Australian Reconciliation story that, though not specifically labelled as 'reconciliation' at the time, can be labelled as evidence of attempts to heal injustices or acknowledge wrongdoing by the colonisers/settlers. These events include the Referendum of 27 May 1967 when more than 90 per cent of the Australian population voted to count First Nations in the census; the year 1975 when Prime Minister Gough Whitlam poured earth into Vincent Lingiari's hand in a gesture to acknowledge Wave Hill land was being given back to the Gurindji nation; the delivery of what became known as 'The Redfern Address' by the Hon Paul Keating in 1992 (Australians for Native Title and Reconciliation (ANTaR), 1992); and the *Mabo v Queensland* decision of 3 June 1992, when the High Court of Australia ruled that the concept of *terra nullius* was a lie and that the First Peoples had a unique ongoing connection to the land and waters of Australia. The Mabo decision is celebrated as part of Australia's annual National Reconciliation Week.

Another important date is National Sorry Day, first commemorated on 26 May 1998, in order to address the recommendations advocated by the 'Bringing Them Home Report' (Human Rights and Equal Opportunity Commission [HREOC], 1997). Sorry Day is now an annually observed day that reminds Australians of a group of Indigenous Australians, known as the 'Stolen Generations', who as Indigenous children were taken away from their families and countries between 1905 and 1970s using the *Aborigines Act* (1905). Ten years later, on 13 February 2008, Prime Minister Kevin Rudd publicly said 'sorry' on behalf of the Australian government to the country's Stolen

Generations after many years of the previous Prime Minister declaring he would never 'apportion blame' (Gunstone, 2007, p. 73) for any past wrongs. However, it was during the formal Reconciliation process, which includes the formation of Reconciliation Australia, where Reconciliation as a social justice initiative was brought into Australian universities.

The realisation of an official movement

Reconciliation was mentioned in the Australian political arena in 1983 in a speech by Minister for Aboriginal Affairs Clyde Holding (Hattam & Matthews, 2012, p. 13). However, Reconciliation as a formal process was first connected to the paper presented at a law conference in 1988, which proposed the establishment of an Australian Recognition Commission to recognise the rights of Australia's First Nations (Brennan, 2007; Brennan & Crawford, 1990). The authors had wanted to resurrect the idea of recognition and treaty from the 1979 National Aboriginal Conference where Senator Fred Chaney, as the Liberal Minister for Aboriginal Affairs, had welcomed and then worked to progress the idea with the Prime Minister, Malcolm Fraser. Chaney's successor, Senator Peter Baume, also worked to promote the proposed 'makarrata'. However, the idea did not materialise (Brennan & Crawford, 1990, p. 197).

By 1988, the year in which Australia held many public events to celebrate the 200 years since the British had landed and claimed the country for the British Empire, Prime Minister Bob Hawke noted this work by Brennan and Crawford. Hawke summoned one of the authors, Frank Brennan, to Canberra for discussions and eventually announced there would be a preamble for the *Australian Constitution* and a version of a treaty and stated:

> The government is committed to a real and lasting reconciliation, achieved through full consultation and honest negotiation between Aboriginal and non-Aboriginal citizens of this nation.
> (Cited in De Costa, 2006, p. 151)

Hawke's announcement resulted in much debate and strong opposition such that it failed to be supported. Later, Minister for Aboriginal Affairs Robert Tickner, in Paul Keating's government, noted that, since the idea of treaty was too hard, 'the associated issues were addressed through the strategic advancement of the reconciliation process' (cited in De Costa, 2006, p. 151). In what became known as 'The Redfern Address', Prime Minister Paul Keating (ANTaR, 1992) publicly acknowledged the wrongs done to Indigenous Australians and the responsibility of non-Indigenous people in perpetrating these injustices. He went on to say:

> [T]he starting point might be to recognize that the problem starts with us non-Aboriginal Australians. It begins, I think, with the act of recognition.

Recognition that it was we who did the dispossessing. We took the traditional lands and smashed the traditional way of life. We brought the disasters. The alcohol. We committed the murders. We took the children from their mothers. We practiced discrimination and exclusion. It was our ignorance and our prejudice. And our failure to imagine these things being done to us. With some noble exceptions, we failed to make the most basic human response and enter into their hearts and minds. We failed to ask – how would I feel if this were done to me? As a consequence, we failed to see that what we were doing degraded all of us.

The political processes moved from pursuing treaty-making towards practices that they hoped would be more acceptable to the voting majority of non-Indigenous Australians – that of Reconciliation. On 2 September 1991, CAR was formed as a direct response to recommendations from the *Royal Commission into Aboriginal Deaths in Custody* and the ensuing final report by Elliott Johnston QC (Johnston, 1991). The focus of the *Johnston Report*, as determined by these recommendations, was on the 'process of Reconciliation' and the concepts of education and social justice. It instructed: '[A]ll political leaders and their parties recognise that Reconciliation between the Aboriginal and non-Aboriginal communities in Australia must be achieved if community division, discord and injustice to Aboriginal people are to be avoided' (*Johnston Report*, point 339).

Reflecting an inclusive, nationalistic tone, CAR (1995) described the destination of the national Reconciliation process as being 'a united Australia which respects this land of ours; values the Indigenous and Torres Strait Islander heritage; and provides social justice for all' (p. 23). CAR's primary focus on educating non-Indigenous people about the social justice imperative of reconciliation with Indigenous people 'rather than towards the kinds of structural justice that Indigenous people were calling for' (Clark, De Costa, & Maddison, 2017, p. 394) meant that they were often criticised by Indigenous Australians.

Practical Reconciliation

By 1996, on taking office, Prime Minister John Howard stepped back from Keating's position and refused to apologise for the wrongs that non-Indigenous Australians had done to Indigenous Australians. He also committed his government to 'practical reconciliation', to addressing practical issues of health, housing, and education in Indigenous communities. At Corroboree 2000, which opened Reconciliation Week, Prime Minister John Howard called on all Australians 'to honour the contribution' of Indigenous Australians to the life of the country; 'to honour the special character of their cultures'; to 'thank them for the generosity of their spirit; and to "recognize the richness that their cultures bring to modern Australian life"' (Australian Government: Department of the Prime Minister and Cabinet, 2000).

Ma Rhea and Seddon (2006) argued that where Keating had affirmed Indigenous Australians as part of the 'we' of modern Australia, Howard delineated 'them' and remaindered them as 'one of many cultures' that make up Australia and as a 'profoundly disadvantaged' group. 'Disadvantage', not citizen right, was the justification for policy action aimed at addressing this group's social disadvantage. Where Keating sought to construct an inclusive understanding of 'we' in Australia by building on the legal framework of citizenship, Howard indicated that his government would target funds to support health, education, and housing initiatives for disadvantaged communities – funding that was, in any case, a citizen entitlement that 'every Australian should enjoy' (M. Dodson, 2000 cited in Burridge, 2009, p. 117). When the CAR handed over its report at Corroboree 2000, not only did Prime Minister John Howard refuse to tender an official apology for the past injustices on behalf of the nation, but he also 'rubbed salt into the wound' (Houston, Martin, & McLaren, 2012, p. 128) by announcing that a new private body, Reconciliation Australia, would replace the government-supported body. The new organisation was to be self-funded from philanthropic donations, signalling a clear move away from the 'political' aspects of the idea of reconciliation towards an economically focused approach favoured by the Howard government. With such a significant recasting of public policy with the change of government, the concept of Reconciliation changed in its focus. Moving away from an approach guided by the principles of social justice *per se*, the concept of 'Practical Reconciliation' came to be regarded by many as 'a neo-assimilationist view that argued the need to concentrate on improving the socio-economic outcomes' (Gunstone, 2008, p. 174). Patrick Dodson loudly opposed this version and resigned as chairperson of CAR in protest (Behrendt, 2003). Though the formal political process was fraught and largely a compromise process for Indigenous Australians, it remained a movement of possibilities and hope. Even Patrick Dodson, in declaring his rejection of Howard's idea of practical reconciliation, in early 2000, said:

> It's the people's movement and, thankfully, there are Australians who are continuing this process. They see we are in need of coming to one spirit, one view, one feeling about our position as Australians. ... Just by resorting to some social policy about health, housing and education is not going to do it. It's about how we as people are going to feel about ourselves.
> (Dodson, as cited in Keeffe, 2003, p. 319)

Twenty-first-century Reconciliation

By the 21st century, the various expressions of Reconciliation in Australia have made it difficult to ascertain a single approach to its operationalisation. There have been several options for how to enact it. It is noteworthy that, unlike places like South Africa, 'truth-telling' was never a part of the formal Australian national Reconciliation process (Fleay & Judd, 2019) though First Nations have been calling for this for many years. Now that the Canadians since 2015, as noted earlier, have had this concept as part of their formal Reconciliation process, it may also become a more populist notion in Australia. Indeed, truth-telling was the theme for the 2019 National Reconciliation Week (Reconciliation Australia, 2019).

There are those who question the purpose of a national Reconciliation movement. Discourses of reconciliation, such as the Recognise Campaign and the Referendum Council, show how reconciliation can reflect 'a well-meaning, non-Indigenous project to manage the colonial past as it spills into the present' (Elder, 2017, p. 91). Equally, it makes visible the ongoing insistence by many Indigenous people that the 'unfinished business of colonialism is not going to go away' (Elder, 2017, p. 91). In a call to action, as part of the annual ANU Reconciliation Lecture in 2018, one of Australia's most senior First Nations men, Peter Yu (2018), despondently critiqued the formal Reconciliation process as being aimless and without meaning:

> Reconciliation has lost its moral and political gravitas. While I know and believe sections of the general community remain committed to the concept and aspiration of Reconciliation, it has become a nebulous and meaningless term and used by anyone as a throwaway concept to apply their interpretation about the relationship between Indigenous people and the Australian State. It has become part of Australia's lazy dialogue concerning Indigenous people dominated by symbolism which has little connection with the realities of people's lives.

The organisation Reconciliation Australia would probably disagree with Yu's negative assessment. Their appraisal is more positive and advocates for their services and resources, linking much of the success of Reconciliation back to their development of a tool called RAPs. Their approach to the task of Reconciliation has developed during the past decade to include five dimensions: race relations, equality and equity, institutional integrity, historical acceptance, and unity. Each of these 'dimensions' is defined with a stated goal and one broad action. This includes the action, under institutional integrity, to 'create a wider range of opportunities for Aboriginal and Torres Strait Islander Australians' (Reconciliation Australia, 2019). This approach to delivering on Reconciliation has become a tool by which Australian universities were able to operationalise their approach to taking a pro-active stance on the higher education needs and aspirations of Indigenous Australians. The next section provides a brief history of Reconciliation and RAPs and their adoption in Australian universities.

Reconciliation Action Plans

The origin of RAPs can be traced to the outcomes of the Australian Reconciliation Convention in May 1997 and the ensuing discussions in

CAR (1999) who stated on their website that one of the components for the National Strategy to Sustain the Reconciliation Process was to eventually achieve: 'By 2001, Commonwealth, State and Territory Parliaments pass formal motions of support for the Document for Reconciliation including measures to include provisions about agreements in legislation' (CAR, 1999). There is further evidence from a paper by the Chairperson, Evelyn Scott AO, asking 'whether reconciliation would be advanced by a formal document or documents of reconciliation' (Scott, 1998). Because there was never one formal document created at a national government level, such discussions may have been the impetus for the RAP programme that was subsequently announced by Reconciliation Australia, who activated the first RAP in July 2006, to 'maintain the reconciliation momentum' (Aubrey-Poiner & Phillips, 2010, p. 6). Professor Tom Calma AO, the co-chair of Reconciliation Australia, explains his involvement in the origin of RAPs:

> I saw it when they [RAPs] first started. I was Social Justice Commissioner at the time. I saw the value and got behind wanting to improve it. It was quite an interesting issue because in 2005, I launched my social justice report, a chapter of that, was addressed to Closing the Gap. It was health inequality gaps we had to address ... in 2006, we formed the Close the Gap campaign. Then in 2006, RAPs got started. They, in turn, adopted the Close the Gap. So, it was about addressing health inequality. That's really the nucleus of what a RAP was about.
>
> (Goerke, 2019, p. 17)

Since 2006, RAPs have been a significant aspect of the formal Reconciliation process in Australia. RAPs, which exist in many businesses, government departments, and educational institutions throughout Australia, are documents that outline a plan for what those organisations intend to do to enact Reconciliation between the majority non-Indigenous population and the Indigenous peoples of Australia. RAPs were created in 2006 by Reconciliation Australia with the key purpose of helping organisations to 'turn their good intentions into real actions' (Reconciliation Australia, 2016). Explanations for RAPs on the Reconciliation Australia website have been refined and developed between 2006 and 2019 depending on Australian government policies and broader sentiments in the Australian community. For example, in the early years, the first sentence stated that 'through the RAP programme, organizations develop business plans that document what they will do within their sphere of influence to contribute to Reconciliation' (Reconciliation Australia, 2013). In April 2019, this was changed to 'the RAP programme provides a framework for organizations to support the national reconciliation movement' (Reconciliation Australia, 2019).

The RAPs had their strategic roots in the key principles developed by Reconciliation Australia, which have changed little over the years. Therefore, the explanation for what they are belongs to that organisation. The definition for a RAP on the website in 2015 was 'a business plan that turns good intentions into actions. A RAP publicly formalises an organization's contribution to Reconciliation by identifying clear actions with realistic targets' (Reconciliation Australia, 2013). In 2019, the definition for a RAP was 'a strategic document that supports an organization's business plan. It includes practical actions that will drive an organization's contribution to reconciliation both internally and in the communities in which it operates' (Reconciliation Australia, 2019). In 2019, Reconciliation Australia stated on their website that the terms

> Reconciliation Action Plan and RAP are valued trademarks of Reconciliation Australia. We are proud to share the RAP logo with organizations that work with us through our feedback and quality assurance process to develop a RAP that meets quality requirements.
> (Reconciliation Australia, 2019)

By 2013, an online template for a RAP had evolved to allow organisations to choose between four levels of RAPs: reflect, innovate, stretch, or elevate. These four RAP templates or models had different criteria, and Reconciliation Australia advised and eventually gave their approval as to which level was the most appropriate for an organisation to choose, depending on what that organisation was proposing for their RAP.

Corporate social responsibility and Reconciliation in Australian universities

These preliminary discussions assist in understanding how the concept of Reconciliation is being undertaken in Australian universities for them to be able to demonstrate that they are addressing the educational aspirations and needs of Indigenous Australians. All Australian universities display evidence of Reconciliation practices in their relationships and good intentions regarding First Nations students, scholars, and community. Universities have public-facing strategic plans, sophisticated websites, social media platforms and other forms of community engagement and projections of themselves. Further, universities have additional evidence of delivering on their espoused values that other businesses may not have, such as successful First Nation students, scholars and alumni along with written and visual evidence in publications and research projects.

The early discussion on social justice, as outlined earlier, changed over time to fit in with the ideals expressed in the phrase 'Corporate Social Responsibility' (CSR). This shift heralded a move from Reconciliation being regarded as a social process to a business process and something that could be embraced by businesses, including Australia's universities. There is no commonly accepted definition for CSR due to differing cultural and community contexts. However, a relevant description of CSR for the Australian context is that it is about 'what companies do in order to be socially responsible' (Black, 2006, p. 25). This has led many organisations to articulate the concept of Reconciliation into their CSR programmes, which is often evidenced by a RAP. Reconciliation Australia began promoting RAPs as tools to enact this aspect of organisations and, as universities have also become more corporatised, it appears that RAPs should fit into their strategic governance and planning frameworks. Within the context of this chapter, universities can be said to use CSR to label how they will build better relationships with and provide career opportunities for Indigenous Australians.

Universities are also large corporations that aim to be perceived as good corporate citizens by conforming with other large non-educational organisations in the demonstration of their CSR (Banerjee, 2008). RAPs allow universities to be comparable with such businesses, even if the extent to which universities meet RAP targets is mostly unknown and there are no significant consequences for failing to meet or report on targets. The discourse employed in RAPs is a mixture of 'management speak' with words such as 'governance, capacity building, partnerships, whole of government, benchmarks, stakeholders, leadership, targets, measurable, outcomes, role models' (Sutton, 2009, p. 209), alongside words such as 'deep respect', and 'culturally safe' and words in the local First Nations language.

According to the Reconciliation Australia website, as of April 2019, there were 10 of 39 universities in Australia with RAPs. Maddison (2017) notes that they are 'a rare example of economic elites demonstrating preparedness to engage with questions of reconciliation and socio-economic redistribution' (p. 162), which provides other 'economic elites' with good practices to emulate. Such practices in universities regarding social justice, social inclusion and notions of equality and equity combine to evolve into what could be called CSR, of which, as already noted, the RAP is an expression.

Rarely have Indigenous Australians been asked about the idea of reconciliation or of Reconciliation and RAPs. Over a period of five years, Goerke undertook a national study that specifically engaged various people in discussion about their perception of Reconciliation and RAPs specifically focusing on Australia's universities; groups included Indigenous leaders, other education leaders and those working in reconciliation-related work connected to the universities that had been engaged early in the RAP process. Many of the people involved in Goerke's research and in discussion over the past 20 years display distinctive Reconciliation wisdom that, if listened to, could transform how universities move into the future. Goerke (2019) names these older, mostly First Nations people whom she interviewed within the universities as 'Reconciliation Elders' (Goerke). She extended this title to some of the non-Indigenous interviewees who displayed evidence of deep understanding, had worked for many decades beside First Nations colleagues and who knew that 'we have to listen [to First Nations in our university] and we will have to implement' (Interviewee #20).

Goerke's respondents expressed a range of answers and, in her analysis, she proposed that reconciliation in the university sector exists along a complex and dynamic Reconciliation Spiralling Continuum (RSC), which is evidenced by well-intentioned though sometimes assimilationist practices through to those that demonstrated reciprocal partnerships and Indigenous rights-based reconciliation. This RSC is informed by Burridge's (2009, p. 116) 'reconciliation typologies', which were named on a continuum, with one end labelled 'rights-based', the centre labelled 'symbolic' and the other end 'assimilationist'.

Reconciliation within universities

The explanations for reconciliation in a university given by participants in the Goerke study span from it being the almost dismissive concept of being 'just a word' (Interviewee #23) to an idea that had been 'kidnapped away' (Interviewee #22), which alluded especially to the time when Australia was being led by John Howard. The definition could also be about 'assisting the people that have been discriminated against to move together in a way in which we can support them but which is guided by them ... the need for respectful change' (Interviewee #14). In whatever way it was presented, both in the words of the RAPs and that of the interviewees, reconciliation always came across as having some moral value (Allen, 1999, p. 325), and what was always central was the idea of relationship – a relationship that was a 'right' relationship. It was about 'reconciliation as the relationships that we build between Aboriginal and non-Aboriginal people in meeting positive outcomes for our communities and in relation to higher education' (Interviewee #24). There was also an expectation by many First Nations participants in the Goerke study, that the non-Indigenous people should initiate the reconciling. It was noted by several that as First Nations have nothing to be reconciled about, non-Indigenous people need to do the work: 'Take two steps even if the Aboriginal community take one-step, take four steps towards them so that we can actually reconcile in the end' (Interviewee #29). Just as Brounéus (2003, p. 57) recommended, each country needs to find its own way to define and enact reconciliation because what may work in one place will not have any meaning in another – and this is true for the different university communities in Australia.

The first university RAP was created in 2008 (by Curtin University) and by 2011, all universities were encouraged to 'create either reconciliation statements and/or RAPs to reflect the university's Indigenous education strategy and commitment to meaningful engagement with local Indigenous communities and organizations' (Universities Australia & IHEAC, 2011, p. 24). As noted in the key Australian documents of 2011–2012, this was followed up in the *Behrendt Review* (Behrendt et al., 2012; see Chapters 5 and 10, this edition), which encouraged reconciliation within universities and gave only qualified support for RAPs because the authors noted that RAPs appeared to be 'primarily the responsibility of the Indigenous Education units rather than truly strategic whole of university documents they are intended to be' (p. 148). They cited the report by Moreton-Robinson, Walter, Singh, and Kimber (2011) and Pechenkina and Anderson's (2011) background paper to support their recommendations and went on to advise universities that wanted to have a RAP about how this should be done, including suggesting that RAPs 'be incorporated into annual business planning cycle outcomes' (Behrendt et al., 2012, pp. 148).

The next significant national paper relevant to Indigenous tertiary education in 2017 was also cautious about RAPs saying: 'While universities have specific Indigenous strategies or Reconciliation Action Plans, these should serve as complementary to, not a replacement for, central policy documents' (Universities Australia, 2017, p. 18). The *Buckskin Report* (Buckskin & Tranthim-Fryer, 2018) echoed these cautions and instructed universities that if they chose a RAP, it must be led in partnership with First Peoples:

> Choose to engage with external bodies, such as Reconciliation Australia, through the development of a RAP to show their commitment in a public forum and add another level of accountability. Importantly, if this path is chosen it must be driven by the senior executive of the university in collaboration with senior Aboriginal roles in the true sense of reconciliation.
>
> (p. 83)

These were all strong messages to make Indigenous education part of core university business and should not be determined by an outside body, which perhaps explains the reluctance of most universities to developing a RAP. Although the *Universities Australia Indigenous Strategy First Annual Report* (Universities Australia, 2019) included self-reporting by the universities that could be more 'rosy coloured' because of the self-chosen metrics to be achieved (Larkin et al., 2018), the actual existence of the strategy and the apparent growing strength of the Universities Australia partnership with the *National Aboriginal and Torres Strait Islander Higher Education Consortium* (NATSIHEC [AC]) were signs of positive change for the future (Universities Australia, 2019).

Enacting reconciliation within universities clearly involves not just questioning the hegemony of Western knowledges in the institution, but also disrupting it and asking for other ways of being and knowing. Reconciliation raises the question as to whether universities really can be innovative, engage with 'other' ways of knowing and lead students in learning for tomorrow. Reconciliation Elders consistently argue that universities must enact the aspirations and agreements of the UNDRIP and make way for the knowledges of this country's First Peoples. This includes evidence of integrating these knowledges into the curriculum as well as reshaping university governance, learning On-Country and promoting Indigenous research methodologies. Therefore, the idea promoted so strongly by the Truth and Reconciliation Commission of Canada (2015a) about 'truth-telling' – the theme chosen by Reconciliation Australia for the 2019 National Reconciliation Week (Reconciliation Australia, 2019b) – can be easily actualised in universities that are innovative enough to explore different ways of being and knowing. This form of Reconciliation does not mean being apologetic for Western knowledges but, instead, being confident enough to stop using the labels 'mainstream' and 'other'. Australian universities must go forth with courage and make changes.

The opportunities of Reconciliation

Promoting employment

Interviewees discussed how utilitarian RAPs could be, not necessarily the specificities of the plans but rather the fact that the plans existed at their universities. First Nations interviewees spoke about the opportunities for employment prompted by RAPs as being the best aspect of a RAP. However, evidence of other more influential documents in a university indicated that the RAPs were not essential for creating these employment opportunities. As Larkin (2014) noted in his research, the intent of RAPs is commendable in terms of offering opportunities but 'it is the employment strategies of the organizations that holds them to account' (p. 147). These strategies have Key Performance Indicators (KPIs) that senior staff are accountable for; all the universities have an Indigenous employment strategy independent of their RAPs and all have governance structures that afford Indigenous people a voice in at least an advisory role to the Vice-Chancellor.

Even if RAPs have this positive role, it was the publicly available annual Indigenous Education Statements – and the Indigenous Student Success Program Performance Reports from 2017 – that universities were obligated to produce and publish annually that were more powerful. These reports ensured ongoing government funding and it is these documents that capture most of the opportunities, which were then reflected in the RAPs. Universities are also required to have Indigenous employment strategies which cover such strategies as participation and retention of Aboriginal and Torres Strait Islander students – the employment strategy for the university – and even require an indication of how the university is demonstrating increased participation by First Nations people in decision-making processes. These statements are reporting requirements to the Department of the Prime Minister and Cabinet (Australian Government: Department of the Prime Minister and Cabinet, 2019).

Even with these documents and requirements, the fact that improving employment opportunities for First Nations people was seen as the primary benefit of the RAP cannot be overstated. As one senior First Nations interviewee stated about the transformational changes that had resulted from the inclusion of a RAP in workplaces:

Hand on my heart and all due respect to all the effort that's put into RAP, the best outcome is really in employment. Everything else – like the hanging of artwork – it's all very symbolic, and acknowledgements and stuff are really important things, but the tangible outcome for RAPs that I've seen is definitely associated with employment.

(Goerke, 2019)

A tool to facilitate positive change

There was a strong theme addressed by the First Nations interviewees regarding how they could use RAPs as 'a powerful tool' (Interviewee # 7), 'a very important device within this university' (Interviewee #22) to get Indigenous matters addressed. However, they acknowledged that 'a RAP is never going to be a silver bullet to solve everything. It is a workplace tool that can help within workplaces' (Interviewee #3). One participant who had initially stated that reconciliation was problematic and that the RAP was not always useful also emphatically stated that she found the plan to be a strategically useful device for getting attention paid to First Peoples and their matters in the university:

We constantly use the RAP – as I do – I will pull it out and I use it where I need to use it. So it's about employment, it's about culture, our culture and the way we do things, the way we work in the centre, because we are owned by the university and many of my staff think we can do what we want, but we can't. But for me it's about again crossing the two, going into one world and crossing over. And if there's something that I really need to bring up and say that this is totally inappropriate and it's not the way that we work, I will use the RAP to also bring about trying to get change; trying to support what I want to do culturally. I find that that's a good thing with the RAP. It doesn't always work, but there are times – and I use the RAP quite often and bring people's attention to the RAP: this is what the RAP says!

(Interviewee #13)

An enabler of Indigenous rights

The concept of equality aligns with the concept of Indigenous rights (Ma Rhea, 2014; see Chapter 10, this edition). If a RAP has this focus, it would support what Reconciliation Elders, as one senior First Nation's leader and Reconciliation Elder, argued: 'a RAP should give prominence and place to First Nations' (Goerke, 2019, p. 147). Indigenous rights were barely mentioned in the RAP documents but the words spoken by most of the interviewees indicated those who worked in Reconciliation understood and promoted Indigenous rights. This same Reconciliation Elder shared words that encapsulated the key themes of translating reconciliation within RAPs that advocate for rights. In relation to rights, it was the fact that the RAP existed as an artefact of the university that appeared to be of more significance to the interviewees, rather than the words written in the documents. This Reconciliation Elder defined what RAPs represent in terms of rights by referring to the position that universities take regarding equality and inclusivity, as well as the need to give unique prominence to First Nations:

> I think it's [the RAP] central to the 'we' I mentioned earlier, because it should never be seen as 'Oh, we're doing something for "the Blacks!"' We're doing something for other Australians who we've ostracised and isolated and marginalised and dispossessed. We need to treat them like we want to be treated ourselves and to treat them like all Australians ought to be treated, fairly and justly and we understand their special position in the country. They were here first, we came and took it off them; this is one way of trying to make amends.
>
> (Goerke, 2019, p. 147)

The restrictions of RAPs

The RAP can also be constraining on how a university shapes reconciliation. One of the bureaucratic limitations of RAPs is that they are usually created to articulate reconciliation for a two- to four-year period, with the opportunity to revise slightly each year. For some, the more explicit and definitive people were in naming the actions and the targets in their RAP, the more constrained they were about reflecting and revising their RAP-related activities. Reconciliation Australia, in their attempt to encourage measurable outputs for which people can write reports to be submitted to them, edited and advised universities on their proposed RAPs until they met their requirements. Several interviewees referred to being frustrated by how prescriptive and constraining this process could be.

Falling outside the KPIs

This need to rethink and reshape how Reconciliation is actualised was evidenced by the current four RAP templates on the Reconciliation Australia website, which determine levels for RAPs. As the data have shown, a process created for an organisation that is a business will not always suit an organisation whose primary focus is education and knowledge creation. However, just like a business, if something is not named and measured in a university's strategic plan and does not have associated explicit KPIs assigned to an executive leader, then it is unlikely to happen. There is tension between using RAPs to exhibit a desire to be doing something right with First Nations people and the lack of consequences when organisations do not deliver on their targets. As the RAPs belong to an outside body that does not have regulatory legislative authority, unless identical KPIs are in an organisation's strategic plans, there are no consequences for not meeting the targets named in RAPs. As Larkin (2014) argued, 'even then, such organization plans are noted as being only part of the solution as these targeted strategic plans, policy frameworks and performance-based programmes to achieve Indigenous outcomes' (p. 228).

RAPs sit outside university strategic plans, although they can be linked to them, and can fail to have legitimacy and acknowledgement by everyone in the leadership team. This is another indication of the limitations of the requirements and templates offered by Reconciliation Australia. However, as an educational resource and as a place for guidance for universities that are starting to engage in formal and public reconciliation, they have much to offer:

> If it takes a RAP to actually be able to have the conversations internally and externally to the university, then to me, that's what should happen. I think the RAP is about conversations, providing a framework to have some dialogue and discussion. So I think for those universities that are having trouble actually getting off the starting blocks, or have tripped over on the first hurdle or the second hurdle and have got their scraped knees and not really being able to heal and keep going, then maybe a RAP would be a good tool to actually help them in having the conversations.
>
> (Interviewee #23)

However, for a university that has a mature, established relationship among Australia's First Nations and all others, the current trademarked RAP can sometimes be restrictive: 'I think it depends on where the university is at. I don't believe that there's a one size fits all for every university. I think that we'd be silly to think that was the case' (Interviewee #23).

The university as business versus the university as educator

Reconciliation Australia surveys that sought to measure the impact of the RAP programme have indicated that it has been successful in changing attitudes and that they had started with eight organisations having a RAP in 2006 to 650 organisations with RAPs by 2016 and a further 500 organisations in the process of developing a RAP (Reconciliation Australia, 2016). Although the RAP programme appears to be thriving across many organisations, as already noted, because only one-quarter of Australian universities have a RAP, it is evident for many in the sector that senior university leaders are not convinced of the ability of RAPs to strengthen their approach to addressing the aspirations and needs of Indigenous scholars.

Although RAPs can be viewed as very important to the universities that have them, because it gives them a connection and common attribute with other businesses who have RAPs, it was noteworthy that the Reconciliation Australia interviewees did not compare the university sector with the school sector in which Reconciliation Australia has an extensive RAP programme. Instead of being considered part of the education sector, Reconciliation Australia staff referred to the universities as being part of the business sector and noted that 'the university market has been a bit trying for us to actually progress universities to have a RAP'. The concept of the university sector as a market or a marketplace and a business was referred to many times by the interviewees. Also, the positioning of a RAP as a marketing tool was apparent. As was said to me by staff from Reconciliation Australia, 'a university is a business' and they referenced RAP activity:

> There would be a whole range of things that, in a corporate sense, a university would do and would do as a matter or course in the general conduct of its business ... It's going to the future we'd love to be able to convert those [universities] to RAPs. They were saying they're a corporate commercial entity. They're a work place. We'd certainly love to get them on board.
> (Reconciliation Australia Interviewee)

Using RAPs – given the current controls by Reconciliation Australia – can sometimes clash with what it means to actually be in the reconciliation space within universities. RAPs were created to 'make real' reconciliation in a commercial world. However, universities have more ways of being in the world other than as businesses and, as noted by one participant, 'RAP conditions are just too confining for what we need' (Interviewee #15). A RAP may, therefore, be useful for enacting reconciliation for some universities but, as the majority of Australian universities have shown by their lack of engagement, it is not the only way.

Situating the RAP based on equity pragmatics

One problematic issue can be the place where RAP work is managed from within universities. While it was fine that such work was situated in the building that was the university's Indigenous centre, if this meant the RAP work was then done by Indigenous peoples, the interviewees of this research project argued, it implied that reconciliation was the responsibility of the First Peoples, which is simply wrong. Several interviewees noted that positioning the RAP so that it implied – and often became – extra work for First Nations was wrong. Calma (Goerke, 2019, p. 149) noted this was a mistake made when RAPs were first introduced in Australia, but he believed this was no longer done in most organisations, saying:

> It started off early in the days but it's just changing a lot now. Organizations thought – government departments were champions at this – that it's a RAP so we'll get the Aboriginal people in the organizations to develop it up. That was defeating the whole intent of it. So it's now moved fortunately,

in most organizations: that the organization takes responsibility and is supported by Aboriginal Torres Strait Islander people in that whole process.

(Calma)

Explicit work related to RAPs and reconciliation could also be led from the equity and diversity offices of the universities. The report by Moreton-Robinson et al. (2011) indicated that universities should avoid placing any work that is associated with First Nations with such administrative offices and, instead, endorse the UNDRIP. In doing this, universities are challenged to be unequivocal about giving First Nations people their places and voices completely separate to any work being done in such offices:

> Predictably, Indigenous higher education provision is often yoked to equity and diversity plans. Indigenous Australians are corralled with other low SES groups without regard to First Peoples status as defined in the UNDRIP and recognised in most universities' Reconciliation Statements.
> (Moreton-Robinson et al., 2011, p. 51)

This relegation of reconciliation activities and RAPs to diversity and equity offices in universities diminished the Indigenous rights of the First Nations within those universities. It relegated the conversation and the activities to a smaller place to be one of many other social justice issues. Although Goerke's project focused on how this reconciliation played out within university settings, a similar finding regarding reconciliation in the broader Australian landscape was comprehensively covered by Short (2008, pp. 165–168), who argued that the narrow focus on social justice ignored larger, more significant matters from land rights to self-determination. Gunstone (2007, 2008) also argued that the reconciliation process, including the focus on educating the populace, had been stymied by several factors, including the focus on 'the nationalist discourse of reconciliation' (Gunstone, 2008, p. 175).

Certainly, the sentiments expressed by some interviewees in this project echoed declarations made in the first years of Reconciliation Australia and the formal reconciliation process in Australia by First Nations writer Moran (2003), who viewed the process as 'a government-funded attempt at creating a unified Australian national category from the settler/Indigene opposition, whilst leaving intact the fundamental colonial structures and lingering colonial fantasies shaped by this opposition and its implied hierarchy' (p. 189). However, there was also evidence of the hope and potential of what reconciliation could be, which is at the forefront of the findings in this project and is supported by work already done within education environments by the many scholars cited in this project. Along with Langton (2001, p. 13, as cited in Hattam & Matthews, 2012), we believe that Reconciliation is about 'constructing an honourable place for Indigenous Australians in the modern nation state' (p. 12).

The impact of Reconciliation and RAPs in the Australian higher education sector

Expressions of the idea of reconciliation and the concept of Reconciliation can be best understood as lying on a continuum. Our analysis has revealed that the concept of Reconciliation as a lever for change in Australian universities has been dynamic and evolving. RAPs, which are a key expression of formal Reconciliation in universities, have played an important part, albeit probably more influential in changing the ideas of non-Indigenous Australians than pro-actively engaging Indigenous Australians. More significantly, we believe that the concept of Reconciliation is larger than the RAPs.

The ways in which the concept of Reconciliation is expressed are complex and understood differently by those who work in universities that have RAPs. At one extreme, it can be perceived as having messy overtones of a system that conspires to be unintentionally racist in its fear of conversations regarding sovereignty and its assimilationist structures and, at the other extreme, it can have individuals who are inclusive, creative and work together to engender First Nations knowledges to be at the fore. These extremes and potential polarisations were clearly part of Indigenous people's reflections on Reconciliation with one participant saying:

> I think that the further it takes you into a kind of a deep look at what are the institutional barriers to change, the more that the issues like racism, anti- racism need to come to the fore. But if the RAP is really a fairly superficial and symbolic agenda – like flagpole raising, NAIDOC Week, that sort of stuff – it's not going to take you to that point.
>
> (Interviewee #7)

Though RAPs may be imperfect, engagement in a Reconciliation process, however messy, was critical. The Reconciliation Elders and most of the other interviewees in the Goerke project would also perhaps resonate with Burridge (2009), who had argued a decade earlier that 'mainstream Australia must ask the question, is reconciliation to be merely symbolic expression of nationhood or are there more complex realities we must face as a nation before we are truly reconciled?' (p. 118).

As one Reconciliation Elder concluded, after admitting their initial cynicism of formal Reconciliation, the process had created spaces for dialogue and positive changes:

> Reflecting back on those early discussions in the 1990s, what I think is extraordinary is how much activity and thinking has matured. Rolling forward to ... early in the week, I was having a conversation with a senior business leader who chairs the Indigenous Engagement Group for the Business Council of Australia and I just reflected: it would not have been

possible for that individual to actually be so deeply engaged in the project of Indigenous development if it had not been for the reconciliation movement.

(Interviewee #7)

Indigenous rights-based reconciliation

Many of the interviewees alluded to Indigenous rights as the ideal foundational concept for shaping Reconciliation. This idea can be linked to the UNDRIP, namely Article 14, which advises that First Nations explicitly lead and shape their education: 'Indigenous peoples have the right to establish and control their educational systems and institutions providing education in their own languages, in a manner appropriate to their cultural methods of teaching and learning'. Such leadership in Australia is held by NATSIHEC, who partner with Universities Australia to give direction about Indigenous higher education. As the peak body for Indigenous Education, their advice and direction need to be sought and adhered to by all universities. Michael Dodson (quoted in Maddison, 2009, p. ix) referred to his brother, Patrick Dodson, saying that unless it was rights-based reconciliation, it could not be considered reconciliation: 'For the vast majority of Indigenous people and a significant number of Settler Australians, the substantial recognition of Indigenous people's inclusion as a distinct and unique people is a fundamental condition for a reconciled nation'. However, this stance must contend with those who are drawn towards assimilating First Peoples and their knowledges in with everyone else – those who work from the other end of the continuum and as evidenced by the policy swings discussed in earlier sections of this chapter. Chaney (Goerke, 2019, p. 155) clearly explains this predisposition by the Australian community to see everyone as the same in enacting Reconciliation. He explains that whereas one aspect of reconciliation is about 'Closing the Gap', this second important aspect is 'the more difficult second stream' because:

> Australians are instinctively assimilationist and think that all these other problems [connected to Closing the Gap] would be solved if Aboriginal people simply became like us.... Whether you look at it at an international level in terms of constitutional recognition, treaty, all those things or you look at it in terms of relationships in the classroom, in workplaces, in streets and villages, that's actually the harder part and the counterintuitive part of reconciliation for most Australians is that it involves recognition of continuing difference, and respect for continuing difference.
>
> (Goerke, 2019, p. 155)

This insight about assimilative propensities not only captures the spirit of our analyses and discussions but also resonates with words written more than a decade earlier by Burridge (2007) when she noted that the formal reconciliation process was 'no more than a normative movement acting to reinforce old style assimilationist tendencies' (p. 73). In contrast, the requirement for a more rights-based partnering expression of Reconciliation was the strongest call by the Reconciliation Elders and was encapsulated by the words of Michael Dodson at the Corroboree 2000 speech (cited in Burridge, 2009, p. 117) during his response to Prime Minister Howard's promotion of 'practical reconciliation'. Dodson reminded people that all that Howard promised was basic human rights to which everyone was already entitled. Dodson was clear that Reconciliation was about more than this when he said:

> Don't be distracted by notions of practical reconciliation because they mean practically nothing now. Also issues of health housing and education of Indigenous Australians are of course key concern to us as a nation, they are not issues that are at the very heart or the very soul of reconciliation. But they are, to put it quite simply and plainly, the entitlements every Australian should enjoy ... Reconciliation is about deeper things, to do with nation, soul and spirit. Reconciliation is about the blood and flesh of the lives we must lead together and not the nuts and bolts of the entitlements as citizens we should enjoy.
>
> (Dodson, 27 May 2000)

Conclusions

The idea of reconciliation and the concept of Reconciliation have been examined here in some detail to assess their usefulness in guiding universities towards meeting the aspirations and needs of Indigenous people in Australia in education and employment within the education sector. The summary of findings from the analysis of Goerke's (2019, p. 120) data indicated that there were a number of successful common elements in the approach of universities to operationalising the idea of reconciliation such as progress towards valuing Indigenous Knowledge and a growing respect for Indigenous leadership. All recognised that for the concept of Reconciliation to work, it needed courageous leadership from all the people involved in the work. With respect to her interviewees' sense of the potential for Reconciliation to be supported in universities, they reported: the need to establish 'right relationships'; deep listening; that it is an always evolving, dynamic process and a slowly built relationship; and that it needs to be seen as justice rather than as only social justice.

She found that the pursuit of Reconciliation outcomes in those universities with a RAP was problematic because some universities seemed to use the RAP as a 'tick-box' exercise, meaning they had 'done' Reconciliation by achieving their own performance targets rather than there being some accountability measure of their success or failure. Feedback from Indigenous people suggested RAPs are both problematic and useful as a policy tool for furthering Reconciliation in Australian universities. This meant that RAPs: could be used to capture everything related to First Peoples; could be symbolic as opposed to substantive; could be tools to challenge racism; could be prompts for employment opportunities for First Peoples; were most importantly about increasing employment opportunities for First Peoples; were also about compliance and outputs; could be work-creating for First Nations people; could be lost among several equity plans or issues; and were useful for articulating 'how to'. Significantly, most respondents felt strongly that RAPs were not essential for Reconciliation to be enacted in a university into the future.

Overall, we conclude that the concept of Reconciliation in universities needs to be founded on 'right' relationship between the majority non-Indigenous peoples and First Nations peoples. It is evident that the RAPs could be a useful tool to enact this Reconciliation. We argue that, while the current RAP templates are worthwhile devices for universities which require direction about the articulation and evaluation of Reconciliation-related activities, sustainable, embedded change in universities can occur without a RAP. Rather, as Reconciliation Elders advised, the transformational changes of creating a more reconciled society – not only within universities – must be evolutionary and realised differently with future generations. Finally, 'true' Reconciliation needs to be led by First Nations' voices and knowledges, as per the UNDRIP.

References

Allen, J. (1999). Balancing justice and social unity: Political theory and the idea of a truth and reconciliation commission. *University of Toronto LJ, 49*(3), 315–353.

Aubrey-Poiner, K., & Phillips, J. (2010). *Are we there yet? Ten years on from the decade of reconciliation: A reconciliation progress report.* Retrieved 31 May 2020 from http://antar.org.au/reports/are-we-there-yet-a-reconciliation-progress-report-2010-0

Retrieved 31 May 2020 from Australian Government: Department of the Prime Minister and Cabinet. (2000). *Address to Corroboree 2000 – Towards reconciliation.* Transcript of speech delivered by prime minister, John Howard. Retrieved 31 May 2020 from https://pmtranscripts.pmc.gov.au/release/transcript-22720

Australian Government: Department of the Prime Minister and Cabinet. (2019). *Higher education.* Retrieved 31 May 2020 from www.pmc.gov.au/indigenous-affairs/education/higher-education

Australians for Native Title and Reconciliation (ANTaR). (1992). *Redfern speech.* Transcript of speech delivered by Paul Keating. Retrieved 31 May 2020 from https://antar.org.au/sites/default/files/paul_keating_speech_transcript.pdf

Banerjee, S. B. (2008). Corporate social responsibility: The good, the bad and the ugly. *Critical Sociology, 34*(1), 51–79.

Behrendt, L. (2003). *Achieving social justice: Indigenous rights and Australia's future.* Sydney, Australia: Federation Press.

Behrendt, L., Larkin, S., Griew, R., & Kelly, P. (2012). *Review of Higher Education access and outcomes for Aboriginal and Torres Strait Islander people: Final report.* Canberra, Australia: Commonwealth of Australia.

Black, L. D. (2006). Corporate social responsibility as capability. *Journal of Corporate Citizenship, 23*(14), 25–38.

Brennan, F. (2007). *Whatever happened to reconciliation?* Retrieved 31 May 2020 from www.acu.edu.au/__data/assets/pdf_file/0006/51594/Whatever_Happened_to_Rec72.pdf

Brennan, F., & Crawford, J. (1990). Aboriginality, recognition and Australian law: The need for a bipartisan approach. *The Australian Quarterly, 62*(2), 145–169.

Brounéus, K. (2003). *Reconciliation: Theory and practice for development cooperation.* Stockholm, Sweden: Swedish International Development Cooperation Agency (SIDA) (1–75). Retrieved 31 May 2020 from urn.kb.se/resolve?urn=urn:nbn:se:uu:diva-45814

Buckskin, P., & Tranthim-Fryer, M. (Eds.). (2018). *Accelerating Indigenous higher education consultation paper: Whole of university; academic taskforce; science, technology, engineering and mathematics.* Adelaide, South Australia: NATSIHEC(AC). Retrieved 31 May 2020 from eprints.qut.edu.au/123520/1/NATSIHEC_%20AIHE_FinaL_%20Report%20Jan%202018_updated_031218.pdf

Burridge, N. (2009). Perspectives on reconciliation and Indigenous rights. *Cosmopolitan Civil Societies: An Interdisciplinary Journal, 1*(2), 111–128.

Clark, T., De Costa, R., & Maddison, S. (2017). Non-Indigenous Australians and the 'responsibility to engage'? *Journal of Intercultural Studies, 38*(4), 381–396.

Council for Aboriginal Reconciliation (CAR). (1995). *Going forward: Social justice for the first Australians – A submission to the Commonwealth government.* Canberra, Australia: Australian Government Publishing Service.

Council for Aboriginal Reconciliation (CAR). (1999). *National strategy to sustain the reconciliation process.* Retrieved 31 May 2020 from www5.austlii.edu.au/au/orgs/car/docrec/policy/natstrat/6sustain.htm

De Costa, R. (2006). *A higher authority: Indigenous transnationalism and Australia.* Sydney, Australia: UNSW Press.

Dodson, P. (2007). Whatever happened to reconciliation? In J. Altman & M. Hinkson (Eds.). *Coercive reconciliation: Stabilise, normalise, exit Aboriginal Australia* (pp. 21–29). Melbourne, Australia: North Carlton Arena Publications Association.

Elder, C. (2017). Unfinished business in (post)reconciliation Australia. *Australian Humanities Review, 61*, 74–93. Retrieved 31 May 2020 from australianhumanitiesreview.org/2017/06/13/unfinished-business-in-postreconciliation-australia/

Fleay, J., & Judd, B. (2019). The Uluru statement. *International Journal of Critical Indigenous Studies, 11*(1). Retrieved 31 May 2020 from doi.org/10.5204/ijcis.v12i1.532

Freer, J. (2018). Teaching respect to support reconciliation. *Journal of International Education* (Nihon Kokusaikyoiku Gakkai Kiyo), *24*, 118–126.

Goerke, V. (2019). *The idea of reconciliation in Australian universities and how it has been articulated through reconciliation action plans.* (Unpublished PhD thesis). Melbourne, Australia: Monash University.

Gunstone, A. (2007). *Unfinished business: The Australian formal reconciliation process.* Melbourne, Australia: Australian Scholarly Publishing.

Gunstone, A. (2008). The Australian reconciliation process: An analysis. In P. Rothfield, C. Fleming, & P. A. Komesaroff (Eds.). *Pathways to reconciliation: Between theory and practice* (1st ed., pp. 169–178). Aldgate, England: Ashgate.

Hattam, R., & Matthews, J. (2012). Reconciliation as a resource for critical pedagogy. In P. Ahluwalia, S. Atkinson, P. Bishop, P. Christie, R. Hattam, & J. Matthews (Eds.). *Reconciliation and pedagogy* (pp. 10–28). New York: Taylor and Francis.

Hattam, R., Atkinson, S., & Bishop, P. (2012). Rethinking reconciliation and pedagogy in unsettling times. In P. Ahluwalia, S. Atkinson, P. Bishop, P. Christie, R. Hattam, & J. Matthews (Eds.). *Reconciliation and pedagogy* (pp. 1–9). New York: Taylor and Francis.

Houston, D., Martin, G., & McLaren, P. (2012). In the market for reconciliation? In P. Ahluwalia, S. Atkinson, P. Bishop, P. Christie, R. Hattam, & J. Matthews (Eds.). *Reconciliation and pedagogy* (pp. 118–135). New York: Routledge.

Human Rights and Equal Opportunity Commission (HREOC). (1997). *Bringing them home: Report of the national inquiry into the separation of Aboriginal and Torres Strait Islander children from their families*. Sydney, Australia: Commonwealth of Australia.

James, P. (2008). Reconciliation: From the usually unspoken to the almost unimaginable. In P. Rothfield, C. Fleming, & P. A. Komesaroff (Eds.). *Pathways to reconciliation: Between theory and practice* (pp. 115–126). Aldershot, England: Ashgate.

Johnston, E. (1991). *Royal commission into Aboriginal deaths in custody – National report: Recommendations*. Retrieved 31 May 2020 from www.austlii.edu.au/au/other/IndigLRes/rciadic/national/

Keeffe, K. (2003). *Paddy's road: Life stories of Patrick Dodson*. Canberra, Australia: Aboriginal Studies Press.

Larkin, S. R. (2014). Race matters: Indigenous employment in the Australian public service (Unpublished Doctoral dissertation). Queensland University of Technology, Australia.

Larkin, S., Ireland, S., MacGibon, L., Small, T., Butler, K., & Chatfield, T. (2018). Academic Workforce. In P. Buckskin & M. Tranthim-Fryer (Eds.). *Accelerating Indigenous higher education* (pp. 90–155). Adelaide, South Australia: NATSIHEC(AC).

Ma Rhea, Z. (2014). Educational equality, equity and sui generis rights in Australian higher education. In H. Zhang, P. W. K. Chan, & C. Boyle (Eds.). *Equality in education: Fairness and inclusion* (pp. 35–49). Rotterdam, The Netherlands: Sense.

Ma Rhea, Z., & Seddon, T. (2006). Negotiating nation: Globalization and knowing. In D. Coulby & E. Zambeta (Eds.). *Globalization and nationalism in education: World education yearbook 2005* (pp. 252–271). London, England: RoutledgeFalmer.

Maddison, S. (2009). *Black politics: Inside the complexity of Aboriginal political culture*. Crows Nest, Australia: Allen & Unwin.

Maddison, S. (2017). Can we reconcile? Understanding the multi-level challenges of conflict transformation. *International Political Science Review, 38*(2), 155–168.

Moran, S. (2003). Imagining reconciliation. *Journal of Australian Studies, 27*(76), 181–191. Retrieved 31 May 2020 from doi:10.1080/14443050309387836.

Moreton-Robinson, A., Walter, M., Singh, D., & Kimber, M. (2011). *On stony ground: Governance and Aboriginal and Torres Strait Islander participation in Australian universities. Report to the review of higher education access and outcomes for Aboriginal and Torres Strait Islander people*. Canberra, Australia: Department of Education, Employment and Workplace Relations. Retrieved 31 May 2020 from docs.education.gov.au/documents/stony-ground-governance-and-Aboriginal-and-torres-strait-islander-participation-australian

Morrison, M. L. (2011). Peace education. In D. K. Chatterjee (Ed.). *Encyclopedia of global justice* (pp. 820–824). Dordrecht, Germany: Springer.
Pechenkina, E., & Anderson, I. (2011). *Background paper on Indigenous Australian higher education: Trends. initiatives and policy implications*. Retrieved 31 May 2020 from sydney.edu.au/documents/about/higher_education/2011/20110930%20Indigen ousHigherEducationReview-ReseachPaper.pdf
Queen's University. (2019). *Truth and reconciliation commission task force*. Retrieved 31 May 2020 from www.queensu.ca/provost/committees-and-reports/truth-and-reconciliation-commission-task-force
Reconciliation Australia. (2013). *Getting started*. Retrieved 31 May 2020 from raphub. reconciliation.org.au/program/getting-started/#Understanding-the-template
Reconciliation Australia. (2016). *The state of reconciliation in Australia: Our history, our story, our future*. Retrieved 31 May 2020 from www.reconciliation.org.au/wp-content/ uploads/2018/06/ra_stateofreconciliation_report_a4_revised-2018.pdf
Reconciliation Australia. (2019). *National reconciliation Australia week*. Retrieved 31 May 2020 from www.reconciliation.org.au/national-reconciliation-week/
Rodman, K. A. (2011). Peace versus justice. In D. K. Chatterjee (Ed.). *Encyclopedia of global justice* (Vol. 2, pp. 824–827). Salt Lake City, UT: Springer-Verlag New York.
Sasakamoose, J., & Pete, S. M. (2015). Towards indigenizing university policy [kakwe-iyiniwasta kihci-kiskinwahamâtowikamikohk wiyasiwâcikanisa]. *Education Matters: The Journal of Teaching and Learning, 3*(1). Retrieved 31 May 2020 from journalhosting. ucalgary.ca/index.php/em/article/view/62922
Scott, E. (1998). *Documents of reconciliation – Briefing paper introduction*. For the Council for Aboriginal Reconciliation (CAR). Retrieved 31 May 2020 from www5.austlii. edu.au/au/orgs/car/docrec/policy/brief/intro.htm
Short, D. (2008). *Reconciliation and colonial power: Indigenous rights in Australia*. Hampshire, England: Ashgate.
Smith, D. W. (2017). Reconciliation and the academy: Experience at a small institution in Northern Manitoba. *Canadian Journal of Educational Administration and Policy, 183*, 61–81.
Sutton, P. (2009). *The politics of suffering: Indigenous Australia and the end of the liberal consensus*. Carlton, Australia: Melbourne University Press.
Truth and Reconciliation Commission of Canada. (2015a). *Our mandate*. Retrieved 31 May 2020 from www.trc.ca/about-us/our-mandate.html#Principles
Truth and Reconciliation Commission of Canada. (2015b). *Truth and Reconciliation Commission of Canada: Calls to action*. Retrieved 31 May 2020 from nctr.ca/assets/ reports/Calls_to_Action_English2.pdf
Universities Australia. (2017). *Indigenous strategy 2017–2020*. Retrieved 31 May 2020 from socialsciences.arts.unsw.edu.au/media/SOSSFile/FINAL_Indigenous_Strategy. pdf
Universities Australia & IHEAC. (2011). *Guiding principles for developing Indigenous cultural competency in Australian universities*. Canberra, Australia: Universities Australia. Retrieved 31 May 2020 from www.universitiesaustralia.edu.au/lightbox/ 1313
University of Waterloo. (2019). *Truth and reconciliation response projects*. Retrieved 31 May 2020 from uwaterloo.ca/truth-and-reconciliation-response-projects/

Woodward, S. A. E. (1974). *Aboriginal land rights commission: Second report April 1974*. Canberra, Australia: Australian Government Publishing Service. Retrieved 31 May 2020 from www.austlii.edu.au/cgi- bin/download.cgi/au/other/IndigLRes/1974/1

Yu, P. (Producer). (2018). *ANU reconciliation lecture: Reconciliation, treaty making and nation building*. Retrieved 31 May 2020 from www.anu.edu.au/news/all-news/2018-anu-reconciliation-lecture-full-speech-by-peter-yu

Zinga, D. (2018). *Reconciliation in higher education contexts: Tensions and challenges*. Retrieved 31 May 2020 from www.openaccessgovernment.org/reconciliation-higher- education/46562/

Legislation

Aborigines Act No. 1905/014 (5 Edw. VII No.14)

Appendix

Key Australian government statements and reports

Source: Koleth, E. (2010). *Multiculturalism: A review of Australian policy statements and recent debates in Australia and overseas* (Report No. 6 2010–11). Canberra, Australia: Parliament of Australia. Retrieved 31 May 2020 from www.aph.gov.au/About_Parliament/Parliamentary_Departments/Parliamentary_Library/pubs/rp/rp1011/11rp06

1973: A Grassby. (1973). *A multi-cultural society for the future*. Speech made at the Cairnmillar Institute's Symposium Strategy: Australia for Tomorrow. 11 August 1973. Retrieved 31 May 2020 from www.multiculturalaustralia.edu.au/doc/grassby_1.pdf

1977: The Australian Ethnic Affairs Council. (1977). Australia as a multicultural society (Submission to the Australian Population and Immigration Council on the green paper: Immigration policies and Australia's population). Canberra, Australia: Australian Government Publishing Service. Retrieved 31 May 2020 from www.multiculturalaustralia.edu.au/doc/auscouncilpop_2.pdf

1978: (*Galbally Report*) *Review of post arrival programs and services for migrants, migrant services and programs*. (1978) Canberra, Australia: Australian Government Publishing Service, 1978, pp. 3–13 and 15–28. Retrieved 31 May 2020 from www.multiculturalaustralia.edu.au/doc/galbally_1.pdf

1978: Fraser, Malcolm, Hon. (1978, April). Statement by the Prime Minister, the Right Honourable Malcolm Fraser. In *Background to the review of post arrival programs and services for migrants*. Canberra, Australia: Commonwealth Government Printer. Retrieved 31 May 2020 from www.multiculturalaustralia.edu.au/doc/fraser_2.pdf

1981: Fraser, M. (30 November 1981). Multiculturalism: Australia's unique achievement. In *Inaugural address on multiculturalism to the Institute of Multicultural Affairs*. AIMA The Malcolm Fraser Collection at the University of Melbourne. Retrieved 31 May 2020 from www.unimelb.edu.au/malcolmfraser/speeches/nonparliamentary/multiculturalism.html

1982: Australian Council on Population and Ethnic Affairs. (1982). *Multiculturalism for all Australians – Our developing nationhood*. Canberra, Australia: Australian Government Publishing Service.

1986: (*Jupp Report*) Review of migrant and multicultural programs and services, Committee for Stage 1. (1986). *Don't settle for less* (Report of the committee: Summary). Canberra, Australia: Australian Government Publishing Service. Retrieved 31 May 2020 from www.multiculturalaustralia.edu.au/doc/jupp_3.pdf

1986: AIMA. (1986). Future directions for multiculturalism (Final report of the Council of AIMA, pp. 7–13). Melbourne, Australia. Retrieved 31 May 2020 from www.multiculturalaustralia.edu.au/doc/multinst_3.pdf

1988: (*Fitzgerald Report*) Committee to advise on Australia's immigration policies. (1988). *Immigration: A commitment to Australia*. (Report, pp. xi–xvi) Canberra, Australia: Australian Government Publishing Service. Retrieved 31 May 2020 from www.multiculturalaustralia.edu.au/doc/fitzgerald_2.pdf

1989: Office of Multicultural Affairs. (1989, July). *National agenda for a multicultural Australia*. Canberra, Australia: DIAC website. Retrieved 31 May 2020 from www.immi.gov.au/media/publications/pdf/na-multicultural-australia-sharing-our-future.pdf

1995: National Multicultural Affairs Council (NMAC). (1005). *Multicultural Australia – The next steps: Towards and beyond 2000* (vol. 1, pp. vii–viii and 49–54). Canberra, Australia: Australian Government Publishing Service. Retrieved 31 May 2020 from www.multiculturalaustralia.edu.au/doc/multadvis_1.pdf

1997: National Multicultural Affairs Council (NMAC). (1997). *Multicultural Australia: The way forward*. Canberra, Australia: Department of Immigration and Multicultural Affairs. Retrieved 31 May 2020 from www.immi.gov.au/about/charters/_pdf/culturally-diverse/charter.pdf

1999: National Multicultural Advisory Council (NMAC). (1999). Australian multiculturalism for a new century: Towards inclusiveness. Canberra, Australia: Department of Immigration and Multicultural Affairs. Retrieved 31 May 2020 from www.immi.gov.au/media/publications/multicultural/nmac/report.pdf

1999: Australian Government. (1999). *A new agenda for multicultural Australia* (p. 3). Retrieved 31 May 2020 from www.immi.gov.au/media/publications/multicultural/pdf_doc/agenda/agenda.pdf

2003: Australian Government. (2003). *Multicultural Australia: United in diversity: Updating the 1999 New agenda for multicultural Australia: Strategic directions for 2003–2006*. Retrieved 31 May 2020 from www.immi.gov.au/media/publications/settle/_pdf/united_diversity.pdf

2003: Department of Immigration, Multicultural and Indigenous Affairs (DIMIA), Report on the review of settlement services for migrants and humanitarian entrants, Commonwealth of Australia, Canberra, Australia,

May 2003. Retrieved 31 May 2020 from www.immi.gov.au/living-in-australia/delivering-assistance/government-programs/settlement-policy/review-settlement-services.htm

2007: Howard, J. (Prime Minister). (23 January). *Transcript of press conference.* Canberra, Australia: Parliament House [Media release]. Retrieved 31 May 2020 from http://parlinfo.aph.gov.au/parlInfo/search/display/display.w3p;query=Id%3A%22media%2Fpressrel%2FYR0M6%22

2010: Australian Multicultural Advisory Council (AMAC). (2010). *The people of Australia.* Retrieved 31 May 2020 from www.immi.gov.au/about/stakeholder-engagement/_pdf/people-of-australia.pdf

Evans, C. (Minister for Immigration and Citizenship) and L. Ferguson (Parliamentary Secretary for Multicultural Affairs and Settlement Services). (2010, April 30). *Multicultural policy to speak to all Australians* [Media release]. Canberra, Australia. Retrieved 31 May 2020 from http://parlinfo.aph.gov.au/parlInfo/search/display/display.w3p;query=Id%3A%22media%2Fpressrel%2FL6MW6%22

DIAC. (2007, June). *The evolution of Australia's multicultural policy* (Fact Sheet no. 6). Retrieved 31 May 2020 from www.immi.gov.au/media/fact-sheets/06evolution.htm

For a list of key multicultural reports see DIAC, 'Multicultural publications', DIAC website. Retrieved 31 May 2020 from www.immi.gov.au/media/publications/multicultural/

For key immigration-related research see DIAC. (2009, September). *Immigration research* (Fact Sheet no. 16). Retrieved 31 May 2020 from www.immi.gov.au/media/fact-sheets/16research.htm

Index

Note: Page numbers in *italics* indicate figures and in **bold** indicate tables on the corresponding pages.

Aboriginal 69; advisory committees 95, 100; affairs 68; child-rearing 31; children 92; consultative group 92; epistemologies 95; leadership 186; parents 31; protectors 67–68; and respect, key concept maps *142*; and student, concepts with *144*; students, with non-Aboriginal students 99; studies 59, 98; teachers initiative 97; and Torres Strait Islander Australians 235; and Torres Strait Islander education 10, 93–103; *see also* Ainu; Australian Aboriginal; Indigenous Peoples; Torres Strait Islander communities

Aboriginal education 55, 92, 96, 107; Aboriginal Education Programme 96; challenges in 93; educationalists 134; experts 56; policy 95; teacher training and 94

Aboriginal Education Consultative Group (AECG) 10, 51

Aboriginal Education Policy Task Force 55, 100

Aboriginal Institute of Aboriginal Studies Act 1964 (Cth) (AIAS Act) 10

Aboriginal Protection Act (NSW) 1909 9

Aboriginal Protection Board (APB) 9

Aborigines 2, 5; *Aborigines Act* 9, 231; conversion to Christianity 9

academic appointment, Level A–Level E 188

academic employment *201*

accrediting volunteering activities 159–160

Act on Promoting Measures to Realize a Society in Which the Pride of the Ainu People Is Respected 7, 73, 122, 176–177, 217

Act on the Promotion of Ainu Culture and Dissemination and Enlightenment of Knowledge About Ainu Tradition, etc. 73, 81, 83, 174, 217

Adelaide Declaration 11

Advisory Council for Future Ainu Policy (ACFAP) 2, 7, 114, 175

affirmative action 18, 82, 86–87, 176, 179–180, 215–216, 222

Ainu 2, 5, 46, 51, 53, **70**, 87, 211; activism 46, 71, 213–214; assimilation policy 42; association of Hokkaido 46–47; child naming 30–31; child-rearing wisdom 28; cultural promotion policies 169; discrimination 174; economic poverty 174; education 17; education activists 72; educational philosophy 174; employment and educational achievement 212; ethnic identity 211; financial assistance and scholarships 215; higher education in 80–88; Indigenous education 6–8, 169; Japanese families 30, *30*; language 28, 42, 47, 86, 217; participation in higher education 212; *Resolution to Recognize the Ainu as an Indigenous People* 7; self-determination 6, 86–87; telling *yukara* to a Wajin *29*; women, empowerment 87; *see also* Ainu children; Okinawans

Ainu Bunka Shinkō Kenkyū Suishin Kikō 217

Ainu children: comprehensive education for 47; graduation rate 73; post-compulsory retention rate 214; retention to university **73**; retention to upper secondary school **72**

Ainu Cultural Promotion Act (ACPA) 6, 53, 81, 83, 88, 174, 176, 217
Ainu culture 86; educational systems and institutions 87; lower-secondary schools 116; protection 220
Ainu Folklore Museum 120
Ainu Japanese 46
Ainu Kyōkai 213
Ainu-led higher education system 211–212; Ainu policies and the impact of UNDRIP 215–217; assimilation and marginalisation 212–215; collaboration advocated in UNDRIP 217–219; Urespa Project 219–223
Ainu Liberation League 71
Ainu-minzoku ni kansuru Hōritsu 216
Ainu Policy Promotion Act (2019) 2, 5, 7, 18, 31, 177, 181
Ainu seisaku no arikata nikansuru yūshikisha kondankai 216
Ainu Seisaku Sokushin Kaigi 216
Ainu seisaku suishinn kaigi 213
Amerasians in Okinawa **70**
ancestral educational approaches 3, 25
Anderson, P. J. 16–17, 114, 117–119, 128, 131, 203, 227
Anglo-Australian society 68
Anning, B. 101
anti-racist education 153, 177
anti-slavery movement 9
Aoki, M. 154
approximation 33–39, *34*
Asmar, C. 196, 201
assessment approaches 129
assimilation 67–68
Australia: Aboriginal People 5; *Aboriginal Protection Act* (NSW) 1909 9; *Aborigines Act* No. 1905/014 9; diverse cultural groups 94; Enclaves and Support Systems/Services 99; immigration policies 68; *National Education Policy* 12; Native Institution 8–9; parliamentary democracy 3
Australia, Indigenous higher education in 91; Aboriginal and Torres Strait Islander education, advisory committees 101–103; Aboriginal and Torres Strait Islander education, funding 95–96; *Coolangatta Statement* 101; deprivation and exclusion 92–93; National Aboriginal Education Committee 93–95; National Aboriginal Education Policy 100–101; national and international priorities 104–106; review of 103–104; United Nations Declaration on the Rights of Indigenous Peoples (UNDRIP) 106–107
Australian Aboriginal: assimilation 67–68; children 31; constitutional recognition of 68, 74; education of 95; feast and mothers *32*; on improving the lives 40; integration 67; knowledge and understanding 95; non-Indigenous Australians 74; normalisation 67; protection 67–68; right to self-determination 74; self-determination 67; self-determination for 92; societal framework 93–94; sustainability 14
Australian Council for Education Research (ACER) 201
Australian Curriculum 122; analysis of 116–117; cross-curriculum priorities (CCP) 116, 123; Indigenous histories, languages and cultures 116; Indigenous lifeways 117
Australian Education Council 10, 55
Australian higher education 14; reconciliation for guiding 17
Australian Human Rights Commission (AHRC) 130
Australian Indigenous peoples 130; CALD minoritised groups 67
Australian Indigenous Studies 58
Australian Institute of Aboriginal and Torres Strait Islander Studies (AIATSIS) 10, 136
Australian Institute of Teaching and School Leadership (AITSL) 15, 126, 136
Australian pre-service teacher education: evidence-based Indigenist curriculum design 134–138; Indigenist 132–133; Indigenist approach, resources evaluation and curriculum 133–134; participatory action research (PAR) 138–141; rights-based approach 130–132; teacher professionalisation 123–129
Australian Professional Standards for Teachers (APST) 15, 122, 126, **127**
Australian Public Service 203
Australian Public Service Commission (APSC) 191
Australian teachers 126
auto-ethnographical account 179
autonomy 31–33; into public Ainu education 180

Bakufu, E. 56
Ballot paper 1967 Referendum *52*

Barnhardt, R. 173
Batchelor, J. 28, 34–35
Batchelor Institute 107
Behrendt, L. 192, 198, 201–202
Behrendt Report 193–194; Review 197
Bell, H. 39
Bloom, B. S. 39
Bohr, Y. 31
'Both Ways' approach 60
Bourke, C. 101
Brayboy, B. 170, 177
'Bringing Them Home Report' 231
Buckskin, P. 55, 195
Buraku Liberation League (BLL) 75
Buraku liberation movement 46
Buraku People 67, 69, **70**, 74, 76; Special Measures for Regional Improvement 71; state-institutionalised marginalisation 75
Burridge, N. 8

Cadzow, A. 8
careers in higher education: academic appointments 188; professional 187–188; senior leadership 187–188
Castagno, A. 170, 177
celebration 135
Chaney, F. 232
Chavez, A. F. 196, 203
Chiba University 179
children of mixed descent **70**
Chishima Ainu *43*
Chodkiewicz, A. 8
Christianity, conversion of Aboriginals 8–9
Christie, M. J. 33, 40
civilisation 40–41
Closing the Gap 104–105
co-educational schools 71
colonialism 30, 130, 152–153, 230; colonial education 134; island of Ezochi 41
Commonwealth Aboriginal and Torres Strait Islander Employment Strategy 2015–2018 191
Commonwealth Education Commission 95–96
Commonwealth Government of Australia 133
Commonwealth Schools Commission 51
Commonwealth-State National Aboriginal Education Policy, 1989 69
community-controlled organisations 92
comparative institutional analysis (CIA) 16, 154

Considine, M. 189, 203
Coolangatta Statement 101, 170, 173
Coombs Report 189–191
Cooper, S. *44*
Cooper, W. 44, *44*
Corporate Social Responsibility (CSR) 237
Council for Aboriginal Reconciliation (CAR) 229, 235–236
Council for Ainu Policy Promotion 7
Council on Teacher Professional Development in the Okinawa Prefecture 161
Crafts Education Centre 180
cross-curriculum priorities (CCP) 116
Cultural Bearer's Training Initiative 179–180
cultural competency training 103
cultural disrespect 201
cultural diversity 66, 68–69, 172; *see also* multiculturalism
cultural knowledge 48
cultural leadership 204
Culturally Competent Curriculum 135
Culturally Competent Teacher 135
culturally and linguistically diverse (CALD) 66, 69, 74, 77
cultural promotion policies 169
Cummeragunja Mission 48
Cummeragunja Reserve 44
Cummeragunja school *45*
cumulative marginalisation 74
curriculum 113, 115–117, 123, 126, 130; content 25; design 128; development 129

Dai Nippon Teikoku 13
Declaration on the Rights of Indigenous Peoples 174
decolonisation, pedagogy for 153
decolonising methodologies 172
deficit thinking in education 128, 130
Deloria, V. 172
Delugan, R. 200
Department of Education Victoria 132
Development Commission 212
Development Commission (1869), Tokyo 71
Diamond, Z. M. 1, 13, 15–16, 25, 113, 126, 186
Diet Resolution to Recognize Ainu People as Indigenous People 175–176
discrimination 46, 84, 114; elimination 47; nature and extent **85**; racial 100; situation **86**

Index

Draft Law Concerning the Ainu People (Draft Law) 14, 47, 81, 83–84, 88; Article 4 86; policies for the Ainu People 84; provisions 84, 87

EDF2031 Indigenous Perspectives in Teaching and Learning 140
EDF5657 Indigenous Perspectives in Professional Practice 140
Edith Cowan University (Western Australia CAE) 98
education, Indigenous history of 42
education, recognition of 114
Education for Aborigines: Report to the Schools Commission 68, 92–93
education for Ainu People before UNDRIP 173–175
Educational Administration 16
Educational Leadership 16
educational systems, control of 170
Educational Volunteer Practice I (EVPI) 159–160
Educational Volunteer Practice II (EVPII) 159–160
education curricula 159
The Education and Employment of Aboriginal and Torres Strait Islander Teachers (report) (EEATSIT) 93–94
education of Indigenous children 27–28; Ainu 42–46; approximation 33–39; autonomy and belonging 31–33; boys 35; curriculum-level changes 56–60; elder knowledge-keepers, language, and story 28–29; first-wave Indigenous activism in formal education 46–53; girls 35; imperial and colonial schooling 39–42; internationalisation 53–54; mastery learning 33–39; national identity 53–54; observation and repetition 29; oral traditions 28; policy-level developments 54–56; relatedness 29–31; second wave 53–60; *Yorta Yorta* 42–46; *see also* Aboriginal; Ainu; Australia, Indigenous higher education in
Education Personnel Certification Act 120–121
education of pre-service teachers 132
education systems 1, 5; and Indigenous perspectives 2–3; right to establish and control 4
Eisa 153, 162
Elder knowledge-keepers 28–29
embedded education systems 186
employment: Indigenous and non-Indigenous 186; of Indigenous people in Australia's universities, 187; operationalisation 188
enclaves and support systems/services 99
equality 242
equality and access 92
ethnic Chinese **70**
ethnic Koreans **70**
ethnic minorities 87
ethno-cultural perspectives 164
ethno-linguistic perspectives 164
eurocentrism 230

face-to-face environment 136
Federal Council for Aboriginal Reconciliation 11
Federal Council for the Advancement of Aborigines & Torres Strait Islanders (FCAATSI) 9–10, 50–51
Federal Department of Aboriginal Affairs 68
fire mastery 36, *38*
First Nation 18, 67, 69, 231–232, 234–250
First People 18, 231, 240, 242–250
Fletcher, J. J. 8, 41
formal education 40, *41*
formative feedback 132
Foundation for Research and Promotion of Ainu Culture 73
Four Rs model 173
Fraser, M. 232
Funding Priorities in Aboriginal and Torres Strait Islander Education (report) 96

Gayman, J. 16, 169
geographical isolation 100
global Indigenous Peoples' Movement 2
Goerke, V. 17, 227
Gooda, M. 130
Google-sourced resources 134
grass weaving *36*
growing your own philosophy 196–198, 204

Haisai-Haitai Undo (Hello Movement) 158
Harris, S. 39–40, 60
Harvard University Native American Program 172
Hawke, B. 232–233
HEIMS data 196, *201*, 204n1
Hello Movement 162

higher education 3; definition of 126; nature and purpose 126
higher education for Ainu People 80–82, 169–170, 177–179; Ainu Cultural Promotion Act 83; Indigenous education, standards and frameworks 170–171; Indigenous education status 180–182; Indigenous higher education 171–173; requirements 83–88; specific programmes 179–180; before UNDRIP 173–175; UNDRIP and its impact on Japan 175–177
higher education employment 202
Higher Education Student Support Act 2003 98
Higher Education Worker (HEW) 188
highly accomplished teachers 128
Hobart Declaration 11
Hodson, J. 113
Hokkaido 5, 41, 71, 176; *Saru-gun Biratori-cho Nibutani* 84
Hokkaido Ainu Association 88n1, 177
Hokkaido Education Board 214
Hokkaido Former Aboriginal Protection Act (1899) 6, 46, 71, 81, 83–84, 115, 213
Hokkaido Government Board of Education 56
Hokkaido-kōtōgakkō-kyōshokuinkumiai 214
Hokkaido Kyū-dojin hogo-hō (Former Aboriginal Protection Act [1899]) 44
Hokkaido University Centre for Ainu and Indigenous Studies (HUCAIS) 178–180
Hokkaido University of Education (HUE) 119
Hokkaido Utari Association 6
Hokkaido Utari Welfare Measures 213
Holding, C. 232
Holt, L. 16, 91, 186
Honda, Y. 219
Howard, J. 234
Howard, S. M. 98–99
Hughes, P. 12, 55, 60, 97
Hughes Report 55
Human Rights and Equal Opportunity Commission (HREOC) 231
Human Rights Commission (AHRC) 192
Hyllus Maris (1934–1986): A visionary with a passion for education 61n1

imperial and colonial education 39–42
Indigenising of the academy 171
Indigenist 132–133; resources evaluation and curriculum development 133–134
Indigenist rights-based approach 138
Indigenous academics 197–198, 201
Indigenous Ainu education 67
Indigenous Australian Higher Education Association (IAHEA) 101
Indigenous Australians 130
Indigenous-controlled education institution 106
Indigenous cultural competency framework 126
Indigenous culture on students' learning styles 39
Indigenous education 2, 67, 69, 87, 101, 136; Ainu education 73; approximation 33–39; APSTs for 138; in Australia, timeline 8–13; curriculum-level changes 56–60; first-wave Indigenous activism 46–53; higher education 171–173; higher education institutions in Japan and Australia 14; internationalisation and national identity 53–54; in Japan, timeline 5–8; lectures in 60; mastery learning 33–39; multicultural education policies 67; policy-level developments in 54–56; right to all levels and forms of education 170; right to establish and control their educational systems 169; rights-based education 60; second-wave Indigenous activism 53–60; standards and frameworks 170–171; status 180–182; teacher education programs 59; teacher educators in 26; watching and learning 33–39
Indigenous educational programmes 183n1
Indigenous employment 196
Indigenous enculturation 39
Indigenous Higher Education Advisory Committee (IHEAC) 188
Indigenous higher education in Australia 91, 171; Aboriginal and Torres Strait Islander education, advisory committees 101–103; Aboriginal and Torres Strait Islander education, funding 95–96; *Coolangatta Statement* 101; deprivation and exclusion 92–93; National Aboriginal Education Committee 93–95; National Aboriginal Education Policy 100–101; national and international priorities 104–106; review of 103–104; UNDRIP 106–107

Indigenous leadership in Australian universities 186–187, 203; academic roles 198–203; leadership and management 192; leadership pipeline 189–196; pathways 187–189; professional roles 197–198; university employment plans 196–197
Indigenous and non-Indigenous Australians, reconciliation between **128**
Indigenous Okinawans 153, 158
Indigenous peoples 3; Ainu and Okinawan 69–73; ancestral education systems 3; definition of 66; image usage and advises 27; intergenerational cumulative disadvantage 73; lifeways 128; normative framework for policies 7; Okinawans 151; recognition of special place 5; rights 4–5; *sui generis* rights 3; UNDRIP's Articles 14, 15, 21, and 31, 4–5
Indigenous readers, acknowledgement and warning 26–27
Indigenous Referendum of 1967 51
Indigenous rights 47, 242; based reconciliation 248–249
Indigenous self-determination 172
Indigenous Student Success Program 98
Indigenous Studies 2
Indigenous Support Program (ISP) 98
Indigenous teaching and learning approaches 39
Indigenous traditional pedagogical models 152–153
Indigenous and Tribal Peoples Convention (ILO 169) 86
In-service training courses 11
institutional racism 67
intellectual leadership 202–203
inter-ethnic alliances 76
International Association for the Evaluation of Educational Achievement (IEA) 1
International Convention on the Elimination of All Forms of Racial Discrimination 82–83
International rights mechanism 186
Introduction to Teaching Internship (ITI) 160
Inuit in Canada 31
involuntary minority groups 67
Ishihara, M. 179

James, T. 44, 227
James Cook University (Townsville CAE) 98

Japan: Buraku People 69; CALD minoritised groups 67; Indigenous peoples (Ainu and Okinawan) 69–73; Meiji Restoration, 1868 3, 5; multiculturalism 69–73; 'newcomer' migrants 69–70; Zainichi descendants 69; *zainichi gaikokujin* foreigners 211; *see also* Aboriginal; Ainu; Australian Aboriginal
Japan Communist Party 46, 72
Japanese Constitution, Article 98-2 of 1947 82
Japanese legal system 81
Japanese returnees **70**
Japan Socialist Party 72
Johnson, R. 200
Jordan, D. F. 98–99

Kaitaku-shi (Development Commission) 42, *43*
Kakazu, K. 15, 151, 157–158
kamui yukara 28
Kantō utari-kai shinpojiumu 86
Karafuto Ainu *43*
kari-gakkō 42
Kayano, S. 28, 35, 53–54, *54*
key performance indicators (KPIs) 241
kigyō no shakaiteki sekinin 222
Kimber, M. 188
Kirkness, V. J. 173
Kitahara, J. 179–180
Kitchen, J. 113
Koleth, E. 68, 255
Komazawa Tomakomai University 179
Koseki-hō Family Register Act (1871) 46
kotan 28
Kotter, J. P. 131
Kotter's principles in evaluating student responses 131
Kulin Nations 132
Kurils *43*
Kushiro 120
Kussharo Kotan Ainu Folklore Museum 120
Kyōikusho (education place) *43*
Kyū-dojin Aboriginals 46
Kyū-dojin jidō kyōiku-kitei: in 1901 46; in 1922 46

Labor Party, Australia 97
language 28–29, 135; rights 181
Larkin, S. 188, 195–196, 198, 201–202, 204
lateral violence 201

leadership pipeline 187, 189–196
Leximancer analysis 140–141
Leximancer-generated concept maps *142–144*
lifeways 2–3, 10, 15, 18, 27, 55–59, 113–114, 117, 119, 122–123, 126, 128, 134, 147, 202–203
Lincoln, A. 229
local boards of education (LBEs) 157
localisation mode 161, **161**
Lois Peeler, A. M. 117, *119*
Loos, N. 1–3
lower-secondary Social Studies 115

Mabo v Queensland 231
Macfarlane, B. 202
Macquarie, L. 8, 40
Maeda, K. 1, 14, 17, 80, 211, 223n1
mainstream education 3, 13, 123, 131, 172–173, 176
makarrata 232
Maloga Mission 44
marginalisation 67, 71; collective identity of 76
Marginson, S. 189, 203
Ma Rhea, Z. 59, 114, 116–119, 128–129, 191, 234
Marika-Munuŋgiritj, R. 60
Maris, H. 48, 50, *50*, 117
Martin, K. 29
Masaru, O. 176
master–apprentice model 199–200
mastery learning 33–39; fishing 33, *33–34, 37*; hunting 35, *35, 37*; making, fire-making for preparing food 36, *38*; ropemaking *38*; sewing 36
Matthews, D. 43
Matthews, J. 43
Meiji government 41, 115
Meiji Restoration, 1868 3, 5, 13
Melbourne Declaration 11, 122
Mercier, O. R. 196
Ministry of Education, Culture, Sports, Science and Technology (MEXT) 115, 119, 121, 157
Minthorn, R. S. 196, 203
modernisation (Japan) 71, 114, 213
Monash University 129
Moore, M. H. 152
More Aboriginal and Torres Strait Islander Teachers Initiative (MATSITI) 104–105
Moreton-Robinson, A. 129, 188

mother tongue 36
Muir, N. 31
multiculturalism 66–67; Australia's case, Indigenous peoples 67–69; Buraku People 69; co-living 220; definition of 66–67; education 47, 53, 66–67; Indigenous peoples (Ainu and Okinawan) 69–73; in Japan 211; Japan's case, Indigenous Ainu People 67, 69–73; panethnic identities, and strategies 73–77; Zainichi descendants 69
multicultural symbiosis 74
multi-ethnic co-living 216
mutual nurturing *see* Urespa Project

Naha City Board of Education (NCBE) 158
Nakano, I. 86
narratives: about events 28; about wisdom of their Elders 28; genres of language 28
National Aboriginal Conference 232
National Aboriginal Consultative Council (NACC) 190
National Aboriginal Education Committee (NAEC) 10–11, 51, 55, 93–97, 99–101
National Aboriginal and Torres Strait Islander Education Joint Policy Statement 100–101
National Aboriginal and Torres Strait Islander Education Policy (NATSIEP) 12, 55
National Aboriginal and Torres Strait Islander Higher Education Consortium (NATSIHEC) 102–103, 195, 240
National Ainu Museum and Park, Hokkaido 8, 182
National Association for Research into the Education of Resident Koreans in Japan 75
National Indigenous Australian Agency (NIAA) 69
National Indigenous Higher Education Network (NIHEN) 102
National Indigenous Higher Education Workforce Strategy 188, 193
National Inquiry into Teacher Education (NITE) 93
national integration 164
National Review of Education for Aboriginal and Torres Strait Islander Peoples 68
National Tertiary Education Union (NTEU) 201

nation-state formation 3, 42
Native Institution 8–9
NATSIHEC (AC) 195
Naturalised Japanese citizens **70**
neo-classical framework 153
New Ainu Cultural Promotion Act 73
'newcomer' migrants, Japan: Japan 69–70
Nicholls, Doug 48, 50
Nomoto, H. 87
non-Ainu settlers 41
non-Anglo-Whites 76
non-Indigenous academics 113, 189, 202; workforce 198
non-Indigenous Australian 17
non-Indigenous children 69, 123
non-Indigenous employment 201
non-Indigenous Japanese society 81
non-Indigenous learners 123
non-Indigenous majority 106
non-White ethnic migrants and refugees 76
non-White workers exploitation 76
NSW Aboriginal Education Consultative Group 12
NSW Aboriginal Protection Board 50
NSW Department of Education (DET) 12

observation and repetition 29, 34
Oda, H. 182
O'Donoghue, L. 190
Ogawa, M. 47
Ogbu, J. 75
Okano, K. 13, 66, 211
Okinawa, teacher education issues in 151–154; comparative institutional analysis (CIA) 154–155; 'Okinawan' teacher 157–160; re-commencement after Second World War 155–156; teacher education programmes after reintegration since 1972 157; teacher education programmes in universities, 1950–1972 156
Okinawan Bunkyō Gakkō (Okinawa Teacher College) 155
Okinawan language 151–152, 158
Okinawans 5, **70**, 74, 81, 155, 157
Okinawa University 157–160; programmes 163
Okinawa University Teaching Support Centre (OUTSC) 158
Okuda, O. 28
online environment 136
Osanai, T. 1–3
Otani University, Kyoto 121

Page, S. 196, 201
panethnicity 76
parliamentary democratic system 3
participatory action research (PAR) 137, 139; data analysis 139–140; data collection 139; inspired evaluation strategies 146
Pearson, N. 130
pedagogies for learning 39, 113, 117, 123, 126, 130; anti-racist education 153; data analysis 139–140; data collection 139; Indigenous traditional pedagogical models 152–153; leadership 128; pedagogy for decolonisation 153; place-based education 153; technical aspects 129
People of *Buraku* descent 69, **70**
perseverance 39
personhood 31
Phillip, A. 231
Philosophy, aims and policy guidelines for Aboriginal and Torres Strait Islander education (1985) 95
Pidgeon, M. 173
place-based education 153
policy formulation 128
Policy Statement on Tertiary Education for Aboriginal and Torres Strait focused 99
political reconciliation 229; *see also* reconciliation
post-colonialism 170
post-imperialism 170
post-secondary courses 169
post-UNDRIP schooling changes 114; curriculum changes 115–117; pedagogical challenges 117; policy level changes 114–115
Practice of Teaching Internship (PTI) 160
pre-service teachers 134; classrooms 123; education 129
Price, K. 113
primary teacher education programmes 153
Professional Knowledge Standard 127
Progress in International Reading Literacy Study (PIRLS) 1
Promotion of Ainu Culture and Dissemination and Enlightenment of Knowledge About Ainu Tradition, etc. 174
Protectors for Aboriginal people in Victoria 9
Protocols of Engagement 137
psychology 39
public service agency 195

racial discrimination 71, 100, 201
racism 152
Raynor, M. 113
Recognise Campaign 235
reconciliation 134, 227–228; action plans 235–237; Australian higher education sector, impact on 247–248; Australian narratives 230–235; Canadian higher education perspective 229–230; colonial understandings 230–231; corporate social responsibility 237–239; definition 227; formal 231–232; idea and concept 228; Indigenous rights 242–243; Indigenous rights-based reconciliation 248–249; international reconciliation narratives 229; official movement 232–233; opportunities of 241–243; positive change 242; practical reconciliation 233–234; promoting employment 241–242; RAP, based on equity pragmatics 245–246; RAPs, restrictions of 243; Twenty-first-century Reconciliation 234–235; within universities 239–241; university as business *versus* the university as educator 244–245
Reconciliation Action Plans (RAPs) 18, 230, 235–237, 240–244
'Red Unit' 140
Referendum Council 235
registered foreigners **70**
rehabilitation mode 160, **161**
reintegration of Okinawa in education 157
relatedness 29–30
remote Indigenous school communities 129
Report of the Aboriginal Education Policy Task 68
Research Association for Ainu Education 72
Research Centre for Ainu and Pacific Cultures 178
Resolution to Recognize the Ainu as an Indigenous People 7, 114–115
rights 135
rights-based approach 129–132
rights-based orientation 130
right to self-determination 83, 170
Rigney, L. I. 172
Rogers, J. 163
Royal Commission into Aboriginal Deaths in Custody 11, 54–55
Royal Commission on Australian Government Administration (RCAGA) 189
Rudd, K. 231–232
Russell, L. 59, 116, 128
Ryūkyūan 87
Ryūkyūan people 81
Ryūkyū Kingdom 5–6, 71, 151
Ryūkyūs 156

Sakhalin Ainu 47
Sapporo City Education Board 57
Sarra, C. 113
Sato, C. 1, 13, 15, 25, 53, 113
school-based ethnic Korean 75
Science Council of Japan 115
Second World War 213
Seddon, T. 234
self-adaptation 16, 246
self-affirmation of Ainu children 174
self-determination 87, 169, 216; in education 177; in Indigenous rights 101
Self-Determination Policy 92
self-identification: as Indigenous 66
self-identified Ainu People 211
self-motivation to practise a skill 34
Seminar for Teaching Professions 122
senior academics 199
Senior High School Teachers Union 72
senior leadership 187
settler-colonialism 41
SETU feedback from students 136
Sheils, H. 58
Shelley, W. 8
Shikoku Gakuin University 180, 216
Shima-kutuba 152
Shimizu, Y. 87
Shiritsu gakkō hō Private School Act (1949) 218
Shiro, K. 87
Simons, H. D. 75
Singh, D. 188
Smith, D. W. 229–230
Smith, T. 87
social and cultural alienation 100
Social Democratic Party of Japan 46
socialisation of children 27–28; *see also* education of Indigenous children
socio-economic system 157
South African Truth and Reconciliation Commission (TRC) 229
sovereignty 74–75, 131, 247

Special Activities 122
standardisation mode 160, **161**
Stanner, W. E. H. 58–59
state education committees 93
stories 28–29
Strategic Change Management 16
'student' and 'important' key concept maps *143*
Student Evaluation of Teaching Units (SETU): feedback 139–141, **145**; survey 132
sui generis rights 47
Sutton, P. 227
systematisation 159

Takegahara, Y. 58, 123
Takeshiro Matsuura 56, *57*, 58
Tamai, Y. 119
tattoo 35
teacher education 3, 114; Ainu culture and history 123; cultural identity 127; linguistic background 127; self-reflective restraint 134; system 121, 153
teacher education issues in Okinawa 151–154; comparative institutional analysis (CIA) 154–155; lived experiences 152; 'Okinawan' teacher 157–160; pedagogical matters 152; re-commencement after Second World War 155–156; teacher education programmes after reintegration since 1972 157; teacher education programmes in universities, 1950–1972 156; teacher education systems 152
teacher education programmes 164; after reintegration since 1972 157; in universities, 1950–1972 156
teacher preparedness 128
teacher training courses 11
teacher training programmes 98, 119
teaching Aboriginal and Torres Strait Islander students **127**
teaching methods in social studies 122
teas 60
Teasdale G. R. 60
terra nullius 212, 231
Thaman, K. H. 113
Theory and Practice of Moral Education 122
Think, Plan, Act, and Reflect approach 139, 145
'third wave' of educational reform 14

Thomas, G. 101
Tomakomai Komazawa University 178
Toorong Marnong Committee 132
Torres Strait Islander communities 2, 5, 14, 31; higher education 192; societal framework 93–94; teachers in 94
Torres Strait Islander education 10, 93–103; advisory committees 101–103; funding 95–96; higher education 97–99; universities employees 187
traditional education 14
traditional estates 5
traditionally oriented Aboriginal children 60, 63
Trends in International Mathematics and Science Study (TIMSS) 1
Tribal College Act 173
Tribal Colleges 172
Trow, M. A. 80
Tsuishikari 43
Tsuishikari Ainu school 47
Tsuishikari kyōiku-sho school *43*
Tsunemoto, T. 211
tu-itak 28

Uchi-nanchu 151
Uchinanchu Okinawan 87
Ueno, M. 16, 169
uepeker 28
UN Human Rights Council in Geneva 130
United Nations Declaration on the Rights of Indigenous Peoples (UNDRIP) 2, 13–15, 42, 73, 80, 106–107, 113–114, 129, 165, 169, 181, 212, 230; Ainu policies and 215–217; Article 14 4, 84, 169–170, 230; Article 14(2) 18, 217; Article 14(3) 217; Article 15 4, 84; Article 15(2) 218; Article 17(2) 218; Article 21 4; Article 31 4–5; articles of direct relevance to education 4–5; Australia's endorsement of 195; contemporary best practices 117–118; curriculum changes 115–117; and education services in Japan and Australia 113–122; Indigenous children in education 25; Japan's support 175; Okinawans under 151; pedagogical challenges 117; policy level changes 114–115; post-UNDRIP schooling changes 114–117; teacher education responses 118–122
Universal Declaration of Human Rights 130

Universities Australia Indigenous Strategy First Annual Report 240
Universities Australia's Indigenous Strategy 2017–2020 195
University Council, Japan 80
University of South Australia (South Australian Institute of Technology) 98
University of the Ryūkyūs (UR) 156
university-related reconciliation 230
UN Permanent Forum for Indigenous Issues (UNPFII) 106
Urespa Project 17, 212, 219–224n1–2
Utari Association 71–72, 88n1
Utari Kyōkai 213
Utari Special Welfare Project 71, 213
Utari taisaku no arikata nikansuru yūshikisha kondan-kai 82

Victorian Aboriginal Education Association Incorporated (VAEAI) 132
Victorian Honour Roll of Women 50
voluntary minorities 75

Wajin Japanese 17, 41, 211; mother tongue 219

Walter, M. 188
Western education system 40, 107
Willmot, E. 97
women, priority for 35–36
Woodward, S. A. E. 231
Worawa Aboriginal College 48, 117–118, *118*
Working Group on Indigenous Populations (WGIP) 174
World Indigenous Peoples Conference on Education (WIPCE) 170
Wyatt, K. 69

Yoneda, Y. 56
Yorta Yorta 42–46, 51
yukara 28
Yunupiŋu, M. 27, 60

Zainichi descendants 69
zainichi gaikokujin foreigners 211
Zainichi Koreans 67, 74–76
Zinga, D. 230
Zōjyō-ji Temple in Tokyo 42